Beginning JavaScript with DOM Scripting and Ajax

Second Edition

Russ Ferguson
Christian Heilmann

Apress·

Beginning JavaScript with DOM Scripting and Ajax: Second Edition

ISBN-13 (pbk): 978-1-4302-5092-0

ISBN-13 (electronic): 978-1-4302-5093-7

President and Publisher: Paul Manning
Lead Editor: Louise Corrigan
Technical Reviewer: Paddy Byers
Editorial Board: Steve Anglin, Mark Beckner, Ewan Buckingham, Gary Cornell, Louise Corrigan, Morgan Ertel, Jonathan Gennick, Jonathan Hassell, Robert Hutchinson, Michelle Lowman, James Markham, Matthew Moodie, Jeff Olson, Jeffrey Pepper, Douglas Pundick, Ben Renow-Clarke, Dominic Shakeshaft, Gwenan Spearing, Matt Wade, Tom Welsh
Coordinating Editor: Anamika Panchoo
Copy Editor: Roger LeBlanc
Compositor: SPi Global
Indexer: SPi Global
Artist: SPi Global
Cover Designer: Anna Ishchenko

Distributed to the book trade worldwide by Springer Science+Business Media New York, 233 Spring Street, 6th Floor, New York, NY 10013. Phone 1-800-SPRINGER, fax (201) 348-4505, e-mail orders-ny@springer-sbm.com, or visit www.springeronline.com. Apress Media, LLC is a California LLC and the sole member (owner) is Springer Science + Business Media Finance Inc (SSBM Finance Inc). SSBM Finance Inc is a Delaware corporation.

For information on translations, please e-mail rights@apress.com, or visit www.apress.com.

Apress and friends of ED books may be purchased in bulk for academic, corporate, or promotional use. eBook versions and licenses are also available for most titles. For more information, reference our Special Bulk Sales–eBook Licensing web page at www.apress.com/bulk-sales.

Any source code or other supplementary materials referenced by the author in this text is available to readers at www.apress.com. For detailed information about how to locate your book's source code, go to www.apress.com/source-code/.

For Dad.
Thanks for Saturdays full of cartoons, Doctor Who and Atari Basic

—Russ Ferguson

To Ioanna, who can sleep and look like an angel while some geek next to her hacks on the keyboard of a laptop and constantly mutters "Why won't you work" under his breath.

—Christian Heilmann

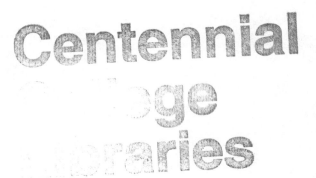

Contents at a Glance

Contents

About the Authors

Russ Ferguson is a freelance developer and instructor in the New York City area. His interest in computers goes back to Atari Basic, CompuServe, and BBS systems in the mid 1980s. For over 10 years, he has been fortunate to teach at Pratt Institute, where subjects have been as diverse as the student body. Working in New York has given him the opportunity to work with a diverse group of companies whose projects ranged from developing real-time chat/video applications for start-ups to developing and managing content-management systems for established media and advertising agencies like MTV and DC Comics.

Christian Heilmann grew up in Germany and, after a year working with people with disabilities for the Red Cross, spent a year as a radio producer. From 1997 onwards, he worked for several agencies in Munich as a web developer. In 2000, he moved to the US to work for eToys. After the dot-com crash, he moved to the UK, where he led the web-development department at Agilisys. In April 2006, he joined Yahoo! UK as a web developer. He is now Principal Developer Evangelist of the Mozilla Developer Network in the lovely town of London, England. You can find out more about him on his website: http://christianheilmann.com/.

About the Technical Reviewer

Dr. Paddy Byers is an independent developer and consultant with a long-standing interest in web technology and the mobile web in particular. He has been prominent in a series of efforts to enable web applications to deliver the same functionality and experiences as native apps, including authoring the BONDI specification and participating in multiple World Wide Web Consortium (W3C) API standardization groups. Paddy now develops extensively with server-side JavaScript using node.js and is an active contributor in the open-source ecosystem around it.

Paddy's programming experience includes working with a wide range of platforms and languages going back over 30 years. He trained originally as a mathematician, and he maintains an academic interest in security, privacy, and formal assurance.

Acknowledgments

I want to thank everyone at Apress for the help in putting this together: Louise for giving me a chance to work on this, Anamika for keeping me on track, and Paddy for helping me explain everything better. I really appreciate it.

I also need to thank my family for being supportive after a rough year and, more recently, dealing with me as I worked on this.

Introduction

JavaScript has gone though a huge transformation, from being something that was nice to know to being essential to developing web sites that are fully featured and take full advantage of the new capabilities built into browsers. The amount of attention given to JavaScript though libraries and frameworks has grown at an accelerated rate.

This was not always the case. JavaScript was first introduced as LiveScript in 1995 by Netscape. Over time, Microsoft's Internet Explorer adopted it and Netscape changed the name to JavaScript with the release of Netscape Navigator 2. As the two companies continued to compete, support was not that good. At worst, developers had to make two different versions of a site to support the most popular browsers (which, at the time, were Netscape 4 and Internet Explorer 4).

Browser support has improved greatly. The World Wide Web Consortium (W3C), working with browser makers, developed a standard way of representing and interacting with HTML documents, called the Document Objet Model (DOM), and a scripting language, called ECMAScript. Over the years, compliance with these standards has improved.

This book starts with the basics and gives you a good foundation on how to write JavaScript in an unobtrusive way, keeping your structure (HTML), presentation (CSS), and behavior (JavaScript) separate. There are also examples of how to keep your sites accessible for visitors using screen readers, as well as examples of how to develop your site if JavaScript is not available. We also cover subjects like objected detection versus browser detection, AJAX, HTML 5 Form validation, and an introduction to jQuery.

The goal of this book is to help you understand JavaScipt. If you haven't looked at JavaScript in a while, you'll be glad to know a lot has changed for the better. You can use this book as a guide to update your skills. If you are new to JavaScript, this book helps you from the beginning. We start with explaining what a variable is and later move on to how to add Google Maps to your site.

This book is full of examples you can use to enhance your site and add features based on the enhanced capabilities built into current browsers.

CHAPTER 1

Getting Started with JavaScript

This book will teach you about JavaScript and how to use it in a practical manner. After you read it, you'll be able to

- Understand JavaScript syntax and structures.

- Create scripts that are easy to understand and maintain.

- Write scripts that do not interfere with others.

- Write scripts that make web sites easier to use without blocking out non-JavaScript users.

- Write scripts that are independent of the browser or user agent trying to understand them—which means that in some years they will still be usable and won't rely on obsolete technology.

- Enhance a web site with JavaScript, and allow developers without any scripting knowledge to change the look and feel.

- Enhance a web document with JavaScript, and allow HTML developers to use your functionality by simply adding a CSS class to an element.

- Use progressive enhancement to make a web document nicer only when and if the user agent allows for it.

- Use Ajax to bridge the gap between the back end and client side, thus creating sites that are easier to maintain and appear much slicker to the user.

- Use JavaScript as part of a web methodology that enables you to maintain it independently without interfering with the other development streams.

What you will not find here are

- JavaScript applications that are browser specific

- JavaScript that is only there to prove that it can be used and does not enhance the visitor's experience

- JavaScript that promotes unwanted content, such as pop-up windows or other flashy techniques like tickers or animation for animation's sake

JavaScript is essential in modern web development, but you cannot take it for granted that the visitor will be able to use or even experience all the effects and functionality you can achieve with JavaScript. You can use JavaScript to completely change the web page by adding and removing or showing and hiding elements. You can offer users richer interfaces such as drag-and-drop applications or multilevel drop-down menus. However, some visitors cannot use a drag-and-drop interface because they can only use a keyboard or rely on voice recognition to use our sites.

Other visitors might be dependent on hearing our sites rather than seeing them (via screen readers) and might not be notified of changes achieved via JavaScript. Last but not least, there are users who just cannot have JavaScript enabled—for example, in high-security environments like banks. Therefore, you need to back up a lot of the things you do in JavaScript with solutions on the server side.

■ **Note** Web design has matured over the years—long ago we stopped using FONT tags, and we deprecated visual attributes like bgcolor and started moving all the formatting and presentational attributes to a CSS file. The same cleaning process has also happened to JavaScript. Now the content, structure, presentation, and behavior of web sites are all separated from each other. Web development now is done for business and for helping the user rather than done for the sake of putting something out there and hoping it works in most environments.

JavaScript is now part of an overall development methodology, which means that you develop it not to interfere with other technologies like HTML or CSS, but to interact with them or complement them.

Web development has come quite a way since the 1990s, and there is not much sense in creating web sites that are static and fixed in size. Any modern web design should allow for growth as needed. It should also be accessible to everyone (which does not mean that everybody gets the same appearance—a nice multicolumn layout, for example, might make sense on a high-resolution monitor but is hard to use on a mobile phone or a tablet)—and ready for internationalization. You cannot afford any longer to build something and think it'll last forever. Because the Web is about content and change, it'll become obsolete if we don't upgrade our web products constantly and allow other data sources to feed into it or get information from it.

Enough introductions—you got this book to learn about JavaScript, so let's start by talking quickly about JavaScript's history and assets before diving right into it.

In this chapter, you'll learn

- What JavaScript is, and what it can do for you

- The advantages and disadvantages of JavaScript

- How to add JavaScript to a web document, and what its essential syntax is

- Object-oriented programming (OOP) in relation to JavaScript

- How to write and run a simple JavaScript program

Chances are that you have already come across JavaScript and already have an idea of what it is and what it can do, so we'll move quite swiftly through some basics of the language and its capabilities first. If you know JavaScript well already, and you simply want to know more about the newer and more accessible features and concepts, you might skip to Chapter 3. However, there might be some information you've forgotten, and a bit of a review doesn't hurt, either.

The Why of JavaScript

In the beginning of the Web, there was HTML and the Common Gateway Interface (CGI). HTML defines the parts of a text document and instructs the user agent (usually the web browser) how to show it—for example, text surrounded by the tags <p></p> becomes a paragraph. Within that paragraph, you might have <h1></h1> tags that define the main page heading. Notice that for most opening tags, there is a corresponding closing tag that begins with </.

HTML has one disadvantage—it has a fixed state. If you want to change something, or use data the visitor entered, you need to make a round-trip to a server. Using a *dynamic technology* (such as ColdFusion, Ruby on Rails, ASP.NET, PHP, or JSP), you send the information from forms, or from parameters, to a server, which then performs calculations, tests, database lookups, and other such tasks. The application server associated with these technologies then writes an HTML document to show the results, and the resulting HTML document is returned to the browser for viewing.

The problem with that is it means every time there is a change, the entire process must be repeated (and the page reloaded). This is cumbersome and slow. It is true that at least the Western world has the benefit of fast Internet connections these days, but displaying a page still means a reload, which could be a slow process that frequently fails. (Ever get an `Error 404`?)

Some information, such as the results of performing calculations and verifying the information on a form, might not need to come from the server. JavaScript is executed by the user agent (normally a browser) on the visitor's computer. We call this *client-side code*. This could result in fewer trips to the server and faster-running web sites.

What Is JavaScript?

JavaScript started life as *LiveScript*, but Netscape changed the name—possibly because of the excitement being generated by Java—to JavaScript. The name is confusing, though, because there is no real connection between Java and JavaScript—although some of the syntax looks similar.

> *Java is to JavaScript what Car is to Carpet*
>
> —From a JavaScript discussion group on Usenet

Netscape created the JavaScript language in 1996 and included it in their Netscape Navigator (NN) 2.0 browser via an interpreter that read and executed the JavaScript added to `.html` pages. The language has steadily grown in popularity since then, and it is now supported by all browsers and some applications as a way to customize them.

The good news is that this means JavaScript can be used in web pages for all browsers. The not-quite-so-good news is that there are differences in the way the different browsers implement JavaScript, although the core JavaScript language is much the same. However, JavaScript can be turned off by the user. I will discuss this further shortly, as well as throughout this book.

The great thing about JavaScript is that once you've learned how to use it for browser programming, you can move on to use it in other areas. Microsoft Windows 8 and Surface tablets both let you use JavaScript to develop applications, PDF files use JavaScript, and applications such as Dreamweaver and Photoshop are scriptable with JavaScript. Now mobile applications can be developed with JavaScript and converted to native code. JavaScript can even be used on the server side using things like Node.js.

A lot of large companies also offer software development kits (SDKs) that let you access data or integrate services on your site. For example, if you want your visitors to log in with their Facebook ID, you can use Facebook's JavaScript SDK located at `http://developers.facebook.com/web/`.

Even better is the fact that JavaScript is a lot easier to develop than higher programming languages or server-side scripting languages. It does not need any compilation like Java or C++, and it doesn't need to be run on a server or command line like Perl, PHP, or Ruby. All you need to write, execute, debug, and apply JavaScript is a text editor and a browser—both of which are supplied with any operating system. There are, of course, tools that make it a lot easier for you—for example, JavaScript debuggers like Firebug, Opera Dragonfly, and Chrome Developer tools.

Problems and Merits of JavaScript

As mentioned at the outset of this chapter, JavaScript has been an integral part of web development over the last few years, but it has also been used incorrectly. As a result, it has received a bad reputation. The reason for this is the use of gratuitous JavaScript effects, like moving page elements and pop-up windows. These effects might have been impressive the first time you saw them, but they soon become just a "nice to have" feature and, in some cases, even a "nice to not have any longer" element. A lot of this comes from the days of *DHTML* (which I'll say more about in Chapter 3).

The term *user agent* and the lack of understanding of what a user agent is can also be a problem. Normally, the user agent is a browser like Microsoft Internet Explorer (IE), Chrome, Firefox (Fx), Opera, or Safari. However, browsers are not the only user agents on the Web. Others include

- Assistive technology that helps users to overcome the limitations of a disability—like text-to-speech software or Braille displays

- Text-only agents like Lynx

- Web-enabled applications

- Browsers in game consoles

- Browsers in smartphones

- Browsers in tablets

- Interactive TV and set-top boxes

- Search engines and other indexing programs

- And many more

This large variety of user agents, of different levels of technical finesse (and old user agents that don't get updated), is also a great danger for JavaScript.

Not all visitors to your web site will experience the JavaScript enhancements you applied to it. A lot of them will also have JavaScript turned off—for security reasons. JavaScript can be used for good and for evil. If the operating system—like unpatched Windows—allows you to, you can install viruses or Trojan Horses on a computer via JavaScript or read out user information and send it to another server.

■ **Note** There is no way of knowing what the visitor uses or what his computer is capable of. Furthermore, you never know what the visitor's experience and ability are. This is one of the beautiful aspects of the Web—everyone can participate. However, this can introduce a lot of unexpected consequences for the JavaScript programmer.

In many cases, you might want to have a server-side backup plan. It would test to see whether the user agent supports the functionality desired and, if it doesn't, the server takes over.

Independence of scripting languages is a legal requirement for web sites, as defined in the Digital Discrimination Act for the UK, section 508 in the US law, and many more local legal requirements throughout the world. This means that if the site you developed cannot be used without JavaScript, or your JavaScript enhancements are expecting a certain ability of the users or their user agent without a fallback, your client could be sued for discrimination.

However, JavaScript is not evil or useless, and it is a great tool to help your visitors to surf web sites that are a lot slicker and less time-consuming.

The merits of using JavaScript are

- **Less server interaction** You can validate user input before sending the page off to the server. This saves server traffic, which means saving money.

- **Immediate feedback to the visitors** They don't have to wait for a page reload to see if they forgot to enter something

- **Informing the visitor of minor errors** For example, if you need your visitors to fill out a form, JavaScript can provide instant feedback on how the form was filled out. If a required field is missing, the site can inform the user before submitting any data to the server.

- **Increased usability by allowing visitors to change and interact with the user interface without reloading the page**   For example, by collapsing and expanding sections of the page or offering extra options for visitors with JavaScript. A classic example of this is selection boxes that allow immediate filtering, such as only showing the available destinations for a certain airport, without making you reload the page and wait for the result.

- **Increased interactivity**   You can create interfaces that react when the user hovers the pointer over them or activates them via the keyboard. This is partly possible with cascading style sheets (CSS) and HTML as well, but JavaScript offers you a lot wider—and more widely supported— range of options.

- **Richer interfaces**   If your users allow for it, you can use JavaScript to include such items as drag-and-drop components and sliders—something that originally was possible only in thick client applications your users had to install, such as Java applets or browser plug-ins like Flash.

- **Lightweight environment**   Unlike Java applets or Flash movies, which are large files that must be downloaded, scripts are small in file size and get cached (temporary storage) once they have been loaded. JavaScript also uses the browser controls for functionality rather than its own user interfaces like Flash or Java applets do. This makes it easier for users, because they already know these controls and how to use them. Modern Flash and Apache Flex applications do have the option to stream media and—being vector based—are visually scalable, something JavaScript and HTML controls aren't. On the other hand, SVG (Scalable Vector Graphics) is something native to the browser and can be controlled by JavaScript.

JavaScript in a Web Page and Essential Syntax

Applying JavaScript to a web document is very easy; all you need to do is use the `script` tag. The `type` attribute is optional in HTML5 but required in HTML4:

```
<script type="text/javascript">
  // Your code here
</script>
```

For older browsers, you'll need to comment out the code to make sure the user agent does not display it inside the page or try to render it as HTML markup. There are two different syntaxes for commenting out code but we are showing one. For HTML documents, you use the normal HTML comments:

```
<script type="text/javascript">
<!--
 // Your code here
-->
</script>
```

Technically, it is possible to include JavaScript anywhere in the HTML document, and browsers will interpret it. However, there are reasons in modern scripting why this is a bad idea. For now, though, we will add JavaScript examples to the body of the document to allow you to see immediately what your first scripts are doing. This will help you get familiar with JavaScript a lot more easily than the more modern and advanced techniques awaiting you in Chapter 3.

▓ **Note** There is also an "opposite" to the `script` tag—`noscript`—which allows you to add content that will be displayed only when JavaScript is not available. However, `noscript` is deprecated in XHTML and strict HTML, and there is no need for it—if you create JavaScript that is unobtrusive.

JavaScript Syntax

Before we go any further, we should discuss some JavaScript syntax essentials:

- `//` indicates that the rest of the current line is a comment and not code to be executed, so the interpreter doesn't try to run it. Comments are a handy way of putting notes in the code to remind you what the code is intended to do, or to help anyone else reading the code see what's going on.

- `/*` indicates the beginning of a multiline comment.

- `*/` indicates the end of a comment that covers more than one line. Multiline comments are also useful if you want to stop a certain section of code from being executed but don't want to delete it permanently. If you are having problems with a block of code, for example, and you aren't sure which lines are causing the problem, you can comment one portion of it at a time to isolate the problem.

- Curly braces (`{` and `}`) are used to indicate a block of code. They ensure that all the lines inside the braces are treated as one block. You will see more of these when I discuss structures such as `if` or `for`, as well as functions.

- A semicolon or a newline defines the end of a statement, and a statement is a single command. Semicolons are in fact optional, but it's still a good idea to use them to make clear where statements end, because doing so makes your code easier to read and debug. (Although you can put many statements on one line, it's best to put them on separate lines to make the code easier to read.)

Let's put this syntax into a working block of code:

```
<!DOCTYPE html>
<html>
<head>
<body>
<script type="text/JavaScript">
  // One-line comments are useful for reminding us what the code is doing

  /*
     This is a multiline comment. It's useful for longer comments and
     also to block out segments of code when you're testing
  */

  /*
     Script starts here. We're declaring a variable myName, and assigning to it the
     value of whatever the user puts in the prompt box (more on that in Chapter
     2), finishing the instruction with a semicolon because it is a statement
  */
  var myName = prompt ("Enter your name","");
```

```
    // If the name the user enters is Chris Heilmann
    if (myName == "Chris Heilmann")
    {
        // then a new window pops up saying hello
        alert("Hello Me");
    }

    // If the name entered isn't Chris Heilmann
    else
    {
        // say hello to someone else
        alert("hello someone else");
    }
</script>
</body>
</html>
```

Some of the code might not make sense yet, depending on your previous JavaScript experience. All that matters for now is that it's clear how comments are used, what a code block is, and why there are semicolons at the end of some of the statements. You can run this script if you like—just copy it into an HTML page, save the document with the file extension .html, and open it in your browser.

Although statements like if and else span more than one line and contain other statements, they are considered single statements and don't need a semicolon after them. The JavaScript interpreter knows that the lines linked with an if statement should be treated as one block because of the curly braces, {}. Although it's not mandatory, you should indent the code within the curly braces. This makes reading and debugging much easier. We'll be looking at variables and conditional statements (if and else) in the next chapter.

Code Execution

The browser reads the page from top to bottom, so the order in which code executes depends on the order of the script blocks. A *script block* is the code between the <script> and </script> tags. (Also note that it's not just the browser that can read your code; the user of a web site can view your code, too, so you shouldn't put anything secret or sensitive in there.) There are three script blocks in this next example:

```
<!DOCTYPE html>
<html>
<head>
<script type="text/javascript">
  alert( 'First script Block ');
  alert( 'First script Block - Second Line ');
</script>
</head>
<body>
<h1>Test Page</h1>
<script type="text/javascript">
  alert( 'Second script Block' );
</script>
<p>Some more HTML</p>
<script type="text/JavaScript">
```

```
    alert( 'Third script Block' );
  function doSomething() {
    alert( 'Function in Third script Block' );
  }
</script>
</body>
</html>
```

If you try it out, you'll see that the alert() dialog in the first script block appears and displays the message

```
First script Block
```

That's followed by the next alert() dialog in the second line displaying the message

```
First script Block - Second Line.
```

The interpreter continues down the page and comes to the second script block, where the alert() function displays this dialog:

```
Second script Block
```

And the third script block follows it with an alert() statement that displays

```
Third script Block
```

Although there's another alert statement inside the function a few lines down, it doesn't execute and display the message. This is because it's inside a function definition (function doSomething()) and code inside a function executes only when the function is called.

An Aside About Functions

I'll be talking about functions in much more depth in Chapter 3, but I introduce them here because you can't get very far in JavaScript without an understanding of functions. A *function* is a named, reusable block of code, surrounded by curly braces, that you create to perform a task. JavaScript contains functions that are available for you to use and perform tasks like displaying a message to the user. The proper use of functions can save a programmer from writing a lot of repetitive code.

You can also create our own functions, which is what we did in the previous code block. Let's say you create some code that writes out a message to a page in a certain element. You'd probably want to use it again and again in different situations. Although you could cut and paste code blocks wherever you wanted to use them, this approach can make the code excessively long; if you want the same piece of code three or four times within one page, it'll also get pretty hard to decipher and debug. Instead, you can wrap the messaging code into a function and then pass in any information that the function needs in order to work using *parameters*. A function can also return a value to the code that called the function into action originally.

To call the function, you simply write its name followed by parentheses, (). (Note—you use the parentheses to pass the parameters. However, even when there are no parameters, you must still use the parentheses.) But you can't call the function, as you might expect, until the script has created it. You can call it in this script by adding it to the third script block like this:

```
<script type="text/javascript">
  alert( 'Third script Block ');
function doSomething(){
  alert( 'Function in Third script Block ');
}
// Call the function doSomething
doSomething();
</script>
</body>
</html>
```

So far in this chapter, you've looked at the pros and cons of the JavaScript language, seen some of the syntax rules, learned about some of the main components of the language (albeit briefly), and run a few JavaScript scripts. You've covered quite a lot of distance. Before we move on to a more detailed examination of the JavaScript language in the next chapter, let's talk about something key to successful JavaScript development: *objects*.

Objects

Objects are central to the way you use JavaScript. Objects in JavaScript, in many ways, are like objects in the world outside of programming. (It does exist, I just had a look.) In the real world, an object is just a "thing" (many books about object-oriented programming compare objects to nouns): a car, a table, a chair, and the keyboard I'm typing on. Objects have

- **Properties** (analogous to adjectives)   The car is *red*.

- **Methods** (like verbs in a sentence)   The method for starting the car might be *turn ignition key*.

- **Events**   Turning the ignition key results in the *car starting* event.

Object-oriented programming (OOP) tries to make programming easier by modeling real- world objects. Let's say you were creating a car simulator. First, you create a car object, giving it properties like *color* and *current speed*. Then you need to create methods: perhaps a *start* method to start the car, and a *brake* method to slow the car, into which you need to pass information about how hard the brakes should be pressed so that you can determine the slowing effect. Finally, you would want to know when something happens with your car. In OOP, this is called an *event*. For example, when the gas tank is low, the car sends a notification (that light on the dashboard) letting you know it's time to fill up. In this code, you would want to listen for such an event so that you can do something about it.

Object-oriented programming works with these concepts. This way of designing software is now very commonplace and influences many areas of programming—but most importantly to you, it's central to JavaScript and web browser programming.

Some of the objects we'll be using are part of the language specification: the String object, the Date object, and the Math object, for example. The same objects are available to JavaScript in a PDF file and on a web server. These objects provide lots of useful functionality that could save you tons of programming time. You can use the Date object, for example, to obtain the current date and time from the client (such as a user's PC). It stores the date and provides lots of useful date-related functions—for example, converting the date/time from one time zone to another. These objects are usually referred to as *core objects*, because they are independent of the implementation. The browser also makes itself available for programming through objects you can use to obtain information about the browser and to change the look and feel of the application. For example, the browser makes available the Document object, which represents a web page available to JavaScript. You can use this in JavaScript to add new HTML to the web page being viewed by the user of the web browser. If you used JavaScript with a different host, with a Node.js server, for example, you'd find that the server hosting JavaScript exposes a very different set of host objects, because their functionality is related to things you want to do on a web server.

You'll also see in Chapter 3 that you can use JavaScript to create your own objects. This is a powerful feature that allows you to model real-world problems using JavaScript. To create a new object, you need to specify the properties and methods it should have, using a template called a *class*. A class is a bit like an architect's drawing in that it specifies what should go where and do what, but it doesn't actually create the object.

■ **Note**   There is some debate as to whether JavaScript is an object-based language or an object-oriented language. The difference is that an object-based language uses objects for doing programming but doesn't allow the coder to use object-oriented programming in her code design. An object-oriented programming language not only uses objects, but also makes it easy to develop and design code in line with object-oriented design methodology. JavaScript allows you to create your own objects, but this is not accomplished in the same way as in class-based languages like Java or C#. However, we'll be concentrating not on debates about what is or isn't object oriented here, but on how objects are useful in practical terms in this book, and we'll look at some basic object-oriented coding where it helps make life easier for us.

As you progress through the book, you'll get a more in-depth look at objects: the objects central to the JavaScript language, the objects that the browser makes available for access and manipulation using JavaScript, and your own custom objects. For now, though, all you need to know is that objects in JavaScript are *entities* you can use to add functionality to web pages, and that they can have properties and methods. The Math object, for example, has among its properties one that represents the value of pi and among its methods one that generates a random number.

Simple JavaScript Example

I'll finish the chapter with a simple script that determines first the width of the visitor's screen and then applies a suitable style sheet. (It does this by adding an extra LINK element to the page. Something like this would now be done using CCS media queries, but this is still a good example of how to use objects.) You'll do this using the Screen object, which is a representation of the user's screen. This object has an availWidth property that you'll retrieve and use to decide which style sheet to load.

Here's the code:

```
<!doctype html>
<html>
  <head>
    <meta charset="UTF-8">
    <title>CSS Resolution Demo</title>
    <!-- Basic style with all settings -->
    <link rel="StyleSheet" href="basic.css" type="text/css" />
    <!--
    Extra style (applied via JavaScript) to override default settings
    according to the screen resolution
    -->
    <script type="text/javascript">
      // Define a variable called cssName and a message
      // called resolutionInfo
      var cssName;
      var resolutionInfo;
      // If the width of the screen is less than 650 pixels
```

```
    if( screen.availWidth < 650 ) {
    // define the style Variable as the low-resolution style
      cssName = 'lowres.css';
      resolutionInfo = 'low resolution';
    // Or if the width of the screen is less than 1000 pixels
    } else {
      if( screen.availWidth > 1000 ) {
    // define the style Variable as the high-resolution style
        cssName = 'highres.css';
        resolutionInfo = 'high resolution';
    // Otherwise
      } else {
    // define the style Variable as the mid-resolution style
        cssName = 'lowres.css';
        resolutionInfo = 'medium resolution';
      }
    }
    document.write( '<link rel="StyleSheet" href="' + cssName + '" type="text/css" />' );
    </script>
    </head>
  <body>
    <script type="text/javascript">
      document.write( '<p>Applied Style:' + resolutionInfo + '</p>' );
    </script>
  </body>
</html>
```

Although we'll be looking at the details of if statements and loops in the next chapter, you can probably see how this is working already. The if statement on the first line asks whether the screen.availWidth is less than 650:

```
if ( screen.availWidth < 650 )
```

If the user's screen is 640×480, the width is less than 650, so the code within the curly braces is executed and the low-resolution style and message get defined.

```
if ( screen.availWidth < 650 ) {
// define the style Variable as the low-resolution style
  cssName = 'lowres.css';
  resolutionInfo = 'low resolution';
}
```

The code carries on checking the screen size using the else statement. The final else occurs only if neither of the other evaluations have resulted in code being executed, so you assume that the screen is 800×600 and define the medium style and message accordingly:

```
else {
// define the style Variable as the mid-resolution style
  cssName = 'lowres.css';
  resolutionInfo = 'medium resolution';
}
```

Note that you're measuring the screen size here, and the user might have a 800×600 screen, but that doesn't mean his browser window is maximized. You might be applying a style that is not appropriate.

You're using another object, the document object, to write to the page (an HTML document). The document object's write() method allows you to insert HTML into the page. Note that document.write() doesn't actually change the source HTML page, just the page the user sees on his computer.

■ **Note** In fact, you'll find document.write() very useful as you work through the first few chapters of the book. It's good for small examples that show how a script is working, for communicating with the user, and even for debugging an area of a program that you're not sure is doing what you think it should be doing. It also works on all browsers that support JavaScript. More modern browsers have better tools and methods for debugging, but I'll say more on that later in the book.

You use document.write() to write out the appropriate link element with your defined style in the head:

```
document.write( '<link rel="StyleSheet" href="' +
cssName + '" type="text/css" />' );
```

And in the document's body, you write out the message explaining which resolution style was applied:

```
<script type="text/javascript">
  document.write( '<p>Applied Style: '+ resolutionInfo + '</p>' );
</script>
```

Later on, we'll work with more complex examples that use JavaScript to test capabilities of the user's agent and interface. For now, though, I hope this simple example gives you an inkling of the kind of flexibility you can add to your web pages using JavaScript.

Summary

In this chapter, we took a look at what JavaScript is, how it works, and what its advantages and disadvantages are. I noted that the biggest disadvantage is that you cannot rely on it as a given. However, I also mentioned that using JavaScript can make web sites a nicer and slicker experience for your users.

You ran some JavaScript code, saw how to add comments to the code, and saw how to separate JavaScript statements using semicolons. You also saw that you can tell JavaScript to treat a group of lines of code as a single block using curly braces, following an if statement, for example. You learned that JavaScript execution generally runs from top to bottom, and from the first script block to the last, with the exception of functions that execute only when you tell them to.

You also looked at objects, which are central to writing JavaScript. Not only is JavaScript itself very much dependent on objects, but the browser also uses objects and methods to make itself and the document available for scripting. Finally, you looked at a simple example that reads out the user's screen resolution and applies a suitable style sheet.

In the next chapter, I'll cover the language fundamentals of JavaScript. You'll see how JavaScript stores and manipulates data, and uses it in calculations. We'll also look at creating "intelligent" JavaScript programs using decision-making statements that allow you to evaluate data, do calculations with it, and decide on an appropriate course of action. With that chapter under your belt, you'll have most of the fundamental knowledge needed to go on to more exciting and useful web programming.

CHAPTER 2

Data and Decisions

Data and decision making are fundamental to every *intelligent* program. We'll begin this chapter by looking at how JavaScript understands, or represents, data. This is important because JavaScript works with a number of *data types* and manipulates data according to its data type. You can generate unexpected results by mismatching data of different types. We'll look at some of the more common data type problems, and you'll see how to convert one type of data to another.

We'll also be working with *conditional statements* and *loops*: two of the most valuable tools for decision making. To make decisions in a computer language, you need to let the program know what should happen in response to certain conditions, which is where conditional statements come in. Loops, on the other hand, simply allow you to repeat an action until a specified circumstance is met. For example, you might want to loop through each input box in a form and check that the information it contains is valid.

I'll be covering a lot of different facets of JavaScript in this chapter:

- Classifying and manipulating information in JavaScript: data types and data operators

- Variables

- Converting data types

- Introducing data objects: String, Date, and Math objects

- Arrays: storing ordered sets of data, like the items in a shopping basket

- Decision making with conditional statements, loops, and data evaluation

> **Note** The examples in this chapter are kept as simple as possible and therefore use document.write() as a feedback mechanism for you to see the results. You'll learn in later chapters about other methods for doing this that are more modern and versatile.

Data, Data Types, and Data Operators

Data is used to store information, and to do that more effectively, JavaScript needs to have each piece of data assigned a *type*. This type stipulates what can or cannot be done with the data. For example, one of the JavaScript data types is *number*, which you can use to perform certain calculations on the data that it holds.

The three most basic data types that store data in JavaScript are

- **String**: A series of characters—for example, "some characters"

- **Number**: A number, including floating point numbers

- **Boolean**: Can contain a true or false value

These are sometimes referred to as *primitive data types*, because they store only single values. There are two slightly different primitive data types as well. These don't store information, but instead warn you about a particular situation:

- **Null**: Indicates that even though a variable has been created, its current value is null or nothing.

- **Undefined**: Indicates that something has not been defined and given a value. This is important when you're working with variables.

We'll be working extensively with these data types throughout the chapter.

The String Data Type

The JavaScript interpreter expects string data to be enclosed within single or double quotation marks (known as delimiters). The following script, for example, will write some characters on the page:

```
<html>
<body>
<script type="text/javascript">
    document.write("some characters");
</script>
</body>
</html>
```

The quotation marks won't be written to the page because they are not part of the string; they simply tell JavaScript where the string starts and ends. You could just as easily use single quotation marks:

```
<html>
<body>
<script type='text/javascript'>
    document.write('some characters');
</script>
</body>
</html>
```

Both methods are fine, as long as you close the string the same way you opened it and don't try to delimit it like this:

```
document.write('some characters");
document.write("some characters');
```

Of course, you might want to use a single or double quotation mark inside the string itself—in which case, you need to use a distinct delimiter. If you use double quotation marks, the instructions will be interpreted as you intended:

```
document.write("Paul' s characters");
```

But if you used single quotations marks, they won't be:

```
document.write('Paul' s characters');
```

This gives you a syntax error because the JavaScript interpreter thinks the string ends after the *l* in *Paul* and doesn't understand what is happening afterwards.

14

■ **Note**   JavaScript syntax, like English syntax, is a set of rules that makes the language intelligible. Just as a syntax error in English can render a sentence meaningless, a syntax error in JavaScript can render the instruction meaningless.

You can avoid creating JavaScript syntax errors like the following one by using single quotation marks to delimit any string containing double quotes and vice versa:

```
document.write("Paul' s numbers are 123");
document.write('some "characters"');
```

If, on the other hand, you wanted to use both single and double quotation marks in your string, you need to use something called an *escape sequence*. In fact, it's better coding practice to use escape sequences instead of the quotation marks we've been using so far, because they make your code easier to read.

Escape Sequences

Escape sequences are also useful for situations where you want to use characters that can't betyped using a keyboard (like the symbol for the Japanese yen, ¥, on a Western keyboard). Table 2-1 lists some of the most commonly used escape sequences.

Table 2-1. *Common Escape Sequences*

Escape Sequences	Character Represented
\b	Backspace.
\f	Form feed.
\n	Newline.
\r	Carriage return.
\t	Tab.
\'	Single quote.
\"	Double quote.
\\	Backslash.
\xNN	*NN* is a hexadecimal number that identifies a character in the Latin-1 character set. (The Latin-1 character is the norm for English-speaking countries.)
\uDDDD	*DDDD* is a hexadecimal number identifying a Unicode character.

Let's amend the following string, which causes a syntax error

```
document.write( 'Paul' s characters' );
```

so that it uses the escape sequence (\') and is correctly interpreted:

```
document.write( 'Paul\' s characters' );
```

The escape sequence tells the JavaScript interpreter that the single quotation mark belongs to the string itself and isn't a delimiter.

ASCII is a character-encoding method that uses values from 0 to 254. As an alternative, you can specify characters using the ASCII value in hexadecimal with the \xNN escape sequence. The letter C is 67 in decimal and 43 in hex, so you could write that to the page using the escape sequence like this:

```
document.write( "\x43" );
```

The \uDDDD escape sequence works in much the same way but uses the Unicode character-encoding method, which has 65,535 characters. Because the first few hundred ASCII and Unicode character sets are similar, you can write the letter C using this escape sequence as follows:

```
document.write( '\u0043' );
```

ASCII and Unicode information can get quite detailed, so the best place to look for information is on the Web. For Unicode, try http://www.unicode.org.

Operators

JavaScript has a number of operators you can use to manipulate the data in your programs; you'll probably recognize them from math. Table 2-2 presents some of the most commonly used operators.

Table 2-2. *JavaScript Operators*

Operator	What It Does
+	Adds two numbers together or concatenates two strings.
-	Subtracts the second number from the first.
*	Multiplies two numbers.
/	Divides the first number by the second.
%	Finds the modulus—the remainder of a division—for example, 98 % 10 = 8.
--	Decreases the number by 1; only useful with variables, which you'll see at work later.
++	Increases the number by 1; only useful with variables, which you'll see at work later.

Here they are in use:

```
<html>
<body>
<script type="text/javascript">
    document.write( 1 - 1 );
    document.write("<br>" );
    document.write( 1 + 1 );
    document.write("<br>" );
    document.write( 2 * 2 );
    document.write( "<br>" );
    document.write( 12 / 2 );
    document.write("<br>" );
```

```
        document.write( 1 + 2 * 3 );
        document.write("<br>" );
        document.write( 98 % 10 );
</script>
</body>
</html>
```

You should get this output:

0
2
4
6
7
8

JavaScript, just like math, gives some operators precedence. Multiplication takes a higher precedence than addition, so the calculation $1 + 2 * 3$ is carried out like this:

$$2 * 3 = 6$$

$$6 + 1 = 7$$

All operators have an order of precedence. Multiplication, division, and modulus have equal precedence, so when they all appear in an equation, the sum is calculated from left to right. Try this calculation:

$$2 * 10 / 5\%3$$

The result is 1, because the calculation simply reads from left to right:

$$2 * 10 = 20$$

$$20 / 5 = 4$$

$$4\%3 = 1$$

Addition and subtraction also have equal precedence.

You can use parentheses to give part of a calculation higher precedence. For example, you could add 1 to 1 and then multiply by 5 like this:

$$(1 + 1) * 5$$

The result will then be 10, but without the parentheses it would have been 6. In fact, you should use parentheses even when they're not essential because they help make the order of the execution clear.

If you use more than one set of parentheses, JavaScript simply works from left to right or, if you have inner parentheses, from the inside out:

```
document.write( ( 1 + 1 ) * 5 * ( 2 + 3 ) );
```

This is how the calculations for the preceding formula are performed:

$$(1 + 1) = 2$$

$$(2 + 3) = 5$$

$$2 * 5 = 10$$

$$10 * 5 = 50$$

As you've seen, JavaScript's addition operator adds the values. What it actually does with the two values depends on the data type you're using. For example, if you're working with two numbers that have been stored as the number data type, the + operator will add them together. However, if one of the data types you're working with is a string (as indicated by the delimiters), the two values will be concatenated. Try this:

```
<html>
<body>
<script type="text/javascript">
      document.write( 'Java' + 'Script' );
      document.write( 1 + 1 );
      document.write( 1 + '1' );
</script>
</body>
</html>
```

Being able to use the addition operator with strings can be handy (and is called the *concatenation* operator in this case), but it can also generate unexpected results if one of the values you're working with happens to be of a different data type from the one you were expecting. We'll be looking at some examples like this, and resolving them, later on.

It's less of a problem if you're working with *literal* values as you have been doing so far. However, much of the data you'll be working with in your programs will be entered by the user or generated by the script, so you won't know in advance exactly what values you're going to be working with. This is where *variables* come in. Variables are placeholders for data in your script, and they're central to JavaScript.

JavaScript Variables

JavaScript is probably the most forgiving language when it comes to variables. You don't need to define what a variable is before you can use it, and you can change the type of a variable any time in the script. However, having variables be created implicitly (not defined first) will not work if your code is running in *Strict Mode*. For more information about this, the Mozilla Developer Network has a full description of how Strict Mode is different at: https://developer.mozilla.org/en-US/docs/JavaScript/Reference/Functions_and_function_scope/Strict_mode.

You declare a variable by giving it a unique name and using the var keyword. Variable names have to start with a letter of the alphabet or with an underscore, while the rest of the name can be made up only of numbers, letters, the dollar sign ($), and underscore characters. Do not use any other characters.

■ **Note**   Like most things in JavaScript, variable names are case sensitive—for example, thisVariable and ThisVariable are different variables. Be very careful about naming your variables; you can run into all sorts of trouble if you don't name them consistently. To that end, most programmers use *camel notation*, where the name of the variable begins with a lowercase letter while subsequent words are capitalized and run in without spaces. Thus, the name thisVariable.

Always give your variables meaningful names. In the next example, we'll build, we're going to write an exchange-rate conversion program, so we'll use variable names like euroToDollarRate and dollarToPound. There are two advantages to naming variables descriptively: it's easier to remember what the code is doing if you come back to it at a later date, and it's easier for someone new to the code to see what's going on. Code readability and layout are very important to the development of web pages. It makes it quicker and easier to spot errors and debug them, and to amend the code as you want to.

■ **Note** Although it is not technically necessary, variable declarations should begin with the keyword var. Not using it could have implications, which you will see as you progress.

With all that said, let's start declaring variables. You can declare a variable without initializing it (giving it a value):

```
var myVariable;
```

Then it's ready and waiting for when you have a value. This is useful for variables that will hold user input. You can also declare and initialize the variable at the same time:

```
var myVariable = "A String";
var anotherVariable = 123;
```

Or you can declare and initialize a variable by assigning it the return value of the prompt() function or the sum of a calculation:

```
var eurosToConvert = prompt("How many Euros do you wish toconvert", "");
var dollars = eurosToConvert * euroToDollarRate;
```

The prompt() function is a JavaScript function that asks the user to enter a value and then returns it to the code. Here you're assigning the value entered to the variable eurosToConvert.

Initializing your variables is a very good idea, especially if you can give them a default value that's useful to the application. Even initializing a variable to an empty string can be a good idea, because you can check back on it without bringing up the error messages that would have popped up if it didn't have a value.

Let's look at how variables can improve both the readability of your code and its functionality. Here's a block of code without any variables:

```
<html>
<body>
<script type="text/javascript">
    document.write( 0.872 * prompt( "How many Euros do you wish to convert", "" ) );
</script>
</body>
</html>
```

It's not immediately obvious that this code is converting euros to dollars, because there's nothing to tell you that 0.872 is the exchange rate. The code works fine though; if you try it out with the number 10, you should get the following result:

8.72

We are using the prompt() method of the window object to get user feedback in this example. (The window is optional in this instance; to keep the code shorter, you can omit it.) This method has two parameters: one label displayed above an entry field and an initial value for the field. You'll learn more about prompt() and how to use it in Chapter 4. Suppose that you want to make the result a little more informative, like this:

---

10 Euros is 8.72 Dollars

Without variables, the only way to do it is to ask users to enter the amount of euros they want to convert twice, and that really isn't user friendly. Using variables, though, you can store the data temporarily and then call it up as many times as you need to:

```
<html>
<body>
<script type="text/javascript">
      // Declare a variable holding the conversion rate
      var euroToDollarRate = 0.872;
      // Declare a new variable and use it to store the
      // number of euros
      var eurosToConvert = prompt( "How many Euros do you wish to convert", "" );
      // Declare a variable to hold the result of the euros
      // multiplied by the conversion
      var dollars = eurosToConvert * euroToDollarRate;
      // Write the result to the page
      document.write( eurosToConvert + " euros is " + dollars + " dollars" );
</script>
</body>
</html>
```

You've used three variables: one to store the exchange rate from euros to dollars, another to store the number of euros that will be converted, and the final one to hold the result of the conversion into dollars. Then all you need to do is write the result using both variables. Not only is this script more functional, it's also much easier to read.

Converting Different Types of Data

For the most part, the JavaScript interpreter can work out what data types you want to be used. In the following code, for example, the interpreter understands the numbers 1 and 2 to be of the number data type and treats them accordingly:

```
<html>
<body>
<script type="text/javascript">
      var myCalc = 1 + 2;
      document.write( "The calculated number is " + myCalc );
</script>
</body>
</html>
```

This will be written to your page:

```
The calculated number is 3
```

However, if you rewrite the code to allow the user to enter his own number using the prompt() function, you'll get a different calculation altogether:

```
<html>
<body>
<script type="text/javascript">
      var userEnteredNumber = prompt( "Please enter a number","" );
```

```
        var myCalc = 1 + userEnteredNumber;
        var myResponse = "The number you entered + 1 = " + myCalc;
        document.write( myResponse );
</script>
</body>
</html>
```

If you enter 2 at the prompt, you'll be told that

```
The number you entered + 1 = 12
```

Rather than adding the two numbers, the JavaScript interpreter concatenated them. This is because the prompt() function actually returns the value entered by the user as a string data type, even though the string contains number characters. The concatenation happens in this line:

```
var myCalc = 1 + userEnteredNumber;
```

In effect, it's the same as if you'd written

```
var myCalc = 1 + "2";
```

If, however, you use the subtraction operator instead, as shown here:

```
var myCalc = 1 - userEnteredNumber;
```

userEnteredNumber is subtracted from 1. The subtraction operator isn't applicable to string data, so JavaScript works out that you wanted the data to be treated as a number, converts the string to a number, and does the calculation. The same applies to the * and / operators. The typeof() operator returns the type of data that has been passed to it, so you can use that to see which data types the JavaScript interpreter is working with:

```
<html>
<body>
<script type="text/javascript">
        var userEnteredNumber = prompt( "Please enter a number","" );
        document.write( typeof( userEnteredNumber ) );
</script>
</body>
</html>
```

This will write the string into the page. The way to ensure that the interpreter is using the desired number data type is to *explicitly* declare that the data is a number. There are three functions you can use to do this:

- Number(): Tries to convert the value of the variable inside the parentheses into a number.

- parseFloat(): Tries to convert the value to a floating point. It parses the string character by character from left to right, until it encounters a character that can't be used in a number. It then stops at that point and evaluates this string as a number. If the first character can't be used in a number, the result is NaN (which stands for *Not a Number*).

- parseInt(): Converts the value to an integer by removing any fractional part without rounding the number up or down. Anything nonnumerical passed to the function is discarded. If the first character is not +, -, or a digit, the result is NaN.

Let's see how these functions work in practice:

```
<html>
<body>
<script type="text/javascript">
        var userEnteredNumber = prompt( "Please enter a number", "" );
        document.write( typeof( userEnteredNumber ) );
        document.write( "<br>" );
        document.write( parseFloat( userEnteredNumber ) );
        document.write( "<br>" );
        document.write( parseInt( userEnteredNumber ) );
        userEnteredNumber = Number( userEnteredNumber )
        document.write( "<br>" );
        document.write( userEnteredNumber );
        document.write( "<br>" );
        document.write( typeof( userEnteredNumber ) );
</script>
</body>
</html>
```

Try entering the value 23.50. You should get this output:

```
string
23.5
23
23.5
number
```

The data entered is read as a string in the first line. Then parseFloat() converts 23.50 from a string to a floating point number, and in the next line, parseInt() strips out the fractional part (without rounding up or down). The variable is then converted to a number using the Number() function and stored in the userEnteredNumber variable itself (overwriting the string held there). On the final line, you see that userEnteredNumber's data type is indeed number.

Try entering 23.50abc at the user prompt:

```
string
23.5
23
NaN
number
```

The results are similar, but this time Number() has returned NaN. The parseFloat() and parseInt() functions still return a number because they work from left to right, converting as much of the string to a number as they can, and then stop when they hit a nonnumeric value. The Number() function rejects any string that contains nonnumerical characters. (Digits, a valid decimal place, and + and – signs are allowed, but nothing else.)

If you try entering abc, you'll just get

```
string
NaN
NaN
NaN
number
```

None of the functions can find a valid number, and so they all return NaN, which you can see is a number data type, but not a valid number. This is a good way of checking user input for validity, and you'll use it to do exactly that later on.

So let's get back to the problem we started with: using prompt() to retrieve a number. All you need to do is tell the interpreter the data entered by the user should be converted to a number data type, using one of the functions discussed with the prompt()function:

```
<html>
<body>
<script type="text/javascript">
    var userEnteredNumber = Number( prompt( "Please entera number", "" ) );
    var myCalc = 1 + userEnteredNumber;
    var myResponse = "The number you entered + 1 = " + myCalc;
    document.write( myResponse );
</script>
</body>
</html>
```

This will not throw any error, but it does not help the visitor much, because the meaning of *NaN* is not common knowledge. Later on, you will deal with conditions, and you'll see how you could prevent an output that does not make much sense to the non-JavaScript-savvy user.

And that's all you need to know about primitive data types and variables for now. Primitive data types, as you have seen, simply hold a value. However, JavaScript can also deal with complex data, and it does this using *composite* data types.

The Composite Data Types: Array and Object

Composite data types are different from simple data types, because they can hold more than one value. There are two composite data types:

- **Object:** Contains a reference to any object, including the objects that the browser makes available

- **Array:** Contains one or more of other data types

We'll look at the object data type first. As you might recall from the discussion in Chapter1, objects model real-world entities. These objects can hold data and provide you with properties and methods.

Objects JavaScript Supplies You with: `String`, `Date`, and `Math`

This is not a complete list of built-in objects, but you will start to get a feel for how objects work by looking at the following ones:

- `String` object: Stores a string, and provides properties and methods for working with strings

- `Date` object: Stores a date, and provides methods for working with it

- `Math` object: Doesn't store data, but provides properties and methods for manipulating mathematical data

Let's start with the `String` object.

The `String` Object

Earlier, you created string primitives by giving them some characters to hold, like this:

```
var myPrimitiveString = "ABC123";
```

A `String` *object* does things slightly differently, not only allowing you to store characters, but also providing a way to manipulate and change those characters. You can create `String` objects explicitly or implicitly.

Creating a `String` Object

Let's work with the implicit method first: we'll begin by declaring a new variable and assigning it a new string primitive to initialize it. Try that now using `typeof()` to make sure that the data in the variable `myStringPrimitive` is a string primitive:

```
<html>
<body>
<script type="text/javascript">
    var myStringPrimitive= "abc";
    document.write( typeof( myStringPrimitive ) );
</script>
</body>
</html>
```

You can still use the `String` object's methods on it, though. JavaScript will simply convert the string primitive to a temporary `String` object, use the method on it, and then change the data type back to string. You can try that out using the `length` *property* of the `String` object:

```
<html>
<body>
<script type="text/javascript">
    var myStringPrimitive= "abc";
    document.write( typeof( myStringPrimitive ) );
    document.write( "<br>" );
    document.write( myStringPrimitive.length );
    document.write( "<br>" );
    document.write( typeof( myStringPrimitive ) );
</script>
</body>
</html>
```

This is what you should see in the browser window:

```
string
3
String
```

So `myStringPrimitive` is still holding a string primitive after the temporary conversion. You can also create `String` objects explicitly, using the new keyword together with the `String()` *constructor*:

```
<html>
<body>
<script type="text/javascript">
     var myStringObject = new String( "abc" );
     document.write( typeof( myStringObject ) );
     document.write( "<br>" );
     document.write( myStringObject.length );
     document.write( "<br>" );
     document.write( typeof( myStringObject ) );
</script>
</body>
</html>
```

Loading this page displays the following:

```
object
3
object
```

The only difference between this script and the previous one is in the first line, where you create the new object and supply some characters for the `String` object to store:

```
var myStringObject = new String( "abc" );
```

The result of checking the `length` property is the same whether you create the `String` object implicitly or explicitly. The only real difference between creating `String` objects explicitly or implicitly is that creating them explicitly is marginally more efficient if you're going to be using the same `String` object again and again. Explicitly creating `String` objects also helps prevent the JavaScript interpreter getting confused between numbers and strings, as it can do.

Using the `String` Object's Methods

The `String` object has a lot of methods, so I'll limit this discussion to two of them here, the `indexOf()` and `substring()` methods.

JavaScript strings, as you've seen, are made up of characters. Each of these characters is given an index. The index is zero-based, so the first character's position has the index 0, the second 1, and so on. The method `indexOf()` finds and returns the position in the index at which a substring begins (and the `lastIndexOf()` method returns the position of the last occurrence of the substring). For example, if you want your user to enter an e-mail address, you could check that she included the @ symbol in her entry. (Although this wouldn't ensure that the address is valid, it would at least go some way in that direction. We'll be working with much more complex data checking later on in the book.)

25

Let's do that next, using the prompt()method to obtain the user's e-mail address and then check the input for the @ symbol, returning the index of the symbol using indexOf():

```
<html>
<body>
<script type="text/javascript">
      var userEmail= prompt("Please enter your emailaddress ", "" );
      document.write( userEmail.indexOf( "@" ) );
</script>
</body>
</html>
```

If the @ is not found, −1 is written to the page. As long as the character is there in the string somewhere, its position in the index—in other words, something greater than −1,will be returned.

The substring() method carves one string from another string, taking the indexes of the start and end positions of the substring as parameters. You can return everything from the first index to the end of the string by leaving off the second parameter.

So, to extract all the characters from the third character (at index 2) to the sixth character (index 5), you'd write

```
<html>
<body>
<script type="text/javascript">
      var myOldString = "Hello World";
      var myNewString = myOldString.substring( 2, 5 );
      document.write( myNewString );
</script>
</body>
</html>
```

You should see llo written out to the browser. Note that the substring() method copies the substring that it returns, and it doesn't alter the original string.

The substring() method really comes into its own when you're working with unknown values. Here's another example that uses both the indexOf() and substring() methods:

```
<html>
<body>
<script type="text/javascript">
      var characterName = "my name is Simpson,  Homer";
      var firstNameIndex = characterName.indexOf( "Simpson," ) + 9;
      var firstName = characterName.substring( firstNameIndex );
      document.write( firstName );
</script>
</body>
</html>
```

You're extracting Homer from the string in the variable characterName, using indexOf() to find the start of the last name and adding 9 to it to get the index of the start of the first name (because "Simpson, " is 9 characters long), and storing it in firstNameIndex. This is used by the substring() method to extract everything from the start of the first name—you haven't specified the final index, so the rest of the characters in the string will be returned.

Now let's look at the Date object. This allows you to store dates and provides some useful date/time-related functionality.

The Date Object

JavaScript doesn't have a primitive date data type, so you can create Date objects only explicitly. You create new Date objects the same way as you create String objects, using the new keyword together with the Date() constructor. This line creates a Date object containing the current date and time:

```
var todaysDate = new Date();
```

To create a Date object that stores a specific date or time, you simply put the date, or date and time, inside the parentheses:

```
var newMillennium = new Date( "1 Jan 2000 10:24:00" );
```

Different countries describe dates in a different order. For example, in the US dates are specified in *MM/DD/YY*, while in Europe they are *DD/MM/YY*, and in China they are *YY/MM/DD*. If you specify the month using the abbreviated name, then you can use any order:

```
var someDate = new Date( "10 Jan 2013" );
var someDate = new Date( "Jan 10 2013" );
var someDate = new Date( "2013 10 Jan" );
```

In fact, the Date object can take a number of parameters:

```
var someDate = new Date( aYear, aMonth, aDate, anHour, aMinute, aSecond, aMillisecond )
```

To use these parameters, you first need to specify year and month, and then use the parameters you want—although you do have to run through them in order and can't select among them. For example, you can specify year, month, date, and hour:

```
var someDate = new Date( 2013, 9, 22, 17 );
```

You can't specify year, month, and then hours, though:

```
var someDate = new Date( 2013, 9, , 17 );
```

■ **Note**   Although you usually think of month 9 as September, JavaScript starts counting months from 0 (January), so September is represented as month 8.

Using the Date Object

The Date object has a lot of methods you can use to get or set a date or time. You can use local time (the time on your computer in your time zone) or UTC (Coordinated Universal Time, once called Greenwich Mean Time). Although this can be very useful, you need to be aware when you're working with Date that many people don't set their time zone correctly.

Let's look at an example that demonstrates some of the methods:

```html
<html>
<body>
<script type="text/javascript">
     // Create a new date object
     var someDate = new Date( "31 Jan 2013 11:59" );
     // Retrieve the first four values using the
     // appropriate get methods
     document.write( "Minutes = " + someDate.getMinutes() + "<br>" );
     document.write( "Year = " + someDate.getFullYear() + "<br>" );
     document.write( "Month = " + someDate.getMonth() + "<br>" );
     document.write( "Date = " + someDate.getDate() + "<br>" );
     // Set the minutes to 34
     someDate.setMinutes( 34 );
     document.write( "Minutes = " + someDate.getMinutes() + "<br>" );
     // Reset the date
     someDate.setDate( 32 );
     document.write( "Date = " + someDate.getDate() + "<br>" );
     document.write( "Month = " + someDate.getMonth() + "<br>" );
</script>
</body>
</html>
```

Here's what you should get:

```
Minutes = 59
Year = 2013
Month = 0
Date = 31
Minutes = 34
Date = 1
Month = 1
```

This line of code might look a bit counterintuitive at first:

```
someDate.setDate( 32 );
```

JavaScript knows that there aren't 32 days in January, so instead of trying to set the date to the January 32, the interpreter counts 32 days beginning with January 1, which gives us February 1.

This can be a handy feature if you need to add days onto a date. Usually, you'd have to take into account the number of days in the different months, and whether it's a leap year, if you wanted to add a number of days to a date, but it's much easier to use JavaScript's understanding of dates instead:

```html
<html>
<body>
<script type="text/javascript">
     // Ask the user to enter a date string
     var originalDate = prompt("Enter a date (Day, Name of the Month, Year"), "31 Dec 2013" );
     // Overwrite the originalDate variable with a new Date
     // object
```

```
        var originalDate = new Date( originalDate );
        // Ask the user to enter the number of days to be
        // added, and convert to number
        var addDays = Number( prompt( "Enter number of daysto be added", "1" ) )
        // Set a new value for originalDate of originalDate
        // plus the days to be added
        originalDate.setDate( originalDate.getDate( ) + addDays )
        // Write out the date held by the originalDate
        // object using the toString( ) method
        document.write( originalDate.toString( ) )
</script>
</body>
</html>
```

If you enter 31 Dec 2013 when prompted, and 1 for the number of days to be added, the answer you'll get is Thu Jan 1 00:00:00 UTC 2014.

Note   Notice that you're using the Number() method of the Math object on the third line of the script. The program will still run if you don't, but the result won't be the same. If you don't want to use the method, there is a trick to convert different data types: if you subtract o from a string that could be converted to a number using parseInt(), parseFloat(), or Number(), you convert it to a number, and if you add an empty string, "", to a number, you convert it to a string, something you normally do with toString().

On the fourth line, you set the date to the current day of the month, which is the value returned by originalDate.getDate() plus the number of days to be added; then comes the calculation, and the final line outputs the date contained in the Date object as a string using the toString() method. In addition, toDateString() produces a nicely formatted string using the date alone. You can use the same methods for get and set if you're working with UTC time—all you need to do is add *UTC* to the method name. So getHours() becomes getUTCHours(), setMonth() becomes setUTCMonth(), and so on. You can also use the getTimezoneOffset() method to return the difference, in hours, between the computer's local time and UTC time. (You'll have to rely on users having set their time zones correctly and be aware of the differences in daylight saving time between different countries.)

Note   For crucial date manipulation, JavaScript might not be the correct technology, becauseyou cannot trust the client computer to be properly set up. You could, however, populate the initial date of your JavaScript via a server-side language and go from there.

The Math Object

The Math object provides you with lots of mathematical functionality, like finding the square of a number or producing a random number. The Math object is different from the Date and String objects in two ways:

- You can't create a Math object explicitly, you just go ahead and use it.
- The Math object doesn't store data, unlike the String and Date objects.

You call the methods of the Math object using the following format:

```
Math.methodOfMathObject( aNumber ):
alert( "The value of pi is " + Math.PI );
```

We'll look at a few of the commonly used methods next. (You can find a complete reference by running a search at https://developer.mozilla.org/en-US/docs/Web_Development.) We'll look at the methods for rounding numbers and generating random numbers here.

Rounding Numbers

You saw earlier that the parseInt() function will make a fractional number whole by removing everything after the decimal point (so 24.999 becomes 24). Pretty often, you'll want more mathematically accurate calculations—if you're working with financial calculations, for example—and for these, you can use one of the Math object's three rounding functions: round(), ceil(), and floor(). This is how they work:

- round(): Rounds a number up when the decimal is .5 or greater
- ceil()(as in *ceiling*): Always rounds up, so 23.75 becomes 24, as does 23.25
- floor(): Always rounds down, so 23.75 becomes 23, as does 23.25

Here they are at work in a simple example:

```
<html>
<body>
<script type="text/javascript">
     var numberToRound = prompt( "Please enter a number", "" )
     document.write( "round( ) = " + Math.round( numberToRound ) );
     document.write( "<br>" );
     document.write( "floor( ) = " + Math.floor( numberToRound ) );
     document.write( "<br>" );
     document.write( "ceil( ) = " + Math.ceil( numberToRound ) );
</script>
</body>
</html>
```

Even though you used prompt() to obtain a value from the user, which as you saw earlier returns a string, the number returned is still treated as a number. This is because the rounding methods do the conversion for you as long as the string contains something that can be converted to a number.

If you enter 23.75, you get the following result:

```
round() = 24
floor() = 23
ceil() = 24
```

If you enter -23.75, you get

```
round() = -24
floor() = -24
ceil() = -23
```

Generating a Random Number

You can generate a fractional random number that is 0 or greater but smaller than 1 using the Math object's random( ) method. Usually, you'll need to multiply the number, and then use one of the rounding methods to make it useful.

For example, to mimic a die throw, you'd need to generate a random number between 1 and 6. You could create this by multiplying the random fraction by 6, to give a fractional number between 0 and 6, and then round the number down to a whole number using the floor( ) method. Here's the code:

```
<html>
<body>
<script type="text/javascript">
        var diceThrow = Math.floor( Math.random( ) * 6 ) + 1;
        document.write( "You threw a " + diceThrow );
</script>
</body>
</html>
```

Arrays

JavaScript allows you to store and access related data using an *array*. An array is a bit like a row of boxes (***elements***), with each box containing a single item of data. An array can work with any of the data types that JavaScript supports. For example, you could use an array to work with a list of items that the users will select from, or for a set of graph coordinates, or to reference a group of images.

Array objects, like String and Date objects, are created using the new keyword together with the constructor. You can initialize an Array object when you create it:

```
var preInitArray = new Array( "First item", "Second item", "Third Item" );
```

Or you can set it to hold a certain number of items:

```
var preDeterminedSizeArray = new Array( 3 );
```

Or you can just create an empty array:

```
var anArray = new Array();
```

You can add new items to an array by assigning values to the elements:

```
anArray[0] = "anItem";
anArray[1] = "anotherItem"
anArray[2] = "andAnother"
```

▦ **Note**   You do not have to use the array() constructor; instead, it is perfectly valid to use a shortcut notation.

```
var myArray = [1, 2, 3];
var yourArray = ["red", "blue", "green"];
```

Once you've populated an array, you can access its elements through their indexes or positions (which, once again, are zero-based) using square brackets:

```
<html>
<body>
<script type="text/javascript">
     var preInitArray = new Array( "First Item" "Second Item", "Third Item" );
     document.write( preInitArray[0] + "<br>" );
     document.write( preInitArray[1] + "<br>" );
     document.write( preInitArray[2] + "<br>" );
</script>
</body>
</html>
```

Using index numbers to store items is useful if you want to loop through the array—we'll look at loops next.

You can create associated arrays (called *hashes* in other languages) by using keywords and assigning them values, like this:

```
<html>
<body>
<script type="text/javascript">
     // Creating an array object and setting index
     // position 0 to equal the string Fruit
     var anArray = new Array( );
     anArray[0] = "Fruit";
     // Setting the index using the keyword
     // 'CostOfApple' as the index.
     anArray["CostOfApple"] = 0.75;
     document.write( anArray[0] + "<br>" );
     document.write( anArray["CostOfApple"] );
</script>
</body>
</html>
```

Keywords are good for situations where you can give the data useful labels, or if you're storing entries that are meaningful only in context, like a list of graph coordinates. You can't, however, access entries using an index number if they have been set using keywords (as you can in some other languages, like PHP). You can also use variables for the index. You can rewrite the previous example using variables (one holding a string and the other a number) instead of literal values:

```
<html>
<body>
<script type="text/javascript">
     var anArray = new Array( );
     var itemIndex = 0;
     var itemKeyword = "CostOfApple";
     anArray[itemIndex] = "Fruit";
     anArray[itemKeyword] = 0.75;
     document.write( anArray[itemIndex] + "<br>" );
     document.write( anArray[itemKeyword] );
</script>
</body>
</html>
```

Let's put what we've discussed about arrays and the Math object into an example. We'll write a script that randomly selects a banner to display at the top of the page.

We'll use an Array object to hold some image source names, like this:

```
var bannerImages = new Array();
bannerImages[0] = "Banner1.jpg";
bannerImages[1] = "Banner2.jpg";
bannerImages[2] = "Banner3.jpg";
bannerImages[3] = "Banner4.jpg";
bannerImages[4] = "Banner5.jpg";
bannerImages[5] = "Banner6.jpg";
bannerImages[6] = "Banner7.jpg";
```

Then you need seven images with corresponding names to sit in the same folder as the HTML page. You can use your own or download mine from http://www.beginningjavascript.com.

Next you'll initialize a new variable, randomImageIndex, and use it to generate a random number. You'll use the same method you used to generate a random die throw earlier, but without adding 1 to the result because you need a random number from 0 to 6:

```
var randomImageIndex = Math.round( Math.random( ) * 6 );
```

Then you'll use document.write() to write the randomly selected image into the page. Here's the complete script:

```
<html>
<body>
<script type="text/javascript">
    var bannerImages = new Array( );
    bannerImages[0] = "Banner1.jpg";
    bannerImages[1] = "Banner2.jpg";
    bannerImages[2] = "Banner3.jpg";
    bannerImages[3] = "Banner4.jpg";
    bannerImages[4] = "Banner5.jpg";
    bannerImages[5] = "Banner6.jpg";
    bannerImages[6] = "Banner7.jpg";
    var randomImageIndex = Math.round( Math.random( ) * 6 );
    document.write( "<img alt=\"\" src=\"" + bannerImages[randomImageIndex] + "\">" );
</script>
</body>
</html>
```

And that's all there is to it. Having the banner change will make it more noticeable to visitors than if you displayed the same banner every time users came to the page—and, of course, it gives the impression that the site is being updated frequently.

The Array Object's Methods and Properties

One of the most commonly used properties of the Array object is the length property, which returns the index one count higher than the index of the last array item in the array. If, for example, you're working with an array with elements with indexes of 0, 1, 2, 3, the length will be 4—which is useful to know if you want to add another element.

33

The Array object provides a number of methods for manipulating arrays, including methods for cutting a number of items from an array or joining two arrays together. We'll look at the methods for concatenating, slicing, and sorting next.

Cutting a Slice of an Array

The slice() method is to an Array object what the substring() method is to a String object. You simply tell the method which elements you want to be sliced. This is useful, for example, if you want to slice information being passed using a URL.

The slice() method takes two parameters: the index of the first element of the slice, which will be included in the slice, and the index of the final element, which won't be. To access the second, third, and fourth values from an array holding five values in all, you use the indexes 1 and 4:

```
<html>
<body>
<script type="text/javascript">
      // Create and initialize the array
      var fullArray = new Array( "One", "Two", "Three","Four", "Five" );
      // Slice from element 1 to element 4 and store
      // in new variable sliceOfArray
      var sliceOfArray = fullArray.slice( 1, 4 );
      // Write out new ( zero-based ) array of 3 elements
      document.write( sliceOfArray[0] + "<br>" );
      document.write( sliceOfArray[1] + "<br>" );
      document.write( sliceOfArray[2] + "<br>" );
</script>
</body>
</html>
```

The new array stores the numbers in a new zero-based array, so slicing indexes 0, 1, and 2 gives you the following:

```
Two
Three
Four
```

The original array is unaffected, but you could overwrite the Array object in the variable by setting it to the result of the slice() method if you needed to:

```
fullArray = fullArray.slice( 1, 4 );
```

Joining Two Arrays

The Array object's concat() method allows you to concatenate arrays. You can add two or more arrays using this method, each new array starting where the previous one ends. Here you're joining three arrays: arrayOne, arrayTwo, and arrayThree:

```
<html>
<body>
<script type="text/javascript">
```

```
        var arrayOne = new Array( "One", "Two", "Three","Four", "Five" );
        var arrayTwo = new Array( "ABC", "DEF", "GHI" );
        var arrayThree = new Array( "John", "Paul", "George","Ringo" );
        var joinedArray = arrayOne.concat( arrayTwo, arrayThree );
        document.write( "joinedArray has " + joinedArray.length + " elements<br>" );
        document.write( joinedArray[0] + "<br>" )
        document.write( joinedArray[11] + "<br>" )
</script>
</body>
</html>
```

The new array, `joinedArray`, has 12 items. The items in this array are the same as they were in each of the previous arrays; they've simply been concatenated together. The original arrays remain untouched.

Converting an Array to a String and Back

Having data in an array is handy when you want to loop through it or select certain elements. However, when you need to send the data somewhere else, you probably should convert that data to a string. You can do that by looping through the array and adding each element value to a string. However, there is no need for that, because the `Array` object has a method called `join()` that does that for you. The method takes a string as a parameter. This string will be added in between each element.

```
<script type="text/javascript">
  var arrayThree = new Array( "John", "Paul", "George","Ringo" );
  var lineUp=arrayThree.join( ',  ' );
  alert( lineUp );
</script>
```

The resulting string, `lineUp`, has the value `"John, Paul, George, Ringo"`. The opposite of `join()` is `split()`, which is a method that converts a string to an array.

```
<script type="text/javascript">
  var lineUp="John,  Paul,  George,  Ringo";
  var members=lineUp.split( ',  ' );
  alert( members.length );
</script>
```

Sorting an Array

The `sort()` method allows you to sort the items in an array into alphabetical or numerical order:

```
<html>
<body>
<script type="text/javascript">
        var arrayToSort = new Array( "Cabbage", "Lemon","Apple", "Pear", "Banana" );
        arrayToSort.sort( );
        document.write(arrayToSort[0] + "<br>" );
        document.write(arrayToSort[1] + "<br>" );
        document.write(arrayToSort[2] + "<br>" );
```

```
      document.write(arrayToSort[3] + "<br>" );
      document.write(arrayToSort[4] + "<br>" );
</script>
</body>
</html>
```

The items are arranged like this:

```
Apple
Banana
Cabbage
Lemon
Pear
```

If, however, you lower the case of one of the letters—the *A* of *Apple*, for example—then you'll end up with a very different result. The sorting is strictly mathematical—by the number of the character in the ASCII set, not like a human being would sort the words.

If you want to change the order in which the sorted elements are displayed, you can use the reverse() method to display the last one in the alphabet as the first element:

```
<script type="text/javascript">
  var arrayToSort = new Array( "Cabbage", "Lemon", "Apple", "Pear", "Banana" );
   arrayToSort.sort( );
sortedArray.reverse( );
  document.write(sortedArray[0] + "<br>" );
  document.write(sortedArray[1] + "<br>" );
  document.write(sortedArray[2] + "<br>" );
  document.write(sortedArray[3] + "<br>" );
  document.write(sortedArray[4] + "<br>" );
</script>
```

The resulting list is now in reverse order:

```
Pear
Lemon
Cabbage
Banana
Apple
```

Making Decisions in JavaScript

Decision making is what gives programs their apparent intelligence. You can't write a good program without it, whether you're creating a game, checking a password, giving the user a set of choices based on previous decisions he has made, or something else.

Decisions are based on conditional statements, which are simply statements that evaluate to true or false. This is where the primitive Boolean data type comes in useful. Loops are the other essential tool of decision making, enabling you to loop through user input or an array, for example, and make decisions accordingly.

The Logical and Comparison Operators

There are two main groups of operators we'll look at:

- **Data comparison operators:** Compare operands and return Boolean values
- **Logical operators:** Test for more than one condition

We'll start with the comparison operators.

Comparing Data

Table 2-3 lists some of the more commonly used comparison operators.

Table 2-3. *Comparisons in JavaScript*

Operator	Description	Example
==	Checks whether the left and right operands are equal	`123 == 234` returns false. `123 == 123` returns true.
===	Checks whether the left and right operands are equal and whether the data types are equal	`123 ==="234"` returns false. `123 === 123` returns true.
!=	Checks whether the left operand is not equal to the right side	`123 != 123` returns false. `123 != 234` returns true.
>	Checks whether the left operand is greater than the right	`123 > 234` returns false. `234 > 123` returns true.
>=	Checks whether the left operand is greater than or equal to the right	`123 >= 234` returns false. `123 >= 123` returns true.
<	Checks whether the left operand is less than the right	`234 < 123` returns false. `123 < 234` returns true.
<=	Checks whether the left operand is less than, or equal to, the right	`234 <= 123` returns false. `234 <= 234` returns true.

■ **Caution**   Beware the `==` equality operator: it's all too easy to create errors in a script by using the assignment operator, `=`, by mistake.

These operators all work with string type data as well as numerical data, and they are case sensitive:

```
<html>
<body>
<script type="text/javascript">
document.write("Apple" == "Apple" )
    document.write("<br>" );
    document.write("Apple"<"Banana" )
```

```
        document.write("<br>" );
        document.write("apple"<"Banana" )
</script>
</body>
</html>
```

This is what you should get back:

```
true
true
false
```

When evaluating an expression comparing strings, the JavaScript interpreter compares the ASCII codes for each character in turn of both strings—the first character of each string, then the second character, and so on. Uppercase *A* is represented in ASCII by the number 65, *B* by 66, *C* by 67, and so on. To evaluate the expression "Apple"<"Banana", the JavaScript interpreter tests the comparison by substituting the ASCII code for the first character in each string: 65 < 66, so *A* sorts first, and the comparison is true. When testing the expression "apple"<"Banana", the JavaScript interpreter does the same thing; however, the lowercase letter *a* has the ASCII code 97, so the expression "a"<"B" reduces to 97 < 66, which is false. You can do alphabetical comparisons using <, <=, >, >= operators. If you need to ensure that all the letters are of the same case, you can use the String object's toUpperCase() and toLowerCase() methods. Comparison operators, just like the numerical operators, can be used with variables. If you want to compare apple and Banana alphabetically, you do this:

```
<html>
<body>
<script type="text/javascript">
        var string1 = "apple";
        var string2 = "Banana";
        string1 = string1.toLowerCase( );
        string2 = string2.toLowerCase( );
        document.write( string1 < string2 )
</script>
</body>
</html>
```

There is something else you need to be aware of when you're comparing String objects using the equality operator, though. Try this:

```
<html>
<body>
<script type="text/javascript">
        var string1 = new String( "Apple" );
        var string2 = new String( "Apple" );
        document.write( string1 == string2 )
</script>
</body>
</html>
```

You'll get false returned. In fact, what we've done here is compare two String *objects* rather than the *characters* of two string primitives and, as the returned false indicates, two String objects can't be the same object even if they do hold the same characters.

If you do need to compare the strings held by two objects, you can use the valueOf() method to perform a comparison of the data values:

```
<html>
<body>
<script type="text/javascript">
      var string1 = new String( "Apple" );
      var string2 = new String( "Apple" );
      document.write( string1.valueOf() == string2.valueOf() );
</script>
</body>
</html>
```

Logical Operators

Sometimes you'll need to combine comparisons into one condition group. You might want to check that the information users have given makes sense, or restrict the selections they can make according to their earlier answers. You can do this using the logical operators shown in Table 2-4.

Table 2-4. Logical Operators in JavaScript

Symbol	Operator	Description	Example
&&	And	Both conditions must be true.	123 == 234 && 123 < 20 (false) 123 == 234 && 123 == 123 (false) 123 == 123 && 234 < 900 (true)
||	Or	Either or both of the conditions must be true.	123 == 234 || 123 < 20 (false) 123 == 234 || 123 == 123 (true) 123 == 123 || 234 < 900 (true)
!	Not	Reverses the logic.	!(123 == 234) (true) !(123 == 123) (false)

Once you've evaluated the data, you need to be able to make decisions according to the outcome. This is where conditional statements and loops are useful. You'll find that the operators that we've looked at in this chapter are most often used in the context of a conditional statement or loop.

Conditional Statements

The if...else structure is used to test conditions and looks like this:

```
if ( condition ) {
// Execute code in here if condition is true
} else {
// Execute code in here if condition is false
}
// After if/else code execution resumes here
```

If the condition being tested is true, the code within the curly braces following the if will be executed, but won't if it isn't. You can also create a block of code to execute should the condition set out in the if *not* be met, by using a final else statement.

Let's improve on the currency exchange converter you built earlier on in the chapter and create a loop to deal with nonnumeric input from the user:

```
<html>
<body>
<script type="text/javascript">
        var euroToDollarRate = 0.872;
        // Try to convert the input into a number
        var eurosToConvert = Number( prompt( "How many Euros do you wish to convert", "" ) );
        // If the user hasn't entered a number,  then NaN
        // will be returned
        if ( isNaN( eurosToConvert ) ) {
          // Ask the user to enter a value in numerals
          document.write( "Please enter the number in numerals" );
          // If NaN is not returned,  then we can use the input
        } else {
          // and do the conversion as before
          var dollars = eurosToConvert * euroToDollarRate;
          document.write( eurosToConvert + " euros is " + dollars + " dollars" );
        }
</script>
</body>
</html>
```

The if statement is using the isNaN() function, which will return true if the value in variable eurosToConvert is not a number.

Note   Remember to keep error messages as polite and helpful as possible. Good error messages that inform users clearly what is expected of them make using applications much more painless.

You can create more complex conditions by using logical operators and nesting if statements:

```
<html>
<body>
<script type="text/javascript">
        // Ask the user for a number and try to convert the
        // input into a number
        var userNumber = Number( prompt( "Enter a number between 1 and 10", "" ) );
          // If the value of userNumber is NaN,  ask the user
          // to try again
        if ( isNaN( userNumber ) ) {
          document.write( "Please ensure a valid number is entered" );
          // If the value is a number but over 10, ask the
          //user to try again
        } else {
```

```
      if ( userNumber > 10 || userNumber < 1 ) {
        document.write( "The number you entered is notbetween 1 and 10" );
      // Otherwise the number is between 1 and 10, so
      // write to the page
      } else {
        document.write( "The number you entered was " + userNumber );
      }
    }
</script>
</body>
</html>
```

You know that the number is fine just so long as it is a numeric value and is under 10.

Note   Observe the layout of the code. You have indented the `if` and `else` statements and blocks so that it's easy to read and to see where code blocks start and stop. It's essential to make your code as legible as possible.

Try reading this code without the indenting or spacing:

```
<html>
<body>
<script type="text/javascript">
// Ask for a number using the prompt() function and try to make it a number
var userNumber = Number(prompt("Enter a number between 1 and 10",""));
// If the value of userNumber is NaN, ask the user to try again
if (isNaN(userNumber)){
document.write("Please ensure a valid number is entered");
}
// If the value is a number but over 10, ask the user to try again
else {
if (userNumber > 10 || userNumber < 1) {
document.write("The number you entered is not between 1 and 10");
}
// Otherwise the number is between 1 and 10, so write to the screen
else{
document.write("The number you entered was " + userNumber);
}
}
</script>
</body>
</html>
```

It's not impossible to read, but even in this short script, it's harder to decipher which code blocks belong to the `if` and `else` statements. In longer pieces of code, inconsistent indenting or illogical indenting makes code very difficult to read, which in turn leaves you with more bugs to fix and makes your job unnecessarily harder.

You can also use else if statements, where the else statement starts with another if statement, like this:

```
<html>
<body>
<script type="text/javascript">
     var userNumber = Number( prompt( "Enter a number between1 and 10", "" ) );
     if ( isNaN( userNumber ) ){
       document.write( "Please ensure a valid number isentered" );
     } else if ( userNumber > 10 || userNumber < 1 ) {
       document.write( "The number you entered is notbetween 1 and 10" );
     } else {
       document.write( "The number you entered was " +userNumber );
     }
</script>
</body>
</html>
```

The code does the same thing as the earlier piece, but it uses an else if statement instead of a nested if and is two lines shorter.

Breaking Out of a Branch or Loop

One more thing before we move on: you can break a conditional statement or loop using the break statement. This simply terminates the block of code running and drops the processing through to the next statement. We'll be using this in the next example.

You can have as many if, else, and else ifs as you like, although they can make your code terribly complicated if you use too many. If there are a lot of possible conditions to check a value against in a piece of code, then the switch statement, which you'll look at next, can be helpful.

Testing Multiple Values: The switch Statement

The switch statement allows you to switch between sections of code based on the value of a variable or expression. This is the outline of a switch statement:

```
switch( expression ) {
  case someValue:
  // Code to execute if expression == someValue;
  break; // End execution
  case someOtherValue:
  // Code to execute if expression == someOtherValue;
  break; // End execution
  case yesAnotherValue:
  // Code to execute if expression == yetAnotherValue;
  break; // End execution
  default:
  // Code to execute if no values matched
}
```

JavaScript evaluates `switch(expression)` and then compares it to each `case`. As soon as a match is found, the code starts executing at that point and continues through all the `case` statements until a break is found. It's often useful to include a default `case` that will execute if none of the `case` statements match. This is a helpful tool for picking up on errors, where, for example, you expect a match to occur but a bug prevents that from happening.

The values of the cases can be of any data type, numbers, or strings, for example. You can have just one case or as many cases as you need. Let's look at a simple example:

```html
<html>
<body>
<script type="text/javascript">
    // Store user entered number between 1 and 4 in userNumber
    var userNumber = Number( prompt( "Enter a number between 1 and 4", "" ) );
    switch( userNumber ) {
      // If userNumber is 1, write out and carry on
      // executing after case statement
      case 1:
        document.write( "Number 1" );
      break;
      case 2:
        document.write( "Number 2" );
      break;
      case 3:
        document.write( "Number 3" );
      break;
      case 4:
        document.write( "Number 4" );
      break;
      default:
        document.write( "Please enter a numeric value between 1 and 4." );
      break;
    }
    // Code continues executing here
</script>
</body>
</html>
```

Try it out. You should just get the number you've entered written out or the sentence "Please enter a numeric value between 1 and 4."

This example also illustrates the importance of the break statement. If you don't include break after each case, execution carries on within the block until the end of the `switch`. Try removing the breaks and then enter 2. Everything after the match will execute, giving you this output:

```
Number 2Number 3Number 4Please enter a numeric value between 1 and 4
```

You can use any valid expression inside the `switch` statement—a calculation, for example:

```
switch( userNumber * 100 + someOtherVariable )
```

You can also have one or more statements in between the case statements.

Repeating Things: Loops

In this section, we look at how you can repeat a block of code for as long as a set condition is true. For example, you might want to loop through each input element on an HTML form or through each item in an array.

Repeating a Set Number of Times: The `for` Loop

The `for` loop is designed to loop through a code block a number of times and looks like this:

```
for( initial-condition; loop-condition; alter-condition ) {
  //
  // Code to be repeatedly executed
  //
}
// After loop completes,  execution of code continues here
```

Like the conditional statement, the `for` keyword is followed by parentheses. This time, the parentheses contain three parts separated by a semicolon.

The first part initializes a variable that will serve as the counter to keep track of the number of loops made. The second part tests for a condition. The loop will keep running as long as this condition is true. The last part either increments or decrements the counter, created in the first part, after each loop. (The fact that it is after is an important one in programming as you shall see.)

For example, take a look at a loop that keeps running for as long as `loopCounter` is less than 10:

```
for( loopCounter = 1; loopCounter <= 10; loopCounter++ )
```

The loop keeps executing as long as the loop condition evaluates to true—for as long as `loopCounter` is less than or equal to 10. Once it hits 11, the looping stops and execution of the code continues at the next statement after the loop's closing parenthesis.

Let's look at an example that uses the `for` loop to run through an array. You'll use a `for` loop to run through an array called `theBeatles` using a variable called `loopCounter` to keep the loop running while the value of `loopCounter` is less than the length of the array:

```
<html>
<body>
<script type="text/javascript">
      var theBeatles = new Array( "John", "Paul", "George","Ringo" );
      for ( var loopCounter = 0; loopCounter < theBeatles.length; loopCounter++ ) {
        document.write( theBeatles[loopCounter] + "<br>" );
      }
</script>
</body>
</html>
```

This example works because you are using a zero-based array in which the items have been added to the index in sequence. The loop won't run if you use keywords to store items in an array like this:

```
theBeatles["Drummer"] = "Ringo";
```

Earlier, when I discussed arrays, I stated that the `Array` object has a property that knows the length (how many elements). When looping through arrays, such as in the previous example, you use the name of the array followed by a dot and length as the condition. This prevents the loop from counting beyond the length of the array, which would cause an "Out of Bounds" error.

JavaScript also supports the `for..in` loop (which has been around since Netscape Navigator 2, although Internet Explorer has supported it only since IE5). Instead of using a counter, the `for...in` loop runs though each item in the array using a variable to access the array. Let's create an array this way and see how it works:

```html
<html>
<body>
<script type="text/javascript">
    // Initialize theBeatles object and store in a variable
    var theBeatles = new Object( );
    // Set the values using keys rather than numbers
    theBeatles["Drummer"] = "Ringo";
    theBeatles["SingerRhythmGuitar"] = "John";
    theBeatles["SingerBassGuitar"] = "Paul";
    theBeatles["SingerLeadGuitar"] = "George";
    var indexKey;
    // Write out each indexKey and the value for that
    // indexKey from the array
    for ( indexKey in theBeatles ) {
      document.write( "indexKey is " + indexKey + "<br>" );
      document.write( "item value is " + theBeatles[indexKey] + "<br><br>" );
    }
</script>
</body>
</html>
```

The results of the item key in `indexKey` at each iteration of the loop is written out alongside the value extracted from the array using that key in the same order as it occurs in the array:

```
indexKey is Drummer
item value is Ringo

indexKey is SingerRhythmGuitar
item value is John

indexKey is SingerBassGuitar
item value is Paul

indexKey is SingerLeadGuitar
item value is George
```

Repeating Actions According to a Decision: The `while` Loop

The loops you have been working with so far take the instruction to stop looping from inside the script itself. There are likely to be times when you'll want the user to determine when the loop should stop, or when you want the loop to stop when a certain user-led condition is met. The `while` and `do...while` loops are intended for just this sort of situation.

In its simplest form, a while loop looks like this:

```
while ( some condition true ) {
  // Loop code
}
```

The condition inside the curly braces can be anything you might use in an if statement. You could use some code like this to allow users to enter numbers and stop the entering process by typing the number **99**.

```
<html>
<body>
<script type="text/javascript">
      var userNumbers = new Array( );
      var userInput = 0;
      var arrayIndex = 0;
      var message = ""
      var total = 0;
      // Loop for as long as the user doesn't input 99
      while ( userInput != 99 ) {
        userInput = prompt( "Enter a number,  or 99 to exit", "99" );
        userNumbers[arrayIndex] = userInput;
        arrayIndex++;
      }
      message += 'You entered the following:\n';
      for ( var i = 0; i < arrayIndex-1; i++ ) {
        message += userNumbers[i] + '\n';
        total += Number( userNumbers[i] );
}
      message += 'Total: ' + total + '\n';
      alert( message );
</script>
</body>
</html>
```

Here the while loop's condition is that userInput is not equal to 99, so the loop will continue as long as that condition is true. When the user enters 99 and the condition is tested, it will evaluate to false and the loop will end. Note the loop doesn't end as soon as the user enters 99, but only when the condition is tested again at the start of another iteration of the loop.

There is one small but significant difference between the while loop and the do...while: the while loop tests the condition before the code is executed, and executes the code block only if the condition is true, while the do...while loop executes the code block before testing the condition, doing another iteration only if the condition is true. In short, the do...while loop is useful when you know you want the loop code to execute at least once before the condition is tested. You could write the previous example with a do...while loop like this:

```
<html>
<body>
<script type="text/javascript">
      var userNumbers = new Array( );
      var message = '';
      var total = 0;
      // Declare the userInput but don't initialize it
      var userInput;
```

```
        var arrayIndex = 0;
        do {
          userInput = prompt( "Enter a number,  or 99 to exit", "99" );
          userNumbers[arrayIndex] = userInput;
          arrayIndex++;
        } while ( userInput != 99 )
        message +='You entered the following:\n';
        for ( var i = 0; i < arrayIndex-1; i++ ) {
          message += userNumbers[i] + '\n';
          total += Number( userNumbers[i] );
}
        message += 'Total: ' + total + '\n';
        alert( message );
</script>
</body>
</html>
```

You don't need to initialize userInput because the code inside the loop sets a value for it before testing it for the first time.

Continuing the Loop

As you've already seen, the break statement is great for breaking out of any kind of loop once a certain event has occurred. The continue keyword works like break in that it stops the execution of the loop. However, instead of dropping out of the loop, continue causes execution to resume with the next iteration.

Let's first alter the previous example so that if the user enters something other than a number, the value is not recorded and the loop finishes, using break:

```
<html>
<body>
<script type="text/javascript">
        var userNumbers = new Array( );
        var userInput;
        var arrayIndex = 0;
        do {
          userInput = Number( prompt( "Enter a number, or 99 to exit", "99" ) );
          // Check that user input is a valid number,
          // and if not,  break with error msg
          if ( isNaN( userInput ) ) {
            document.write( "Invalid data entered: please enter a number between 0 and 99 in numerals" );
            break;
          }
          // If break has been activated,  code will continue from here
          userNumbers[arrayIndex] = userInput;
          arrayIndex++;
        } while ( userInput != 99 )
        // Next statement after loop
</script>
</body>
</html>
```

Now let's change it again, so that you don't break out of the loop but instead just ignore the user's input and keep looping, using the continue statement:

```
<html>
<body>
<script type="text/javascript">
     var userNumbers = new Array( );
     var userInput;
     var arrayIndex = 0;
     do {
       userInput = prompt( "Enter a number, or 99 to exit", "99" );
       if ( isNaN( userInput ) ) {
         document.write( "Invalid data entered: please enter a number between 0 and 99 in numerals " );
         continue;
       }
       userNumbers[arrayIndex] = userInput;
       arrayIndex++;
     } while ( userInput != 99 )
     // Next statement after loop
</script>
</body>
</html>
```

The break statement has been replaced with continue, so no more code will be executed in the loop, and the condition inside the while statement will be evaluated again. If the condition is true, another iteration of the loop will occur; otherwise, the loop ends.

Use the following rules of thumb in deciding which looping structure to use:

- Use a for loop if you want to repeat an action a set number of times.

- Use a while loop when you want an action to be repeated until a condition is met.

- Use a do...while loop if you want to guarantee that the action will be performed at least once.

Summary

We covered a lot of ground in this chapter: in fact, we discussed most of the essentials of the JavaScript language.

You learned how JavaScript handles data and saw that there are a number of data types: string, number, Boolean, and object, as well as some special types of data like NaN, null, and undefined. You saw that JavaScript supplies a number of operators that perform operations on data, such as numerical calculations or joining strings together.

We then looked at how JavaScript allows you to store values using variables. Variables last for the lifetime of the page, or the lifetime of the function if they are inside a user-created function and declared locally via the var keyword. You also looked at how to convert one type of data to another.

Next you worked with three JavaScript built-in objects: the String, Date, and Math objects. You saw that these provide useful functionality for manipulating strings, dates, and numbers. I also showed you the Array object, which allows a number of items of data to be stored in a single variable.

We finished the chapter by looking at decision making, which provides the logic or intelligence of a programming language. You used if and switch statements to make decisions, using conditions to test the validity of data and acting upon the findings. Loops also use conditions and allow you to repeat a block of code for a certain number of times or while a condition is true.

CHAPTER 3

From DHTML to DOM Scripting

In this chapter, you'll learn what DHTML was, why it is regarded as a bad way to go nowadays, and what modern techniques and ideas should be used instead. You'll learn what functions are and how to use them. You'll also hear about variable and function scope and some state-of-the-art best practices that'll teach your scripts how to play extremely well with others.

If you are interested in JavaScript and you have searched the Web for scripts, you surely have come upon the term *DHTML*. DHTML was one of the big buzz words of the IT and web development industry in the late 1990s and beginning of the millennium.

Note   DHTML, or Dynamic HTML, was never a real technology or World Wide Web Consortium (W3C) standard—it was merely a term invented by marketing and advertising agencies.

DHTML is JavaScript interacting with cascading style sheets (CSS) and web documents (written in HTML) to create seemingly dynamic pages. With this, developers have been able to create effects in the browser that were previously difficult or impossible to build in a browser.

At that time, Microsoft Internet Explorer 5 and Netscape Navigator 4 were the dominant browsers. One of the problems developers had to deal with was that the Microsoft DOM and the Netscape DOM were different.

These browsers also had different levels of CSS support. For example, properties that did the same thing had different names. It was enough of a problem that accessing elements in the document required you to write the code twice, once for each browser. Because of that, complex browser-sniffing scripts were written to make sure the right code was being run in the right browser.

Common DHTML scripts had several issues:

- *JavaScript dependence and lack of graceful degradation*: Visitors who had JavaScript turned off (either by choice or because of their company security settings) would not get the functionality; instead, they would get elements that didn't do anything when activate or even pages that couldn't be navigated at all.

- *Browser and version dependence*: A common way to test whether the script could be executed was to read out the browser name in the navigator object. Because a lot of these scripts were created when Netscape 4 and Internet Explorer 5 were state-of-the-art, they failed to support newer browsers—the reason being that browser detection didn't take newer versions into account and just tested for versions 4 or 5.

- *Code forking*: Because different browsers supported different DOMs, a lot of code needed to be duplicated and several browser quirks needed to be avoided. This also made it difficult to write modular code.

- *High maintenance*: Because most of the look and feel of the site or application was kept in the script, any change meant you needed to know at least basic JavaScript. Because JavaScript was developed for several different browsers, you needed to apply the change in all of the different scripts targeted to each browser.

- *Markup dependence*: Instead of generating or accessing HTML via the DOM, a lot of scripts wrote out content via the document.write directive and added to each document body instead of keeping everything in a separate—cached—document.

All of these issues stand in a stark contrast to the requirements we currently have to fulfill:

- Code should be cheap to maintain and possible to reuse in several projects.

- Legal requirements like the Digital Discrimination Act (DDA) in the UK and Section 508 in the US strongly advise against or, in some cases, even forbid web products to be dependent on scripting.

- More browsers, user agents (UAs) on devices such as mobile phones, or assistive technology helping disabled users to take part in the Web make it impossible to keep our scripts dependent on browser identification.

- Newer marketing strategies make it a requirement to change the look and feel of a web site or a web application quickly and without high cost—possibly even by a content-management system.

There is a clear need to rethink the way we approach JavaScript as a web technology if we still want to use and sell it to clients and keep up with the challenge of the changing market.

The first step is to make JavaScript less of a show-stopper by making it a "nice to have" item rather than a requirement—no more empty pages or links that don't do anything when JavaScript is not available. The term *unobtrusive JavaScript* was christened by Stuart Langridge at http://www.kryogenix.org.

Unobtrusive JavaScript refers to a script that does not force itself on users or stand in their way. It tests whether it can be applied and does so if it is possible. Unobtrusive JavaScript is like a stagehand—doing what she is good at backstage for the good of the whole production rather than being a diva who takes the whole stage for herself and shouts at the orchestra and her colleagues every time something goes wrong or is not to her liking.

Later on, the term *DOM scripting* got introduced, and in the aftermath of the @media conference in London 2004, the WaSP DOM Scripting Task Force was formed. The task force consists of many coders, bloggers, and designers who want to see JavaScript used in a more mature and user-centered manner—you can check out what it has to say at http://domscripting.webstandards.org.

Because JavaScript did not have a fixed place in common web development methodologies—instead, it was considered as either "something you can download from the web and change" or "something that will be generated by the editing tool if it is needed"—the term *behavior layer* came up in various web publications.

JavaScript as the Behavior Layer

Web development can be thought of as being made up of several different *layers*, as shown in Figure 3-1:

- *The behavior layer*: Is executed on the client and defines how different elements behave when the user interacts with them (JavaScript or ActionScript for Flash sites).

- *The presentation layer*: Is displayed on the client and specifies the look of the web page (CSS, imagery).

- *The structure layer*: Is converted or displayed by the user agent. This is the markup defining what a certain text or media is (HTML).

- *The content layer*: Is stored on the server and consists of all the text, images, and multimedia content that are used on the site (XML, database, media assets).

- *The business logic layer (or back end)*: Runs on the server and determines what is done with incoming data and what gets returned to the user.

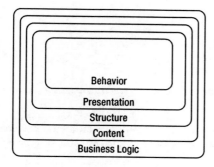

Figure 3-1. *The different layers of web development*

Notice that this simply defines what layers are available, not how they interact. For example, something needs to convert content to structure (such as XSLT), and something needs to connect the upper four layers with the business logic.

If you manage to keep all these layers separate yet talking to each other, you will have succeeded in developing an accessible and easy-to-maintain web site. In the real development and business world, this is hardly ever the case. However, the more you make this your goal, the fewer annoying changes you'll have to face at a later stage. Cascading style sheets are powerful because they allow you to define the look and feel of numerous web documents in a single file that will be cached by the user agent. JavaScript can act in the same fashion by using the `src` attribute of the `script` tag and a separate `.js` file.

In earlier chapters of this book, we embedded JavaScript directly in HTML documents. We will not do that from this point on; instead, we'll create separate JavaScript files and link to them in the head of the document:

```
<!doctype html>
<html>
<head>
<meta charset="UTF-8">
<title>Demo</title>
<link rel="stylesheet" type="text/css" href="styles.css">
<script type="text/javascript" src="scripts.js"></script>
<script type="text/javascript" src="morescripts.js"></script>
</head>
<body>
</body>
</html>
```

We should also try not to use any script blocks inside the document any longer, mainly because that would mix the structure and the behavior layers and can cause a user agent to stop showing the page if a JavaScript error occurs. It is also a maintenance nightmare—adding all JavaScript to separate `.js` files means we can maintain the scripts for a whole site in one place rather than searching through all the documents. Security is also a reason to keep your JavaScript separate. The Content Security Policy (CSP) will make sure that only code being loaded from separate files will run.

■ **Note** While Firefox, Chrome, Safari, and Opera display .js files as text, Microsoft Internet Explorer tries to execute them. If the file is assigned to a program (which you can tell by the icon), when you double-click, it will launch that program. If you drag it into the browser, it will warn you before trying to execute the code. If your file is associated with a program when you do this, it will just launch the program anyway.

Figure 3-2. Microsoft Internet Explorer on Windows 7 shows a warning message when you try to execute JavaScript locally

This separation of JavaScript into its own file makes it simpler to develop a web site that still works when the script is not available; and if a change in the site's behavior is needed, it is easy to change only the script files.

Object Detection vs. Browser Dependence

One way to determine which browser is in use is by testing the navigator object, which reveals the name and the version of the browser in its appName and appVersion attributes.

For example, the following script gets the browser name and version and writes it to the document:

```
<script type="text/javascript">
  document.write("You are running " + navigator.appName);
  document.write(" and its version is " + navigator.appVersion);
</script>
```

On my computer, inside Adobe Dreamweaver's design view, this script reports the following (because Dreamweaver uses the WebKit engine for previewing HTML):

```
You are running Netscape and its version is 5.0 (Macintosh; U; Intel Mac OS X; en_US)
AppleWebKit/533.19.4 (KHTML, like Gecko) Dreamweaver/12.1.0.5949 Version/5.0.3 Safari/533.19.4
```

If I run the same script in Firefox 17.0.2 on the same computer, I get the following:

```
You are running Netscape and its version is 5.0 (Macintosh)
```

■ **Note** Running the same code on a Windows 7 Machine with Internet Explorer (IE) 10. The + navigator.appVersion shows up as version 5.0

A lot of older scripts use this information to determine whether a browser is capable of supporting their functionality:

```
<script type="text/javascript">
 if(navigator.appName.indexOf('Internet Explorer')!=-1  && browserVersion.indexOf('6')!=-1)
  {
    document.write('<p>This is MSIE! 6</p>');
  }
  else
  {
    document.write('<p>This isn\'t MSIE</p>');
  }
</script>
```

This appears rather clever at first glance, but it is not a bulletproof method of finding out which browser is in use. For example, suppose you display the results of navigator.appName like this:

```
<script type="text/javascript">
 if(navigator.appName.indexOf('Internet Explorer')!=-1  && browserVersion.indexOf('6')!=-1)
  {
    document.write('<p>This is MSIE! 6</p>');
    document.write('<p>navigator.appName</p>');
  }
  else
  {
    document.write('<p>This isn\'t MSIE</p>');
    document.write('<p>'+navigator.appName+'</p>');
  }
</script>
```

The results will show that in Chrome, Safari, and Firefox the appName is displayed as "Netscape", a browser that has not been developed since 2007. It only gets worse from here. Looking for navigator.userAgent will give you more mixed results. For example, IE shows up as "Mozilla/4.0 (compatible, MSIE 7.0)" for IE 10 on Windows 7.

Reading out the browser name and version—commonly known as ***browser sniffing***—is not advisable, not only because of the inconsistencies I just pointed out, but also because it makes your script dependent on a certain browser rather than supporting any user agent that is actually capable of supporting the script.

The solution to this problem is called ***object detection***, and it basically means that we determine whether a user agent supports a certain object and makes this our key differentiator. In really old scripts, like the first image rollovers, you might have seen something like this:

```
<script type="text/javascript">
  // preloading images
  if(document.images)
  {
    // Images are supported
    var home=new Image();
    home.src='home.gif';
    var aboutus=new Image();
    aboutus.src='home.gif';
  }
</script>
```

The if condition checks whether the browser gives you access to the images property, and it runs the code inside the condition only if that is the case. For a long time, scripts like these were the standard way of dealing with images. In newer browsers, a lot of the JavaScript image effects can be achieved with CSS, effectively rendering scripts of this kind obsolete. However, JavaScript can manipulate images in ways CSS cannot, and we will come back to this in Chapter 6.

Every browser offers us the document it displays for manipulation, via something called the **Document Object Model**, or **DOM** for short. Older browsers supported their own DOMs, now called *Legacy DOM* or *DOM Level 0*. All modern browsers support the W3C DOM, which is the standard DOM as defined by the W3C. At the time of this writing, the latest version is DOM Level 3. You might have encountered test scripts like this one in the past:

```
<script type="text/javascript">
  if(document.all)
  {
    // MSIE
  }
  else if (document.getElementById)
  {
    // W3C DOM (MOZ, Chrome, Safari, Opera and IE)
  }
</script>
```

The document.all DOM was invented by Microsoft and supported by IE only. If you are expecting users to have really old browsers, you can test for the W3C-recommended DOM via document.getElementById. Currently, all modern browsers understand the W3C DOM.

There might be an instance where you want to try something experimental and don't know if the users' browser supports it yet. For example, accessing the microphone and camera, which is not supported across all browsers at this time.

```
<script type="text/javascript">
  if (navigator.getUserMedia || navigator.webkitGetUserMedia || navigator.mozGetUserMedia ||
navigator.msGetUserMedia)
  {
document.write('<p>getUserMedia() is supported in your browser</p>');
  }else{
document.write('<p>getUserMedia() is not supported in your browser</p>');
}
</script>
```

As you can see from the example, Opera, webkit (Chrome in this case), Mozilla (Firefox), and Microsoft (Internet Explorer) all implement it slightly differently. Because you're checking for the object and not a specific browser version, you do not have to worry about someone not having the exact browser version you are targeting. And if you need to, it's easy to update in the future.

Rather than catering to specific user agents, you test for the UA's capabilities before you apply your functionality—a process that is part of a bigger modern web design idea called *progressive enhancement*.

Progressive Enhancement

Progressive enhancement is the practice of providing functionality only to those who can see and use it by starting with a lowest common denominator and then testing whether successive improvements are supported. Users who don't have the capability to support those higher features will still be able to use the web site perfectly adequately. A comparable real-life process is putting on your clothes in the morning:

- You start with a naked body that is, hopefully, in full working condition—or at least in the same condition as it was yesterday so that it is no shock to you. (We discount pajamas and/or underwear to keep this example easy.)

- You might have a wonderful nude body, but it is insufficient in cold weather and might not appeal to other people around you—you'll need something to cover it with.

- If there are clothes available, you can check which articles of clothing fit the weather, your mood, the group of people you'll be seeing this day, and whether the different garments are in good order, clean, and the right sizes.

- You put them on, and you can face the day. If you want to, you can start accessorizing, but you should make sure to take other people into consideration when doing so. (Too much perfume might not be a good idea in a crowded train carriage.)

In web development terms, this means the following:

- You start with a valid, semantically correct HTML document with all the content—including relevant images with text alternatives as `alt` attributes—and a meaningful structure.

- You add a style sheet to improve this structure's appearance, legibility, and clarity—possibly you even add some simple rollover effects to liven it up a little.

- You add JavaScript:

  - The JavaScript starts when the document is loaded, by using the `window` object's `onload` event handler.

  - The JavaScript tests whether the current user agent supports the W3C DOM.

  - It then tests whether all the necessary elements are available and applies the desired functionality to them.

Before you can apply the idea of progressive enhancement in JavaScript, you'll need to learn how to access and interact with HTML and CSS from your scripts. I devote two chapters of this book to that task—Chapters 4 and 5. For the moment, however, it is enough to realize that the object detection you practiced earlier helps you implement progressive enhancement—you make sure that only those browsers understanding the right objects will try to access them.

JavaScript and Accessibility

Web accessibility is the practice of making web sites usable for everybody, regardless of any disabilities they might have. For example, users with visual impairments might use special software called ***screen readers*** to read out the web page content to them, and users with motor disabilities might use a tool of some kind to manipulate the keyboard for navigating around the web because they are unable to use the mouse. People with disabilities form a significant portion of web users, so companies that choose not to allow them to use their web sites could be missing out on a lot of business. In some countries, legislation (such as Section 508 in the US) means that any sites that provide a public service have to be accessible, by law.

So where does JavaScript come into this? Outdated JavaScript techniques can be very bad for accessibility, because they can mess up the document flow. For example, screen readers cannot read JavaScript elements back to the user properly. (This situation is especially bad when essential content is generated by JavaScript—there's a chance that the screen reader won't see it at all!).Thus, users are forced to use the mouse to navigate their sites (for example, in the case of complicated DHTML whiz-bang navigation menus). The whole issue goes a lot deeper than this, but this is just to give you a feel for issues in this area.

■ **Tip**　If you want to read more about web accessibility, pick up a copy of *Web Accessibility: Web Standards and Regulatory Compliance*, by Jim Thatcher et al. (friends of ED, 2006).

JavaScript and accessibility is holy war material. Many a battle between disgruntled developers and accessibility gurus is fought on mailing lists, in forums, and in chats, and the two sides all have their own—very good—arguments.

The developers who had to suffer bad browsers and illogical assumptions by marketing managers ("I saw it on my cousin's web site. Surely, you can also use it for our multinational portal.") don't want to see years of research and trial and error go down the drain and not use JavaScript any longer.

The accessibility gurus point out that JavaScript can be turned off, that the accessibility guidelines by the W3C seem not to allow for it at all (and there's a lot of confusion on that in the guidelines), and that a lot of scripts just assume that the visitors have and can use a mouse with the precision of a neurosurgeon.

Both are right, and both can have their cake: ***there is no need to completely remove JavaScript from an accessible web site***.

What has to go is JavaScript that assumes too much. Accessible JavaScript has to ensure the following:

- The web document has to have the same content with and without JavaScript—no visitor should be blocked or forced to turn on JavaScript (because it is not always the visitor's decision whether he can turn it on).

- If there is content or there are HTML elements that make sense only when JavaScript is available, this content and those elements have to be created by JavaScript. Nothing is more frustrating than a link that does nothing or text explaining some slick functionality that is not available to you.

- All JavaScript functionality has to be independent of the input device—for example, the user might be able to use a drag-and-drop interface, but she should also be able to activate the element via clicking it or pressing a key.

- Elements that are not interactive elements in a page (practically anything but links and form elements) should not become interactive elements—unless you provide a fall back option. Confusing? Imagine headlines that collapse and expand the piece of text that follows them. You can easily make them clickable in JavaScript, but that would mean that a visitor dependent on a keyboard will never be able to get to them. If you create a link inside the headlines while making them clickable, even that visitor will be able to activate the effect by "tabbing" to that link and hitting Enter.

- Scripts should not redirect the user automatically to other pages or submit forms without any user interaction. This is to avoid the premature submission of forms—because some assistive technology will have problems with onchange event handlers. Furthermore, viruses and spyware send the user to other pages via JavaScript, and this is therefore blocked by some software these days.

That is all there is to making a web site with JavaScript accessible. That, of course, and all the assets of an accessible HTML document, such as allowing elements to resize with larger font settings and providing enough contrast and colors that work for the color-blind as well as for people with normal vision.

Good Coding Practices

Now that I have put you into the mindset of practicing forward-compatible and accessible scripting, let's go through some general best practices of JavaScript.

Naming Conventions

JavaScript is case dependent, which means that a variable or a function called moveOption is different than moveoption or Moveoption. Any name—no matter whether it is a function, an object, a variable, or an array—must contain only letters, numbers, the dollar sign, or the underscore character and must not start with a number.

```
<script type="text/javascript">
  // Valid examples
  var dynamicFunctionalityId = 'dynamic';
  var parent_element2='mainnav';
  var _base=10;
  var error_Message='You forgot to enter some fields: ';

  // Invalid examples
  var dynamic ID='dynamic';  // Space not allowed!
  var 10base=10; // Starts with a number
  var while=10; // while is a JavaScript statement
</script>
```

The last example shows another issue: JavaScript has a lot of reserved words—basically, all the JavaScript statements use reserved words like while, if, continue, var, or for. If you are unsure what you can use as a variable name, it might be a good idea to get a JavaScript reference. Good editors also highlight reserved words when you enter them to avoid the issue.

There is no length limitation on names in JavaScript; however, to avoid huge scripts that are hard to read and debug, it is a good idea to keep them as easy and descriptive as possible. Try to avoid generic names such as the following:

- function1

- variable2

- doSomething()

These do not mean much to somebody else (or even to your two months down the line) who tries to debug or understand the code. It is better to use descriptive names that tell exactly what the function does or what the variable is:

- createTOC()

- calculateDifference()

- getCoordinates()

- setCoordinates()

- maximumWidth

- address_data_file

As mentioned in previous chapters, you can use underscores or *camelCase* (that is, camel notation—lowercasing the first word and then capitalizing the first character of each word after that) to concatenate words; however, camelCase is more common (DOM itself uses it), and getting used to it will make it a lot easier for you to move on to more complex programming languages at a later stage. Another benefit of camelCase is that you can highlight a variable with a double-click in almost any editor, while you need to highlight an underscore-separated name with your mouse.

Caution Beware the lowercase letter *1* and the number *1*! Most editors will use a font face like Courier, and they both look the same in this case, which can cause a lot of confusion and make for hours of fun trying to find bugs.

Code Layout

First and foremost, code is there to be converted by the interpreter to make a computer do something—or at least this is a very common myth. The interpreter will swallow the code without a hiccup when the code is valid—however, the real challenge for producing really good code is that a human will be able to edit, debug, amend, or extend it without spending hours trying to figure out what you wanted to achieve. Logical, succinct variable and function names are the first step to make it easier for the maintainer—the next step is proper code layout.

▓ **Note**   If you are really bored, go to any coder forum and drop an absolute like "Spaces are better than tabs" or "Every curly brace should get a new line." You are very likely to get hundreds of posts that point out the pros and cons of what you claimed. Code layout is a hotly discussed topic. The following examples work nicely for me and seem to be a quite common way of laying out code. It might be a good idea to check whether there are any contradictory standards to follow before joining a multi developer team on a project and using the ones mentioned here.

Simply check the following code examples; you might not understand now what they do. (They present a small function that opens every link that has a CSS class of small popup in a new window and add a message that this is what will happen). However, just consider which one would be easier to debug and change.

Here they are without indentation:

```
function addPopUpLink(){
var popupClass='smallpopup';
var popupMessage= '(opens in new window)';
var pop,t;
var as=document.getElementsByTagName('a');
for(var i=0;i<as.length;i++){
t=as[i].className;
if(t&&t.toString().indexOf(popupClass)!=-1){
as[i].appendChild(document.createTextNode(popupMessage));
as[i].onclick=function(){
pop=window.open(this.href,'popup','width=400,height=400');
returnfalse;
}}}}
window.onload=addPopUpLink;
```

Here they are with indentation:

```
function addPopUpLink(){
  var popupClass='smallpopup';
  var popupMessage= '(opens in new window)';
  var pop,t;
  var as=document.getElementsByTagName('a');
for(var i=0;i<as.length;i++){
    t=as[i].className;
    if(t && t.toString().indexOf(popupClass)!=-1){
      as[i].appendChild(popupMessage);
      as[i].onclick=function(){
        pop=window.open(this.href,'popup','width=400,height=400');
```

```
          return false;
        }
      }
    }
  }
}
window.onload=addPopUpLink;
```

Here they are with indentation and curly braces on new lines:

```
  function addPopUpLink()
  {
    var popupClass='smallpopup';
    var popupMessage= ' (opens in new window)';
var pop,t;
    var as=document.getElementsByTagName('a');
for(var i=0;i<as.length;i++)
    {
      t=as[i].className;
      if(t && t.toString().indexOf(popupClass)!=-1)
      {
        as[i].appendChild(document.createTextNode(popupMessage));
        as[i].onclick=function()
        {
          pop=window.open(this.href,'popup','width=400,height=400');
          return false;
        }
      }
    }
  }
  window.onload=addPopUpLink;
```

I think it is rather obvious that indentation is a good idea; however, there is a big debate whether you should indent via tabs or spaces. I like tabs, mainly because they are easy to delete and less work to type in. Developers that work a lot on very basic (or pretty amazing, if you know all the cryptic keyboard shortcuts) editors like vi or emacs frown upon that, because the tabs might display as very large horizontal gaps. If that is the case, it is not much of a problem to replace all tabs with double spaces with a simple regular expression.

The question of whether the opening curly braces should get a new line or not is another you need to decide for yourself. The benefit of not using a new line is that it is easier to delete erroneous blocks, because they have one line less. The benefit of new lines is that the code does look less crammed. I keep the opening one on the same line in JavaScript and on a new line in PHP—because these seem to be the standard in those two developer communities.

Another issue is line length. Most editors these days have a line-wrap option that makes sure you don't have to scroll horizontally when you want to see the code. However, not all of them print out the code properly, and perhaps the person maintaining the code later will not have a fancy editor like the one you were using. Therefore, you should keep lines short—approximately 80 characters at most.

Commenting

Commenting is something that only humans benefit from—although in some higher programming languages, comments are indexed to generate documentation. (One example is the PHP manual, which at times is a bit cryptic for nonprogrammers exactly because of this.) Although commenting is not a necessity for the code to work—if you use clear names and indent your code, it should be rather self-explanatory—it can speed up debugging immensely. The previous example might make more sense for you with explanatory comments:

```
/*
  addPopUpLink
  opens the linked document of all links with a certain
  class in a pop-up window and adds a message to the
  link text that there will be a new window
*/
function addPopUpLink(){
    // Check for DOM and leave if it is not supported
   // Assets of the link - the class to find out which link should
   // get the functionality and the message to add to the link text
   var popupClass='smallpopup';
   var popupMessage= ' (opens in new window)';
   // Temporary variables to use in a loop
   var pop,t;
   // Get all links in the document
   var as=document.getElementsByTagName('a');
   // Loop over all links
   for(var i=0;i<as.length;i++)
   {
     t=as[i].className;
     // Check if the link has a class and that the class is the right one
     if(t && t.toString().indexOf(popupClass)!=-1)
     {
       // Add the message
       as[i].appendChild(document.createTextNode(popupMessage));
       // Assign a function when the user clicks the link
       as[i].onclick=function()
       {
         // Open a new window with
         pop=window.open(this.href,'popup','width=400,height=400');
         // Don't follow the link (otherwise, the linked document
         // would be opened in the pop-up and the document).
         return false;
       }
     }
   }
}
window.onload=addPopUpLink;
```

That's a lot easier to grasp, isn't it? It is also overkill. An example like this can be used in training documentation or a self-training course, but it is a bit much in a final product. Moderation is always the key when it comes to commenting. In most cases, it is enough to explain what something does and what can be changed.

```
/*
  addPopUpLink
  opens the linked document of all links with a certain
  class in a pop-up window and adds a message to the
  link text that there will be a new window
*/
function addPopUpLink()
{

  // Assets of the link - the class to find out which link should
  // get the functionality and the message to add to the link text
  var popupClass='smallpopup';
  var popupMessage=document.createTextNode(' (opens in new window)');
  var pop;
  var as=document.getElementsByTagName('a');
  for(var i=0;i<as.length;i++)
  {
    t=as[i].className;
    if(t && t.toString().indexOf(popupClass)!=-1)
    {
      as[i].appendChild(popupMessage);
      as[i].onclick=function()
      {
        pop=window.open(this.href,'popup','width=400,height=400');
        return false;
      }
    }
  }
}
window.onload=addPopUpLink;
```

These comments make it easy to grasp what the whole function does and to find the spot where you can change some of the settings. This makes quick changes easier—changes in functionality would require the maintainer to analyze your code more closely, anyway.

Functions

Functions are reusable blocks of code and are an integral part of most programs today, including those written in JavaScript. Imagine you have to do a calculation or need to perform a certain conditional check over and over again. You could copy and paste the same lines of code where necessary; however, it is much more efficient to use a function.

Functions can get values as parameters (sometimes called *arguments*), and they can return values after they are finished testing and changing what has been given to them.

You create a function by using the function keyword followed by the function name and the parameters separated by commas inside parentheses:

```
function createLink(linkTarget, LinkName)
{
  // Code
}
```

There is no limit to how many parameters a function can have, but you should not use too many, because it can become rather confusing. If you check some DHTML code, you can find functions with 20 parameters or more, and remembering their order when calling those in other functions will make you almost want to simply write the whole thing from scratch. When you do that, remember that using too many parameters means a lot more maintenance work and makes debugging a lot harder than it should be.

Unlike PHP, JavaScript has no option to preset the parameters if they are not available. You can work around this issue with some if conditions that checks first whether there are any arguments to work with. Using arguments.length, you can see how many arguments have been passed over to your function. Once you do that, you can check the value of the parameters:

```
function createLink(linkTarget, LinkName)
{
   if(arguments.length == 0 ) {return false}
  if (linkTarget === undefined)
  {
    linkTarget = '#';
  }
  if (linkName == null)
  {
    linkName = 'dummy';
  }
}
```

Functions report back what they have done via the return keyword. If a function that's invoked by an event handler returns the Boolean value false, the sequence of events that is normally triggered by the event gets stopped. This is very handy when you want to apply functions to links and stop the browser from navigating to the link's href. You saw this in the "Object Detection vs. Browser Dependence" section earlier in the chapter.

Any other value following the return statement will be sent back to the calling code. Let's change our createLink function to create a link and return it once the function has finished creating it:

```
function createLink(linkTarget,linkName)
{
  if (linkTarget == null) { linkTarget = '#'; }
  if (linkName == null) { linkName = 'dummy'; }

  var tempLink=document.createElement('a');
  tempLink.setAttribute('href',linkTarget);
  tempLink.appendChild(document.createTextNode(linkName));

  return tempLink;
}
```

Another function could take these generated links and append them to an element. If there is no element ID defined, it should append the link to the body of the document:

```
function appendLink(sourceLink,elementId)
{
  var element=false;
  if (elementId==null || !document.getElementById(elementId))
  {
    element=document.body;
  }
```

```
  if(!element) {
    element=document.getElementById(elementId);
  }
  element.appendChild(sourceLink);
}
```

Now, to use both these functions, you can have another one call them with the appropriate parameters:

```
function linksInit()
{
  var openLink=createLink('#','open');
  appendLink(openLink);
  var closeLink=createLink('closed.html','close');
  appendLink(closeLink,'main');
}
```

The function `linksInit()` checks whether DOM is available. (Because it is the only function calling the others, you don't need to check for it inside them again.) Then it creates a link with a target of # and opens as the link text.

It then invokes the `appendLink()` function and sends the newly generated link as a parameter. Notice it doesn't send a target element, which means elementId is null and `appendLink()` adds the link to the main body of the document.

The second time `initLinks()` invokes `createLink()`, it sends the target closed.html and close as the link text and applies the link to the HTML element with the ID main via the `appendLink()` function. If there is an element with the ID main, `appendLink()` adds the link to this one; if not, it uses the document body as a fallback option.

If this is confusing now, don't worry—you will see more examples later on. For now, it is just important to remember what functions are and what they should do:

- Functions are there to do one task over and over again. Keep each task inside its own function; don't create monster functions that do several things at once.

- Functions can have as many parameters as you want, and each parameter can be of any type—string, object, number, variable, or array.

- You cannot provide default values for parameters in the function definition itself, but you can check whether they were defined or not and set defaults with an `if` condition. You can do this succinctly via the ternary operator, which you will get to know in the next section of this chapter.

- Functions should have a logical name describing what they do. Try to keep the name close to the task topic, as a generic `init()`, for example, could be in any of the other included JavaScript files and overwrite their functions. Object literals can provide one way to avoid this problem, as you'll see later in this chapter.

Short Code via the Ternary Operator

Looking at the `appendLink()` function shown earlier, you might get a hunch that a lot of `if` conditions or `switch` statements can result in long and complex code. A trick to avoid some of this bloating involves using something called the *ternary operator*. The ternary operator has the following syntax:

```
var variable = condition ? trueValue:falseValue;
```

This is handy for Boolean conditions or very short values. For example, you can replace this long `if` condition with one line of code:

```
// Normal syntax
var direction;
if(x<200)
{
  direction=1;
}
else
{
  direction=-1;
}
// Ternary operator
var direction = x < 200 ? 1 : -1;
```

Here are a few other examples:

```
t.className = t.className == 'hide' ? '' : 'hide';
var el = document.getElementById('nav')
        ? document.getElementById('nav')
        : document.body;
```

You can also nest the ternary selector, but that gets rather unreadable:

```
y = x <20 ? (x > 10 ? 1 : 2) : 3;
// equals
if(x<20)
{
  if(x>10)
{
    y=1;
  }
  else
  {
    y=2;
  }
}
else
{
 y=3
}
```

Sorting and Reuse of Functions

If you have a large number of JavaScript functions, it might be a good idea to keep them in separate `.js` files and apply them only where they are needed. Name the `.js` files according to what the functions included in them do—for example, `formvalidation.js` or `dynamicmenu.js`.

This has been done to a certain extent for you, because there are a lot of prepackaged JavaScript libraries (collections of functions and methods) that help create special functionality. We will look at some of them in Chapter 11 and create our own during the next few chapters.

Variable and Function Scope

Variables defined inside a function with a new var are valid only inside this function, not outside it. This might seem like a drawback, but it actually means that your scripts will not interfere with others—which could be fatal when you use JavaScript libraries or your own collections.

Variables defined outside functions are called *global variables* and are dangerous. You should try to keep all your variables contained inside functions. This ensures that your script will play nicely with other scripts that might be applied to the page. Many scripts use generic variable names like navigation or currentSection. If these are defined as global variables, the scripts will override each other's settings. Try running the following function to see what problems omitting a var keyword can cause:

```
<script type="text/javascript">
  var demoVar=1 // Global variable
  alert('Before withVar demoVar is' +demoVar);
  function withVar()
  {
    var demoVar=3;
  }
  withVar();
  alert('After withVar demoVar is' +demoVar);
  function withoutVar()
  {
    demoVar=3;
  }
  withoutVar();
  alert('After withoutVar demoVar is' +demoVar);
</script>
```

While withVar keeps the variable untouched, withoutVar changes it:

```
Before withVar demoVar is 1
After withVar demoVar is 1
After withoutVar demoVar is 3
```

Keeping Scripts Safe with the Object Literal

Earlier, I talked about keeping variables safe by defining them locally via the var keyword. The reason was to avoid other functions relying on variables with the same name and the two functions overwriting each other's values. The same applies to functions. Because you can include several JavaScripts to the same HTML document in separate script elements, your functionality might break because another included document has a function with the same name. You can avoid this issue by using a naming convention, like myscript_init() and myscript_validate() for your functions. However, this is a bit cumbersome, and JavaScript offers a better way to deal with this in the form of objects.

You can define a new object and use your functions as methods of this object—this is how JavaScript objects like Date and Math work. For example:

```
<script type="text/javascript">
  myscript=new Object();
  myscript.init=function()
```

```
  {
    // Some code
  };
  myscript.validate=function()
  {
    // Some code
  };
</script>
```

Notice that if you try to call the functions init() and validate(), you get an error, because they don't exist any longer. Instead, you need to use myscript.init() and myscript.validate().

Wrapping all your functions in an object as methods is analogous to the programming classes used by some other languages such as C++ or Java. In such languages, you keep functions that apply to the same task inside the same class, thus making it easier to create large pieces of code without getting confused by hundreds of functions.

The syntax we used is still a bit cumbersome, because you have to repeat the object name over and over again. There is a shortcut notation called the *object literal* that makes it a lot easier.

The object literal has been around for a long time but has been underused. It is becoming more and more fashionable nowadays, and you can pretty much presume that a script you find on the web using it is good, modern JavaScript.

What the object literal does is use a shortcut notation to create the object and apply each of the functions as object methods instead of stand-alone functions. Let's see our three functions from the dynamic links example as a big object using the object literal:

```
var dynamicLinks={
  linksInit:function()
  {
    var openLink=dynamicLinks.createLink('#','open');
    dynamicLinks.appendLink(openLink);
    var closeLink=dynamicLinks.createLink('closed.html','close');
    dynamicLinks.appendLink(closeLink,'main');
  },
  createLink:function(linkTarget,linkName)
  {
    if (linkTarget == null) { linkTarget = '#'; }
    if (linkName == null) { linkName = 'dummy'; }
    var tempLink=document.createElement('a');
    tempLink.setAttribute('href',linkTarget);
    tempLink.appendChild(document.createTextNode(linkName));
    return tempLink;
  },
  appendLink:function(sourceLink,elementId)
  {
    var element=false;
    if (elementId==null || !document.getElementById(elementId))
    {
      element=document.body;
    }
    if(!element){element=document.getElementById(elementId)}
    element.appendChild(sourceLink);
  }
}
window.onload=dynamicLinks.linksInit;
```

As you can see, all the functions are contained as methods inside the dynamicLinks object, which means that if you want to call them, you need to add the name of the object before the function name. Another way of handling functions is to have them nested. The outer function would have a name, and the inner function (called an *anonymous function*) would just run.

The syntax is a bit different; instead of placing the function keyword before the name of the function, you add it behind the name preceded by a colon. Additionally, each closing curly brace except for the very last one needs to be followed by a comma.

If you want to use variables that should be accessible by all methods inside the object, you can do that with syntax that is quite similar:

```
var myObject=
{
  objMainVar:'preset',
  objSecondaryVar:0,
  objArray:['one','two','three'],
  init:function(){},
  createLinks:function(){},
  appendLinks:function(){}
}
```

This might be a lot of information to digest right now, but don't worry. This chapter is meant as a reference for you to come back to and as a reminder of a lot of good practices. We will continue in the next chapter with more tangible examples and rip open an HTML document to play with the different parts.

Summary

You have done it: you finished this chapter. You should now be able to distinguish between modern and old scripts when you see them on the Web. Older scripts are likely to

- Use a lot of document.write().

- Check for browsers and versions instead of objects.

- Write out a lot of HTML instead of accessing what is already in the document.

- Use proprietary DOM objects like document.all for Microsoft IE and document.getElementById for modern browsers including Microsoft IE.

- Appear anywhere inside the document (rather in the <head> or included via <script src="----.js">), and rely on javascript: links instead of assigning events.

You've learned about putting JavaScript into stand-alone .js documents instead of embedding it into HTML and thereby separating behavior from structure.

You then heard about using object detection instead of relying on browser names. I explained what *progressive enhancement* means and how it applies to web development. Testing user agent capabilities instead of names and versions will ensure that your scripts also work for user agents you might not have at hand to test yourself. It also means that you don't have to worry every time a new version of a browser is released—if it supports the standards, you'll be fine.

I talked about accessibility and what it means for JavaScript, and you got a peek at a lot of coding practices. The general things to remember are

- Test for the objects you want to use in your scripts.

- Make improvements in an existing site that already works well without client-side scripting instead of adding scripts first and adding nonscripting fallback options later on.

- Keep your code self-contained, and don't use any global variables that might interfere with other scripts.

- Code with the idea in mind that you will have to hand this code over to someone else to maintain. This person might be you in three months' time, and you should be able to immediately understand what is going on.

- Comment your code's functionality, and use readable formatting to make it easy to find bugs or change the functions.

This is the lot—except for something called an *event handler*, which I talked about but did not actually define. I'll do so in Chapter 5. But for now, sit back, get a cup of coffee or tea, and relax for a bit, until you're ready to proceed with learning how JavaScript interacts with HTML and CSS.

CHAPTER 4

■ ■ ■

HTML and JavaScript

In this chapter, you finally get your hands dirty in real JavaScript code. You'll learn how JavaScript interacts with the page structure—defined in HTML—and how to receive data and give back information to your visitors. I start with an explanation of what an HTML document is and how it is structured, and then I explain several ways to create page content via JavaScript. You'll then hear about the JavaScript developer's Swiss Army knife—the Document Object Model (DOM)—and how to separate JavaScript and HTML to create now-seamless effects that developers used to create in an obtrusive manner with DHTML.

The Anatomy of an HTML Document

Documents displayed in user agents are normally HTML documents. Even if you use a server-side language like ASP.NET, PHP, ColdFusion, or Perl, the outcome is HTML if you want to use browsers to their full potential. Modern browsers like Firefox or Safari also support XML, SVG, and other formats, but for 99 percent of your day-to-day web work, you'll go the HTML route.

An HTML document is a text document that starts with a DOCTYPE that tells the user agent what the document is and how it should be dealt with. HTML has evolved over time, and the current DOCTYPE tells the browser that the page being delivered should be rendered as HTML5 in Standards Mode. The next element in a document is the HTML tag. This element contains everything else that makes up a document. All elements in the document can have an optional lang attribute. The lang attribute defines the language the page is using (think human-readable languages, not computer languages)—in the following example, "en" stands for *English*. Inside the HTML element are the HEAD and TITLE elements. An optional element on the same level as HEAD and TITLE is the META element. The charset attribute inside META describes *character encoding*, or the way text should be displayed on screen. This can be set on the server, but because most people don't have access to the webserver, it can be defined here. On the same level as the HEAD element, but after the closing <head> tag, is the BODY—the element that contains all the page content.

```
<!doctype html>
<html lang="en">
<head>
<meta charset="UTF-8">
<title>Our HTML Page</title>
</head>
<body>
</body>
</html>
```

A markup document like this consists of *tags* (words or letters enclosed in tag brackets, like <p>) and text content. Documents should be well formed (meaning that every opening tag like <p> must be matched by a closing tag like </p>).

HTML elements are everything in the brackets, <>, with a starting tag like <h1> followed by content and a closing tag of the same name—like </h1>. Each element can have content in between the opening and the closing tags. Each element might have several *attributes*. The following example is a P element with an attribute whose name is class. The attribute has the value intro. The P contains the text *Lorem Ipsum*.

```
<p class="intro">Lorem Ipsum</p>
```

The browser checks the element it encounters and knows that P is a paragraph and that the class attribute is valid for this element. It also realizes that the class attribute should check the linked cascading style sheets (CSS) style sheet, get the definitions for a P with that class, and render it accordingly.

There are several reasons why you should strive for standards compliance—even in HTML generated via JavaScript:

- It is easier to trace errors when you know the HTML is valid.

- It is easier to maintain documents that adhere to the rules—because you can use a validator to measure its quality.

- It is a lot more likely that user agents will render or convert your pages properly when you develop against an agreed-upon standard.

- The final documents can be easily converted to other formats if they are valid HTML.

Now, if you add some more elements to the example HTML and open it in a browser, you get rendered output as shown in Figure 4-1:

```
<!doctype html>
<html lang="en">
<head>
<meta charset="utf-8">
<title>DOM Example</title>
</head>
<body>
<h1>Heading</h1>
<p>Paragraph</p>
<h2>Subheading</h2>
<ul id="eventsList">
<li>List 1</li>
<li>List 2</li>
<li><a href="http://www.google.com">Linked List Item</a></li>
<li>List 4</li>
</ul>
<p>Paragraph</p>
<p>Paragraph</p>
</body>
</html>
```

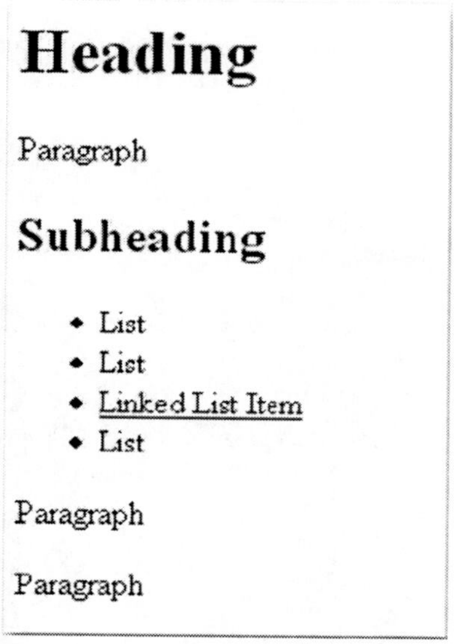

Heading

Paragraph

Subheading

- List
- List
- Linked List Item
- List

Paragraph

Paragraph

Figure 4-1. *An HTML document rendered by a browser*

A QUICK WORD ON XHTML

Browsers use DOCTYPE to decide how to render documents. The previous version of HTML (XHTML 4.01) had a longer DOCTYPE. One of the things that it described was whether it should render things in *Quirks Mode* or *Standards Mode*. As the name suggests, Quirks Mode was created to accommodate the way HTML was rendered in early browsers to maintain backward–compatibility, essentially keeping all the quirks so that pages would display properly. Standards Mode maintains strict compliance with standards established by the World Wide Web Consortium (W3C).

The user agent "sees" the document a bit differently. The DOM models a document as a set of nodes, including element nodes, text nodes, and attribute nodes. Both elements and their text content are separate *nodes*. Attribute nodes are the *attributes* of the elements. The DOM includes other sorts of nodes for other parts of a markup document, but these three—element nodes, text nodes, and attribute nodes—are the important ones if you keep your JavaScript and HTML hat on. If you want to see the document through the eyes of the browser, right-click (control-click on a Mac) and choose Inspect Element. This opens the bottom half of the browser to display the document as a tree structure, and it gives you access to the built-in debugging tools, as depicted in Figure 4-2.

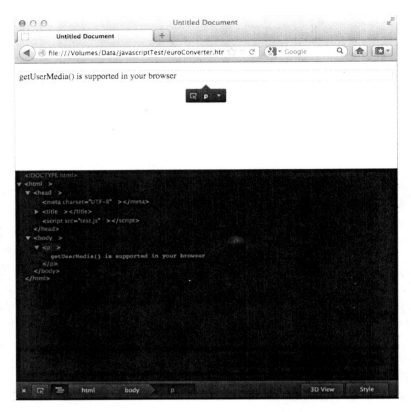

Figure 4-2. *The DOM representation of a document illustrated in the Mozilla DOM Inspector*

■ **Tip** You can access similar tools in Chrome, Safari, Opera, and Internet Explorer. Not only can you see how the document is represented, you can also edit the code and see the results directly in the browser. In the appendix, I'll cover validation and debugging.

■ **Note** Notice all the #text nodes between the elements? This is not text I added to the document, but the line breaks I added at the end of each line. Some browsers see those as text nodes, while others don't—which can be very annoying when you try to access elements in the document via JavaScript later on.

Figure 4-3 shows another way you can visualize the document tree.

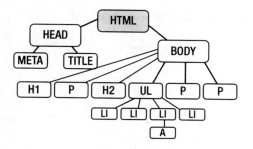

Figure 4-3. *The structure of an HTML document*

It is very important to recognize HTML for what it is: HTML is structured content, not a visual construct like an image with elements placed at different coordinates. When you have a proper, valid HTML document, the sky is the limit, and you can access and change it via JavaScript. An invalid HTML document might trip up your scripts, no matter how much testing you do. A classic mistake is using the same id attribute value twice in a single document, which negates the purpose of having a unique identifier (ID).

Providing Feedback in Web Pages via JavaScript: The Old-School Ways

You already saw one way—document.write()—of giving feedback to the user in an HTML document by writing out content. We also discussed the problems this method has—namely, mixing the structure and the presentation layer and losing the maintenance benefits of keeping all JavaScript code in a separate file.

Using window Methods: prompt(), alert(), and confirm()

A different way of giving feedback and retrieving user-entered data is using methods the browser offers you via the window object—namely, prompt(), alert(), and confirm().

The most commonly used window method is alert(), an example of which appears in Figure 4-4. What it does is display a value in a dialog (and perhaps play a sound, if the user's hardware supports it). The user has to click OK or press the Enter key to get rid of the message.

Figure 4-4. *A JavaScript alert (on Firefox on a Mac OS)*

Alerts look different from browser to browser and from operating system to operating system.

As a user feedback mechanism, alert() has the merit of being supported by most user agents, but it also keeps you from interacting with anything else on the page—you call such windows *modal*. An *alert* is a message that normally bears bad news or warns someone of danger ahead—which is not necessarily your intention.

Suppose you want to tell the visitor to enter something in a search field before submitting a form. You could use an alert for that:

```html
<!doctype html>
<html lang="en">
<head>
<meta charset="utf-8">
<title>Search example</title>
<script type="text/javascript">
      function checkSearch()
      {

if(!document.getElementById("search")){return;}
var searchValue=document.getElementById("search").value;
        if(searchValue=='')
        {
          alert("Please enter a search term");
          return false;
        }
        else
        {
          return true;

        }
      }
</script>
</head>
<body>
<form action="sitesearch.php" method="post" onsubmit="return checkSearch();">
<p>
<label for="search">Search the site:</label>
<input type="text" id="search" name="search" />
<input type="submit" value="Search" />
</p>
</form>
</body>
</html>
```

If a visitor tries to submit the form via the Submit button, he'll get the alert, and the browser will not send the form to the server after he activates the OK button. Chrome on Mac OS looks like what you see in Figure 4-5.

Figure 4-5. *Giving feedback on a form error via an alert*

Alerts do not return any information to the script—they simply give a message to the user and stop any further code execution until the OK button is activated.

This is different for prompt() and confirm(). The former allows visitors to enter something, and the latter asks users to confirm an action.

■ **Tip**   As a debugging measure, alert() is simply too handy not to use. All you do is add an alert(variableName) in your code where you want to know what the variable value is at that time. You'll get the information and stop the rest of the code from executing until the OK button is activated—which is great for tracing back where and how your script fails. Beware of using it in loops, though—there is no way to stop the loop, and you might have to press Enter a hundred times before you get back to your editing. There are other debugging tools such as the JavaScript consoles of Opera and Safari, as well as Mozilla. I'll say more about these in the appendix.

You could extend the earlier example as shown in the following code sample to ask the visitor to confirm a search for the common term *JavaScript* (and the results are shown in Figure 4-6):

```
function checkSearch()
{

  if(!document.getElementById("search'"){return;}
  var searchValue=document.getElementById("search").value;
  if(searchValue=='')
  {
   alert("Please enter a search term before sending the form");
   return false;
  }
  else if(searchValue=="JavaScript")
  {
    var really=confirm('"JavaScript" is a very common term.\n' +'Do you really want to search for this?');
    return really;
  }
```

```
    else
    {
      return true;
    }
}
```

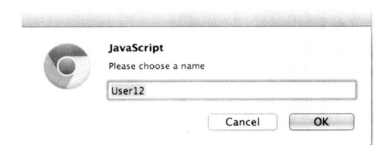

Search the site: JavaScript   Search

JavaScript

"JavaScript" is a very common term.
Do you really want to search for this?

Cancel   OK

Figure 4-6. Example of asking for user confirmation via confirm()

Notice that confirm() is a method that returns a Boolean value (true or false) depending on whether the visitor activates OK or Cancel. Confirm dialogs are an easy way to stop visitors from taking really bad steps in web applications. Although they are not the prettiest way of asking a user to confirm a choice, they are really stable and offer some functionality your own confirmation functions most probably will not have—for example, playing the alert sound.

Both alert() and confirm() send information to the user, but what about retrieving information? A simple way to retrieve user input is via the prompt() method. This method takes two parameters: the first one is a string displayed above the entry field as a label, and the second is a preset value for the entry field. Buttons labeled OK and Cancel (or something similar) will be displayed next to the field and the label, as shown in Figure 4-7.

```
var user=prompt('Please choose a name','User12');
```

JavaScript

Please choose a name

User12

Cancel   OK

Figure 4-7. Allowing the user to enter data in a prompt

When the visitor activates the OK button, the value of the variable user will be either User12 (when she hasn't changed the preset) or whatever she entered. When she activates the Cancel button, the value will be null.

You can use this functionality to allow a visitor to change a value before sending a form to the server:

```html
<!doctype html>
<html lang="en">
<head>
<meta charset="utf-8">
<title>Date example</title>
<script type="text/javascript">
      function checkDate()
      {
        if(!document.getElementById("date")){return;}
        // Define a regular expression to check the date format
        var checkPattern=newRegExp("\\d{2}/\\d{2}/\\d{4}");
        // Get the value of the date entry field
        var dateValue=document.getElementById("date").value;
        // If there is no date entered, don't send the form
        if(dateValue=='')
        {
          alert("Please enter a date");
          return false
        }
        else
        {
          // Tell the user to change the date syntax either until
          // she presses Cancel or enters the right syntax
          while(!checkPattern.test(dateValue) && dateValue!=null)
          {
            dateValue=prompt("Your date was not in the right format." + "Please enter it as
DD/MM/YYYY.", dateValue);
          }
          return dateValue!=null;
        }
      }
</script>
</head>
<body>
<h1>Events search</h1>
<form action="eventssearch.php" method="post" onsubmit="return checkDate();">
<p>
<label for="date">Date in the format DD/MM/YYYY:</label><br>
<input type="text" id="date" name="date">
<input type="submit" value="Check">
<br>(example 26/04/1975)
</p>
</form>
</body>
</html>
```

Don't worry if the regular expression and the test() method are confusing you at the moment; these will be covered in Chapter 9. All that is important now is that you use a while loop with a prompt() inside it. The while loop displays the same prompt over and over again until either the visitor presses Cancel (which means dateValue becomes null) or enters a date in the right format (which satisfies the test condition of the regular expression checkPattern).

Quick Review

You can create pretty nifty JavaScripts using the `prompt()`, `alert()`, and `confirm()` methods, and they have some points in their favor:

- They are easy to grasp, because they use the functionality and look and feel of the browser and offer a richer interface than HTML. (Specifically, the alert sound, when present, can help a lot of users.)

- They appear outside and above the current document—which gives them the utmost importance.

However, there are some points that speak against the use of these methods to retrieve data and give feedback:

- You cannot style the messages, and they obstruct the web page. This does give them more importance, but it also makes them appear clumsy from a design point of view. Because they are part of the user's operating system or browser UI, they are easy to recognize for the user, but they break design conventions and guidelines the product might have to adhere to.

- Feedback mechanisms do not have the same look and feel as the web site—which renders the site design less important and stops dead the user's journey through your usability-enhancing design elements.

- They are dependent on JavaScript—feedback should also be available when JavaScript is turned off.

Accessing the Document via the DOM

In addition to the window methods you now know about, you can access a web document via the DOM. In a manner of speaking, you did that already with the `document.write()` examples. The `document` object is what you want to alter and add to, and using `write()` is one method to do that. However, `document.write()` adds a string to the document and not a set of nodes and attributes, and you cannot separate the JavaScript out into a separate file—`document.write()` works only where you put it in the HTML. What you need is a way to reach where you want to change or add content, and this is exactly what the DOM and its methods provide you with. Earlier on, you found out that user agents read a document as a set of nodes and attributes, and the DOM gives you tools to grab these. You can reach elements of the document via three methods:

- `document.getElementsByTagName('p')`

- `document.getElementById('id')`

- `document.getElementsByClassName('cssClass')`

The `getElementsByTagName('p')` method returns a list of all the elements with the name p as objects (where p can be any HTML element) and `getElementById('id')` returns you the element with the ID as an object. The third method, `getElementsByClassName('cssClass')`, returns all the elements using that class name.

■ **Note** One of interesting things about `getElementsByClassName()` is that you can retrieve elements that are using more than one class. For example, `getElementsByClassName("one two")` retrieves only the elements that are using those classes together. Keep in mind that this method is available in IE starting with version 9.

If you go back to the HTML example we used earlier, you can write a small JavaScript example that shows how to use these two methods:

```
<!doctype html>
<html>
<head>
<meta charset="UTF-8">
<title>DOM Example</title>
<script src="exampleFindElements.js"></script>
</head>
<body>
<h1>Heading</h1>
<p>Paragraph</p>
<h2>Subheading</h2>
<ul id="eventsList">
<li>List 1</li>
<li>List 2</li>
<li><a href="http://www.google.com">Linked List Item</a></li>
<li>List 4</li>
</ul>
<p class='paraStyle'>Paragraph</p>
<p class='paraStyle'>Paragraph</p>
</body>
</html>
```

Our script could now read the number of list items and paragraphs in the document by calling the getElementsByTagName() method and assigning the return value to variables—one time with the tag name li, and the other time with p.

```
var listElements=document.getElementsByTagName('li');
var paragraphs=document.getElementsByTagName('p');
var msg='This document contains '+listElements.length+' list items\n';
msg+='and '+paragraphs.length+' paragraphs.';
alert(msg);
```

As Figure 4-8 shows, if you open the HTML document in a browser, you will find that both values are zero!

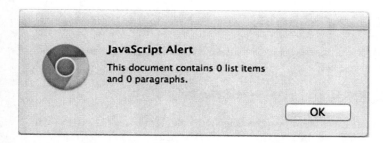

Figure 4-8. Unwanted result when trying to reach elements before the page was rendered

There aren't any list elements because the document has not yet been rendered by the browser when you try to read its content. You need to delay that reading until the document has been fully loaded and rendered.

79

You can achieve this by calling a function when the document has finished loading. The document has finished loading when the DOMContentLoaded event of the document object gets triggered. This event tells JavaScript that the structure of the page (the DOM) is ready for your code to work with it, and when it's ready, call the function. Similar to getElementsByClassName, DOMContentLoaded works in IE starting with version 9.

```
function findElements()
{
  var listElements = document.getElementsByTagName('li');
  var paragraphs = document.getElementsByTagName('p');
  var msg = 'This document contains ' + listElements.length +
' list items\n';
  msg += 'and ' + paragraphs.length + ' paragraphs.';
  alert(msg);
}
document.addEventListener("DOMContentLoaded", findElements, false);
```

If you open the HTML document in a browser now, you'll see an alert like the one in Figure 4-9 with the right number of list elements and paragraphs.

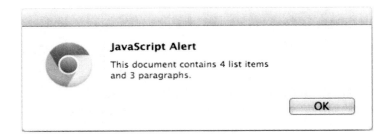

JavaScript Alert

This document contains 4 list items and 3 paragraphs.

OK

Figure 4-9. *Output alert indicating the number of found elements*

You can access each of the elements of a certain name like you access an array—once again bearing in mind that the counter of an array starts at 0 and not at 1:

```
// Get the first paragraph
var firstpara = document.getElementsByTagName('p')[0];
// Get the second list item
var secondListItem = document.getElementsByTagName('p')[1];
```

You can combine several getElementsByTagName() method calls to read child elements directly. For example, to reach the first link item inside the third list item, you use

```
var targetLink=document.getElementsByTagName('li')[2].getElementsByTagName('a')[0];
```

This can get pretty messy, though, and there are more clever ways to reach child elements—we'll get to these in a second. If you want to reach the last element, you can use the length property of the array:

```
var lastListElement = listElements[listElements.length - 1];
```

The length property also allows you to loop through elements and change all of them, one after the other:

```
var linkItems = document.getElementsByTagName('li');
for(var i = 0; i < linkItems.length; i++)
{
  // Do something...
}
```

Element IDs need to be unique to the document; therefore, the return value of getElementById() is a single object rather than an array of objects:

```
var events = document.getElementById('eventsList');
```

You can mix both methods to cut down on the number of elements to loop through. While the earlier for loop accesses all LI elements in the document, this one will go through only those that are inside the element with the ID eventsList (the name of the object with the ID replaces the document object):

```
var events = document.getElementById('eventsList');
var eventlinkItems = events.getElementsByTagName('li');
for(var i = 0; i < eventLinkItems.length; i++)
{
  // Do something...
}
```

Accessing elements based on the CSS class (or classes) being used in the document can be done with getElementsByTagName(). Just like the previous methods, you can access the results like an array:

```
var firstClass = document.getElementsByClassName('paraStyle')[0];
```

```
var classNum = document.getElementsByClassName('paraStyle').length;
```

With the help of getElementsByTagName(), getElementById(), and getElementsByClassName(), you can reach every element of the document or specifically target one single element. The methods getElementById() and getElementsByClassName() are methods of document, and getElementsByTagName() is a method of any element. Now it is time to look at ways to navigate around the document once you reach the element.

Of Children, Parents, Siblings, and Values

You know already that you can reach elements inside other elements by concatenating getElementsByTagName methods. However, this is rather cumbersome, and it means that you need to know the HTML you are altering. Sometimes that is not possible, and you have to find a more generic way to travel through the HTML document. The DOM already planned for this, via *children*, *parents*, and *siblings*.

These relationships describe where the current element is in the tree and whether it contains other elements or not. Let's take a look at our simple HTML example once more, concentrating on the body of the document:

```
<body>
<h1>Heading</h1>
<p>Paragraph</p>
<h2>Subheading</h2>
<ul id="eventsList">
<li>List 1</li>
```

```
<li>List 2</li>
<li><a href="http://www.google.com">Linked List Item</a></li>
<li>List 4</li>
</ul>
<p class="paraStyle">Paragraph</p>
<p class="paraStyle">Paragraph</p>
</body>
```

All the indented elements are children of the BODY. H1, H2, UL, and P are siblings, and the LI elements are children of the UL element—and siblings to one another. The link is a child of the third LI element. All in all, they are one big happy family.

However, there are even more children. The text inside the paragraphs, headings, list elements, and links also consists of nodes, as you might recall from Figure 4-2 earlier, and while they are not elements, they still follow the same relationship rules.

Every node in the document has several valuable properties:

- The most important property is nodeType, which describes what the node is—an element, an attribute, a comment, text, or one of several more types (12 in all). For our HTML examples, only the nodeType values 1 and 3 are important, where 1 is an element node and 3 is a text node.

- Another important property is nodeName, which is the name of the element or #text if it is a text node. Depending on the document type and the user agent, nodeName can be either uppercase or lowercase, which is why it is a good idea to convert it to lowercase before testing for a certain name. You can use the toLowerCase() method of the string object for that: if(obj.nodeName.toLowerCase()=='li'){};. For element nodes, you can use the tagName property.

- nodeValue is the value of the node: null if it is an element, and the text content if it is a text node.

In the case of text nodes, nodeValue can be read and set, which allows you to alter the text content of the element. If, for example, you want to change the text of the first paragraph, you might think it is enough to set its nodeValue:

```
document.getElementsByTagName('p')[0].nodeValue='Hello World';
```

However, this doesn't work (although—strangely enough—it does not cause an error), because the first paragraph is an element node. If you want to change the text inside the paragraph, you need to access the text node inside it or, in other words, the first child node of the paragraph:

```
document.getElementsByTagName('p')[0].firstChild.nodeValue='Hello World';
```

From the Parents to the Children

The firstChild property is a shortcut. Every element can have any number of children, listed in a property called childNodes. Here are a few things to keep in mind about childNodes:

- childNodes is a list of all the first-level child nodes of the element—it does not cascade down into deeper levels.

- You can access a child element of the current element via the array counter or the item() method.

- The shortcut properties yourElement.firstChild and yourElement.lastChild are easier versions of yourElement.childNodes[0] and yourElement.childNodes[yourElement. childNodes.length-1] and make it quicker to reach them.

- You can check whether an element has any children by calling the method hasChildNodes(), which returns a Boolean value.

Returning to the earlier example, you can access the UL element and get information about its children as shown here:

HTML

```
<ul id="eventsList">
<li>List 1</li>
<li>List 2</li>
<li><a href="http://www.google.com">Linked List Item</a></li>
<li>List 4</li>
</ul>
```

JavaScript

```
function myDOMinspector()
{
  var DOMstring='';
var demoList=document.getElementById('eventsList');
if (!demoList){return;}
  if(demoList.hasChildNodes())
  {
    var ch=demoList.childNodes;
    for(var i=0;i<ch.length;i++)
    {
      DOMstring+=ch[i].nodeName+'\n';
    }
    alert(DOMstring);
  }

}
```

You create an empty string called DOMstring and check for DOM support and whether the UL element with the right id attribute is defined. Then you test whether the element has child nodes and, if it does, store them in a variable named ch. You loop through the variable (which automatically becomes an array) and add the nodeName of each child node to DOMString, followed by a line break (\n). You then look at the outcome using the alert() method.

If you run this script in a browser, you will see four LI elements and the line breaks in between the elements as text nodes, like in Figure 4-10.

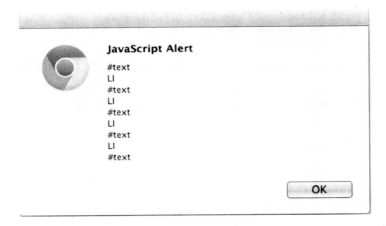

Figure 4-10. *Nodes found by our script, including text nodes that in reality are line breaks*

From the Children to the Parents

You can also navigate from child elements back to their parents, via the parentNode property. First let's make it easier for you to reach the link—by adding an ID to it:

```
<ul id="eventsList">
<li>List</li>
<li>List</li>
<li>
<a id="linkedItem" href="http://www.google.com">
Linked List Item
</a>
</li>
<li>List</li>
</ul>
```

Now assign a variable to the link object and read the parent node's name:

```
var myLinkItem=document.getElementById("linkedItem");
alert(myLinkItem.parentNode.nodeName);
```

The result is LI, and if you add another parentNode to the object reference, you get UL, which is the link's grandparent element:

```
alert(myLinkItem.parentNode.parentNode.nodeName);
```

You can add as many of those as you want—that is, if there are parent elements left in the document tree and you haven't reached the top level yet. If you use parentNode in a loop, it is important that you also test the nodeName and end the loop when it reaches the BODY. Say, for example, you want to check whether an object is inside an element with a class called dynamic. You can do that with a while loop:

```
var myLinkItem = document.getElementById("linkedItem");
var parentElm = myLinkItem.parentNode;
```

```
while(parentElm.className != "dynamic")
{
  parentElm = parentElm.parentNode;
}
```

However, this loop will end in an "`TypeError: Cannot read property 'className' of null`" error when there is no element with the right class. If you tell the loop to stop at the body, you can avoid that error:

```
var myLinkItem = document.getElementById('linkedItem');
var parentElm = myLinkItem.parentNode;
while(!parentElm.className != 'dynamic'&& parentElm != document.body')
{
  parentElm=parentElm.parentNode;
}
alert(parentElm);
```

Among Siblings

The family analogy continues with siblings, which are elements on the same level. (They don't come in different genders like brothers or sisters, though.) You can reach a different child node on the same level via the previousSibling and nextSibling properties of a node. Let's go back to our list example:

```
<ul id="eventsList">
<li>List Item 1</li>
<li>List Item 2</li>
<li>
<a id="linkedItem" href="http://www.google.com/">
    Linked List Item
</a>
</li>
<li>List Item 4</li>
</ul>
```

You can reach the link via getElementById() and the LI containing the link via parentNode. The properties previousSibling and nextSibling allow you to get List Item 2 and List Item 3, respectively:

```
var myLinkItem = document.getElementById("linkedItem");
var listItem = myLinkItem.parentNode;
var nextListItem = myLinkItem.nextSibling;
var prevListItem = myLinkItem.previousSibling;
```

If the current object is the last child of the parent element, nextSibling will be undefined and cause an error if you don't test for it properly. Unlike with childNodes, there are no shortcut properties for the first and last siblings, but you could write utility methods to find them. For example, suppose you want to find the first and the last LI in our demo HTML:

```
document.addEventListener("DOMContentLoaded",init,false);

function init()
{
  var myLinkItem=document.getElementById("linkedItem");
  var first=firstSibling(myLinkItem.parentNode);
  var last=lastSibling(myLinkItem.parentNode);
```

```
  alert(getTextContent(first));
  alert(getTextContent(last));
}
function lastSibling(node){
  var tempObj=node.parentNode.lastChild;
  while(tempObj.nodeType!=1 && tempObj.previousSibling!=null)
  {
    tempObj=tempObj.previousSibling;
  }
  return (tempObj.nodeType==1)?tempObj:false;
}
function firstSibling(node)
{
  var tempObj=node.parentNode.firstChild;
  while(tempObj.nodeType!=1 && tempObj.nextSibling!=null)
  {
    tempObj=tempObj.nextSibling;
  }
  return (tempObj.nodeType==1)?tempObj:false;
}
function getTextContent(node)
{
  return node.firstChild.nodeValue;
}
```

Notice that you need to check for nodeType, because the last or first child of the parentNode might be a text node and not an element.

Let's make our date-checking script less obtrusive by using DOM methods to provide text feedback instead of sending an alert to the user. First, you need a container to show your error message:

```
<!doctype html>
<html>
<head>
<meta charset="UTF-8">
<title>Date example</title>
<style type="text/css">
      .error{color:#c00;font-weight:bold;}
</style>
<script type="text/javascript" src="checkdate.js"></script>
</head>
<body>
<h1>Events search</h1>
<form action="eventssearch.php" method="post"onsubmit="return checkDate();">
<p>
<label for="date">Date in the format DD/MM/YYYY:</label><br />
<input type="text" id="date" name="date" />
<input type="submit" value="Check " />
<br />(example 26/04/1975) <span class="error"></span>
</p>
</form>
</body>
</html>
```

The checking script more or less stays the same as it was before—the difference is that you use the SPAN as a means of displaying the error:

```
function checkDate(){
  var dateField=document.getElementById('date');
  if(!dateField){return;}
  var errorContainer=dateField.parentNode.getElementsByTagName("span")[0];
  if(!errorContainer){return;}
  var checkPattern=new RegExp("\\d{2}/\\d{2}/\\d{4}");
  var errorMessage='';
  errorContainer.firstChild.nodeValue='""';
  var dateValue=dateField.value;
  if(dateValue=='')
  {
    errorMessage="Please provide a date.";
  }
  else if(!checkPattern.test(dateValue))
  {
    errorMessage="Please provide the date in the defined format.";
  }
  if(errorMessage!='')
  {
    errorContainer.firstChild.nodeValue=errorMessage;
    dateField.focus();
    return false;
  }
  else
  {
    return true;
  }
}
```

First, test to see if all the needed elements are there:

```
var dateField=document.getElementById("date");
  if(!dateField){return;}
  var errorContainer=dateField.parentNode.getElementsByTagName("span")[0];
  if(!errorContainer){return;}
```

Then define the test pattern and an empty error message. Set the text value of the error span to a single space. This is necessary to avoid multiple error messages to display when the visitor sends the form a second time without rectifying the error:

```
var checkPattern=new RegExp("\\d{2}/\\d{2}/\\d{4}");
  var errorMessage='';
  errorContainer.firstChild.nodeValue=" ";
```

Next is the validation of the field. Read the value of the date field, and check whether there is an entry. If there is no entry, the error message will be that the visitor should enter a date. If there is a date, but it is in the wrong format, the message will indicate so.

```
var dateValue=dateField.value;
  if(dateValue=='')
  {
    errorMessage="Please provide a date.";
  }
  else if(!checkPattern.test(dateValue))
  {
    errorMessage="Please provide the date in the defined format.";
  }
```

All that is left, then, is to check whether the initial empty error message was changed or not. If it wasn't changed, the script should return true to the form onsubmit="return checkDate();"—thus submitting the form and allowing the back end to take over the work. If the error message was changed, the script adds the error message to the text content (the nodeValue of the first child node) of the error SPAN, and it sets the focus of the document back to the date entry field without submitting the form:

```
if(errorMessage!='')
{
  errorContainer.firstChild.nodeValue+=errorMessage;
  dateField.focus();
  return false;
}
else
{
  return true;
}
```

As Figure 4-11 shows, the result is a lot more visually appealing than the alert message, and you can style it in any way you want to.

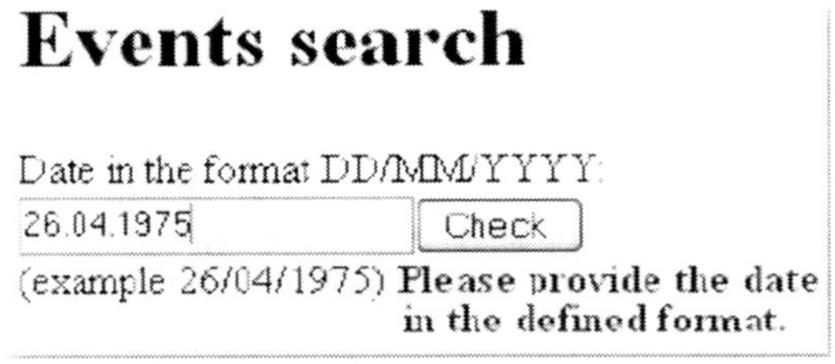

Figure 4-11. *Displaying a dynamic error message*

Now you know how to access and change the text value of existing elements. But what if you want to change other attributes or you need HTML that is not necessarily provided for you?

Changing Attributes of Elements

Once you reach the element you want to change, you can read and change its attributes in two ways: in an older way, having you talk directly to the elements; and in another way, using DOM methods.

Older and newer user agents allow you to get and set element attributes as object properties:

```
var firstLink=document.getElementsByTagName("a")[0];
if(firstLink.href=="search.html")
{
  firstLink.href="http://www.google.com";
}
var mainImage=document.getElementById('nav').getElementsByTagName('img')[0];
mainImage.src="dynamiclogo.gif";
mainImage.alt="Generico Corporation - We do generic stuff";
mainImage.title="Go back to Home";
```

All the attributes defined in the HTML specifications are available and can be accessed. Some are read-only for security reasons, but most can be set and read. You can also come up with your own attributes—JavaScript does not mind. Sometimes storing a value in an attribute of an element can save you a lot of testing and looping.

Caution Beware of attributes that have the same name as JavaScript commands—for example, `for`. If you try to set `element.for='something'`, it will result in an error. Browser vendors came up with workarounds for this. In the case of `for`—which is a valid attribute of the `label` element—the property name is `htmlFor`. Even more bizarre is the `class` attribute—something you will need a lot in the next chapter. This is a reserved word; you need to use `className` instead.

The DOM specifications provide two methods to read and set attributes—`getAttribute()` and `setAttribute()`. The `getAttribute()` method has one parameter—the attribute name. The `setAttribute()` method takes two parameters: the attribute name and the new value.

The earlier example using the newer methods looks like this:

```
var firstLink=document.getElementsByTagName("a")[0];
if(firstLink.getAttribute('href') =='search.html')
{
  firstLink.setAttribute('href') ="http://www.google.com";
}
var mainImage=document.getElementById("nav").getElementsByTagName("img")[0];
mainImage.setAttribute("src") ="dynamiclogo.gif";
mainImage.getAttribute("alt") ="Generico Corporation - We do generic stuff";
mainImage.getAttribute("title") ="Go back to Home";
```

This might seem a bit superfluous and bloated, but the benefit is that it is a lot more consistent with other—higher—programming languages. It is also more likely to be supported by future user agents than the property way of assigning attributes to elements, and they work easily with arbitrary attribute names.

Creating, Removing, and Replacing Elements

DOM also provides methods for changing the structure of the document you can use in an HTML/JavaScript environment. (There are more if you do XML conversion via JavaScript.) Not only can you change existing elements, you also can create new ones and replace or remove old ones as well. These methods are as follows:

- `document.createElement('element')`: Creates a new element node with the tag name `element`.

- `document.createTextNode('string')`: Creates a new text node with the node value of `string`.

- `node.appendChild(newNode)`: Adds `newNode` as a new child node to `node`, following any existing children of `node`.

- `newNode=node.cloneNode(bool)`: Creates `newNode` as a copy (clone) of `node`. If `bool` is `true`, the clone includes clones of all the child nodes and attributes of the original.

- `node.insertBefore(newNode,oldNode)`: Inserts `newNode` as a new child node of `node` before `oldNode`.

- `node.removeChild(oldNode)`: Removes the child `oldNode` from `node`.

- `node.replaceChild(newNode, oldNode)`: Replaces the child node `oldNode` of `node` with `newNode`.

- `node.nodeValue`: Returns the value of the current node.

▓ **Note** Both `createElement()` and `createTextNode()` are methods of `document`; all the others are methods of any node.

All of these are indispensable when you want to create web products that are enhanced by JavaScript but don't rely exclusively on it. Unless you give all your user feedback via alert, confirm, and prompt pop-ups, you will have to rely on HTML elements to be provided to you—like the error message SPAN in the earlier example. However, because the HTML you need for your JavaScript to work makes sense only when JavaScript is enabled, it should not be available when there is no scripting support. An extra SPAN does not hurt anybody—however, form controls that offer the user great functionality (like date-picker tools) but don't work are a problem.

Let's use these methods in our next example. We are going to replace a Submit button with a link.

Links are nicer, because you can style them with CSS. They resize, and they can be easily populated from a localized dataset. The problem with links, though, is that you need JavaScript to submit a form with them. That is why the lazy or too-busy developer's answer to this dilemma is a link that simply submits the form using the `javascript:`protocol (a lot of code generators or frameworks will come up with the same):

```
<a href="javascript:document.forms[0].submit()">Submit</a>
```

A lot earlier in this book, I established that this is just not an option—because without JavaScript this will be a dead link, and there won't be any way to submit the form. If you want to have the best of both worlds—a simple Submit button for non-JavaScript users and a link for the ones with scripting enabled—you'll need to do the following:

1. Loop through all INPUT elements of the document.

2. Test whether the `type` is `submit`.

3. If that is not the case, `continue` the loop, skipping the rest of it.

4.   If it is the case, create a new link with a text node.

5.   Set the node value of the text node to the value of the INPUT element.

6.   Set the href of the link to javascript:document.forms[0].submit(), which allows you to submit the form when you click on the link.

7.   Replace the input element with the link.

▨ **Note**   Setting the href attribute to the javascript: construct is not the cleanest way of doing this. In the next chapter, you'll learn about event handlers—a much better way to achieve this solution.

In code, this could be

```
<!doctype html>
<html>
<head>
<meta charset="UTF-8">
<title>Example: Submit buttons to links</title>
<style type="text/css"></style>
<script type="text/javascript" src="submitToLinks.js"></script>
</head>
<body>
<form action="nogo.php" method="post">
<label for="Name">Name:</label>
<input type="text" id="Name" name="Name" />
<input type="submit" value="send" />
</form>
</body>
</html>
function submitToLinks()
{
var inputs,i,newLink,newText;
  inputs=document.getElementsByTagName('input');
  for (i=0;i<inputs.length;i++)
  {
    if(inputs[i].getAttribute('type').toLowerCase()!='submit') {continue;i++}
    newLink=document.createElement('a');
    newText=document.createTextNode(inputs[i].getAttribute('value'));
    newLink.appendChild(newText);
    newLink.setAttribute('href','javascript:document.forms[0] .submit()');
    inputs[i].parentNode.replaceChild(newLink,inputs[i]);
  }
}
document.addEventListener("DOMContentLoaded", submitToLinks,false);
```

When JavaScript is available, the visitor gets a link to submit the form; otherwise, he gets a Submit button, as shown in Figure 4-12.

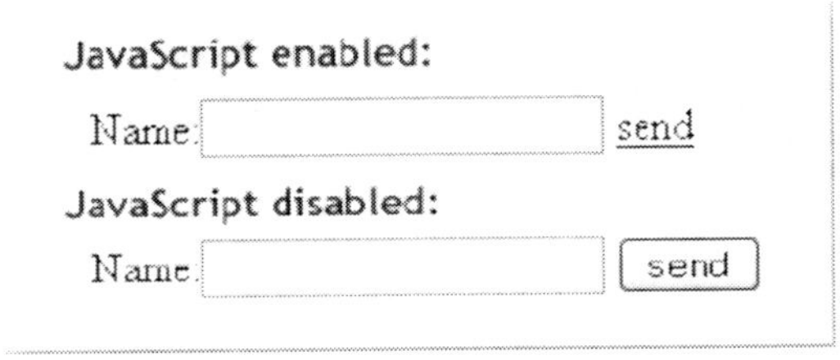

JavaScript enabled:

Name: [   ] send

JavaScript disabled:

Name: [   ] [send]

Figure 4-12. Depending on JavaScript availability, the user gets a link or a button to send the form

However, the function has one major flaw: it will fail when there are more input elements following the Submit button. Change the HTML to have another input after the Submit button:

```
<form action="nogo.php" method="post">
<p>
<label for="Name">Name:</label>
<input type="text" id="Name" name="Name" />
<input type="submit" value="check" />
<input type="submit" value="send" />
</p>
<p>
<label for="Email">email:</label>
<input type="text" id="Email" name="Email" />
</p>
</form>
```

You will see that the "send" Submit button does not get replaced with a link. This happens because you removed an input element, which changes the size of the array, and the loop gets out of sync with the elements it should reach. A fix for this problem is to decrease the loop counter every time you remove an item. However, you need to check whether the loop is already in the final iteration by comparing the loop counter with the length of the array (simply decreasing the counter would cause the script to fail, because it tries to access an element that is not there):

```
function submitToLinks()
{

  var inputs,i,newLink,newText;
  inputs=document.getElementsByTagName('input');
  for (i=0;i<inputs.length;i++)
  {
    if(inputs[i].getAttribute('type').toLowerCase()!='submit') {continue;i++}
    newLink=document.createElement('a');
    newText=document.createTextNode(inputs[i].getAttribute('value'));
    newLink.appendChild(newText);
    newLink.setAttribute('href','javascript:document.forms[0] .submit()');
    inputs[i].parentNode.replaceChild(newLink,inputs[i]);
    if(i<inputs.length){i--};
  }
}
document.addEventListener("DOMContentLoaded", submitToLinks,false);
```

This version of the script will not fail, and it replaces both buttons with links.

Note There is one usability aspect of forms that this script will break: you can submit forms by pressing the Enter button when there is a Submit button in them. When you remove all Submit buttons, this will not be possible any longer. A workaround is to add a blank image button or hide the Submit buttons instead of removing them. I'll get back to that option in the next chapter. The other usability concern is whether you should change the look and feel of forms at all—because you lose the instant recognizability of form elements. Visitors are used to how forms look on their browser and operating system—if you change that, they'll have to look for the interactive elements and might expect other functionality. People trust forms with their personal data and money transactions—anything that might confuse them is easily perceived as a security issue.

Avoiding NOSCRIPT

The SCRIPT element has a counterpart in NOSCRIPT. This element was originally intended to provide visitors alternative content when JavaScript was not available. Semantic HTML discourages the use of script blocks inside the document. (The body should contain only elements that contribute to the document's structure, and SCRIPT does not do that.) NOSCRIPT became deprecated. However, you will find a lot of accessibility tutorials on the Web that advocate the use of NOSCRIPT as a safety measure. It is tempting to simply add a message inside a <noscript> tag to the page that explains that you'll need JavaScript to use the site to its full extent, and it seems to be a really easy approach to the problem. This is why a lot of developers frowned upon the W3C deprecating NOSCRIPT or simply sacrificed HTML validity for the cause. However, by using DOM methods, you can work around the issue.

In a perfect world, there wouldn't be any web site that needed JavaScript to work—only web sites that work faster and are sometimes easier to use when scripting is available. In the real world, however, you will sometimes have to use out-of-the-box products or frameworks that simply generate code that is dependent on scripting. When reengineering or replacing those with less obtrusive systems is not an option, you might want to tell visitors that they need scripting for the site to work.

With NOSCRIPT, this was done quite simply:

```
<script type="text/javascript">myGreatApplication();</script>
<noscript>
  Sorry but you need to have scripting enabled to use this site.
</noscript>
```

A message like that is not very helpful—the least you should do is allow visitors who cannot have scripting enabled (for example, workers in banks and financial companies who turn off scripting because it poses a security threat) to contact you.

Modern scripting tackles this problem from the other side: we give some information and replace it when scripting is available. In the case of an application dependent on scripting, this can be

```
<p id="noscripting">
  We are sorry, but this application needs JavaScript
  to be enabled to work. Please <a href="contact.html">contact us</a>
  If you cannot enable scripting and we will try to help you in other
  ways.
</p>
```

93

You then write a script that simply removes it and even use this opportunity to test for DOM support at the same time:

```html
<!doctype html>
<html>
<head>
<meta charset="UTF-8">
<title>Example: Replacing noscript</title>
<script type="text/javascript">
      function noscript()
      {
         if(!document.getElementById || !document.createTextNode){return;}
         // Add more tests as needed (cookies, objects...)
         var noJSmsg=document.getElementById('noscripting');

         if(!noJSmsg){return;}
         var headline='Browser test succeeded';

         replaceMessage='We tested if your browser is capable of ';
         replaceMessage+='supporting the application, and all checkedout fine. ';
         replaceMessage+='Please proceed by activating the following link.';
         var linkMessage='Proceed to application.';

         var head=document.createElement('h1');

         head.appendChild(document.createTextNode(headline));
         noJSmsg.parentNode.insertBefore(head,noJSmsg);
         var infoPara=document.createElement('p');

         infoPara.appendChild(document.createTextNode(replaceMessage));
         noJSmsg.parentNode.insertBefore(infoPara,noJSmsg);
         var linkPara=document.createElement('p');

         var appLink=document.createElement('a');

         appLink.setAttribute('href','application.aspx');
         appLink.appendChild(document.createTextNode(linkMessage));
         linkPara.appendChild(appLink);
         noJSmsg.parentNode.replaceChild(linkPara,noJSmsg);
}
      document.addEventListener("DOMContentLoaded", noscript,false);
</script>
</head>
<body>
<p id="noscripting">
      We are sorry, but this application needs JavaScript to be
      enabled to work. Please <a href="contact.html">contact us</a>
      if you cannot enable scripting and we will try to help you in
      other ways
</p>
</body>
</html>
```

You can see that generating a lot of content via the DOM can be rather cumbersome, which is why for situations like these—where you really don't need every node you generate as a variable—a lot of developers use innerHTML instead.

Shortening Your Scripts via InnerHTML

Microsoft implemented the nonstandard property innerHTML quite early in the development of Internet Explorer. It is now supported by most browsers; there has even been talk of adding it to the DOM standard. What it allows you to do is define a string containing HTML and assign it to an object. The user agent then does the rest for you—all the node generation and adding of the child nodes. The NOSCRIPT example using innerHTML is a lot shorter:

```
<!doctype html>
<html>
<head>
<meta charset="UTF-8">
<title>Example: Replacing noscript</title>
<script type="text/javascript">
     function noscript()
     {
       if(!document.getElementById || !document.createTextNode){return;}
       // Add more tests as needed (cookies, objects...)
       var noJSmsg=document.getElementById('noscripting');
       if(!noJSmsg){return;}
       var replaceMessage='<h1>Browser test succeeded</h1>';
       replaceMessage='<p>We tested if your browser is capable of ';
       replaceMessage+='supporting the application, and all checkedout fine. ';
       replaceMessage+='Please proceed by activating the following link.</p>';
       replaceMessage+='<p><a href="application.aspx">Proceed to application</a></p>';
       noJSmsg.innerHTML=replaceMessage;
     }
document.addEventListener("DOMContentLoaded", noscript,false);

</script>
</head>
<body>
<p id="noscripting">
     We are sorry, but this application needs JavaScript to be
     enabled to work. Please <a href="contact.html">contact us</a>
     if you cannot enable scripting and we will try to help you in
     other ways.
</p>
</body>
</html>
```

You also can read out the innerHTML property of an element, which can be extremely handy when debugging your code—because not all browsers have a "view-generated source" feature. It is also very easy to replace whole parts of HTML with other HTML, which is something we do a lot when we display content retrieved via Ajax from the back end.

DOM Summary: Your Cheat Sheet

That was a lot to take in. It might be good to have all the DOM features you need in one place to copy and have on hand, so here you go:

- Reaching elements in a document

    - `document.getElementById('id')`: Retrieves the element with the given `id` as an object

    - `document.getElementsByTagName('tagname')`: Retrieves all elements with the tag name `tagname`, and stores them in an array-like list

    - `document.getElementsByClassName('cssClass')`: Retrieves all elements with the class name `cssClass`, and stores them in an array-like list

- Reading element attributes, node values, and other node data

    - `node.getAttribute('attribute')`: Retrieves the value of the attribute with the name `attribute`

    - `node.setAttribute('attribute', 'value')`: Sets the value of the attribute with the name `attribute` to `value`

    - `node.nodeType`: Reads the type of the node (1 = element, 3 = text node)

    - `node.nodeName`: Reads the name of the node (either the element name or `#textNode`)

    - `node.nodeValue`: Reads or sets the value of the node (the text content in the case of text nodes)

- Navigating between nodes

    - `node.previousSibling`: Retrieves the previous sibling node, and stores it as an object.

    - `node.nextSibling`: Retrieves the next sibling node, and stores it as an object.

    - `node.childNodes`: Retrieves all child nodes of the object and stores them in a list. There are shortcuts for the first and last child nodes, named `node.firstChild` and `node.lastChild`.

    - `node.parentNode`: Retrieves the node containing `node`.

- Creating new nodes

    - `document.createElement(element)`: Creates a new element node with the name `element`. You provide the element name as a string.

    - `document.createTextNode(string)`: Creates a new text node with the node value of `string`.

    - `newNode = node.cloneNode(bool)`: Creates `newNode` as a copy (clone) of `node`. If `bool` is true, the clone includes clones of all the child nodes of the original.

    - `node.appendChild(newNode)`: Adds `newNode` as a new (last) child node to `node`.

    - `node.insertBefore(newNode,oldNode)`: Inserts `newNode` as a new child node of `node` before `oldNode`.

    - `node.removeChild(oldNode)`: Removes the child `oldNode` from `node`.

    - `node.replaceChild(newNode, oldNode)`: Replaces the child node `oldNode` of `node` with `newNode`.

    - `element.innerHTML`: Reads or writes the HTML content of the given `element` as a string—including all child nodes with their attributes and text content.

DOMhelp: Your Own Helper Library

The most annoying thing when working with the DOM is browser inconsistencies—especially when this means you have to test the nodeType every time you want to access a nextSibling, because the user agents for very old browsers might or might not read the line break as its own text node. Therefore, you should have a set of tool functions handy to work around these issues and allow you to concentrate on the logic of the main script instead.

Let's start our own helper method library right here and now to illustrate the issues you'd have to face without it otherwise.

Note You'll find the DOMhelp.js file and a test HTML file in the code demo .zip file accompanying this book. The version in the .zip file has more methods, which will be discussed in the next chapter, so don't get confused.

The library will consist of one object called DOMhelp with several utility methods. The following is the skeleton for the utility that we will flesh out over the course of this chapter and the next one:

```
DOMhelp=
{
  // Find the last sibling of the current node
  lastSibling:function(node){},

  // Find the first sibling of the current node
  firstSibling:function(node){},

  // Retrieve the content of the first text node sibling of the current node
  getText:function(node){},

  // Set the content of the first text node sibling of the current node
  setText:function(node,txt){},

  // Find the next or previous sibling that is an element
  //  and not a text node or line break
  closestSibling:function(node,direction){},

  // Create a new link containing the given text
  createLink:function(to,txt){},

  // Create a new element containing the given text
  createTextElm:function(elm,txt){},  // Simulate a debugging console to avoid the need for alerts
  initDebug:function(){},
  setDebug:function(bug){},
  stopDebug:function(){}
}
```

You already encountered the last and first sibling functions earlier in this chapter; the only thing that was missing in those examples was a test for whether there really is a previous or next sibling to check before trying to assign it to the temporary object. Each of these two methods checks for the existence of the sibling in question and returns false if it isn't available:

```
lastSibling:function(node)
{
  var tempObj=node.parentNode.lastChild;
  while(tempObj.nodeType!=1 && tempObj.previousSibling!=null)
  {
    tempObj=tempObj.previousSibling;
  }
  return (tempObj.nodeType==1)?tempObj:false;
},
firstSibling:function(node)
{
  var tempObj=node.parentNode.firstChild;
  while(tempObj.nodeType!=1 && tempObj.nextSibling!=null)
  {
    tempObj=tempObj.nextSibling;
  }
  return (tempObj.nodeType==1)?tempObj:false;
},
```

Next up is the getText method, which reads out the text value of the first text node of an element:

```
getText:function(node)
{
  if(!node.hasChildNodes()){return false;}
  var reg=/^\s+$/;
  var tempObj=node.firstChild;
  while(tempObj.nodeType!=3 && tempObj.nextSibling!=null ||reg.test(tempObj.nodeValue))
  {
    tempObj=tempObj.nextSibling;
  }
  return tempObj.nodeType==3?tempObj.nodeValue:false;
},
```

The first problem you might encounter is that the node has no children whatsoever; therefore, you check for hasChildNodes. The other problems are embedded elements in the node and whitespace such as line breaks and tabs being read as nodes. Therefore, you test the first child node and jump to the next sibling until the nodeType is text (3) and the node does not consist solely of whitespace characters. (This is what the regular expression checks.) You also test whether there is a next sibling node to go to before trying to assign it to tempObj. If all works out fine, the method returns the nodeValue of the first text node; otherwise, it returns false.

The same testing pattern works for setText, which replaces the first real text child of the node with new text and avoids any line breaks or tabs:

```
setText:function(node,txt)
{
  if(!node.hasChildNodes()){return false;}
  var reg=/^\s+$/;
  var tempObj=node.firstChild;
```

```
  while(tempObj.nodeType!=3 && tempObj.nextSibling!=null ||reg.test(tempObj.nodeValue))
  {
    tempObj=tempObj.nextSibling;
  }
  if(tempObj.nodeType==3){tempObj.nodeValue=txt}else{return false;}
},
```

The next two helper methods help you with the common tasks of creating a link with a target and text inside it and creating an element with text inside:

```
createLink:function(to,txt)
{
  var tempObj=document.createElement('a');
  tempObj.appendChild(document.createTextNode(txt));
  tempObj.setAttribute('href',to);
  return tempObj;
},
createTextElm:function(elm,txt)
{
  var tempObj=document.createElement(elm);
  tempObj.appendChild(document.createTextNode(txt));
  return tempObj;
},
```

They contain nothing you haven't already seen here earlier, but they are very handy to have in one place.

The fact that some browsers read line breaks as text nodes and others don't means that you cannot trust nextSibling or previousSibling to return the next element—for example, in an unordered list. The utility method closestSibling() works around that problem. It needs node and direction (1 for the next sibling, –1 for the previous sibling) as parameters:

```
closestSibling:function(node,direction)
{
  var tempObj;
  if(direction==-1 && node.previousSibling!=null)
  {
    tempObj=node.previousSibling;
    while(tempObj.nodeType!=1 && tempObj.previousSibling!=null)
    {
      tempObj=tempObj.previousSibling;
    }
  }
  else if(direction==1 && node.nextSibling!=null)
  {
    tempObj=node.nextSibling;
    while(tempObj.nodeType!=1 && tempObj.nextSibling!=null)
    {
      tempObj=tempObj.nextSibling;
    }
  }
  return tempObj.nodeType==1?tempObj:false;
},
```

The final set of methods is there to simulate a programmable JavaScript debug console. Using alert() as a means to display values is handy, but it can become a real pain when you want to watch changes inside a large loop—who wants to press Enter 200 times? Instead of using alert(), you add a new DIV to the document and output any data you want to check as new child nodes of that one. With a proper style sheet, youcould float that DIV above the content. You start with an initialization method that checks whether the console already exists and removes it if that is the case. This is necessary to avoid several consoles existing simultaneously. You then create a new DIV element, give it an ID for styling, and add it to the document:

```
initDebug:function()
{
  if(DOMhelp.debug){DOMhelp.stopDebug();}
  DOMhelp.debug=document.createElement('div');
  DOMhelp.debug.setAttribute('id',DOMhelp.debugWindowId);
  document.body.insertBefore(DOMhelp.debug,document.body.firstChild);
},
```

The setDebug method takes a string called bug as a parameter. It tests whether the console already exists and calls the initialization method to create the console if necessary. It then adds the bug string followed by a line break to the HTML content of the console:

```
setDebug:function(bug)
{
  if(!DOMhelp.debug){DOMhelp.initDebug();}
  DOMhelp.debug.innerHTML+=bug+'\n';
},
```

The final method is the one that removes the console from the document if it exists. Notice that you need to both remove the element and set the object property to null; otherwise, testing for DOMhelp.debug would be true even if there is no console to write to.

```
stopDebug:function()
{
  if(DOMhelp.debug)
  {
    DOMhelp.debug.parentNode.removeChild(DOMhelp.debug);
    DOMhelp.debug=null;
  }
}
```

We will extend this helper library over the course of the next chapters.

Summary

After reading this chapter, you should be fully equipped to tackle any HTML document, get the parts you need, and change or even create markup via the DOM.

You learned about the anatomy of an HTML document and how the DOM offers you what you see as a collection of element, attribute, and text nodes. You also saw the window methods alert(), confirm(), and prompt(). These are quick and widely supported—albeit insecure and clumsy—ways of retrieving data and giving feedback.

You then learned about the DOM, how to reach elements, navigate between elements, and how to create new content.

In the next chapter, you'll learn how to deal with presentation issues and track how a visitor has interacted with the document in her browser, and to react accordingly via event handling.

CHAPTER 5

Presentation and Behavior (CSS and Event Handling)

In the last chapter, you took apart an HTML document to see what was under the hood. You fiddled with some of the cables, exchanged some parts, and got the engine in pristine condition. Now it is time to take a look at how to give the document a new lick of paint with Cascading Style Sheets (CSS) and kick-start it via events. If beauty is what you are after, you are in luck, because we start with the presentation layer.

Changing the Presentation Layer via JavaScript

Every element in the HTML document has as one of its properties a `style` attribute that is a collection of all its visual properties. You can read or write the attribute's value, and if you write a value into the attribute, you will immediately change the look and feel of the element.

Note   We use the DOMhelp library we created in the previous chapter throughout the whole chapter (and, indeed, in the rest of the book).

Try this script for starters:

exampleStyleChange.html

```
<!doctype html>
<html>
<head>
<meta charset="UTF-8">
<title>Example: Accessing the style collection</title>
<style type="text/css">
</style>
<script type="text/javascript" src="DOMhelp.js"></script>
<script type="text/javascript" src="styleChange.js"></script>
</head>
<body>
<h3>Contact Details</h3>
```

```
<address>
  Awesome Web Production Company<br>
  Going Nowhere Lane 0<br>
  Catch 22<br>
N4 2XX<br>
  England<br>
</address>
</body>
</html>
```

styleChange.js

```
var sc = {
  init:function(){
    sc.head = document.getElementsByTagName('h3')[0];
    if(!sc.head){return;}
    sc.ad = DOMhelp.closestSibling(sc.head,1);
    sc.ad.style.display='none';
    var t = DOMhelp.getText(sc.head);
    var collapseLink = DOMhelp.createLink('#',t);
    sc.head.replaceChild(collapseLink,sc.head.firstChild);
    DOMhelp.addEvent(collapseLink,'click',sc.peekaboo,false)
    collapseLink.onclick = function(){return;} // Safari fix
  },
  peekaboo:function(e){
    sc.ad.style.display=sc.ad.style.display=='none'? '':'none';
    DOMhelp.cancelClick(e);
  }
}
DOMhelp.addEvent(window,'load',sc.init,false);
```

■ **Note** Patience is the key. The addEvent() and cancelClick() parts will be explained in the second part of this chapter.

The script grabs the first H3 element in the document and gets the ADDRESS element via the closestSibling helper method of the DOMhelp library. (The method makes sure that it retrieves the next element and not line breaks that are seen as text nodes.) It then modifies the display property of its style collection to hide the address. It replaces the text inside the heading with a link pointing to the function peekaboo. The link is necessary to allow keyboard users to expand and collapse the address. Although mouse users could easily click the heading, it is not accessible by tabbing through the document. The peekaboo() function reads the display value of the style collection of the address and replaces it with an empty string if display is set to none and with none when the display is set to something other than an empty string—effectively hiding and showing the address as shown in Figure 5-1.

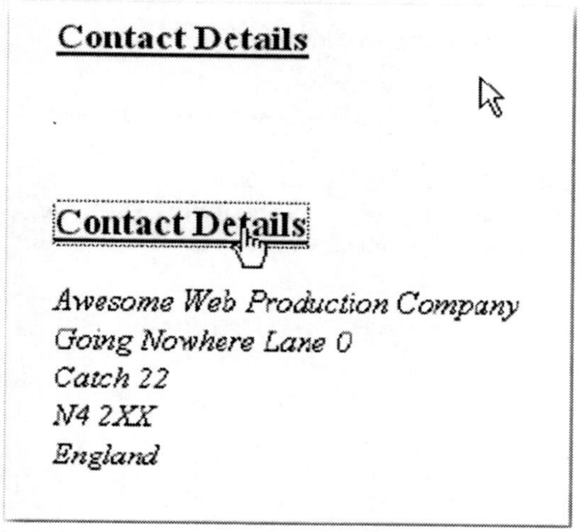

Contact Details

Contact Details

Awesome Web Production Company
Going Nowhere Lane 0
Catch 22
N4 2XX
England

Figure 5-1. *The two states of the address (collapsed and expanded)*

▓ **Note**   You might have encountered scripts in the past that use `element.style.display='block'` as the opposite of none. This works for most elements, but simply setting the display value to nothing resets it to the initial display value—which does not necessarily have to be `block`; it could be `inline` or `table-row`. If you add an empty string, you leave it to the browser to set the appropriate value; otherwise, you have to add a `switch` block or `if` conditions for different elements.

The `style` collection contains all the style settings of the current element that you can modify by using the property notation of the different CSS selectors. A rule of thumb for the property notation is that you remove the dash in the CSS selector and use camelCase for the whole selector. For example, `line-height` becomes `lineHeight` and `border-right` becomes `borderRight`. There is a long list of properties available, but they break down into these categories:

- Background
- Border/Outline
- Generated Content
- List
- Misc
- Margin/Padding
- Positioning/Layout
- Printing
- Table
- Text

■ **Note** A reference guide that includes vendor-prefixed CSS is on the Mozilla Developer Network at https://developer.mozilla.org/en-US/docs/CSS/CSS_Reference.

You can read and write style properties using getAttribute() and setAttribute(); however, if you write them, it might be quicker to simply set the style attribute to a string value using JavaScript object property syntax. For the browser, both of the following examples are the same, but the latter might be a bit quicker to render and it keeps your JavaScript shorter:

```
var warning=document.createElement('div');

warning.style.borderColor='#c00';
warning.style.borderWidth='1px';
warning.style.borderStyle='solid';
warning.style.backgroundColor='#fcc';
warning.style.padding='5px';
warning.style.color='#c00';
warning.style.fontFamily='Arial';

// is the same as
warning.setAttribute( 'style' , 'font-family:arial;color:#c00;
padding:5px;border:1px solid #c00;background:#fcc');
```

Although setting style attributes directly is frowned upon in modern web design (because you are effectively mixing the behavior and presentation layers and making maintenance a lot harder), there are situations where you will have to set style attributes directly via JavaScript—for example:

- Fixing browser shortcomings when it comes to CSS support
- Dynamically changing the dimensions of elements to fix layout glitches
- Animating parts of the document
- Creating rich user interfaces with drag-and-drop functionality

■ **Note** You will hear about the first two items in the list later in this chapter. However, you won't find animation or drag-and-drop examples here, because these are advanced JavaScript topics and need a lot of explanation that falls outside of the scope of this book. You will find examples you can use out of the box in Chapter 11.

For simple styling tasks, you should avoid defining the look and feel in JavaScript in order to simplify the maintenance of your script. In Chapter 3, I talked about the main feature of modern web development: separation of the development layers.

If you use a lot of style definitions in JavaScript, you mix the presentation and behavior layers. If months later the look and feel of your application has to change, you—or some third-party developer—will have to revisit your script code and change all the settings in it. This is neither necessary nor advisable, because you can separate the look and feel by putting it in the CSS document.

You can achieve this separation by dynamically changing the class attribute of elements. That way, you can apply or remove style settings defined in your site's style sheet. The CSS designer does not have to worry about your script code, and you don't have to know about all the problems browsers have when it comes to supporting CSS. All you need to communicate is the names of the classes.

For example, to apply a class called dynamic to an element with the ID nav, you change its className attribute:

```
var n=document.getElementById('nav');
n.className='dynamic';
```

Note Logically, you should also be able to change the class via the setAttribute() method, but browser support for this is flaky (for example, Internet Explorer does not allow class or style as the attribute), which is why for the moment it is a good plan to stick with className. The name of the property is className and not class, because class is a reserved word in JavaScript and results in an error when used as a property.

You can remove the class by setting its value to an empty string. Again, removeAttribute() does not work reliably across different browsers.

As you might be aware, HTML elements can have more than one CSS class assigned to them. A construct of the following kind is valid HTML—and sometimes a good idea:

```
<p class="intro special kids">Lorem Ipsum</p>
```

In JavaScript, you can achieve this by simply appending a value preceded by a space to the className value. However, there is a danger that browsers will not display your class settings correctly, especially when adding or removing results in leading or trailing spaces in the className value. The following two examples will display properly in current browsers (and in Internet Explorer as far back as IE 7):

```
<p class="intro special kids ">Lorem Ipsum</p>
<p class=" intro special kids">Lorem Ipsum</p>
```

You can work around this problem with a helper method. Writing this helper method to dynamically add and remove classes should be easy: you append a class value preceded by a space if the className attribute is not empty and without the space if it is empty. You remove the class name from the original value just like you would remove a word from a string. However, because you need to cater to browser problems with orphan spaces, it gets a bit more complicated than this. The following tool method is included in DOMhelp, and you can use it to dynamically add and remove classes from an element. You also can use this method to test whether a certain class is already added to the element:

```
function cssjs(a,o,c1,c2){
  switch (a){
    case 'swap':
      if(!DOMhelp.cssjs('check',o,c1)){
       o.className.replace(c2,c1);
      }else{
        o.className.replace(c1,c2);
      }
    break;
    case 'add':
      if(!domtab.cssjs('check',o,c1)){
       o.className+=o.className?' '+c1:c1;
      }
```

```
      break;
    case 'remove':
      var rep=o.className.match(''+c1)?''+c1:c1;
      o.className=o.className.replace(rep,'');
      break;
    case 'check':
      var found=false;
      var temparray=o.className.split('');
      for(var i=0;i<temparray.length;i++){
        if(temparray[i]==c1){found=true;}
      }
      return found;
      break;
  }
}
```

Don't worry too much about the inner workings of this method—it will get clearer to you once you master the match() and replace() methods, which will be covered in Chapter 8. For now, all you need to know is how to use it, and for that you use the method's four parameters:

- a is the action that has to be taken and has the following options:

  - swap replaces one class with another.

  - add adds a new class.

  - remove removes a class.

  - check tests whether the class is already applied or not.

- o is the object you want to add classes to or remove classes from.

- c1 and c2 are the class names—c2 is needed only when the action is swap.

Let's use the method to recode the earlier example—this time hiding and showing the address by dynamically applying and removing a class.

exampleClassChange.html

```
<!doctype html>
<html>
<head>
<meta charset="UTF-8">
<title>Example: Dynamically changing classes</title>
<link rel="stylesheet" href="classChange.css">
<script type="text/javascript" src="DOMhelp.js"></script>
<script type="text/javascript" src="classChange.js"></script>
</head>
<body>
<h3>Contact Details</h3>
<address>
  Awesome Web Production Company<br>
  Going Nowhere Lane 0<br>
  Catch 22<br>
N4 2XX<br>
  England<br>
```

```
</address>
</body>
</html>
```

The style sheet contains, among others, a class called hide that will hide any element it gets applied to. This is done is by using a CSS clip. The clip defines the visible areas of this absolutely positioned element. For the screen readers to be able to read the content, it has a size of 1 pixel all around. The !important rule tells the browser to override any other declaration in the CSS. The problem with altering the visibility or display properties to hide elements is that screen readers helping blind users might not make content available to them, although it is visible in a browser.

classChange.css (excerpt)

```css
.hide{
position: absolute !important;
clip: rect(1px 1px 1px 1px); /* IE6, IE7 */
clip: rect(1px, 1px, 1px, 1px);
padding: 0 !important;
border: 0 !important;
height: 1px !important;
width: 1px !important;
overflow: hidden;
}
```

You specify the name of the class as a parameter at the start of the script, which means that if someone needs to change the name at a later stage, he won't have to check the whole script.

If you develop a really complex site with lots of different classes to be added and removed, you could move them out into their own JavaScript include file with their own object. For this example, such a move would be overkill—but I'll come back to this option later.

■ **Note** DOMhelp already includes the cssjs() method; therefore, you don't need to include it in this example.

classChange.js

```javascript
var sc={

  // CSS classes
  hidingClass:'hide', // Hide elements

 init:function(){
   sc.head=document.getElementsByTagName('h3')[0];
   if(!sc.head){return;}
   sc.ad=DOMhelp.closestSibling(sc.head,1);

   DOMhelp.cssjs('add',sc.ad,sc.hidingClass);

   var t=DOMhelp.getText(sc.head);
   var collapseLink=DOMhelp.createLink('#',t);
```

```
        sc.head.replaceChild(collapseLink,sc.head.firstChild);
        DOMhelp.addEvent(collapseLink,'click',sc.peekaboo,false)
        collapseLink.onclick=function(){return;} // Safari fix
    },
    peekaboo:function(e){

        if(DOMhelp.cssjs('check',sc.ad,sc.hidingClass)){
            DOMhelp.cssjs('remove',sc.ad,sc.hidingClass)
        } else {
            DOMhelp.cssjs('add',sc.ad,sc.hidingClass)
        }

        DOMhelp.cancelClick(e);
    }
}
DOMhelp.addEvent(window,'load',sc.init,false);
```

Helping the CSS Designer

DOM scripting and separating the CSS out into classes that get applied and removed dynamically allows you to make the life of web designers a lot easier. Using DOM and JavaScript, you can reach much further into the document than you can by using CSS selectors. One common request is for a way to reach a parent element in CSS for hover effects, for example. In CSS, this is impossible; in JavaScript, it is pretty easy to achieve via parentNode. With JavaScript and DOM, you can provide the designer with dynamic hooks for her style sheet by altering the HTML content to apply classes and IDs, generate content, or even add and remove whole style sheets by adding or removing STYLE and LINK elements.

Styling Dynamic Pages Made Easy

It is very important to make it as easy as possible for the designer to create different styles for the scripting-enhanced version of a site and the nonscripting version. The nonscripting version can be much simpler, and the styles needed for it tend to be fewer. (For example, in the HTML address example, you need link styles defined for inside the H3 only when JavaScript is enabled, because the link is generated via JavaScript.) A really easy option to give the designer a unique identifier when scripting is enabled is to apply a class to the body or to the main element of the layout.

dynamicStyling.js—used in exampleDynamicStyling.html

```
var sc={

    // CSS classes
    hidingClass:'hide', // Hide elements
    DOMClass:'dynamic', // Indicate DOM support

    init:function(){

        // Check for DOM and apply a class to the body if it is supported
        if(!document.getElementById || !document.createElement){return;}
        DOMhelp.cssjs('add',document.body,sc.DOMClass);

        sc.head=document.getElementsByTagName('h3')[0];
        if(!sc.head){return;}
        sc.ad=DOMhelp.closestSibling(sc.head,1);
```

```
      DOMhelp.cssjs('add',sc.ad,sc.hidingClass);
      var t=DOMhelp.getText(sc.head);
      var collapseLink=DOMhelp.createLink('#',t);
      sc.head.replaceChild(collapseLink,sc.head.firstChild);
      DOMhelp.addEvent(collapseLink,'click',sc.peekaboo,false)
      collapseLink.onclick=function(){return;} // Safari fix
   },
   peekaboo:function(e){
      if(DOMhelp.cssjs('check',sc.ad,sc.hidingClass)){
         DOMhelp.cssjs('remove',sc.ad,sc.hidingClass)
      } else {
         DOMhelp.cssjs('add',sc.ad,sc.hidingClass)
      }
      DOMhelp.cancelClick(e);
   }
}
DOMhelp.addEvent(window,'load',sc.init,false);
```

That way, the CSS designer can define in the style sheet which settings to apply when JavaScript is disabled and overwrite them with others when JavaScript is enabled by using the body with the class name in a descendant selector:

dynamicStyling.css

```
*{
  margin:0;
  padding:0;
}
body{
  font-family:Arial,Sans-Serif;
  font-size:small;
  padding:2em;
}

/* JS disabled */
address{
  background:#ddd;
  border:1px solid #999;
  border-top:none;
  font-style:normal;
  padding:.5em;
  width:15em;
}
h3{
  border:1px solid #000;
  color:#fff;
  background:#369;
  padding:.2em .5em;
  width:15em;
  font-size:1em;
}
```

```css
/* JS enabled */
body.dynamic address{
  background:#fff;
  border:none;
  font-style:normal;
  padding:.5em;
  border-top:1px solid #ccc;
}
body.dynamic h3{
  padding-bottom:.5em;
  background:#fff;
  border:none;
}
body.dynamic h3 a{
  color:#369;
}

/* dynamic classes */
.hide{
position: absolute !important;
clip: rect(1px 1px 1px 1px); /* IE6, IE7 */
clip: rect(1px, 1px, 1px, 1px);
padding: 0 !important;
border: 0 !important;
height: 1px !important;
 width: 1px !important;
overflow: hidden;
}
```

The address example now—depending on whether or not JavaScript and DOM are available—can have two completely different looks (one of these having two states), as shown in Figure 5-2.

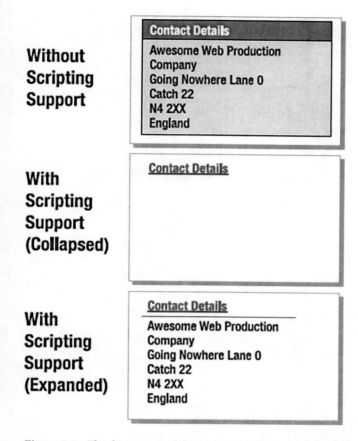

Figure 5-2. *The three states of the address (nondynamic version, collapsed, and expanded)*

This works nicely if your site is not overly complex and does not have many dynamic elements. For more complex sites, you could use a different style sheet for the non-JavaScript versions and the JavaScript versions and add the latter via JavaScript. This also has an added benefit: the low-level user does not have to load a style sheet that isn't of any use to him. You can add dynamic style sheets by creating a new LINK element in the head of the document. In this example, you start by including a low-level style sheet:

exampleStyleSheetChange.html

```
<!doctype html>
<html>
<head>
<meta charset="UTF-8">
<title>Example: Dynamically applying new Style Sheets </title>
<link href="lowlevel.css" rel="stylesheet">
<script type="text/javascript" src="DOMhelp.js"></script>
<script type="text/javascript" src="styleSheetChange.js"></script>
</head>
<body>
```

```
<h3>Contact Details</h3>
<address>
  Awesome Web Production Company<br>
  Going Nowhere Lane O<br>
  Catch 22<br>
N4 2XX<br>
  England<br>
</adress>
</body>
</html>
```

The script checks for DOM support and adds a new link element pointing to the high-level style sheet:

styleSheetChange.js

```
sc={
  // CSS classes

  hidingClass:'hide', // Hide elements
  highLevelStyleSheet:'highlevel.css', // Style sheet for dynamic site

  init:function(){

    // Check for DOM and apply a class to the body if it is supported
    if(!document.getElementById || !document.createElement){return;}

    var newStyle=document.createElement('link');
    newStyle.setAttribute('type','text/css');
    newStyle.setAttribute('rel','stylesheet');
    newStyle.setAttribute('href',sc.highLevelStyleSheet);
    document.getElementsByTagName('head')[0].appendChild(newStyle);

    sc.head=document.getElementsByTagName('h3')[0];
    if(!sc.head){return;}
    sc.ad=DOMhelp.closestSibling(sc.head,1);
    DOMhelp.cssjs('add',sc.ad,sc.hidingClass);
    var t=DOMhelp.getText(sc.head);
    var collapseLink=DOMhelp.createLink('#',t);
    sc.head.replaceChild(collapseLink,sc.head.firstChild);
    DOMhelp.addEvent(collapseLink,'click',sc.peekaboo,false)
    collapseLink.onclick=function(){return;} // Safari fix
  },
  peekaboo:function(e){
    if(DOMhelp.cssjs('check',sc.ad,sc.hidingClass)){
       DOMhelp.cssjs('remove',sc.ad,sc.hidingClass)
    } else {
       DOMhelp.cssjs('add',sc.ad,sc.hidingClass)
    }
    DOMhelp.cancelClick(e);
  }
}
DOMhelp.addEvent(window,'load',sc.init,false);
```

The head of the HTML example is the following after the script has executed. (You can test this in Firefox by selecting the whole document via Ctrl+A or Cmd+A and then right-clicking anywhere and choosing View Selected Source.)

exampleStyleSheetChange.html after script execution (excerpt)

```
<head>
<meta charset=utf-8">
<title>Example: Using dynamic classes</title>
<link href="lowlevel.css" rel="stylesheet">
<script type="text/javascript" src="DOMhelp.js"></script>
<script type="text/javascript" src="styleSheetChange.js"></script>
<link href="highlevel.css" rel="StyleSheet" type="text/css">
</head>
```

You might have encountered the dynamic changing of styles earlier. As early as 2001, so-called *style switchers* became fashionable. These are small page widgets that allow the user to choose a page's look and feel by selecting a style from a given list. Some modern browsers have this option built in—in Firefox, for example, you can choose View, Page Style and get all the available styles to select from.

The demo exampleStyleSwitcher.html shows how this is done. In the HTML, you define a main style sheet and alternate style sheets for large print and high contrast:

exampleStyleSwitcher.html (excerpt)

```
<link href="demoStyles.css" title="Normal"
      rel="stylesheet" type="text/css">
<link href="largePrint.css" title="Large Print"
      rel="alternate stylesheet" type="text/css">
<link href="highContrast.css" title="High Contrast"
      rel="alternate stylesheet" type="text/css">
```

The script is not complex. You loop through all LINK elements in the document and, for each one, determine whether its attribute is either stylesheet or alternate stylesheet. You create a new list with links pointing to a function that disables all but the currently chosen style sheet and add this list to the document.

You start with two properties: one to store the ID of the *style menu* to allow for CSS styling, and one to store a label to show as the first list item preceding all the available styles.

styleSwitcher.js

```
switcher={
  menuID:'styleswitcher',
  chooseLabel:'Choose Style:',
```

An initialization method called init() creates a new HTML list and adds a list item with the label as text content. You set the ID of the list to the one defined in the property.

styleSwitcher.js (continued)

```
init:function(){
  var tempLI,tempA,styleTitle;
  var stylemenu=document.createElement('ul');
  tempLI=document.createElement('li');
  tempLI.appendChild(document.createTextNode(switcher.chooseLabel));
```

```
stylemenu.appendChild(tempLI);
stylemenu.id=switcher.menuID;
```

You loop through all the LINK elements in the document. For each element, test for the value of its rel attribute. If the value is neither stylesheet nor alternate stylesheet, skip this LINK element. This is necessary to avoid other alternative content offered via the LINK tags—like an RSS feed—from being disabled.

styleSwitcher.js (continued)

```
var links=document.getElementsByTagName('link');
for(var i=0;i<links.length;i++){
  if(links[i].getAttribute('rel')!='stylesheet'&& links[i].getAttribute('rel')!='alternate stylesheet'){
    continue;
  }
```

Create a new list item with a link for each style, and set the text value of the link to the value of the LINK element's title attribute. Set a dummy href attribute to make the link appear as a link; otherwise, the user might not recognize the new link as an interactive element.

styleSwitcher.js (continued)

```
tempLI=document.createElement('li');
tempA=document.createElement('a');
styleTitle=links[i].getAttribute('title');
tempA.appendChild(document.createTextNode(styleTitle));
tempA.setAttribute('href','#');
```

Apply an event handler to the link that triggers the setSwitch() method and sends the link itself as a parameter via the this keyword. You can then continue to add the new list items to the menu list and append the list to the document body when the loop is complete.

styleSwitcher.js (continued)

```
    tempA.onclick=function(){
    switcher.setSwitch(this);
    }
    tempLI.appendChild(tempA);
    stylemenu.appendChild(tempLI);
  }
  document.body.appendChild(stylemenu);
},
```

In the setSwitch() method, you'll retrieve the link that was activated as the parameter o. Loop through all LINK elements, and test each to see whether the title attribute is the same as the text content of the link. (You can safely read the text via firstChild.nodeValue without testing for the node type, because you generated the links.) If the title is different, set the disabled property of the LINK to true; if it is the same, set disable to false and the rel attribute to stylesheet instead of alternate stylesheet. Then stop the link from being followed by returning false.

styleSwitcher.js (continued)

```
  setSwitch:function(o){
    var links=document.getElementsByTagName('link');
    for(var i=0;i<links.length;i++){
```

```
      if(links[i].getAttribute('rel')!='stylesheet'&&
      links[i].getAttribute('rel')!='alternate stylesheet'){
        continue;
      }
      var title=o.firstChild.nodeValue;
      if(links[i].getAttribute('title')!=title){
        links[i].disabled=true;
      } else {
        links[i].setAttribute('rel','stylesheet');
        links[i].disabled=false;
      }
    }
  }
  return false;
  }
}
```

You can test the functionality by opening exampleStyleSwitcher.html in a browser that has JavaScript and CSS enabled.

Style switchers can be a useful feature, especially when you offer styles that might help users overcome problems like poor eyesight, such as larger fonts or a higher contrast between the foreground and background. On the other hand, they can be quite pointless eye candy if you use them exclusively for the sake of offering different styles.

Over the years, switchers have gone though a lot of changes. In 2005, Dustin Diaz took up the idea and mixed the stability of the PHP switcher with the slickness of a JavaScript-enhanced interface, which uses Ajax to bridge the gap. You can read more about this in his blog post titled "Unobtrusive Degradable Ajax Style Sheet Switcher" (http://24ways.org/advent/introducing-udasss).

This evolution of the style-switcher idea shows that JavaScript solutions are never set in stone. They need testing in the real world and feedback from users and other developers to be really applicable in a production environment or a live site. If you surf the web these days, you'll see many experimental scripts promising a lot, but on closer inspection they turn out to be slow, unstable, or just a neat trick that could be done a lot better with another technology. Just because you can do anything in JavaScript doesn't mean you should.

Easing the Maintenance of Your Scripts

Keeping the whole look and feel out of your scripts and inside the style sheet (and thereby keeping it as the responsibility of the CSS designer) is just half the battle. During maintenance of a project, the CSS class names might have to change—for example, to support a certain back end or Content Management System (CMS). Therefore, it is important to make it easy for the designer to change the names of your dynamically applied classes. The most basic trick is to keep the class names in their own variables or parameters. You've done that in the earlier examples already. You could apply the class names directly:

```
sc={
  init:function(){
    // Check for DOM and apply a class to the body if it is supported
    if(!document.getElementById || !document.createElement){return;}
    DOMhelp.cssjs('add',document.body, 'dynamic');
    sc.head=document.getElementsByTagName('h3')[0];
    if(!sc.head){return;}
    sc.ad=DOMhelp.closestSibling(sc.head,1);
    DOMhelp.cssjs('add',sc.ad, 'hide');
    var t=DOMhelp.getText(sc.head);
    var collapseLink=DOMhelp.createLink('#',t);
```

```
      sc.head.replaceChild(collapseLink,sc.head.firstChild);
      DOMhelp.addEvent(collapseLink,'click',sc.peekaboo,false)
      collapseLink.onclick=function(){return;} // Safari fix
    },
    peekaboo:function(e){
      if(DOMhelp.cssjs('check',sc.ad,sc.hidingClass)){
         DOMhelp.cssjs('remove',sc.ad,sc.hidingClass)
      } else {
         DOMhelp.cssjs('add',sc.ad,sc.hidingClass)
      }
      DOMhelp.cancelClick(e);
    }
}
DOMhelp.addEvent(window,'load',sc.init,false);
```

Instead, you moved them out of the methods as properties of the main object and commented them to allow those who don't know JavaScript to change the class names without endangering the quality or functionality of your methods:

```
sc={

    // CSS classes
    hidingClass:'hide',       // Hide elements
    DOMClass:'dynamic',       // Indicate DOM support

    init:function(){
      if(!document.getElementById || !document.createElement){return;}
      DOMhelp.cssjs('add',document.body,sc.DOMClass);
      sc.head=document.getElementsByTagName('h3')[0];
      if(!sc.head){return;}
      sc.ad=DOMhelp.closestSibling(sc.head,1);
      DOMhelp.cssjs('add',sc.ad,sc.hidingClass);
      var t=DOMhelp.getText(sc.head);
      var collapseLink=DOMhelp.createLink('#',t);
      sc.head.replaceChild(collapseLink,sc.head.firstChild);
      DOMhelp.addEvent(collapseLink,'click',sc.peekaboo,false);
      collapseLink.onclick=function(){return;} // Safari fix
    },
    peekaboo:function(e){
      // More code snipped
    }
}
DOMhelp.addEvent(window,'load',sc.init,false);
```

For smaller scripts and projects that don't have many different JavaScript includes, this is enough—if accompanied by some documentation on the matter. If you have a lot of dynamic classes scattered over several documents, or you are rather paranoid about noncoders changing your code, you could use a separate JavaScript include file containing an object called CSS with all the classes as parameters. Give it an obvious file name like cssClassNames.js, and document its existence in the project documentation.

cssClassNames.js

```
css={
  // Hide elements
  hide:'hide',

  // Indicator for support of dynamic scripting
  // will be added to the body element
  supported:'dynamic'
}
```

You can apply it to the document just like any of the other scripts in use:

exampleDynamicStylingCSSObject.html

```
<head>
<meta charset="utf-8">
<title>Example: Importing class names from a CSS names object</title>
<link href="demoStyles.css" title="Normal" rel="stylesheet" type="text/css">
<script type="text/javascript" src="DOMhelp.js"></script>
<script type="text/javascript" src="cssClassNames.js"></script>
<script type="text/javascript" src="dynamicStylingCSSObject.js"></script>
</head>
```

The practical upshot of this method is that you don't have to come up with parameter names for the different CSS class names (which normally contain "class" and therefore are confusing for programmers). Instead, use the following:

dynamicStylingCSSObject.js

```
sc={
  init:function(){
    if(!document.getElementById || !document.createElement){return;}

    DOMhelp.cssjs('add',document.body,css.supported);

    sc.head=document.getElementsByTagName('h3')[0];
    if(!sc.head){return;}
    sc.ad=DOMhelp.closestSibling(sc.head,1);

    DOMhelp.cssjs('add',sc.ad,css.hide);

    var t=DOMhelp.getText(sc.head);
    var collapseLink=DOMhelp.createLink('#',t);
    sc.head.replaceChild(collapseLink,sc.head.firstChild);
    DOMhelp.addEvent(collapseLink,'click',sc.peekaboo,false);
    collapseLink.onclick=function(){return;} // Safari fix
  },
  peekaboo:function(e){
    // More code snipped
  }
}
DOMhelp.addEvent(window,'load',sc.init,false);
```

117

In this example, the cssClassNames.js file uses object literal notation. You could go even further and get rid of the comments if you use JSON (http://www.json.org/), which is a format for transferring data from one program or system to another. You will hear more about JSON and its merits in Chapter 7. For now, it is enough to notice that JSON allows you to make the file with the class names a lot more readable for humans:

cssClassNameJSON.js

```
css={
"hide elements" : "hide",
"dynamic scripting enabled" : "dynamic"
}
```

Instead of the attribute notation used earlier, you'll now have to read the data as if it were an associative array:

dynamicStylingJSON.js

```
sc={
  init:function(){
    if(!document.getElementById || !document.createElement){return;}

  DOMhelp.cssjs('add',document.body, css['dynamic scripting enabled']);

    sc.head=document.getElementsByTagName('h3')[0];
    if(!sc.head){return;}
    sc.ad=DOMhelp.closestSibling(sc.head,1);

    DOMhelp.cssjs('add',sc.ad,css['hide elements']);

    var t=DOMhelp.getText(sc.head);
    var collapseLink=DOMhelp.createLink('#',t);
    sc.head.replaceChild(collapseLink,sc.head.firstChild);
    DOMhelp.addEvent(collapseLink,'click',sc.peekaboo,false);
    collapseLink.onclick=function(){return;} // Safari fix
  },
  peekaboo:function(e){
    // More code snipped
  }
}
DOMhelp.addEvent(window,'load',sc.init,false);
```

It is really up to you whether you want to go that far to separate presentation from behavior. Depending on the complexity of the project and the knowledge of the maintenance staff, it might just prevent a lot of avoidable errors.

Overcoming CSS Support Problems

In recent years, CSS has become increasingly important for web development. All page layouts are now being handled by CSS, separating the content of our page from the design. One of the benefits of this separation is that you have the ability to have different layouts for the site based on where it's being displayed. For example, because the size of the screen varies between a desktop, tablet, and phone, you can use different CSS files to layout the site out accordingly.

Browser support for CSS has improved, but as new features are added you might run into things like vendor prefixes:

```
background-color:#444444;
background-image: -webkit-gradient(linear, left top, left bottom, from(#444444), to(#999999));
/*Safari 4+,Chrome*/

background-image:-webkit-linear-gradient(top,#444444,#999999);
/*Chrome 10+,Safari5.1+,iOS5+*/

background-image:-moz-linear-gradient(top,#444444,#999999);
/*Firefox 3.6-15*/

background-image:-o-linear-gradient(top,#444444,#999999);
/*Opera 11.10-12.0*/

background-image:linear-gradient(top,bottom,#444444,#999999);
/* Firefox 16+, IE10, Opera 12.50+ */
```

Here is an example of what vendor prefixes look like. Depending on the version or type of the browser (mobile or desktop), some of these features might need to have a prefix. Although you will get the same effect, the ability for the browser to add that effect using CSS might be dependent on whether you use the vendor prefix.

Multiple Columns with the Same Height

One of the most annoying things about CSS layouts for designers who only dealt with table layouts before is that, if you use CSS float techniques for columns, they don't have the same height, as shown in Figure 5-3.

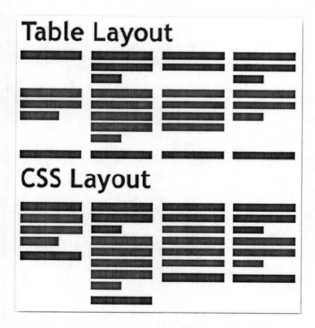

Figure 5-3. *The multiple-column height problem*

Let's start with a list of news items, each containing a heading, a "teaser" paragraph and a "more" link.

exampleColumnHeightIssue.html (with dummy content)

```
<ul id="news">
<li>
<h3><a href="news.php?item=1">News Title 1</a></h3>
<p>Description 1</p>
<p class="more"><a href="news.php?item=1">more link 1</a></p>
</li>
<li>
<h3><a href="news.php?item=2">News Title 2</a></h3>
<p>Description 2</p>
<p class="more"><a href="news.php?item=2">more link 2</a></p>
</li>
<li>
<h3><a href="news.php?item=3">News Title 3</a></h3>
<p>Description 3</p>
<p class="more"><a href="news.php?item=1">more link 3</a></p>
</li>
<li>
<h3><a href="news.php?item=1">News Title 1</a></h3>
<p>Description 4</p>
<p class="more"><a href="news.php?item=4">more link 4</a></p>
</li>
</ul>
```

If you now apply a style sheet that floats the list items and the main list to the left and then set some more text and layout styles, you get a multicolumn layout. The CSS to achieve this is pretty basic:

columnHeightIssue.css

```
#news{
  width:800px;
  float:left;
}
#news li{
  width:190px;
  margin:0 4px;
  float:left;
  background:#eee;
}
#news h3{
  background:#fff;
  padding-bottom:5px;
  border-bottom:2px solid #369;
}
#news li p{
  padding:5px;
}
```

As you can see in the example, each column has a different height, and neither the paragraphs nor the "more" links are in the same position. This makes the design look uneven and can confuse the reader. There might be a CSS way to fix this issue (I am always impressed what kind of hacks and workarounds people find), but let's use JavaScript to work around this problem.

The following script—called in the HEAD of the document, will fix the problem:

fixColumnHeight.js—used in exampleFixedColumnHeightIssue.html

```
fixcolumns={

  highest:0,
  moreClass:'more',

  init:function(){
    if(!document.getElementById || !document.createTextNode){return;}
    fixcolumns.n=document.getElementById('news');
    if(!fixcolumns.n){return;}
    fixcolumns.fix('h3');
    fixcolumns.fix('p');
    fixcolumns.fix('li');
  },
  fix:function(elm){
    fixcolumns.getHighest(elm);
    fixcolumns.fixElements(elm);
  },
  getHighest:function(elm){
    fixcolumns.highest=0;
    var temp=fixcolumns.n.getElementsByTagName(elm);
    for(var i=0;i<temp.length;i++){
      if(!temp[i].offsetHeight){continue;}
      if(temp[i].offsetHeight>fixcolumns.highest){
        fixcolumns.highest=temp[i].offsetHeight;
      }
    }
  },
  fixElements:function(elm){
    var temp=fixcolumns.n.getElementsByTagName(elm);
    for(var i=0;i<temp.length;i++){
      if(!DOMhelp.cssjs('check',temp[i],fixcolumns.moreClass)){
        temp[i].style.height=parseInt(fixcolumns.highest)+'px';
      }
    }
  }
}
DOMhelp.addEvent(window, 'load', fixcolumns.init, false);
```

First, define a parameter to store the height of the highest element and the class used for the "more" links. (The latter is very important, and I'll explain it soon.) Inside the init()method, test for DOM support and check whether the necessary element with the ID news is available. Store the element in the property n for reuse in other methods. Then call the fix() method for each element contained in the list—the headings, the paragraphs, and finally the list items. It is important to change the list items last, because their maximum heights might have changed when those of the other elements were fixed.

fixColumnHeight.js (excerpt)

```
fixcolumns={

  highest:0,
  moreClass:'more',

  init:function(){
    if(!document.getElementById || !document.createTextNode){return;}
    fixcolumns.n=document.getElementById('news');
    if(!fixcolumns.n){return;}
    fixcolumns.fix('h3');
    fixcolumns.fix('p');
    fixcolumns.fix('li');
  },
```

The `fix()` method invokes two additional methods: one to find out the maximum height to apply to each of the items and another to apply this height.

fixColumnHeight.js (excerpt)

```
fix:function(elm){
  fixcolumns.getHighest(elm);
  fixcolumns.fixElements(elm);
},
```

The `getHighest()` method first sets the parameter `highest` to 0 and then loops through all the elements inside the list that match the element name that was sent as the `elm` parameter. It then retrieves the element's height by reading the `offsetHeight` attribute. This attribute stores the height of the element after it has been rendered by the browser. The method then checks whether the height of the element is larger than the property `highest` and sets the property to the new value if that is the case. That way, you find out which element is the highest.

fixColumnHeight.js (excerpt)

```
getHighest:function(elm){
  fixcolumns.highest=0;
  var temp=fixcolumns.n.getElementsByTagName(elm);
  for(var i=0;i<temp.length;i++){
    if(!temp[i].offsetHeight){continue;}
    if(temp[i].offsetHeight>fixcolumns.highest){
      fixcolumns.highest=temp[i].offsetHeight;
    }
  }
},
```

■ **Caution** You need to reset the `highest` parameter to 0 here, because `getHighest()` needs to find the highest of the elements that were sent as a parameter, not of all the elements you fix. If by some freak accident an H3 is higher than the highest paragraph, you'll get gaps between the paragraphs and the "more" links.

The `fixElements()` method then applies the maximum height to all the elements with the given name. Notice that you need to test for the class determining the "more" links; otherwise, the links would get the same height as the highest content paragraph.

```
fixElements:function(elm){
  var temp=fixcolumns.n.getElementsByTagName(elm);
  for(var i=0;i<temp.length;i++){
    if(!DOMhelp.cssjs('check',temp[i],fixcolumns.moreClass)){
      temp[i].style.height = fixcolumns.highest +'px';
    }
  }
}
```

■ **Note**   You need to turn the highest parameter into a number and add a *px* suffix before you apply it to the height of the element. This is always the case; you cannot simply assign a number without a unit when it comes to CSS dimensions of elements.

Lacking Support for `:hover`

The CSS specifications allow you to use the `:hover` pseudo-class on any element of the document, and many browsers support this. This allows the designer to highlight larger parts of the document or even simulate dynamic foldout navigation menus that were hitherto only possible with JavaScript. Although it is worthy of discussion whether something that is not interactive without CSS or JavaScript should get a different state when the mouse hovers over it, it is a feature designers can use a lot—highlighting a current section of a document might make it easier to read after all.

To see an example, take the list of news items once more and apply a different style sheet. If you want to highlight a full list item in CSS-2–compliant browsers, all you need to do is define a hover state on the list item:

listItemRolloverCSS.css (excerpt) used with exampleListItemRollover.html

```
#news{
  font-size:.8em;
  background:#eee;
  width:21em;
  padding:.5em 0;
}
#news li{
  width:20em;
  padding:.5em;
  margin:0;
}
#news li:hover{
  background:#fff;
}
```

On Firefox 19.0.2, the effect appears as shown in Figure 5-4.

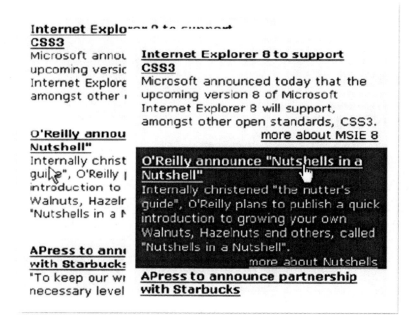

Figure 5-4. *A rollover effect in CSS using the* :hover *pseudo-selector*

In IE 6, you will not get this effect, because it does not support :hover for list items. However, it supports JavaScript, which means that you can use the cssjs method to add a class dynamically when the user hovers the pointer over the list items:

listItemRollover.css (excerpt)

```css
#news{
  font-size:.8em;
  background:#eee;
  width:21em;
  padding:.5em 0;
}
#news li{
  width:20em;
  padding:.5em;
  margin:0;
}
#news li:hover{
  background:#fff;
}
#news li.over{
  background:#fff;
}
```

You add the class via the onmouseover and onmouseout event handlers and by using the this keyword—which we will examine more closely later in this chapter.

listItemRollover.js (excerpt)

```
newshl={
  overClass:'over',
  init:function(){
if(!document.getElementById || !document.createTextNode){return;}
    var newsList=document.getElementById('news');
    if(!newsList){return;}
    var newsItems=newsList.getElementsByTagName('li');
    for(var i=0;i<newsItems.length;i++){
      newsItems[i].onmouseover=function(){
        DOMhelp.cssjs('add',this,newshl.overClass);
      }
      newsItems[i].onmouseout=function(){
        DOMhelp.cssjs('remove',this,newshl.overClass);
      }
    }
  }
}
DOMhelp.addEvent(window,'load',newshl.init,false);
```

If you check this example in IE 6, you will get the same effect you get in more modern browsers.

You can use the pseudo-class selectors of CSS for dynamic effects (:hover, :active, and :focus), but they apply their settings only to elements contained in the current element.

With JavaScript, you have the whole DOM family (including parentNode, nextSibling, firstChild, and so on) at your disposal.

For example, if you want to have a different rollover state when the user hovers the pointer over the links, you can extend the script easily to do so. First you need a new class for the active state:

listItemDoubleRollover.css as used in exampleListItemDoubleRollover.html

```
#news{
  font-size:.8em;
  background:#eee;
  width:21em;
  padding:.5em 0;
}
#news li{
  width:20em;
  padding:.5em;
  margin:0;
}
#news li:hover{
  background:#fff;
}
#news li.over{
  background:#fff;
}
#news li.active{
  background:#ffc;
}
```

Then you need to apply the events to the links inside the list items and change the class of their parent node's parent node (because the link in this example is either in a heading or in a paragraph):

listItemDoubleRollover.js

```
newshl={
  // CSS classes
  overClass:'over',      // Hover state of list item
  activeClass:'active',  // Hover state on a link

  init:function(){
    if(!document.getElementById || !document.createTextNode){return;}
    var newsList=document.getElementById('news');
    if(!newsList){return;}
    var newsItems=newsList.getElementsByTagName('li');
    for(var i=0;i<newsItems.length;i++){
      newsItems[i].onmouseover=function(){
        DOMhelp.cssjs('add',this,newshl.overClass);
      }
      newsItems[i].onmouseout=function(){
        DOMhelp.cssjs('remove',this,newshl.overClass);
      }
    }
    var newsItemLinks=newsList.getElementsByTagName('a');
    for(i=0;i<newsItemLinks.length;i++){
      newsItemLinks[i].onmouseover=function(){
        var p=this.parentNode.parentNode;
        DOMhelp.cssjs('add',p,newshl.activeClass);
      }
      newsItemLinks[i].onmouseout=function(){
        var p=this.parentNode.parentNode;
        DOMhelp.cssjs('remove',p,newshl.activeClass);
      }
    }
  }
}
DOMhelp.addEvent(window, 'load', newshl.init, false);
```

The result is two different states for the news item, as shown in Figure 5-5, depending on whether the user's pointer is hovering over the text or over the links.

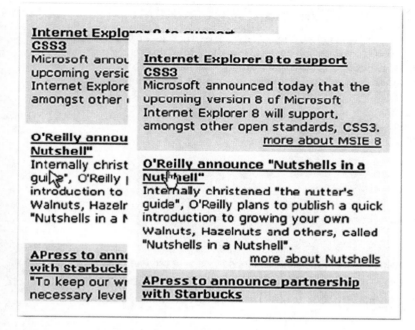

Figure 5-5. *Different rollover states for a single element*

Using JavaScript, you can also make the whole news item clickable, and this is where more events come into play.

If You Have a Hammer, Everything Looks Like a Nail

These few examples should make it clear to you that JavaScript and the DOM are very powerful when it comes to making the browser behave and allow for effects you'd like to achieve.

The questions, however, are whether it is worth the effort and where to draw the line. One idea is to discuss with your client or team how many versions back you need to support. Browsers like Firefox and Chrome have six-week release cycles. This has made it better for developers, who expect a larger amount of consistency when targeting the DOM or CSS3. Some development shops have a policy of supporting the current browser plus three versions back.

JavaScript has one big advantage over CSS: communication with the document works in both directions. While CSS only styles or deals with what is already given, JavaScript can read values, test for support, check whether elements are available and what they are, and even create elements on the fly if they are needed. CSS can only read the document, much like you can only read a newspaper, but JavaScript can also alter it.

This capability of JavaScript is used in a lot of CSS tricks. Many effects are possible only with extraneous markup—nested elements, clearing elements, and so on. Therefore, developers started generating these via JavaScript rather than expecting them in the HTML. This makes the source document appear a lot cleaner;however, for the end user, the final DOM tree—including all generated content—is what he has to deal with. Bloated HTML does not get better by generating the bloat via JavaScript. Maybe it is sometimes better to look at simplifying an interface or making it more flexible from the start than trying to make it behave like tables via lots of CSS and JavaScript sorcery.

Changing the Document's Behavior via Event Handling

Event handling is probably the best thing JavaScript offers to a user-interface-focused developer. It is also one of the most confusing JavaScript topics—not because it is complex, but because there have been different ways to implement them. I will now explain to you what an event is; show an old, tried-and-true approach to dealing with events; and then explain the approach that the W3C recommends. Finally, you'll learn how to tweak the W3C-compliant approach to allow browsers that don't support it to understand your scripts.

Events can be many things, for example:

- The initial loading and rendering of the document

- The loading of an image

- The user clicking a button

- The user pressing a key

- The user moving the mouse over a certain element

Note Picture an event handler like a motion detector or the contacts of a door bell—if someone moves closer to the door, the lights are turned on; and if that someone presses the button of the door bell, the circuit is closed and the ringing mechanism is triggered to play a sound. In the same way, you can detect when a user hovers the mouse over a link to trigger one function and to trigger another one when the user clicks this link.

You can apply event handlers to make your scripts aware of what is happening in several ways. The most obtrusive way and a way that will not work when Content Security Policy (CSP) is enforced, is to use inline event calls in the HTML:

```
<a href="moreinfo.html"onclick="return infoWindow(this.href)">more information</a>
```

A cleaner way was already described in earlier chapters: you identify the element via a class or an ID and then set the event handler in your script instead. It's also important to remember that when CSP is enabled, this code will not work. The easiest and most widely supported way is to apply the event handler directly to the object as a property:

HTML

```
<a href="moreinfo.html" id="info">more information</a>
```

JavaScript

```
var triggerLink=document.getElementById('info');
triggerlink.onclick=infoWindow;
```

Note You do not need to test for the element with the ID info, because the function can only have been called by it.

Triggering events in this way raises several issues:

- You don't send the element to the function; instead, you need to find the element again.

- You can assign only one function at a time.

- You hijack the event of this element for your script exclusively—methods of other scripts trying to use this element for other events will not work any longer.

Unless you defined triggerLink as a global variable or object property, the function infoWindow() needs to find the trigger element before it can be used.

```
function infoWindow(){
  var url=document.getElementById('info').getAttribute('href');
  // Other code
}
```

This and the problem of multiple functions connected to one event can be solved by applying an anonymous function that calls your real function or functions, which also allows you to send the current object via the this keyword:

```
var triggerLink=document.getElementById('info');
triggerlink.onclick=function(){
  showInfoWindow(this.href);
  highLight(this);
  setCurrent(this);
}
function showInfoWindow(url){
  // Other code
}
```

The third problem remains. Your script, as long as it is the last one included in the document, will override the event triggers of other scripts, which means it won't easily work together with other scripts. Therefore, you need a way to assign event handlers without overriding other scripts. This is especially important when you want to call different functions when the document is loaded.

Events in the W3C-Compliant World

The W3C DOM-2 specifications approach the event-handling issue a bit differently, expanding them with DOM-3. First of all, they define different parts of the event's occurrence up to the use of the retrieved data in detail:

- The *event* is what happens—for example, click.
- The *event handler*—for example, onclick—is in DOM-1, which is the location where the event gets recorded.
- The *event target* is where the event occurred—in most cases, an HTML element.
- The *event listener* is a function that deals with that event.
- DOM-3 also brings the concept of *event capturing*, which is the ability to control how the event was propagated through the DOM.

Applying Events

You apply an event via the addEventListener() method. This function takes three parameters: the event as a string and without the *on* prefix, the name of the event listener function (without parentheses), and a Boolean value called useCapture, which defines whether event capturing should be used or not. For now, it is safe to set useCapture to false. By using false, your code will work on all browsers that support addEventListener (such as IE before version 9).

If you want to apply the function `infoWindow()` to the link via `addEventListener()`, you use the following:

```
var triggerLink=document.getElementById('info');
triggerLink.addEventListener( 'click', infoWindow, false);
```

If you want to add a hover effect by calling the function `highlight()` when the mouse is over the link and the function `unhighlight()` when the mouse leaves the link, you can add a couple more lines:

```
var triggerLink=document.getElementById('info');
triggerLink.addEventListener( 'click', infoWindow, false);
triggerLink.addEventListener( 'mouseout', highlight, false);
triggerLink.addEventListener( 'mouseover', unhighlight, false);
```

Checking Which Event Was Triggered Where and How

It might seem that in terms of ease of developing, you are back to square one: you once again have to find the element to read the `href` from inside `infoWindow()`. This is true; however, by using `addEventListener`, you prompt standards-compliant browsers to give you the *event object,* which you can read out via a parameter. This parameter could be called anything you like; you'll probably find most developers just call item.

You might have seen this e before and wondered what it was and whether you should trust an e without knowing where it came from. It is very confusing at first to simply use a parameter without sending it when you apply the event, but once you learn about the event object, you'll never go back to using onevent properties. The event object has many attributes you can use in the event listener function:

- `target`: The element that fired the event.

- `type`: The event that was fired (for example, `click`).

- `button`: The mouse button that was pressed: 0 for left, 1 for middle, and 2 for right.

- `keyCode`: The character code of the key that was pressed. The W3C specifications also have key. In IE 9 and above, keywill show you the key that has been pressed. Also, webkit browsers do not display keyCode results for the arrow keys with a keyPress event; use keydown or keyup instead.

- `shiftKey`, `ctrlKey`, and `altKey`: A Boolean—true if the Shift, Ctrl, or Alt key (respectively) was pressed.

The full list of what is available depends on the event you are listening to. You can find the whole list of attributes in the DOM-3 specification at `http://www.w3.org/TR/DOM-Level-3-Events/`.

Using the Event object, you can easily use one function to deal with several events:

```
var triggerLink=document.getElementById('info');
triggerLink.addEventListener( 'click', infoWindow, false);
triggerLink.addEventListener( 'mouseout', infoWindow, false);
triggerLink.addEventListener( 'mouseover', infoWindow, false);
```

You can use the same function for all three events and check the event type:

```
function infoWindow(e){
  switch(e.type){
    case 'click':
       // Code to deal with the user clicking the link
    break;
```

```
    case 'mouseover':
        // Code to deal with the user hovering over the link
    break;
    case 'mouseout':
        // Code to deal with the user leaving the link
    break;
}
```

You could also check the element the event occurred at by checking its nodeName. Notice that you once again have to use toLowerCase() to avoid cross-browser problems:

```
function infoWindow(e){
  targetElement=e.target.nodeName.toLowerCase();
  switch(targetElement){
    case 'input':
        // Code to deal with input elements
    break;
    case 'a':
        // Code to deal with links
    break;
    case 'h1':
        // Code to deal with the main heading
    break;
  }
}
```

Stopping Event Propagation

Assigning events and intercepting them with event listeners also means that you need to take care of two problems: one is that a lot of events have default actions—click, for example, might make the browser follow a link or submit a form, whereas keyup might add a character to a form field.

The other problem is known as *event bubbling*. The term basically means that when an event occurs at an element, it also occurs at all the parent elements of the initial element.

Event Bubbling

Let's go back to the HTML markup for the news list:

exampleEventBubble.html

```
<ul id="news">
<li>
<h3><a href="news.php?item=1">News Title 1</a></h3>
<p>Description 1</p>
<p class="more"><a href="news.php?item=1">more link 1</a></p>
</li>
<!-- and so on -->
</ul>
```

If you now assign a mouseover event to the links in the list, hovering the mouse over them will also trigger any event listener that might be on the paragraphs, the list items, the list, and all the other elements above that in the node tree right up to the document body. As an example, you'll see how to attach event listeners to each element that will then point to the appropriate functions:

eventBubble.js

```
bubbleTest={
  init:function(){
    if(!document.getElementById || !document.createTextNode){return;}
    bubbleTest.n=document.getElementById('news');
    if(!bubbleTest.n){return;}

    bubbleTest.addMyListeners('click',bubbleTest.liTest,'li');
    bubbleTest.addMyListeners('click',bubbleTest.aTest,'a');
    bubbleTest.addMyListeners('click',bubbleTest.pTest,'p');

  },
  addMyListeners:function(eventName,functionName,elements){
    var temp=bubbleTest.n.getElementsByTagName(elements);
    for(var i=0;i<temp.length;i++){
      temp[i].addEventListener(eventName,functionName,false);
    }
  },
  liTest:function(e){
    alert('li was clicked');
  },
  pTest:function(e){
    alert('p was clicked');
  },
  aTest:function (e){
    alert('a was clicked');
  }
}
window.addEventListener('load',bubbleTest.init,false);
```

Now all the list items will trigger the liTest() method when they are clicked, all the paragraphs will trigger the pTest() method, and all the links will trigger the aTest() method.

However, if you click the paragraph, you will get two alerts:

```
p was clicked
li was clicked
```

You can prevent this by using the e.stopPropagation() method, which ensures that only the event listener applied to the links will get the event. This method works in IE in version 9 and above; for other versions, use the cancelBubble property and set it to true. If you change the pTest() method to the following:

stopPropagation.js—used in exampleStopPropagation.html

```
pTest:function(e){
  alert('p was clicked');
  e.stopPropagation();
},
```

the output will be

```
p was clicked
```

Event bubbling is not really that problematic, because you are not often likely to assign different listeners to embedded elements instead of to their parents. However, if you want to learn more about event bubbling and the order of what happens when an event occurs, Peter-Paul Koch has written an excellent explanation, which is available at http://www.quirksmode.org/js/events_order.html.

Preventing Default Actions

The other problem you might have is that events on certain elements have default actions. Forms, for example, submit data to the server. You might not want that to happen just yet, so you can stop the default action and then perform any work you want before the data is sent to the server.

In the DOM-1 event-handler model, you did this by returning a false value in the function that was called:

```
element.onclick=function(){
  // Do other code
  return false;
}
```

If you click any of the links in the earlier example, they load the linked document. You can override this by using the DOM-2 preventDefault() method. This method is also widely supported in most browsers, including IE versions 9 and above. Let's test it by adding it to the aTest method:

preventDefault.js—used in examplePreventDefault.html

```
aTest:function (e){
  alert('a was clicked');
  e.stopPropagation();
  e.preventDefault();
}
```

Clicking the links now just causes the alert to show up:

```
a was clicked
```

The links, on the other hand, are not being followed, and you'll stay on the same page to do something different with the link data.For example, you could initially show only the headlines and expand the content when the headlines are clicked. First, you need some more classes in the style sheet to allow for these changes:

listItemCollapse.css (excerpt)

```
.hide{
position: absolute !important;
clip: rect(1px 1px 1px 1px); /* IE6, IE7 */
clip: rect(1px, 1px, 1px, 1px);
padding: 0 !important;
border: 0 !important;
height: 1px !important;
```

```css
 width: 1px !important;
overflow: hidden;

}
li.current{
    background:#ccf;
}
li.current h3{
    background:#69c;
}
```

The script for collapsing the elements is not complex, but it uses all the event-handling elements I talked about:

newsItemCollapse.js

```javascript
newshl={
  // CSS classes
  overClass:'over', // Rollover effect
  hideClass:'hide', // Hide things
  currentClass:'current', // Open item

  init:function(){
  var ps,i,hl;
  if(!document.getElementById || !document.createTextNode){return;}
    var newsList=document.getElementById('news');
    if(!newsList){return;}
    var newsItems=newsList.getElementsByTagName('li');
    for(i=0;i<newsItems.length;i++){
      hl=newsItems[i].getElementsByTagName('a')[0];
      hl.addEventListener('click',newshl.toggleNews,false);
      hl.addEventListener('mouseover',newshl.hover,false);
      hl.addEventListener('mouseout',newshl.hover,false);
    }
    var ps=newsList.getElementsByTagName('p');
    for(i=0;i<ps.length;i++){
      DOMhelp.cssjs('add',ps[i],newshl.hideClass);
    }
  },
  toggleNews:function(e){
    var section=e.target.parentNode.parentNode;
    var first=section.getElementsByTagName('p')[0];
    var action=DOMhelp.cssjs('check',first,newshl.hideClass)?'remove':'add';
    var sectionAction=action=='remove'?'add':'remove';
    var ps=section.getElementsByTagName('p');
    for(var i=0;i<ps.length;i++){
      DOMhelp.cssjs(action,ps[i],newshl.hideClass);
    }
    DOMhelp.cssjs(sectionAction,section,newshl.currentClass);
    e.preventDefault();
    e.stopPropagation();
  },
```

```
  hover:function(e){
    var hl=e.target.parentNode.parentNode;
    var action=e.type=='mouseout'?'remove':'add';
    DOMhelp.cssjs(action,hl,newshl.overClass);
  }
}
window.addEventListener ('load',newshl.init,false);
```

The results are clickable news headings that show associated news excerpts when you click them. The "more" links stay unaffected and will send the visitor to the full news article when clicked. (See Figure 5-6.)

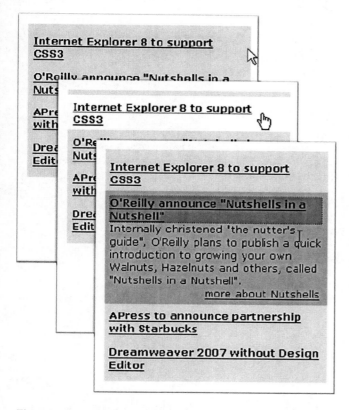

Figure 5-6. *Expanding new items by clicking the headings*

Let's go through the whole script step by step. After defining the CSS class properties and checking for the necessary elements, you loop through the list items, grab the first link (which is the one inside the heading), and assign event listeners for click, mouseover, and mouseout. The click event should fire the newshl.toggleNews() method, while both mouseout and mouseover should trigger newshl.hover().

newsItemCollapse.js (excerpt)

```
for(i=0;i<newsItems.length;i++){
  hl=newsItems[i].getElementsByTagName('a')[0];
  hl.addEventListener('click',newshl.toggleNews,false);
```

```
  hl.addEventListener('mouseover',newshl.hover,false);
  hl.addEventListener('mouseout',newshl.hover,false);
}
```

You hide all paragraphs inside the list item by applying the hiding class to them:

newsItemCollapse.js (excerpt)

```
var ps=newsList.getElementsByTagName('p');
for(i=0;i<ps.length;i++){
  DOMhelp.cssjs('add',ps[i],newshl.hideClass);
}
```

The toggleNews() method grabs the current section by reading out the target of the event object. The target is the link, which means that if you want to reach the list item, you need to go up to the next parent node twice:

newsItemCollapse.js (excerpt)

```
toggleNews:function(e){
  var section=e.target.parentNode.parentNode;
```

You read the first paragraph of the list item and check whether it already has the hiding class assigned to it. If that is the case, define the variable action as remove; otherwise, define it as add. Set another variable called sectionAction and define it as the opposite of action with the same options:

newsItemCollapse.js (excerpt)

```
var first=section.getElementsByTagName('p')[0];
var action=DOMhelp.cssjs('check',first,newshl.hideClass)?'remove':'add';
var sectionAction=action=='remove'?'add':'remove';
```

Loop through all the paragraphs, and either remove the hiding class or add it, depending on the action. Do the same for the section and the current class, but this time use sectionAction. This effectively toggles the visibility of the paragraphs and the styling of the heading:

newsItemCollapse.js (excerpt)

```
var ps=section.getElementsByTagName('p');
for(var i=0;i<ps.length;i++){
  DOMhelp.cssjs(action,ps[i],newshl.hideClass);
}
DOMhelp.cssjs(sectionAction,section,newshl.currentClass);
```

Stop the link that was initially clicked from being followed by calling preventDefault(), and disallow event bubbling by calling stopPropagation():

newsItemCollapse.js (excerpt)

```
  e.preventDefault();
  e.stopPropagation();
},
```

The hover method grabs the list item via parentNode and checks the type of the event that was used to call the method. If the event was mouseout, it defines the action as remove; otherwise, it defines the action as add. It then applies or removes the class from the list item:

newsItemCollapse.js (excerpt)

```
hover:function(e){
  var hl=e.target.parentNode.parentNode;
  var action=e.type=='mouseout'?'remove':'add';
  DOMhelp.cssjs(action,hl,newshl.overClass);
}
```

And finally, add an event listener to the window object that fires off newshl.init() when the window has finished loading:

newsItemCollapse.js (excerpt)

```
}
window.addEventListener ('load',newshl.init,false);
```

Now you know how to make something change once it is clicked in DOM-3–compliant browsers. It is time to think about the other browsers out there and make sure those get support, too.

Fixing Events for the Non-W3C-Compliant World

Now that you know the theory of event handling, it is time to look at the offenders that violate the agreed-upon standard and learn how to deal with them.

Note The helper methods here are already contained inside DOMhelp.js, and you can find them there if you want to use them without DOMhelp.

IE supports addEventListener() starting with version 9. For versions below that, IE has attachEvent(), where instead of passing an event object to each listener, IE keeps one global event object in window.event.

A developer named Scott Andrew came up with a portable function called addEvent() that works around the differences when it comes to adding events:

```
function addEvent(elm, evType, fn, useCapture) {
// Cross-browser event handling for IE5+, NS6+ and Mozilla/Gecko
// By Scott Andrew
  if (elm.addEventListener) {
    elm.addEventListener(evType, fn, useCapture);
    return true;
  } else if (elm.attachEvent) {
    var r = elm.attachEvent('on' + evType, fn);
    return r;
  } else {
    elm['on' + evType] = fn;
  }
}
```

The function uses one more parameter than addEventListener(), which is the element itself. It tests whether addEventListener() is supported and simply returns true when it is able to attach the event in the W3C-compliant way.

Otherwise, it checks whether attachEvent() is supported (effectively meaning IE 8 or below is used) and tries to attach the event that way. Notice that attachEvent() does need the *on* prefix for the event. For browsers that support neither addEventListener() nor attachEvent(), like an extremely old browser, the function points the DOM-1 property to the function.

■ **Note** There is an ongoing discussion about how addEvent() can be improved—for example, to support retaining the option to send the current element as a parameter via this—and many clever solutions have been developed so far. Because each solution has different drawbacks, I won't go into details here, but if you are interested, check the comments at the addEvent() recoding contest page at http://www.quirksmode.org/blog/archives/2005/10/_and_the_winner_1.html.

Because IE uses a global event, you cannot rely on the event object being sent to your listeners. Instead, you need to write a different function to get the element that was activated. Matters get confused even further because the properties of window.event are slightly different from the ones of the W3C event object:

- In Internet Explorer, target is replaced by srcElement.

- button returns different values. In the W3C model, 0 is the left button, 1 is the middle, and 2 is the right; however, IE returns 1 for the left button, 2 for the right, and 4 for the middle. It also returns 3 when the left and right buttons are pressed together, and it returns 7 for all three buttons pressed together.

To accommodate these changes, you can use this function:

```
function getTarget(e){
  var target;
  if(window.event){
    target = window.event.srcElement;
  } else if (e){
    target = e.target;
  } else {
    target = null ;
  }
  return target;
}
```

Or more briefly, using the ternary operator:

```
getTarget:function(e){
  var target = window.event ? window.event.srcElement :
      e ? e.target : null;
  if (!target){return false;}
  return target;
}
```

Safari has a nasty bug (or feature—one is never sure): if you click a link, it does not send the link as the target; instead, it sends the text node contained in the link. A workaround is to check whether the element's node name is really a link:

```
getTarget:function(e){
  var target = window.event ? window.event.srcElement : e ? e.target : null;
  if (!target){return false;}
  if (target.nodeName.toLowerCase() != 'a'){target = target.parentNode;}
  return target;
}
```

Your efforts to prevent default actions and event bubbling also need to accommodate the different browser implementations:

- stopPropagation() is not a method in IE, but a property of the window event called cancelBubble.

- preventDefault() is not a method either, but a property called returnValue.

This means that you have to write your own stopBubble() and stopDefault() methods:

```
stopBubble:function(e){
  if(window.event && window.event.cancelBubble){
    window.event.cancelBubble = true;
  }
  if (e && e.stopPropagation){
    e.stopPropagation();
  }
}
```

▓ **Note** Safari supported stopPropagation() in versions before 5.1 but did nothing with it. This has been fixed in version 5.1 and above.

```
stopDefault:function(e){
  if(window.event && window.event.returnValue){
    window.event.cancelBubble = true;
  }
  if (e && e.preventDefault){
    e.preventDefault();
  }
}
```

Because you normally want to stop both of these things from happening, it might make sense to collect them in one function:

```
cancelClick:function(e){
  if (window.event && window.event.cancelBubble && window.event.returnValue){
    window.event.cancelBubble = true;
    window.event.returnValue = false;
    return;
  }
```

```
  if (e && e.stopPropagation && e.preventDefault){
    e.stopPropagation();
    e.preventDefault();
  }
}
```

Using these helper methods should allow you to handle events unobtrusively and across browsers.

The way around this for versions of Safari prior to 5.1 is to add another dummy function via the old onevent syntax that stops the link from being followed. You'll see this fix in action now. Let's take the collapsing headline example again and replace the DOM-3–compliant methods and properties with the cross-browser helpers:

xBrowserListItemCollapse.js used in exampleXBrowserListItemCollapse.html

```
newshl = {
  // CSS classes
  overClass:'over',        // Rollover effect
  hideClass:'hide',        // Hide things
  currentClass:'current',  // Open item

  init:function(){
  var ps,i,hl;
  if(!document.getElementById || !document.createTextNode){return;}
    var newsList = document.getElementById('news');
    if(!newsList){return;}
    var newsItems = newsList.getElementsByTagName('li');
    for(i = 0;i<newsItems.length;i++){
       hl = newsItems[i].getElementsByTagName('a')[0];
      DOMhelp.addEvent(hl,'click',newshl.toggleNews,false);
      hl.onclick = DOMhelp.safariClickFix;
      DOMhelp.addEvent(hl,'mouseover',newshl.hover,false);
      DOMhelp.addEvent(hl,'mouseout',newshl.hover,false);
    }
    var ps = newsList.getElementsByTagName('p');
    for(i = 0;i<ps.length;i++){
      DOMhelp.cssjs('add',ps[i],newshl.hideClass);
    }
  },
  toggleNews:function(e){
    var section = DOMhelp.getTarget(e).parentNode.parentNode;
    var first = section.getElementsByTagName('p')[0];
    var action = DOMhelp.cssjs('check',first,newshl.hideClass)?'remove':'add';
    var sectionAction = action == 'remove'?'add':'remove';
    var ps = section.getElementsByTagName('p');
    for(var i = 0;i<ps.length;i++){
      DOMhelp.cssjs(action,ps[i],newshl.hideClass);
    }
    DOMhelp.cssjs(sectionAction,section,newshl.currentClass);
    DOMhelp.cancelClick(e);
  },
  hover:function(e){
    var hl = DOMhelp.getTarget(e).parentNode.parentNode;
    var action = e.type == 'mouseout'?'remove':'add';
```

```
      DOMhelp.cssjs(action,hl,newshl.overClass);
  }
}
DOMhelp.addEvent(window,'load',newshl.init,false);
```

> **Note** `hl.onclick = DOMhelp.safariClickFix;` could be a simple `hl.onclick = function(){return false;};`
> however, it will be easier to search and replace this fix once the Safari development team has sorted the problem out.

The clickable headlines now work across all modern browsers; however, it seems that you could streamline the
script a bit. Right now the examples loop a lot, which is not really necessary. Instead of hiding all paragraphs inside the
list items individually, it is a lot easier to simply add a class to the list item and let the CSS engine hide all the paragraphs:

listItemCollapseShorter.css (excerpt)—used in exampleListItemCollapseShorter.html

```css
#news li.hide p{
  display:none;
}
#news li.current p{
  display:block;
}
```

This way, you can get rid of the inner loop through all the paragraphs in the `init()` method and replace it with
one line of code that applies the `hide` class to the list item itself as follows:

listItemCollapseShorter.js (excerpt)—used in exampleListItemCollapseShorter.html

```js
newshl={
  // CSS classes
  overClass:'over',      // Rollover effect
  hideClass:'hide',      // Hide things
  currentClass:'current', // Open item

  init:function(){
    var hl;
    if(!document.getElementById || !document.createTextNode){return;}
    var newsList=document.getElementById('news');
    if(!newsList){return;}
    var newsItems=newsList.getElementsByTagName('li');
    for(var i=0;i<newsItems.length;i++){
      hl=newsItems[i].getElementsByTagName('a')[0];
      DOMhelp.addEvent(hl,'click',newshl.toggleNews,false);
      DOMhelp.addEvent(hl,'mouseover',newshl.hover,false);
      DOMhelp.addEvent(hl,'mouseout',newshl.hover,false);
      hl.onclick = DOMhelp.safariClickFix;
      DOMhelp.cssjs('add',newsItems[i],newshl.hideClass);
    }
  },
```

The next change is in the `toggleNews()` method. There you replace the loop with a simple `if` condition that checks whether the current class is applied to the list item and replaces `hide` with `current` if that is the case and `current` with `hide` if it isn't. This shows or hides all the paragraphs inside the list item:

listItemCollapseShorter.js (excerpt)—used in exampleListItemCollapseShorter.html

```
toggleNews:function(e){
  var section=DOMhelp.getTarget(e).parentNode.parentNode;
  if(DOMhelp.cssjs('check',section,newshl.currentClass)){
    DOMhelp.cssjs('swap',section,newshl.currentClass, newshl.hideClass);
  }else{
    DOMhelp.cssjs('swap',section,newshl.hideClass, newshl.currentClass);
  }
  DOMhelp.cancelClick(e);
},
```

The rest stays the same:

listItemCollapseShorter.js (excerpt)—used in exampleListItemCollapseShorter.html

```
  hover:function(e){
    var hl = DOMhelp.getTarget(e).parentNode.parentNode;
    var action = e.type == 'mouseout'?'remove':'add';
    DOMhelp.cssjs(action,hl,newshl.overClass);
  }
}
DOMhelp.addEvent(window,'load',newshl.init,false);
```

Never Stop Optimizing

You should never cease to analyze your own code in this way to determine what can be optimized, even though it is very tempting in the heat of the moment to merrily code away and create something too complex for its own good. Taking a step back, analyzing the problem you want to solve, and reevaluating what's already in place is sometimes a lot more beneficial than just plowing on. In this case, the optimization is in leaving the hiding of the elements to the cascade in CSS, rather than looping through the child elements and hiding them individually.

When you take another look at code you have created, the following ideas are always good to keep in the back of your mind:

- Any idea that avoids nested loops is a good one.

- Properties of the main object are a good place to store information that is of interest to several methods—for example, which element is active in site navigation.

- If you find yourself repeating bits of code over and over again, create a new method that fulfills this task—if you have to change the code in the future, you'll only have to change it in one place.

- Don't traverse the node tree too much. If a lot of elements need to know about some other element—find it once, and store it in a property. This will shorten the code a lot, because something like `contentSection` is a lot shorter than `elm.parentNode.parentNode.nextSibling`.

- A long list of `if` and `else` statements might be much easier handled as a `switch/case` block.

- If something is likely to change in the future, like the Safari stopPropagation() hack, you should put it in its own method. The next time you see the code and you spot this seemingly useless method, you'll remember what was going on.

- Don't rely on HTML too much. It is always the first thing to change (especially when there is a CMS involved).

The Ugly Page Load Problem and Its Ugly Solutions

When developers started to use CSS extensively, they soon encountered some annoying browser bugs. One of them was the *flash of unstyled content*, otherwise known as FOUC (which you can read more about at http://www.bluerobot.com/web/css/fouc.asp). This effect shows the page without a style sheet for a brief moment before applying it.

You now face the same problem with JavaScript-enhanced pages. If you load the example of the collapsed news items, you'll see all the news expanded for a brief moment. This brief moment is the time needed for the document and all its dependencies, like images and third-party content, to finish loading.

This behavior has been annoying scripting enthusiasts with a designer's eye for a long time; the onload event fired when the page and all contained media (like images) were loaded, and that was it—until a lot of clever DOM scripters put their heads together and had a go at it.

One solution to this is the use the DOMContentLoadedevent, document.addEventListener("DOMContentLoaded",init,false). This event lets you call your function when all the elements of the DOM have been loaded. This is supported in all current browsers (IE as of 9.0, Opera as of 9.0, and Safari as of 3.1).

In earlier versions of IE, you can look for the onReadyStateChange/readyState event and property:

```
document.onreadystatechange = checkState
function checkState(){
if(document.readyState == "complete"){
//run code
}
}
```

Reading and Filtering Keyboard Entries

Probably the most common event for the web you'll use is click, because it has the benefit of being supported by every element and can be triggered by both the keyboard and mouse if the element in question can be reached via keyboard.

However, there is nothing stopping you from checking keyboard entries in JavaScript with the keyup or keypress handler. The former is the W3C standard; the latter is not in the standards and occurs after keydown and keyup, but it is well supported in browsers.

As an example of how you could read out and use keyboard entries, let's write a script that checks whether the entered data in a form field is purely numbers. You tested and converted entries to numbers in Chapter 2 already, but this time you want to check the entry while it occurs rather than after the user submits the form. If the user enters a nonnumerical character, the script should disable the Submit button and show an error message.

You start with a simple HTML form that has one entry field:

exampleKeyChecking.html

```
<!doctype html>
<html>
<head>
<meta charset="UTF-8">
<title>Example: Checking keyboard entry</title>
<link rel="stylesheet" href="keyChecking.css">
```

```
<script type="text/javascript" src="DOMhelp.js"></script>
<script type="text/javascript" src="keyChecking.js"></script>
</head>
<body>
<p class="ex">Keychecking example, try to enter anything but
numbers in the form field below.</p>
<h1>Get Chris Heilmann's book cheaper!</h1>
<form action="nothere.php" method="post">
<p>
<label for="Voucher">Voucher Number</label>
<input type="text" name="Voucher" id="Voucher" />
<input type="submit" value="redeem" />
</p>
</form>
</body>
</html>
```

And after applying the following script, the browser will check what the user enters and both show an error message and disable the Submit button when the entry is not a number, as shown in Figure 5-7.

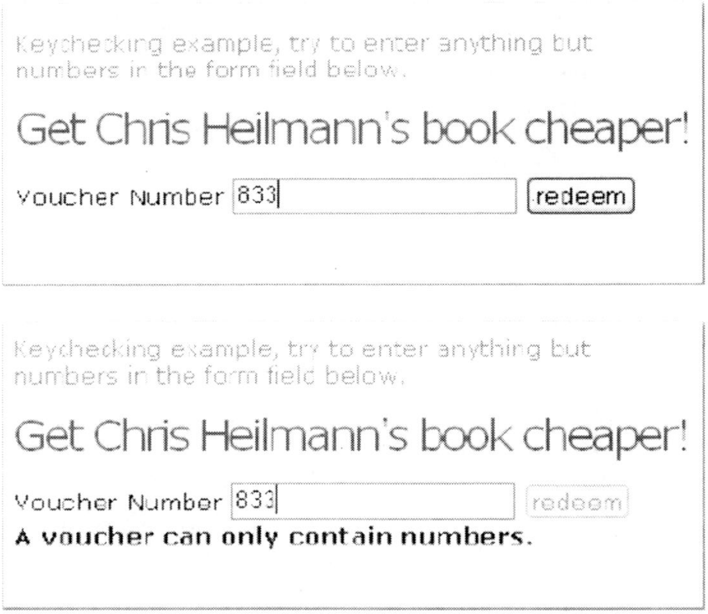

Figure 5-7. *Testing an entry while it is being typed in*

keyChecking.js

```
voucherCheck={
  errorMessage:'A voucher can contain only numbers.',
  error:false,
  errorClass:'error',
  init:function(){
```

144

```
      if (!document.getElementById || !document.createTextNode) { return; }
      var voucher=document.getElementById('Voucher');
      if(!voucher){return;}
      voucherCheck.v=voucher;
      DOMhelp.addEvent(voucher, 'keyup', voucherCheck.checkKey, false);
    },
    checkKey:function(e){
      if(window.event){
        var key = window.event.keyCode;
      } else if(e){
        var key=e.keyCode;
      }
      var v=document.getElementById('Voucher');
      if(voucherCheck.error){
        v.parentNode.removeChild(v.parentNode.lastChild);
        voucherCheck.error=false;
        DOMhelp.closestSibling(v,1).disabled='';
      }
      if(key<48 || key>57){
        v.value=v.value.substring(0,v.value.length-1);
        voucherCheck.error=document.createElement('span');
        DOMhelp.cssjs('add', voucherCheck.error, voucherCheck.errorClass);
        var message = document.createTextNode(voucherCheck.errorMessage)
        voucherCheck.error.appendChild(msg);
        v.parentNode.appendChild(voucherCheck.error);
        DOMhelp.closestSibling(v,1).disabled='disabled';
      }
    }
  }
}
DOMhelp.addEvent(window, 'load', voucherCheck.init, false);
```

First, you'll start by defining some properties, like an error message, a Boolean indicating whether there is an error already displayed, and a class to get applied to the error message. You test for the necessary element and attach a keyup event pointing to the checkKey() method:

keyChecking.js (excerpt)

```
voucherCheck={
  errorMessage:'A voucher can only contain numbers.',
  error:false,
  errorClass:'error',
  init:function(){
    if (!document.getElementById || !document.createTextNode) { return; }
    var voucher=document.getElementById('Voucher');
    if(!voucher){return;}
    voucherCheck.v=voucher;
    DOMhelp.addEvent(voucher, 'keyup', voucherCheck.checkKey, false);
  },
```

145

The checkKey method determines whether window.event or the event object is in use and reads out the keyCode in the appropriate manner:

keyChecking.js (excerpt)

```
checkKey:function(e){
    if(window.event){
      var key = window.event.keyCode;
    } else if(e){
      var key=e.keyCode;
    }
```

It then retrieves the element (in this case via getElementById(), although you could as easily use DOMhelp.getTarget(e), but why make it more complex than needed?) and checks whether the error property is true. If it is true, there is already a visible error message and the Submit button is disabled. In this case, you need to remove the error message, set the error property to false, and enable the Submit button (which is the next sibling of the input element—use closestSibling() here to ensure it is the button and not a line break).

keyChecking.js (excerpt)

```
var v=document.getElementById('Voucher');
if(voucherCheck.error){
  v.parentNode.removeChild(v.parentNode.lastChild);
  voucherCheck.error=false;
  DOMhelp.closestSibling(v,1).disabled='';
}
```

You determine that the key that was pressed is not any of the digits from 0 to 9—that is, that its ASCII code is not between 48 and 57 inclusive.

■ **Tip** You can get the values of each key in any ASCII table, for example, at http://www.whatasciicode.com/.

If the key is not a number key, delete the last key entered from the field value and create a new error message. Create a new span element, add the class, add the error message, append it as a new child to the parent of the text entry box, and disable the form button. The last thing missing is to start voucherCheck.init() when the page has finished loading.

keyChecking.js (excerpt)

```
    if(key<48 || key>57){
      v.value=v.value.substring(0,v.value.length-1);
      voucherCheck.error=document.createElement('span');
      DOMhelp.cssjs('add', voucherCheck.error, voucherCheck.errorClass);
      var message = document.createTextNode(voucherCheck.errorMessage)
      voucherCheck.error.appendChild(msg);
      v.parentNode.appendChild(voucherCheck.error);
      DOMhelp.closestSibling(v,1).disabled='disabled';
  }
 }
}
DOMhelp.addEvent(window, 'load', voucherCheck.init, false);
```

■ **Note**   Normally, it would be enough to check whether the field content is a number on every keyup event, but this demonstrates the power you have with keyboard events.

If you want to read keyboard combinations with Shift, Ctrl, or Alt, you need to check for the shiftKey, ctrlKey, or altKey event properties in your event listener method, for example:

```
if(e.shiftKey && key==48){alert('shift and 0');}
if(e.ctrlKey && key==48){alert('ctrl and 0');}
if(e.altKey && key==48){alert('alt and 0');}
```

The Dangers of Event Handling

With these functions, you can listen and react to any event initiated by the user. You can make navigations that react to rollovers rather than clicks of the links, you can add keyboard shortcuts that are available only to your page, and you can make things react on movements of the mouse.

It is very tempting to use event handling to the fullest and come up with whole new concepts of navigation, user journey flow, and how forms interact with the user. The question is whether that is a good thing or a bad thing.

With your own ideas of what is good and usable in mind, you might sometimes consider a drag-and-drop interface the best there is, but what about users who cannot move a mouse? You can make anything in the document an interactive element by attaching events; however, not all user agents will allow the visitor to reach the element without a mouse. A clickable headline is not available to keyboard users, but a headline with an embedded link is because the user can tab to the link, but he cannot tab to the headline. Basic accessibility guidelines and legal requirements make a strong point that you have to remain input-device-independent if you want to create your own rich interfaces with DOM scripting and HTML.

There is nothing wrong with a drag-and-drop interface, as long as you also allow for keyboard access to it. Because you should not rely on JavaScript being available, you'll need real links on the draggable elements anyway, which could be enhanced with a click event or even keyboard access.

Keyboard event handling is another can of worms. Although all browsers support keydown, you can never know if the keyboard shortcut you want to assign to an element isn't necessary for another piece of software on the user's machine.

Keyboard access is universally part of the operating system, and visitors who need certain key combinations to use it will not take kindly to your hindering them in their work by hijacking those combinations for your purposes. Clever web applications, therefore, make their keyboard shortcuts optional or even customizable by the user.

The same problem occurs in HTML when you use the accesskey attribute. This attribute tells the browser to activate the element when the key defined in the attribute's value is pressed (together with the Alt key on IE and Mozilla—via other combinations on other browsers). In effect, this is adding an event and assigning an event listener that sets the focus of the element or follows the default action of that element. Until recently, it was common practice and deemed safe to use numerical keys for these attributes—which works, until you have a user who has special characters in her name and needs to use Alt and the ASCII number of the character to enter it.

Summary

You've made it to the end of this chapter, and I hope it was not too much information at once.

In the first half, I talked about the interaction of CSS and JavaScript, covering the following:

- How to change presentation in JavaScript via the style collection

- How to help CSS designers by keeping the look and feel of your script in CSS classes

- How to provide the CSS designers with hooks to style the document differently depending on scripting being enabled or disabled

- An introduction to different third-party style switchers and the idea that published JavaScript scripts are not set in stone but can be improved and refined over time

- How to ease the maintenance of CSS and JavaScript working together by introducing objects containing only CSS name information

- Fixing a CSS issue with JavaScript—in this chapter's example, multicolumn displays not having the same height

- Helping the CSS designer by applying cross-browser hover effects

- The dangers of using JavaScript to create lots of HTML elements to support CSS effects instead of implementing these effects via JavaScript from the start

We then moved on to what makes web sites click—literally at times—in other words, event handling. I talked about

- How to apply event handling in old browsers via the DOM-1 onevent properties (like onclick, onmouseover, and so on)

- What the W3C has to say about events in the DOM-3 specifications, and how to use what it recommends

- How to make noncompliant browsers do the same

- How to avoid display glitches when the page is not fully loaded

- How to deal with keyboard entries

- The dangers of event handling

This is it—you should now have all the tools you need to go out there and wow the masses with stable, easy-to-maintain, slick JavaScript. In the next chapter, I'll go through some of the most common uses of JavaScript and have a go at developing up-to-date solutions for them to replace old scripts you might already use.

▓ ▓ ▓

CHAPTER 6

Common Uses of JavaScript: Images and Windows

If you read the last few chapters, you should be well equipped now with your knowledge of JavaScript and its interaction with cascading style sheets (CSS) and HTML. Now you will learn about some of the most common uses of JavaScript on the Web these days, and we'll go through some examples. In these examples, you'll see how to ensure that these implementations of JavaScript work independently of other scripts on the page, and I'll explain what problems might occur. I'll also touch on functionality that is tempting to use but might not be the safest of options.

Note   This chapter has a lot of code examples, and you will be asked to open some of them in a browser to test the functionality for yourself. If you haven't been to `http://www.beginningjavascript.com` yet to download the code examples for this book, it might be a good time to do so now.

Most of the full code examples here use DOM-3 event handling. This makes them a bit more complex than their DOM-1 equivalents, but it also makes them work a lot better with other scripts, and they are much more likely to work in future browsers. Just bear with me, and I promise that by repeatedly using these methods, you will get the hang of them quite quickly.

The examples are also developed with maintenance and flexibility in mind. This means that everything that might be changed at a later stage by non-JavaScript-savvy people is stored in properties and that you can easily have several parts of the same document use the scripts' functionality. This also adds to the complexity of some of the scripts, but it is a real-life deliverable most clients ask for.

Images and JavaScript

Dynamic changing of images was most likely the first "wow" effect JavaScript was used for. When CSS was not supported by browsers yet (and—to be fair—was still in the process of being defined), JavaScript was the only way to change an image when the user moved the mouse over it or clicked it. In recent years, more and more of the image effects traditionally achieved via JavaScript have been replaced by pure CSS solutions that make maintenance a lot easier. I'll discuss these later; for now, let's take a look at the basics of what JavaScript can do to images.

Basics of Image Scripting

In JavaScript, you can reach and amend images in two ways: the DOM-2 way via getElementsByTagName() and getElementById(), or in an older way that involves the images collection that is stored in a property of the document object. As an example, let's take an HTML document with a list of photos:

```
<ul class="slides">
  <li><img src="pictures/thumbs/cat2.jpg" alt="Lazy Cat"></li>
  <li><img src="pictures/thumbs/dog10.jpg" alt="Dog using the shade"></li>
  <li><img src="pictures/thumbs/dog12.jpg" alt="Squinting Dog"></li>
  <li><img src="pictures/thumbs/dog63.jpg" alt="Dog cooling off in the sand"></li>
  <li><img src="pictures/thumbs/dog7.jpg"  alt="Very flat dog"></li>
  <li><img src="pictures/thumbs/donkeycloseup.jpg" alt="Curious Donkey"></li>
  <li><img src="pictures/thumbs/donkeyeating.jpg" alt="Hay-eating Donkey"></li>
  <li><img src="pictures/thumbs/kittenflat.jpg" alt="Ginger and White Cat"></li>
</ul>
```

You can retrieve all these photos in JavaScript to do something to them in both ways:

```
// Old DOM
var photosOldDOM=document.images;
// New DOM
var photos=document.getElementsByTagName('img');
```

Both methods result in an array containing all the images as objects. As with any object, you can read and manipulate their properties. Say, for example, you want to know the alternative text of the third image. All you need to do is read out the alt property of the object:

```
// Old DOM alt property
var photosOldDOM=document.images;
alert(photosOldDOM[2].alt);
// W3C DOM-2 alt attribute
var photos=document.getElementsByTagName('img');
alert(photos[2].getAttribute('alt'));
```

Images have several properties, some of which are obvious. But there are others you might not have heard about:

- border: The value of the border attribute in the HTML

- name: The name attribute of the img tag

- complete: A property that is true if the image has finished loading (this is read-only—you cannot change this attribute)

- height: The height of the image (in pixels—returned as an integer)

- width: The width of the image (in pixels—returned as an integer)

- hspace: The horizontal space around the image

- vspace: The vertical space around the image

- lowsrc: The image preview as defined in the attribute of the same name

- src: The URL of the image

You can use these properties to access and change images dynamically. If you open the example document `exampleImageProperties.html` in a browser, you can read and write the properties of the demonstration image as Figure 6-1 shows.

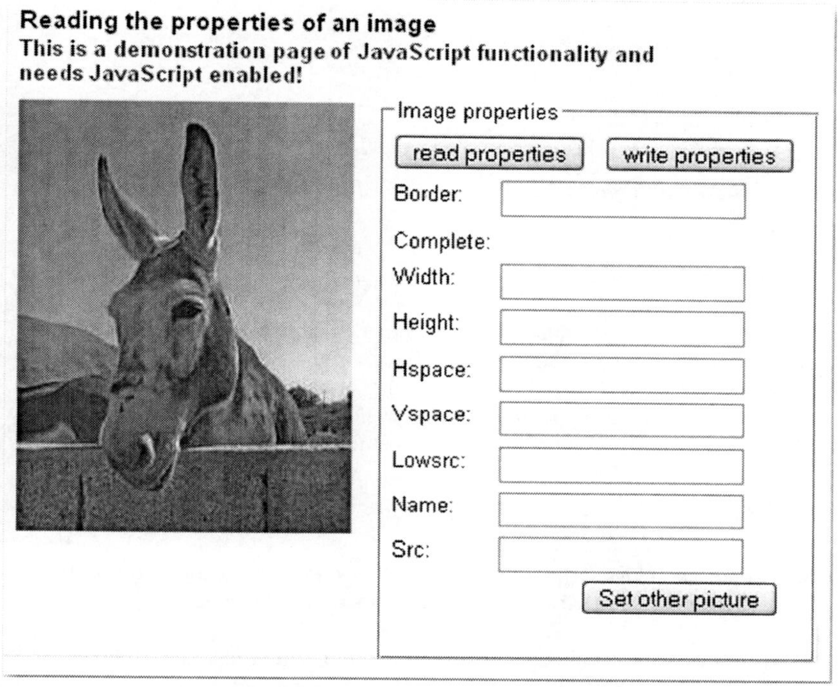

Figure 6-1. *Reading and writing the properties of an image*

■ **Note** If the dimensions of the image have been defined via the HTML `width` and `height` attributes, and you change its source, you don't automatically change its dimensions. For an example, activate the "Set other picture" button in the demo. This can result in an unsightly distortion of the other image, because browsers don't resize images in a sophisticated way.

Preloading Images

If you use images dynamically in the page for rollover or slide-show effects, you'll want to have the images already loaded into the browser's memory cache to give the visitor a smooth experience. You can do this in several ways. One way is to create a new image object for each image you want to preload when you initialize the page:

```
kitten = new Image();
kitten.src = 'pictures/kittenflat.jpg';
```

You'll see an example of this soon in the "Rollover Effects" section:

```
function simplePreload() {
  var args = simplePreload.arguments;
  document.imageArray = new Array( args.length );
  for(var i = 0; i < args.length; i++ ) {
    document.imageArray[i] = new Image;
    document.imageArray[i].src = args[i];
  }
}
```

If you call this function with the images you want to preload, it'll create a new array with all the images in it, loading them one after the other, for example:

```
simplePreload('pictures/cat2.jpg', 'pictures/dog10.jpg');
```

A different, scripting-independent, way of preloading images is putting them as 1×1-pixel images in the HTML inside a container element that you hide via CSS. This mixes structure and behavior and has the same issue as any image-preloading technique: you force the visitor to download a lot of images he might not want to see immediately. If you use preloaders, you might want to keep them optional and let the user decide if he wants to preload all the images.

I'll keep the discussion about image preloading brief here, because there is much more to learn about images.

Rollover Effects

Rollover or hover effects were the absolute craze when JavaScript first got supported widely in the most common user agents. Many scripts were written, and a lot of small tools came out that allowed "instant rollover generation without any need to code."

The idea of a rollover effect is pretty easy: you hover with your mouse over an image and the image changes, indicating that this is a clickable image and not just eye candy. Figure 6-2 shows a rollover effect.

Figure 6-2. *A rollover effect means the element changes its look when the mouse hovers over it*

Rollovers Using Several Images

You can create a rollover effect by changing the src property of the image when the mouse hovers over it. Old-school rollover effects were tied to the name attribute of the <img> tag and used the images collection. A construct like this was not uncommon in web pages in the 1990s:

exampleSimpleRollover.html (excerpts)
HTML

```
<a href="contact.html"
   onmouseover="rollover('contact', 'but_contact_on.gif')"
```

```
onmouseout="rollover('contact', 'but_contact.gif')">
  <img src="but_contact.gif" name="contact" width="103" height="28" alt="Contact Us" border="0">
</a>
```

JavaScript

```
function rollover( img, url ) {
  document.images[img].src=url;
}
```

The problem with rollovers was (and still is) that the second image might not be loaded yet, which is counterproductive. The fact that this is an interactive element is not immediately obvious—it becomes obvious only when the second image is shown. So this would confuse rather than aid the user in this case. This is why the classic rollover functions, like the one that came bundled with Adobe Dreamweaver, use the image object preloading technique explained earlier in conjunction with the name attribute.

Daniel Nolan came up with a very clever solution in 2003 as described at http://www.dnolan.com/code/js/rollover/. His solution uses the file name of the image and assumes a suffix of "_o" for the rollover state. All you need to add to the image you want to have a rollover effect for is a class called imgover.

You can replicate the same functionality easily using DOM-3 handlers. First you need an HTML document that has images with the correct class assigned to them:

exampleAutomatedRollover.html (excerpt)

```
<ul>
  <li>
    <a href="option1.html">
      <img src="but_1.gif" class="roll" alt="option one">Option 1
    </a>
  </li>
  <li>
    <a href="option2.html">
      <img src="but_2.gif" class="roll" alt="option two"> Option 2
    </a>
  </li>
  [... code snipped ...]
</ul>
```

Then you plan your script. The main object of the script will be called ro for *rollover*. Because you want to make things as easy as possible for future maintainers, you keep all the bits and bobs that might change in properties of the main object.

In this script, this is the class that defines which image should get a rollover state and the suffix of the mouseover image. In this case, you'll use "roll" and "_on", respectively. You will need two methods: one to initialize the effect, and one to do the rollover. Furthermore, you will need an array to store the preloaded images. All of this together makes up the skeleton of the rollover script:

automatedRollover.js (skeleton)

```
ro = {
  rollClass : 'roll',
  overSrcAddOn : '_on',
  preLoads : [],
```

```
  init : function(){},
  roll : function( e ){}
}
DOMhelp.addEvent( window, 'load', ro.init, false );
```

Let's start fleshing out the skeleton. First up are the properties and the `init` method. In it, you predefine a variable called `oversrc` and store all the images of the document in an array called `imgs`. You loop through the images and skip those that don't have the right CSS class attached to them:

automatedRollover.js (excerpt)

```
ro = {
  rollClass : 'roll',
  overSrcAddOn : '_on',
  preLoads : [],
  init : function() {
    var oversrc;
    var imgs = document.images;
    for( var i = 0; i < imgs.length; i++ ) {
      if( !DOMhelp.cssjs('check', imgs[i], ro.rollClass ) ) {
        continue;
      }
```

If the image has the right CSS class attached to it, you read its source attribute, replace the full stop in it by the suffix defined in the `overSrcAddOn` property followed by a full stop, and store the result in the `oversrc` variable:

automatedRollover.js (continued)

```
oversrc = imgs[i].src.toString().replace('. ',ro.overSrcAddOn + '. ');
```

■ **Note**   For example, the first image in the document has the `src` `but_1.gif`. The value of `oversrc` with the suffix property defined here would be `but_1_on.gif`.

You then create a new image object and store it as a new item of the `preLoads` array. Set the `src` attribute of the new image to `oversrc`. Use `addEvent()` from the DOMhelp library to add an event handler for both `mouseover` and `mouseout` that points to the `roll` method.

automatedRollover.js (continued)

```
    ro.preLoads[i] = new Image();
    ro.preLoads[i].src = oversrc;
    DOMhelp.addEvent( imgs[i], 'mouseover', ro.roll, false );
    DOMhelp.addEvent( imgs[i], 'mouseout', ro.roll, false );
  }
},
```

The `roll` method retrieves the image the event occurred on via `getTarget(e)` and stores its `src` property in a variable called `s`. You then test which of the events occurred by reading out the event type. If the event type was `mouseover`, you replace the full stop in the file name with the add-on followed by a full stop, and vice versa if the event was `mouseout`. You add an event handler to the window that calls `ro.init()` when the window has finished loading:

automatedRollover.js (continued)

```
roll : function( e ) {
  var t = DOMhelp.getTarget( e );
  var s = t.src;
  if( e.type == 'mouseover' ) {
    t.src = s.replace('.', ro.overSrcAddOn + '. ' );
  }
  if( e.type == 'mouseout' ) {
    t.src = s.replace( ro.overSrcAddOn + '. ', '. ' );
  }
 }
}
DOMhelp.addEvent( window, 'load', ro.init, false );
```

The outcome of the demo page, as shown in Figure 6-3, features rollovers with highlight images that are already loaded into the browser's cache when the user hovers over the original ones.

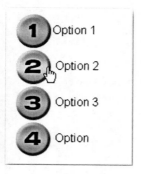

Figure 6-3. *The preloaded and automated rollovers*

As much as you can try to use clever scripting to preload images, it might not always work. The user's browser cache settings or special settings in her connection might make it impossible to sneakily preload something in the back without really adding the image to the document. Therefore, you might find that a safer option is to use a single image for the rollover effect.

Rollover Effects Using a Single Image

When CSS designers started exploring the `:hover` pseudo-selector to do a bit more than just change the underline of a link, CSS-only rollovers were born. These basically mean that you assign different background images to the link and the hover state of the link.

The same problems occurred—images had to get loaded before they were displayed, which made the rollover effect flicker or not happen at all. The solution was to take one single image for both states and use the background-position property to change the location of the image, as shown in Figure 6-4.

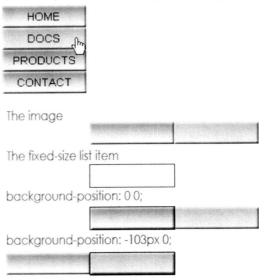

Figure 6-4. *Rollover effects with background position and CSS*

You can see the effect by opening exampleCSSonlyRollover.html in a browser. The CSS in question constrains the link to a certain size and achieves the rollover effect by shifting the background image in the hover state to the left via a negative background-position value that is half the width of the image:

exampleCSSonlyRollover.html (excerpt)

```
#nav a{
  width:103px;
  padding-top:6px;
  height:22px;
  background:url(doublebutton.gif) top left no-repeat #ccc;
}
#nav a:hover{
  background-position:-103px 0;
}
```

You can do the same in JavaScript; however, let's be more creative and do something CSS cannot do.

Rollover Effects on Parent Elements

Let's take an HTML list and turn it into a snazzy navigation bar by adding a nice background image, and then make the links change the background image when the mouse hovers over them. The first thing you need is a background image with all the states of the background, as shown in Figure 6-5.

Figure 6-5. *The navigation background with all states (resized)*

The HTML for the navigation bar is a list of links. Because basic web usability guidelines strongly suggest never linking the current page, the current link is replaced with a `<strong>` tag:

exampleParentRollover.html (excerpt)

```
<ul id="nav">
  <li><a href="index.html">Home</a></li>
  <li><a href="documentation.html">Documentation</a></li>
  <li><strong>Products</strong></li>
  <li><a href="contact.html">Contact Us</a></li>
</ul>
```

However, because this navigation could be the first level in a multilevel navigation menu, the highlight might not be a STRONG element but a class on the list item instead:

```
<ul id="nav">
  <li><a href="index.html">Home</a></li>
  <li><a href="documentation.html">Documentation</a></li>
  <li class="current"><a href="products.html">Products</a></li>
  <li><a href="contact.html">Contact Us</a></li>
</ul>
```

Both scenarios have to be taken into account. Explaining the CSS in the demo page is not the purpose of this book; it suffices to say that you fix the dimensions of the list with the ID nav, float it to the left, and float all list elements in it.

Instead, let's go straight into planning the script. You'll need to define several properties for the main object (which is called pr for *parent rollover*), the ID of the navigation list, the height of the navigation (which is also the height of each of the images and necessary for the background position), and the optional class that might have been used to highlight the current section instead of a `<strong>` tag:

parentRollover.js (excerpt)

```
pr = {
  navId : 'nav',
  navHeight : 50,
  currentLink : 'current',
```

You start with an initialization method that checks for DOM support and whether the necessary list with the right ID is available:

parentRollover.js (continued)

```
init : function() {
  if( !document.getElementById || !document.createTextNode ) {
    return;
  }
  pr.nav = document.getElementById( pr.navId );
  if( !pr.nav ){ return; }
```

The next task is to loop through all the list items contained in this list and check whether there is either a STRONG element inside the item or the item has the "current" class. If either is true, the script should store the counter for the loop in the current property of the main object. This property will be used in the rollover method to reset the background to the original state:

parentRollover.js (continued)

```
var lis = document.getElementsByTagName('li');

for(var i = 0; i < lis.length; i++)
{
  if( lis[i].getElementsByTagName('strong').length > 0 || DOMhelp.cssjs('check', lis[i],
pr.currentLink) ) {
    pr.current = i;
  }
```

Each of the list items gets a new property called index, which contains its counter value in the whole list array. Using this property is a trick that prevents you from having to loop through all the list items and compare them with the target in the event listener method.

You assign two event handlers pointing to the roll() method: one when the mouse is over the list item, and another when the mouse leaves the list item.

parentRollover.js (continued)

```
    lis[i].index = i;
    DOMhelp.addEvent( lis[i], 'mouseover', pr.roll, false );
    DOMhelp.addEvent( lis[i], 'mouseout', pr.roll, false );
  }
},
```

The rollover method starts by predefining a variable called pos that later becomes the offset value needed to show the correct image. It then calls getTarget() to determine which element was rolled over and compares the node name of the target with LI. This is a safety measure: although you assigned the event handler to the LI, browsers might actually send the link instead as the event target. One explanation for this may be that a link is an interactive page element, whereas an LI isn't, and the browser's rendering engine considers a link more important. You won't know, but you should be aware of the fact that some user agents will see the link instead of the list element as the event target.

parentRollover.js (continued)

```
roll : function( e ) {
  var pos;
  var t = DOMhelp.getTarget(e);
  while(t.nodeName.toLowerCase() != 'li' && t.nodeName.toLowerCase() != 'body') {
    t = t.parentNode;
  }
```

Then you define the position needed to show the right background image. This position is either the index value of the list item or the stored current property multiplied by the height of each image.

Which of the two gets applied depends on whether the user hovers his mouse over the list item or not—something you can find out by comparing the event type with mouseover. Set the style of the navigation's background position accordingly, and then call the init() method when the page has finished loading:

parentRollover.js (excerpt)

```
    pos = e.type == 'mouseover' ? t.index : pr.current;
    pos = pos * pr.navHeight;
    pr.nav.style.backgroundPosition = '0 -' + pos + 'px';
  }
}
DOMhelp.addEvent( window, 'load', pr.init, false );
```

When you open exampleParentRollover.html in a browser, you can see that rolling over the different links of the navigation shows the different background images, as demonstrated in Figure 6-6.

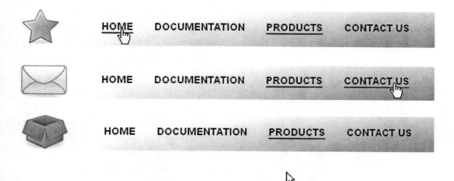

Figure 6-6. *The navigation in different rollover states*

This is a programmatic solution for the problem of rollovers affecting parent elements. However, it has one problem: if the order of the menu items changes, the maintainer of the code also has to change the image accordingly. This is not a very flexible solution, which is why you might be better off dynamically assigning classes to the navigation list to position the background image.

The necessary changes to the script affect the properties and the roll() method; the initialization stays the same. In addition to the currentLink and the navId property, you also need a class name to add to the navigation list. This new property can be called dynamicLink.

In the roll() method, you check once again whether the event triggering the method was mouseover and add or remove a new dynamic class accordingly. This dynamically assigned and named class consists of the dynamicLink property value and the current index plus one (because it is easier for humans to have a first class called item1 class instead of item0):

parentCSSrollover.js as used in parentCSSrollover.html (abbreviated)

```
pr = {
  navId : 'nav',
  currentLink : 'current',
  dynamicLink : 'item',
  init : function() {
   // [... same as in parentRollover.js ...]
  },
  Roll : function( e ) {
    // [... same as in parentRollover.js ...]
    var action = e.type == 'mouseover' ? 'add' : 'remove';
    DOMhelp.cssjs( action, pr.nav, pr.dynamicLink + ( t.index + 1 ) );
  }
}
DOMhelp.addEvent( window, 'load', pr.init, false );
```

This way, you allow the CSS designer to define the different states for the rollover navigation as classes in the CSS:

parentCSSrollover.css as used in parentCSSrollover.html (excerpt)

```
#nav.item1{
  background-position:0 0;
}
#nav.item2{
  background-position:0 -50px;
}
#nav.item3{
  background-position:0 -100px;
}
#nav.item4{
  background-position:0 -150px;
}
```

This also provides the CSS designer with one more hook to design the navigation: the dynamic class can be used to define the current rollover, or highlight state of the link itself, differently from item to item.

Slide Shows

Slide shows are small images embedded in the page with previous and next buttons, or sometimes they even automatically change images after a certain time. They are used to illustrate text or offer different views of a product.

We can distinguish between two kinds of slide shows: embedded ones that have all the images in the same document, and dynamic ones that load the images when they are needed.

Embedded Slide Shows

Probably the easiest way to add a slide show to a page is to add all the images as a list. You can then use JavaScript to turn this list into a slide show by hiding and showing the different list items with the embedded images. The demo document examplePhotoListInlineSlideShow.html does exactly that, as Figure 6-7 shows.

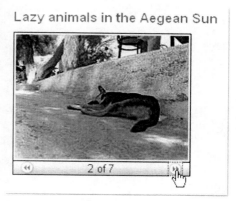

Figure 6-7. An embedded slide show with JavaScript

The underlying HTML is an unordered list with all the images as list items. Notice that this also allows you to set proper alternative text for each of the images:

examplePhotoListInlineSlideShow.html (excerpt)

```
<ul class="slides">
  <li>
     <img src="pictures/thumbs/cat2.jpg" alt="Lazy Cat">
  </li>
  <li>
    <img src="pictures/thumbs/dog10.jpg" alt="Dog using the shade">
  </li>
  <li>
    <img src="pictures/thumbs/dog12.jpg" alt="Squinting Dog">
  </li>
  <li>
    <img src="pictures/thumbs/dog63.jpg" alt="Dog cooling off in the sand">
  </li>
  <li>
    <img src="pictures/thumbs/dog7.jpg"  alt="Very flat dog">
  </li>
  <li>
    <img src="pictures/thumbs/donkeyeating.jpg" alt="Hay-eating Donkey">
  </li>
  <li>
    <img src="pictures/thumbs/kittenflat.jpg" alt="Ginger and White Cat">
  </li>
</ul>
```

All future maintainers have to do to change the order of the images or add or delete images is change the HTML. There is no need to change the JavaScript at all. As long as you supply an appropriate style sheet, visitors without JavaScript will get all the images displayed as shown in Figure 6-8. Users without style sheets will get a list with image thumbnails.

Figure 6-8. *The embedded slide show without JavaScript*

One effect of embedding all images in the document is that they will all be loaded when the visitor loads the page. This could be a good or a bad thing, depending on the visitor's connection speed. Later on, I'll show you an example that loads the larger images only when the user clicks smaller ones.

Let's look at the script that turns this list into a slide show. You will use the DOMhelp library you developed in previous chapters to work around browser issues and shorten the code slightly.

As always, the first thing to do is plan your script. In this case, you should give the CSS designer and HTML developer several classes as hooks to trigger functionality or define the look and feel:

- A class to indicate that the list should be turned into a slide show
- A class to define the look and feel of the dynamic slide show list
- A class to show elements that were previously hidden
- A class to define the look of the image counter (for example, image 1 of 3)
- A class to hide elements that should not be there at a certain state of play

You should also allow the maintainer to change the look and content of the forward and backward links and the text content of the image counter.

As for methods, all you need (apart from the helper methods contained in DOMhelp) is a global initialization method, a method to initialize each slide show, and a method to show a slide. All of this together makes up the skeleton of your script:

photoListInlineSlides.js (skeleton)

```
inlineSlides = {

  // CSS classes
  slideClass : 'slides',
  dynamicSlideClass : 'dynslides',
  showClass : 'show',
  slideCounterClass : 'slidecounter',
  hideLinkClass : 'hide',

  // Labels
  // Forward and backward links, you can use any HTML here
  forwardsLabel : '<img src="control_fastforward_blue.png" lt="next" >',
  backwardsLabel : '<img src="control_rewind_blue.png"alt="previous" >',
  // Counter text, # will be replaced by the current image count
  // and % by the number of all pictures
  counterLabel : '# of %',

  init : function() {},
  initSlideShow : function( o ) {},
  showSlide : function( e ) {}
}
DOMhelp.addEvent( window, 'load', inlineSlides.init, false );
```

■ **Note**   In the preceding code, you offer an HTML-based option in the labels for the forward and backward links. This allows for much more flexible styling of the slide show, because the maintainer can add her own HTML (like images). Furthermore, if you want to allow the maintainer to change dynamic text like the counter, it might be beneficial to use placeholders like # and % and explain what they will be replaced with.

Let's go through the methods in the script step by step. First up is the global initialization method init():

1.   Test for DOM support.

2.   If the test is successful, loop through all the UL elements of the document.

3.   For each UL, check whether it has the class defining it as a slide show (which is stored in the slideClass property), and skip the rest of the steps performed by this function if it doesn't have the class. (Use continue to do this.)

4.   If the current UL is to become a slide show, you replace the class defining it as a slide show with the class defining the dynamic slide show; add a new property called currentSlide to the list and call the method initSlideShow with the list as a parameter.

photoListInlineSlides.js (excerpt)

```
init : function() {
  if( !document.getElementById  || !document.createTextNode ) {
    return;
  }
  var uls = document.getElementsByTagName('ul');
  for( var i = 0; i < uls.length; i++ ) {
    if( !DOMhelp.cssjs('check', uls[i], nlineSlides.slideClass ) ) {
     continue;
    }
    DOMhelp.cssjs('swap', uls[i],inlineSlides.slideClass, nlineSlides.dynamicSlideClass );
    uls[i].currentSlide = 0;
    inlineSlides.initSlideShow( uls[i] );
  }
},
```

You can spare yourself a lot of looping and checking with these tricks. First of all, replacing the class only when JavaScript is available with another class allows you to hide all the list items in the CSS instead of looping through them in the initSlideShow() method:

photoListInlineSlides.css (excerpt)

```
.dynslides li{
  display:none;
  margin:0;
  padding:5px;
}
```

Other dynamically assigned CSS classes you have to define to make the slide show work are a hide class (to remove the backward link when the first image is shown or the forward link when the last image is shown) and a show class (to overrule the hiding you achieved with the .dynslides li selector). All the other CSS selectors and properties inside the demo are of a purely cosmetic nature.

photoListInlineSlides.css (excerpt)

```
.dynslides .hide{
  visibility:hidden;
}
.dynslides li.show{
  display:block;
}
```

By storing the current visible image in a property of the list, you don't need to loop through all the images and hide them before you show the current one. Instead, all you need to do is determine which one will have to be shown, read the property of the parent list element, and hide the previous image stored in this property.

You then reset the property to the new image, and the next time an image gets shown, the cycle starts anew. You could have stored the current image in a property of the main inlineSlides object, but storing it in a property of the list means you allow for several slide shows on the same page.

The `initSlideShow()` method gets each slide show list as a parameter called `lst`. First, define the variables you'll use with the `var` keyword to make sure they don't overwrite global variables with the same name. Then create a new paragraph element to host the forward and backward links and the image counter, and insert it immediately after the list (using `lst.nextSibling`):

photoListInlineSlides.js (continued)

```
initSlideShow : function(lst ) {
  var p, temp, count;
  p = document.createElement('p');
  DOMhelp.cssjs('add', p, inlineSlides.slideCounterClass );
  lst.parentNode.insertBefore( p, lst.nextSibling );
```

Next, create the backward link by means of DOMhelp's `createLink` method, and add the proper label using `innerHTML`. Add an event handler to call the `showSlide` method, hide the link by applying the appropriate CSS class, and add the link to the newly created paragraph. You'll store the link in a property of the list called `rew` to make it easier to reach it later on:

photoListInlineSlides.js (continued)

```
lst.rew = DOMhelp.createLink('#', ' ' );
lst.rew.innerHTML = inlineSlides.backwardsLabel;
DOMhelp.addEvent(lst.rew, 'click', inlineSlides.showSlide, false );
DOMhelp.cssjs('add', lst.rew,inlineSlides.hideLinkClass );
p.appendChild(lst.rew );
```

A new SPAN element that acts as the image counter is next. Get the `counterLabel` property of the main object, and replace the # character with the current list's `currentSlide` property value and add 1 to it (because humans start counting at 1 and not at 0 like computers do). Replace the % character with the number of LI elements in the list, and add the resulting string as a new text node to the SPAN before adding it as a new child node to the paragraph:

photoListInlineSlides.js (continued)

```
lst.count = document.createElement('span');
temp = inlineSlides.counterLabel.replace( /#/, lst.currentSlide + 1 );
temp = temp.replace( /%/, lst.getElementsByTagName('li').length );
lst.count.appendChild( document.createTextNode( temp ) );
p.appendChild(lst.count );
```

Note You store the counter SPAN in a property of the list, called `count`. This is pure laziness, because it saves you having to reach it via `getElementsByTagName('span')[0]` later on. It also makes the script less likely to be broken by maintainers who might add other spans inside the list items at a later stage.

Adding the forward link works analogously to adding the backward link, except that the `forwardsLabel` property is used as the content and a new property called `fwd` is used as the shortcut.

photoListInlineSlides.js (continued)

```
lst.fwd = DOMhelp.createLink('#', ' ' );
lst.fwd.innerHTML = inlineSlides.forwardsLabel;
DOMhelp.addEvent(lst.fwd, 'click', inlineSlides.showSlide, false );
p.appendChild(lst.fwd );
```

The method concludes with taking the list item that corresponds to the currentSlide property and adding the show class to it. You could have just used o.firstChild instead, but a future maintainer might want to initially show a different photo than the first one:

photoListInlineSlides.js (continued)

```
  temp = lst.getElementsByTagName('li')[lst.currentSlide];
  DOMhelp.cssjs('add', temp, inlineSlides.showClass );
},
```

The showSlide() method defines a variable called action and gets the event target via getTarget(e). Because you don't know if the maintainer used an image in the link labels, you need to find the link by testing whether the nodeName of the target's parentNode is A. This also counteracts the bug in older versions of Safari that sends the text contained in a link as the target instead of the link itself. The method then grabs the list the event was triggered in by reading the closestSibling() of the target's parentNode.

photoListInlineSlides.js (continued)

```
showSlide : function( e ) {
  var action;
  var t = DOMhelp.getTarget( e );
  while( t.nodeName.toLowerCase() != 'a' && t.nodeName.toLowerCase() != 'body' ) {
    t=t.parentNode;
  }
  var parentList = DOMhelp.closestSibling( t.parentNode, -1 );
```

■ **Note**   The visitor clicks the content of the link to go one image forward or backward. The event target could be an image (as it is in this example) or text—or anything else the maintainer of this script put in the forwardsLabel and backwardsLabel properties. Therefore—and because Safari sends the text contained in a link as the target rather than the link itself—you need to check for the name of the node and compare it with A. Then you take the parent node of this A—which is the paragraph that was newly created—and get its previous sibling, which is the UL that contains the images.

Next, you need to find the currentSlide property from the list in question and the total number of images by checking the length property of the list item array. Hide the previously shown image by removing the show class:

photoListInlineSlides.js (continued)

```
var count = parentList.currentSlide;
var photoCount = parentList.getElementsByTagName('li').length - 1;
var photo = parentList.getElementsByTagName('li')[count];
DOMhelp.cssjs('remove', photo, inlineSlides.showClass );
```

Determine whether the link that was activated was the forward link by comparing the target with the fwd property of the list, and then increment or decrement the counter accordingly.

If the counter is larger than 0, remove the hide class from the backward link; otherwise, add this class, effectively hiding or showing the link. The same logic applies for the forward link, although the comparison criteria this time is the counter being less than the total number of list items. This prevents the backward link from showing on the first slide and the forward link from showing on the last slide.

photoListInlineSlides.js (continued)

```
count = ( t == parentList.fwd ) ? count+1 : count-1;
action = ( count > 0 ) ? 'remove' : 'add' ;
DOMhelp.cssjs( action, parentList.rew,inlineSlides.hideLinkClass );
action = ( count < photoCount ) ? 'remove' : 'add';
DOMhelp.cssjs( action, parentList.fwd, nlineSlides.hideLinkClass);
```

That took care of the links; now you need to increment the counter display. Because the counter is stored as a property of the list, it is easy to read the first child node of that property—that is, the text inside the SPAN. You can then use the replace() method of the String object to replace the first numerical entry (here via a regular expression) with the new image number, which is count+1—again, because humans do count from 1 and not from 0. Next, reset the currentSlide property, grab the new photo (remember you changed count), and show the current photo by adding the show class. All that is left to do is start the init() method when the window has loaded:

photoListInlineSlides.js (excerpt)

```
    photo = parentList.getElementsByTagName('li')[count];
    var counterText = parentList.count.firstChild
    counterText.nodeValue = counterText.nodeValue.replace( /\d/, count + 1 );
    parentList.currentSlide = count;
    photo = parentList.getElementsByTagName('li')[count];
    DOMhelp.cssjs('add', photo, inlineSlides.showClass );
    DOMhelp.cancelClick( e );
  }
}
DOMhelp.addEvent( window, 'load', inlineSlides.init, false );
```

However, you are not quite finished yet. If you try out the slide show in older versions of Safari, you will realize that the forward and backward links do get hidden, but they are still clickable and cause errors when you try to reach images that are not there.

■ **Caution** This is a common mistake in dynamic web development—hiding things visibly does not necessarily make them disappear for all users. Think of people who are blind or users of textual browsers (such as Lynx). And then there are browser bugs and oddities to consider, too.

Preventing this issue is rather easy though: all you need to amend is the showSlide() method so that nothing is done when the target that was clicked has the hide CSS class assigned to it. And when fixing that, you might as well add the Safari fix to cancel the default action of the newly generated links. The demo examplePhotoListInlineSlideShowSafariFix.html incorporates these changes:

photoListInlineSlidesSafariFix.js

```
inlineSlides = {

  // CSS classes
  slideClass : 'slides',
  dynamicSlideClass : 'dynslides',
  showClass : 'show',
  slideCounterClass : 'slidecounter',
  hideLinkClass : 'hide',
  // Labels
  // Forward and backward links, you can use any HTML here
  forwardsLabel : '<img src="control_fastforward_blue.png" alt="next"> ',
  backwardsLabel : '<img src="control_rewind_blue.png" alt="previous">',
  // Counter text, # will be replaced by the current image count
  // and % by the number of all pictures
  counterLabel : '# of %',

  init : function() {
    if( !document.getElementById || !document.createTextNode ) {
      return;
    }
    var uls = document.getElementsByTagName('ul');
    for( var i = 0; i < uls.length; i++ ) {
      if( !DOMhelp.cssjs('check', uls[i],inlineSlides.slideClass ) ) {
        continue;
      }
      DOMhelp.cssjs('swap', uls[i], inlineSlides.slideClass, inlineSlides.dynamicSlideClass );
      uls[i].currentSlide = 0;
      inlineSlides.initSlideShow( uls[i] );
    }
  },
  initSlideShow : function(lst ) {
    var p, temp, count;
    p = document.createElement('p');
    DOMhelp.cssjs('add', p, inlineSlides.slideCounterClass );
    lst.parentNode.insertBefore( p, lst.nextSibling );
    lst.rew = DOMhelp.createLink('#', ' ' );
    lst.rew.innerHTML = inlineSlides.backwardsLabel;
    DOMhelp.addEvent(lst.rew, 'click', inlineSlides.showSlide, false );
    DOMhelp.cssjs('add', lst.rew, inlineSlides.hideLinkClass );
    p.appendChild(lst.rew );
    lst.count = document.createElement('span');
    temp = inlineSlides.counterLabel._
```

```
      replace( /#/, lst.currentSlide + 1 );
      temp = temp.replace( /%/, o.getElementsByTagName('li').length );
      lst.count.appendChild( document.createTextNode( temp ) );
      p.appendChild(lst.count );
      lst.fwd=DOMhelp.createLink('#', ' ' );
      lst.fwd.innerHTML = inlineSlides.forwardsLabel;
      DOMhelp.addEvent(lst.fwd, 'click', inlineSlides.showSlide, false );
      p.appendChild(lst.fwd );
      temp = lst.getElementsByTagName('li')[ lst.currentSlide];
      DOMhelp.cssjs('add', temp,inlineSlides.showClass );
      lst.fwd.onclick = DOMhelp.safariClickFix;
      lst.rew.onclick = DOMhelp.safariClickFix;
  },
  showSlide : function( e ) {
    var action;
    var t = DOMhelp.getTarget( e );
    while( t.nodeName.toLowerCase() != 'a && t.nodeName.toLowerCase() != 'body' ) {
      t = t.parentNode;
    }
    if( DOMhelp.cssjs('check', t,_inlineSlides.hideLinkClass ) ){
     return;
    }
    var parentList = DOMhelp.closestSibling( t.parentNode, -1 );
    var count = parentList.currentSlide;
    var photoCount = parentList.getElementsByTagName('li').length-1;
    var photo = parentList.getElementsByTagName('li' )[count];
    DOMhelp.cssjs('remove', photo, inlineSlides.showClass );
    count = ( t == parentList.fwd ) ? count + 1 : count - 1;
    action = ( count > 0 ) ? 'remove' : 'add' ;
    DOMhelp.cssjs( action, parentList.rew, inlineSlides.hideLinkClass );
    action = ( count < photoCount ) ? 'remove' : 'add';
    DOMhelp.cssjs( action, parentList.fwd,inlineSlides.hideLinkClass );
    photo = parentList.getElementsByTagName('li')[count];
    var counterText = parentList.count.firstChild
    counterText.nodeValue = counterText.nodeValue.replace( /\d/, count + 1 );
    parentList.currentSlide = count;
    DOMhelp.cssjs('add', photo, inlineSlides.showClass );
    DOMhelp.cancelClick( e );
  }
}
DOMhelp.addEvent( window, 'load', inlineSlides.init, false );
```

Turning embedded image lists into slide shows is an effect that degrades nicely on non- JavaScript user agents, although it is not really image manipulation or even dynamic. The real power of JavaScript is to avoid page reloads and show larger images in the same document instead of just showing them in the browser. Let's take a look at some examples.

Dynamic Slide Shows

Let's take another HTML list and turn it into an example of a dynamic slide show. Start with the HTML—this time a list containing thumbnail images linked to larger images:

exampleMiniSlides.html

```
<ul class="minislides">
<li>
  <a href="pictures/thumbs/cat2.jpg">
     <img src="pictures/minithumbs/cat2.jpg" alt="Lazy Cat">
  </a>
</li>
<li>
  <a href="pictures/thumbs/dog63.jpg">
     <img src="pictures/minithumbs/dog63.jpg" alt="Dog cooling off in the sand"></a>
  </li>
  <li>
   <a href="pictures/thumbs/dog7.jpg">
     <img src="pictures/minithumbs/dog7.jpg"  alt="Very flat dog">
   </a>
  </li>
  <li>
   <a href="pictures/thumbs/kittenflat.jpg">
     <img src="pictures/minithumbs/kittenflat.jpg" alt="Ginger and White Cat">
   </a>
  </li>
</ul>
```

If you open the example in a browser with JavaScript enabled, you get a list of small thumbnails and a larger image. Clicking the thumbnails will replace the larger image with the one the thumbnail points to, as shown in Figure 6-9.

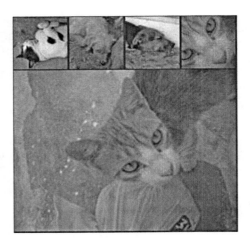

Figure 6-9. *A slide show with small preview images (thumbnails)*

5

Visitors without JavaScript will get only a row of images linking to larger images, as shown in Figure 6-10.

Figure 6-10. *The slide show with small preview images without JavaScript*

Again, let's plan the skeleton of the script: you define a class to recognize which lists are to become slide shows, a class to give to the list item that contains the large photo, and alternative text to add to the large photo.

The methods are the same as the last time: one global initialization method, one method to initialize each slide show, and one method to show the current photo.

miniSlides.js (skeleton)

```
minislides = {
  // CSS classes
  triggerClass : 'minislides',
  largeImgClass : 'photo',
  // Text added to the title attribute of the big picture
  alternativeText : 'large view',

  init : function(){  },
  initShow : function( o ){ },
  showPic : function( e ){  }
}
DOMhelp.addEvent( window, 'load', minislides.init, false );
```

The CSS for the slide show is pretty simple:

miniSlides.css (excerpt)

```
.minislides, .minislides * {
  margin:0;
  padding:0;
  list-style:none;
  border:none;
}
.minislides{
  clear:both;
  margin:10px 0;
  background:#333;
}
.minislides,.minislides li{
  float:left;
}
.minislides li img{
  display:block;
}
```

```
.minislides li{
  padding:1px;
}
.minislides li.photo{
  clear:both;
  padding-top:0;
}
```

First, you do a global reset on anything inside the list with the right class and the list itself. A global reset means setting all margins and paddings to 0 and the borders and list styles to none. This prevents having to deal with cross-browser differences and also makes the CSS document a lot shorter, because you don't need to reset these values for every element.

Then float the lists and all the list items to the left to make them appear inline rather than one under the other. You need to float the main list to make sure it contains the others.

Set the images to display as block elements to avoid gaps around them and add padding on each list item of one pixel to show the background color.

The "photo" list item needs a float clearing to appear below the others. Set its top padding to 0 to avoid a double line between the smaller images and the big image.

The init() method functions analogously to the one in the last slide show. You test for DOM support, loop through all the lists in the document, and skip those that don't have the right class. The ones that have the right class get sent to the initShow() method as a parameter:

miniSlides.js (excerpt)

```
init : function() {
  if( !document.getElementById || !document.createTextNode ) {
    return;
  }
  var lists = document.getElementsByTagName('ul');
  for( var i = 0; i < lists.length; i++ ) {
    if( !DOMhelp.cssjs('check', lists[i],minislides.triggerClass ) ) {
     continue;
    }
    minislides.initShow( lists[i] );
  }
},
```

The initShow() method starts by creating a new list item, creating a new image, and assigning the large image class to the new list item. It adds the image as a child of the list item and the new list item as a child of the main list. Together with the CSS defined earlier, this displays the new image below the others:

miniSlides.js (excerpt)

```
initShow : function( o ) {
  var newli = document.createElement('li');
  var newimg = document.createElement('img');
  newli.appendChild( newimg );
  DOMhelp.cssjs('add', newli, minislides.largeImgClass );
  o.appendChild( newli );
```

Then you grab the first image in the list and read its alternative text stored in the `alt` attribute. Add this text as the alternative text to the new image, add the text stored in the `alternativeText` property to it, and store the resulting string as a `title` attribute of the new image:

miniSlides.js (excerpt)

```
var firstPic = o.getElementsByTagName('img')[0];
var alt = firstPic.getAttribute('alt');
newimg.setAttribute('alt', alt );
newimg.setAttribute('title', alt + minislides.alternativeText );
```

Next, retrieve all the links in the list and apply an event pointing to `showPic` when the user clicks each link. Store the new image as a property called `photo` in the list object and set the `src` attribute of the newly created image to the target location of the first link:

miniSlides.js (excerpt)

```
  var links = o.getElementsByTagName('a');
  for(i = 0; i < links.length; i++){
   DOMhelp.addEvent( links[i], 'click', minislides.showPic,false );

  }
  o.photo = newimg;
  newimg.setAttribute('src', o.getElementsByTagName('a')[0].href );
},
```

Showing the pictures the links point to when they were clicked is a piece of cake. In the `showPic()` method, retrieve the event target via `getTarget()` and get the old picture by reading out the list's `photo` property.

This time, you know the element the visitor will click is an image, which is why you don't need to loop and test the name of the element. Instead, you go up three parent nodes (A, LI, and UL) and read the previously stored image. Then you set the alternative text, the title, and the image `src` and stop the link's default behavior via `cancelClick()`. Add a handler that fires the `init()` method when the window has finished loading to complete your mini slide show.

miniSlides.js (excerpt)

```
  showPic : function( e ) {
    var t = DOMhelp.getTarget( e );
    var oldimg = t.parentNode.parentNode.parentNode.photo;
    oldimg.setAttribute('alt', t.getAttribute('alt') );
    oldimg.setAttribute('title', t.getAttribute('alt') +minislides.alternativeText );
    oldimg.setAttribute('src', t.parentNode.getAttribute('href') );
    DOMhelp.cancelClick( e );
  }
}
DOMhelp.addEvent( window, 'load', minislides.init, false );
```

Summary of Images and JavaScript

This concludes this introduction to images and JavaScript. I hope you are not too overwhelmed by what is possible and what is needed to script in this fashion. I also hope I've sparked your interest in playing with the examples to see what else is possible. Keep these slide shows and how they work in mind, though—at the end of this chapter we will come back to the document-embedded slide show and make it play automatically. In Chapter 10, you will see how to develop a larger JavaScript-enabled gallery.

For now, here are some things to remember about images and JavaScript:

- You can do a lot of preloading with the image objects, but it is not a bulletproof approach. Browser cache settings, broken image links, and proxy servers might mess with your preload script. There are libraries that can help with the preload process. PreloadJS, for example, can help you preload images, sound, and other JavaScript files. If these scripts fail, the user might get stuck or face a constantly changing progress bar, which is frustrating.

- Although you can access the properties of each image directly, it might not be the best approach. Leave the visuals to the CSS, and your scripts will not be changed by others who might not know what is going on.

- CSS has come a long way since the days of DHTML, and these days it might be a better approach to help the CSS designer by providing hooks rather than achieving a visual effect purely by scripting—an example being the parent rollover you saw earlier.

Windows and JavaScript

Spawning new browser windows and altering the current window are common uses for JavaScript. These are also annoying and unsafe practices, because you can never be sure if the visitor of your web page can deal with resized windows or will be notified by her user agent when there is a new window. Think of screen-reader users listening to your site or text-browser users.

Windows have been used for unsolicited advertising (pop-up windows) and executing code in hidden windows for data-retrieval purposes (phishing) in the past, which is why browser vendors and third-party software providers have come up with a lot of software and browser settings to stop this kind of abuse. Mozilla Firefox users, for example, can choose whether they want pop-up windows and what properties of the window can be changed by JavaScript, as shown in Figure 6-11.

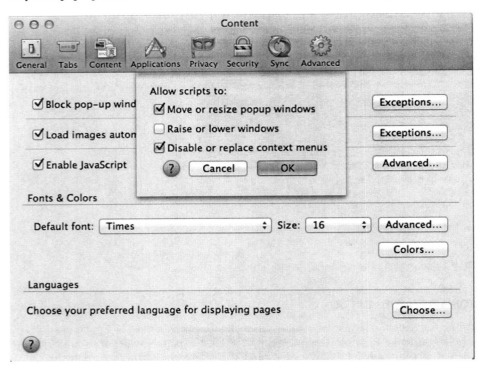

Figure 6-11. *The advanced JavaScript settings in Mozilla Firefox*

Other browsers like Microsoft Internet Explorer 7 or Opera 8 disallow hiding the location bar in new windows and can impose size and position constraints on new windows.

■ **Note** This is a point of agreement between different browser manufacturers that want to stop security vulnerabilities. Opening a new window without a visible location bar can allow a malicious attacker to open a pop-up on a third-party site via *Cross-Site Scripting* (XSS), make it appear as if the window belonged to the site, and ask users to enter information. More about XSS can be found on Wikipedia: `http://en.wikipedia.org/wiki/Cross-site_scripting`.

This is all great news for web surfers, because they can stop unwanted advertising and are less likely to be fooled into giving away their data to the wrong people. It is not such great news for you, because it means that when you want to use windows extensively in JavaScript, you have to test a lot of different scenarios.

Such considerations aside, you can still do a lot with windows and JavaScript. Every JavaScript-capable browser provides you with an object called `window`, whose properties are listed in the next section, as well as some examples on how to use them.

Window Properties

Following is a list of properties for the `window` object:

■ **Note** This partial list does not show all the `window` properties available. If a given property is not supported by a certain browser, I will note that where the property is discussed.

- `closed`: Boolean that indicates whether or not the window was closed (read-only)

- `defaultStatus`: The default status message in the status bar (not supported by Safari)

- `innerHeight`: The height of the document part of the window

- `innerWidth`: The width of the document part of the window

- `outerHeight`: The height of the whole window

- `outerWidth`: The width of the whole window

- `pageXOffset`: Current horizontal start position of the document inside the window (read-only)

- `pageYOffset`: Current vertical start position of the document inside the window (read-only)

- `status`: The text content of the status bar

- `name`: The name of the window

- `toolbar`: Property that returns an object with a visible property of `true` when the window has a toolbar (read-only)

For example, if you want to obtain the inner size of a window, you could use some of these properties:

exampleWindowProperties.html (excerpt)

```
function winProps() {
  var winWidth = window.outerWidth;
  var winHeight = window.outerHeight;
  var docWidth = window.innerWidth;
  var docHeight = window.innerHeight;
  var message = 'This window is ';
  message += winWidth + ' pixels wide and ';
  message += winHeight + ' pixels high.\n';
  message += 'The inner dimensions are: ';
  message += docWidth + ' * ' + docHeight + ' pixels';
  alert( message );
}
```

Some possible output from this function is shown in Figure 6-12.

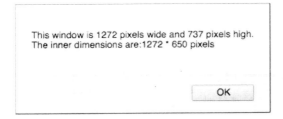

Figure 6-12. *Reading out window properties*

There are other properties that are not supported by Internet Explorer. These are scrollbars, locationbar, statusbar, menubar, and personalbar. Each of them stores an object with a read-only visible property having a value of true or false. To test whether the user has a menu bar open, you check the object and the property:

```
if ( window.menubar && window.menubar.visible == true )
{
 // Code
}
```

Window Methods

The window object also has a number of methods, some of which have been discussed in earlier chapters. The most common ones apart from those that provide user feedback are for opening new windows and timed execution of functions.

User Feedback Methods

The user feedback methods listed here are covered in detail in Chapter 4:

- `alert('message')`: Displays an alert
- `confirm('message')`: Displays a dialog to confirm an action
- `prompt('message', 'preset')`: Displays a dialog to enter a value

Opening New Windows

The opening and closing of windows is technically quite easy. However, with browsers suppressing different properties and methods or badly written pop-up-blocking software even blocking "good" pop-ups, opening and closing windows can become a nightmare and needs proper testing. The specifics of opening new windows are pretty easy. You have four methods at your disposal:

- `open('url', 'name', 'properties')`: Opens a new window called "name", loads the URL in it, and sets the window properties
- `close()`: Closes the window (and if the window is not a pop-up window, this will cause a security alert.)
- `blur()`: Moves the focus of the browser away from the window
- `focus()`: Moves the focus of the browser to the window

The `properties` string of the open method has a very unique syntax: it lists all the properties of the window as strings—each consisting of a name and a value joined with an equal sign—which are separated by commas:

```
myWindow = window.open('demo.html', 'my', 'p1=v1,p2=v2,p3=v3' );
```

Not all of the properties listed here are supported in all browsers. Mobile browsers, for example, might not have every feature a desktop browser will have. But this list will give you an idea of what is available:

- `height`: Defines the height of the window in pixels.
- `width`: Defines the width of the window in pixels.
- `left`: Defines the horizontal position of the window on the screen in pixels.
- `top`: Defines the vertical position of the window on the screen in pixels.
- `location`: Defines whether the window has a location bar or not (yes or no). Due to security concerns. this is always yes and is not editable.
- `menubar`: Defines whether the window has a menu bar or not (yes or no). This does not apply to browsers on MacOS, because the menu is always at the top of the screen.
- `resizable`: Defines whether the user is allowed to resize the window if it is too small or too big. Browsers have overridden this setting. Users have to change their settings to get this to work.
- `scrollbars`: Defines whether the window has scrollbars or not (yes or no). Opera does not allow scrollbars to be suppressed.
- `status`: Defines whether the window has a status bar or not (yes or no). Opera does not allow the status bar to be turned off.
- `toolbar`: Defines whether the window has a toolbar or not (yes or no). Turning the toolbar off is not supported by Opera.

To open a window that is 200 pixels wide and high and 100 pixels from the top-left corner of the screen, and then load into it the document grid.html, you have to set the appropriate properties as shown here:

```
var windowprops = "width=200,height=200,top=100,left=100";
```

You can try to open the window when the page loads:

exampleWindowPopUp.html (excerpt)

```
function popup() {
  var windowprops = "width=200,height=200,top=100,left=100";
  var myWin =  window.open("grid.html", "mynewwin" ,windowprops );
}
window.onload = popup;
```

Notice that the outcome is slightly different from browser to browser. Internet Explorer 9 shows the window without any toolbars; Firefox, Opera, and Chrome warn you that the page is trying to open a new window and ask you whether you want to allow it to do so. Safari does not do anything.

This is handled slightly differently when the window is opened via a link:

exampleLinkWindowPopUp.html

```
<a href="#" onclick="popup();return false">
  Open grid
</a>
```

Opera, Firefox, Chrome, and Safari do not complain about the pop-up window now. However, if JavaScript is disabled, there won't be a new window and the link doesn't do anything. Therefore, you might want to link to the document in the href and send the URL as a parameter instead:

exampleParameterLinkWindowPopUp.html (excerpts)

```
function popup( url ) {
  var windowprops = "width=200,height=200,top=100,left=100";
  var myWin =  window.open( url, "mynewwin", windowprops );
}

<a href="grid.html" onclick="popup(this.href);return false">Open grid</a>
```

Notice the name parameter of window.open() method. This one is seemingly pretty pointless for JavaScript, because it does not do anything. (There is no windows collection you can use to reach the window via windows.mynewwin, for example.) However, it is used in the HTML target attribute to make links open their linked documents in the pop-up window instead of the main window.

In this example, you define the name of the window as mynewwin, and you target a link to open http://www.yahoo.co.uk/ in there:

exampleParameterLinkWindowPopUp.html (excerpts)

```
function popup( url ) {
  var windowprops = "width=200,height=200,top=100,left=100";
  var myWin = window.open( url, "mynewwin", windowprops );
}
<a href="http://www.yahoo.co.uk/" target="mynewwin">Open Yahoo</a>
```

Unless you use nontransitional XHTML or strict HTML (where `target` is deprecated), you can also use the `target` attribute with a value of `_blank` to open a new window regardless of the availability of JavaScript. It is good practice, then, to tell the visitor that the link is going to open in a new window inside the link to avoid confusion or accessibility issues:

```
<a href="grid.html" onclick="popup(this.href);return false" target="blank">
Open grid  (opens in a new window)
</a>
```

However, because you might want to use HTML to have a lot more control over the pop-up using JavaScript, it might be a better solution to not rely on `target` and, instead, turn links into pop-up links only if scripting is available. For that, you need something to hook into and identify the link as a pop-up link. For example, you can use a class called popup:

exampleAutomaticPopupLinks.html (excerpt)

```
<p><a href="grid.html" class="popup">Open grid</a></p>
<p><a href="http://www.yahoo.co.uk/" class="popup">Open Yahoo</a></p>
```

Planning the script doesn't entail much. You need the class to trigger the pop-up, the textual add-on, and the window parameters as properties, you need an `init()` method to identify the links and add the changes, and you need an `openPopup()` method to trigger the pop-ups:

automaticPopupLinks.js (skeleton)

```
poplinks = {
  triggerClass : 'popup',
  popupLabel : ' (opens in a new window)',
  windowProps : 'width=200,height=200,top=100,left=100',
  init : function(){ },
  openPopup : function( e ){ },
}
```

The two methods are pretty basic. The `init()` method checks for DOM support and loops through all the links in the document. If the current link has the CSS trigger class, it adds the label to the link by creating a new text node from the label and adding it as a new child to the link. It adds an event when the link is clicked pointing to the `openPopup()` method, and it applies the fix for old versions of Safari to stop the link from being followed in that browser:

automaticPopupLinks.js (excerpt)

```
init : function() {
  if( !document.getElementById || !document.createTextNode ) {
   return;
  }
  var label;
  var allLinks = document.getElementsByTagName('a');
  for( var i = 0; i < allLinks.length; i++ ) {
    if( !DOMhelp.cssjs('check', allLinks[i],poplinks.triggerClass ) ) {
      continue;
    }
```

```
      label = document.createTextNode( poplinks.popupLabel );
      allLinks[i].appendChild( label );
      DOMhelp.addEvent( allLinks[i], 'click',poplinks.openPopup, false );
      allLinks[i].onclick = DOMhelp.safariClickFix;
  }
},
```

The openPopup() method retrieves the event target, makes sure that it was a link, and opens a new window by calling window.open() with the event target's href attribute as the URL, a blank name, and the window properties stored in windowProps. It finishes by calling the cancelClick() method to stop the link from being followed:

automaticPopupLinks.js (excerpt)

```
openPopup : function( e ) {
  var t = DOMhelp.getTarget( e );
  if( t.nodeName.toLowerCase() != 'a' ) {
    t = t.parentNode;
  }
  var win = window.open( t.getAttribute('href'), '', poplinks.windowProps );
  DOMhelp.cancelClick( e );
}
```

There is more to this topic, especially when it comes to usability and accessibility concerns, and making sure that pop-up windows are used only when they really are opened and not blocked by some software or otherwise fail to open. However, going deeper into the matter is not within the scope of the current discussion. It suffices to say that it is not easy to rely on pop-ups of any kind in today's environment.

Window Interaction

Windows can interact with other windows using a number of their properties and methods. First of all there is focus() and blur(): the former brings the pop-up window to the front; the latter pushes it to the back of the current window.

You can use the close() method to get rid of windows, and you can reach the window that opened the pop-up window via the window.opener property. Suppose you opened two new windows from a main document:

```
w1 = window.open('document1.html', 'win1');
w2 = window.open('document2.html', 'win2');
```

You can hide the first window behind the other by calling its blur() method:

```
w1.blur();
```

Note You don't see it much anymore, but the trick of opening an unsolicited window and hiding it immediately via blur() is called a *pop-under*. This trick is considered by advertisers to be less annoying than pop-up windows, because they don't cover the current page. If you've ever found several windows you don't remember opening when you shut down the browser, this is likely what has happened.

You can close the window by calling its close() method:

```
w1.close();
```

If you want to reach the initial window from any of the documents in the pop-ups, you can do this via

```
var parentWin = window.opener;
```

If you want to reach the second window from the first window, you also need to go through the `window.opener`, because the second window was opened from this one:

```
var parentWin = window.opener;
var otherWin = parentWin.w2;
```

Notice that you need to use the variable name the window was assigned to, not the window name.

You can use any of the window methods of any of the windows this way. Say, for example, you want to close w2 from within `document1.html`; you do this by calling

```
var parentWin = window.opener;
var otherWin = parentWin.w2.close();
```

You can also call functions of the main window. If the main window has a JavaScript function that is called `demo()`, you could reach it from `document1.html` via

```
var parentWin = window.opener;
parentWin.demo();
```

■ **Caution**   If you try to close the initial window with `window.opener.close()`, some browsers will give a security alert asking the user if he wants to allow that. This is another security feature to prevent site owners with malicious intentions from spoofing a different web site. A lot of design agencies used to close the original browser in favor of a window with a predefined size—this is not possible any longer without the aforementioned security alert. It might be a good idea to avoid this kind of behavior unless you want to scare or annoy your visitors.

Changing the Position and the Dimensions of a Window

Each of the methods in the following list has x and y parameters: x is the horizontal position, and y is the vertical position in pixels from the top left of the screen. The `moveBy()`, `resizeBy()`, and `scrollBy()` methods allow for negative values, which would move the window or the content to the left and up or make the window smaller by the stated amount of pixels:

- `moveBy(x,y)`—Moves the window by x and y pixels
- `moveTo(x,y)`—Moves the window to the coordinates x and y
- `resizeBy(x,y)`—Resizes the window by x and y
- `resizeTo(x,y)`—Resizes the window to x and y
- `scrollBy(x,y)`—Scrolls the window's content by x and y
- `scrollTo(x,y)`—Scrolls the window's content to x and y

If you check the example document `exampleWindowPosition.html`, you can test the different methods as shown in Figure 6-13. Note that this example appears in Firefox. In Opera 8 or IE 7, the small window will have a location bar.

Window position and dimensions
This is a demonstration page for a
JavaScript functionality and needs JavaScript enabled!

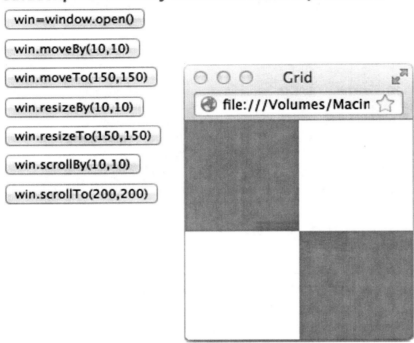

Figure 6-13. *Changing the window position and dimension*

Animation with Window Intervals and Timeouts

You can use the `setInterval()` and `setTimeout()` window methods to allow for the timed execution of code.
`setTimeout` means you wait a certain time before executing the code (once only); `setInterval()` executes the code
every time the given time period has passed.

- `name = setInterval('someCode', x )`: Executes the JavaScript code passed to it as someCode every x milliseconds

- `clearInterval( name )`: Cancels the execution of the interval called name (keeps the code from being executed again)

- `name=setTimeout('someCode', x )`: Executes the JavaScript code someCode once, after waiting x milliseconds

- `clearTimeout( name )`: Stops the timeout called name if the code hasn't yet been run

■ **Note** The parameter someCode in setInterval() and setTimeout() is a function you've defined.

Classic examples for the use of these methods are news tickers, clocks, and animation. However, you can also use them to make your site less obtrusive and more user beneficial. One example of this is a warning message that vanishes after a certain amount of time. The demo exampleTimeout.html shows how you can use setTimeout() to display a very obvious warning message for a short period or allow the user to get rid of it immediately. The HTML has a paragraph warning the user that the document is out of date:

exampleTimeout.html (excerpt)

```
<p id="warning">This document is outdated
 and kept only for archive purposes.</p>
```

A basic style sheet colors this warning red and shows it in bold for non-JavaScript users. For users that have JavaScript enabled, add a dynamic class that makes the warning a lot more obvious.

timeout.css

```
#warning{
  font-weight:bold;
  color:#c00;
}
.warning{
  width:300px;
  padding:2em;
  background:#fcc;
  border:1px solid #c00;
  font-size:2em;
}
```

The difference between the two is shown in Figure 6-14.

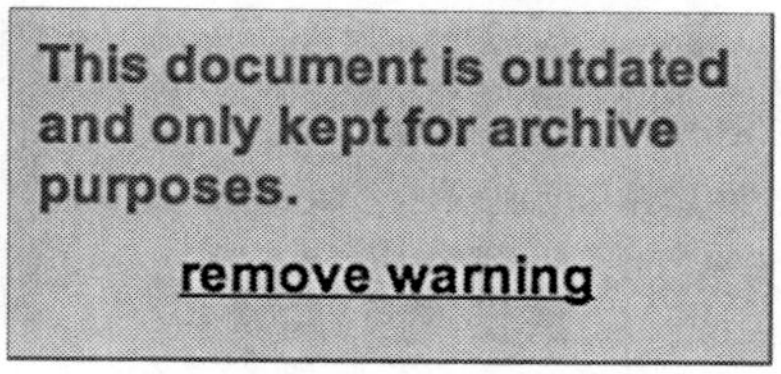

Figure 6-14. *Warning message without and with JavaScript*

The user can click the "remove warning" link to get rid of the warning or wait—it will vanish automatically after 10 seconds.

The script is pretty easy. You check whether DOM is supported and whether the warning message with the right ID exists. Then you add the dynamic warning class to the message and create a new link with an event handler pointing to the removeWarning() method. You append this link as a new child node to the warning message and define a timeout that automatically triggers removeWarning() when 10 seconds are over:

timeout.js (excerpt)

```
warn = {
  init : function() {
    if( !document.getElementById || !document.createTextNode ) {
      return;
    }
```

```
    warn.w = document.getElementById('warning');
    if( !warn.w ){ return; }
    DOMhelp.cssjs('add', warn.w, 'warning');
    var temp = DOMhelp.createLink('#', 'remove warning');
    DOMhelp.addEvent( temp, 'click', warn.removeWarning, false );
    temp.onclick = DOMhelp.safariClickFix;
    warn.w.appendChild( temp );
    warn.timer = window.setTimeout('warn.removeWarning()', 10000 );
  },
```

All the removeWarning() method needs to do is remove the warning message from the document, clear the timeout, and stop the default action of the link.

timeout.js (continued)

```
  removeWarning : function( e ){
    warn.w.parentNode.removeChild( warn.w );
    window.clearTimeout( warn.timer );
    DOMhelp.cancelClick( e );
  }
}
DOMhelp.addEvent( window, 'load', warn.init, false )
```

One web application that pioneered this kind of effect is Basecamp (available at http://www.basecamp.com/), which highlights the recent changes to the document in yellow when the page loads and gradually fades out the highlight. You can see the effect rationale at 37signals (http://www.37signals.com/svn/archives/000558.php).

Timeouts are tempting to use on web sites because they give the impression of a very dynamic site and allow you to transition smoothly from one state to the other.

Tip   There are several JavaScript effect libraries available that offer you premade scripts to achieve transition and animation effects. Although most of them are very outdated, there are some exceptions, like script.aculo.us (http://script.aculo.us/), TweenJS (http://www.createjs.com/#!/TweenJS) and TweenLite (http://www.greensock.com/).

However, you might want to reconsider using a lot of animation and transitions in your web site. Remember that the code is executed on the user's computer, and depending on how old or how busy it is with other tasks, the transitions and animations might look very clumsy and become a nuisance rather than a richer site experience.

Animations can also be an accessibility issue if the functionality of the site is dependent on them, because they might make it impossible for some groups of disabled visitors (such as those with cognitive disabilities or epilepsy) to use the site. The Section 508 accessibility law in the US (which you can read at http://www.section508.gov/) states quite clearly that for software development you need to provide an option to turn off animation:

(h) When animation is displayed, the information shall be displayable in at least one non-animated presentation mode at the option of the user.

```
          http://www.section508.gov/index.cfm?fuseAction=stdsdoc#Software
```

However, for web sites this is not formulated as clearly. The World Wide Web Consortium (W3C) accessibility guidelines, on the other hand, state explicitly in a level-two priority that you should avoid any movement in web pages:

Until user agents allow users to freeze moving content, avoid movement in pages.

http://www.w3.org/TR/WCAG10-TECHS/#tech-avoid-movement

Let's try an example that allows the user to start and stop an animation. Take the embedded slide show developed earlier in the chapter and, instead of giving it forward and backward links, you'll add a link to start and stop an automated slide show using a setInterval().

The HTML and the CSS will stay the same, but the JavaScript has to change a lot.

If you open exampleAutoSlideShow.html in a browser, you'll get a slide show with a Play button that starts the show when you click it. You could easily start the animation when the page loads, but it is a good idea to leave the choice to the user. This is especially the case when you need to comply with accessibility guidelines, because unsolicited animation can cause problems for users suffering from disabilities like epilepsy. Once clicked, the button turns into a Stop button that stops the slide show when activated. You can see how it looks in Firefox in Figure 6-15.

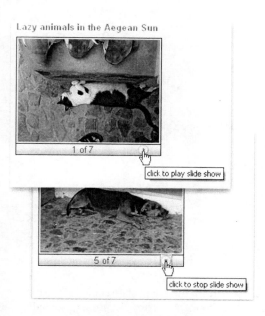

Figure 6-15. *An automatic slide show changing the Play button to a Stop button*

You start with the necessary CSS classes, which are the same as in the first slide show example with the exception of the hide class. Because you won't hide any buttons this time, there is no need for it.

autoSlideShow.js (excerpt)

```
autoSlides = {

  // CSS classes
  slideClass : 'slides',
  dynamicSlideClass : 'dynslides',
  showClass : 'show',
  slideCounterClass : 'slidecounter',
```

The other properties change slightly. Instead of backward and forward labels, you now need play and stop labels. The counter indicating the total number of pictures and which picture in the series is currently shown stays the same. One new property is the delay of the slide show in milliseconds:

autoSlides.js (continued)

```
// Labels
// Play and stop links, you can use any HTML here
playLabel : '<img src="control_play_blue.png" alt="play">',
stopLabel : '<img src="control_stop_blue.png" alt="stop">',
// Counter text, # will be replaced by the current image count
// and % by the number of all pictures
counterLabel : '# of %',

// Animation delay in milliseconds
delay : 1000,
```

The init() method checks for DOM support and adds a new array called slideLists, which will store all the lists that are to be turned into slide shows. This is necessary to be able to tell the function which list to apply the changes to:

autoSlides.js (continued)

```
init : function() {
  if( !document.getElementById || !document.createTextNode ) {
    return;
  }
  var uls = document.getElementsByTagName('ul');
  autoSlides.slideLists = new Array();
```

First, loop through all the lists in the document and check for the class to turn them into slide shows. If a list has the class, you initialize the currentSlide property to 0 and store the loop counter in a new list property called showCounter. Once again, this will be needed to tell the interval which list to change. You call the initSlideShow() method with the list as a parameter and add the lists to the slideLists array:

autoSlides.js (continued)

```
  for( var i = 0; i < uls.length; i++ ) {
    if( !DOMhelp.cssjs('check', uls[i],autoSlides.slideClass ) ){
      continue;
    }
```

```
      DOMhelp.cssjs('swap', uls[i], autoSlides.slideClass,_autoSlides.dynamicSlideClass );
      uls[i].currentSlide = 0;
      uls[i]. showIndex = i;
      autoSlides.initSlideShow( uls[i] );
      autoSlides.slideLists.push( uls[i] );
    }
  },
```

The initSlideShow() method does not differ much from the method of the same name you used in photoListInlineSlidesSafariFix.js. The only difference is that you create one link instead of two and apply the playLabel as the content of the new link:

autoSlides.js (continued)

```
initSlideShow : function( o ){
  var p, temp ;
  p = document.createElement('p');
  DOMhelp.cssjs('add', p, autoSlides.slideCounterClass );
  o.parentNode.insertBefore( p, o.nextSibling );
  o.play = DOMhelp.createLink('#', ' ' );
  o.play.innerHTML = autoSlides.playLabel;
  DOMhelp.addEvent( o.play, 'click', autoSlides.playSlide, false );
  o.count = document.createElement('span');
  temp = autoSlides.counterLabel.replace( /#/, o.currentSlide + 1 );
  temp = temp.replace( /%/, o.getElementsByTagName('li').length );
  o.count.appendChild( document.createTextNode( temp ) );
  p.appendChild( o.count );
  p.appendChild( o.play );
  temp = o.getElementsByTagName('li')[o.currentSlide];
  DOMhelp.cssjs('add', temp,autoSlides.showClass );
  o.play.onclick = DOMhelp.safariClickFix;
},
```

The playSlide() method is new, but it starts pretty much like the old showSlide() method. You check the target and its node name and retrieve the parent list:

autoSlides.js (continued)

```
playSlide : function( e ) {
  var t = DOMhelp.getTarget( e );
  while( t.nodeName.toLowerCase() != 'a' && t.nodeName.toLowerCase() != 'body' ){
    t = t.parentNode;
  }
  var parentList = DOMhelp.closestSibling( t.parentNode, -1 );
```

You test if the parent list already has a property called loop. This is the property that stores the instance of setInterval(). You use a property of the list instead of a variable to allow for more than one automated slide show in the same document.

You define the string to use in setInterval() as a call of the showSlide() method with the showIndex property of the parent list as a parameter. This is necessary because setInterval() is a method of the window object and not in the scope of the main autoSlides object.

You use setInterval() with the delay defined in the autoSlides.delay property and store it in the loop property before changing the content of the link that was activated to the Stop button:

autoSlides.js (continued)

```
if( !parentList.loop ) {
  var loopCall = "autoSlides.showSlide('" + parentList.showIndex + " ' )";
  parentList.loop = window.setInterval( loopCall, utoSlides.delay );
  t.innerHTML = autoSlides.stopLabel;
```

If the list already has a property called loop, the slide show is currently running; therefore, you clear it, set the loop property to null, and change the button back to the Play button. You then stop the default link behavior by calling cancelClick().

autoSlides.js (continued)

```
  } else {
    window.clearInterval( parentList.loop );
    parentList.loop = null;
    t.innerHTML = autoSlides.playLabel;
  }
  DOMhelp.cancelClick( e );
},
```

The showSlide() method changes quite drastically, but you will see that some of the initially confusing parts of the other methods (like what the slideLists array is good for) make the method rather easy.

Remember that you define in playSlide() that the interval should call the showSlide() method with the showIndex property of the list as a parameter. You can use this index now to retrieve the list you need to loop through simply by retrieving the list from the slideLists array.

autoSlides.js (continued)

```
showSlide : function( showIndex ) {
  var currentShow = autoSlides.slideLists[showIndex];
```

Once you have the list, you can read out the current slide and the number of slides. Remove the showClass from the current slide to hide it:

autoSlides.js (continued)

```
var count = currentShow.currentSlide;
var photoCount = currentShow.getElementsByTagName('li').length;
var photo = currentShow.getElementsByTagName('li')[count];
DOMhelp.cssjs('remove', photo, autoSlides.showClass );
```

Increment the counter to show the next slide. Compare the counter with the number of all the slides, and set it to 0 if the last slide was already shown—thus restarting the slide show at the first slide.

Show the slide by retrieving the list element and adding the show class. Update the counter, and reset the currentSlide property of the list to the new list element:

autoSlides.js (continued)

```
    count++;
    if( count == photoCount ){ count = 0 };
    photo = currentShow.getElementsByTagName('li')[count];
    DOMhelp.cssjs('add', photo, autoSlides.showClass );
    var counterText = currentShow.count.firstChild;
    counterText.nodeValue = counterText.nodeValue.replace( /\d/, count + 1 );
    currentShow.currentSlide = count;
  }
}
DOMhelp.addEvent( window, 'load', autoSlides.init, false );
```

This complexity is just a taste of what awaits the JavaScript developer when it comes to animation and timed execution of code. Creating a smooth, stable, cross-browser animation can now be done with JavaScript, as well as CSS3 animations, transforms, and transitions. Luckily, there are ready-made animation libraries available that help you with this task and that have been tested for stability by a lot of developers with different operating systems and browsers. You'll get to know one of them with the examples in Chapter 11.

Navigation Methods of the Browser Window

Following is a list of methods for navigating a browser window:

- back(): Goes back one page in the browser history

- forward(): Goes one page forward in the browser history

- home(): Acts as if the user clicked the home button (only for Firefox and Opera; in IE, its document.location is "about:home")

- stop(): Stops the loading of the document in the window (not supported by IE)

- print(): Starts the browser's print dialog

It is rather tempting to use these methods to provide navigation on pages that should simply link back to the previous page via something like the following:

```
<a href="javascript:window.back()">Back to previous page</a>
```

With accessibility and modern scripting in mind, this means that a user without JavaScript will be promised something that does not exist. A better solution is either to generate a real "back to previous page" link via server-side includes (SSIs) or to provide an actual HTML hyperlink to the right document. If neither is possible, use a placeholder and replace it with a generated link when and if JavaScript is available, as in the following example:

exampleBackLink.html (to reach via exampleForBackLink.html)

```
HTML:
<p id="back">Please use your browser's back button or
keyboard shortcut to go to the previous page</p>
JavaScript:
function backlink() {
```

```
  var p = document.getElementById('back');
  if( p ) {
    var newa = document.createElement('a');
    newa.setAttribute('href', '#');
    newa.appendChild( document.createTextNode('back to previous page') );
    newa.onclick = function() { window.back();return false; }
    p.replaceChild( newa, p.firstChild );
  }
}
window.onload = backlink;
```

■ **Caution**   The danger of these methods is that you offer functionality that the browser already provides the user. The difference is that the browser does it better, because it supports more input devices. In Firefox on a PC, for example, you can print the document by pressing Ctrl+P, close the window or tab by pressing Ctrl+W, and move forward and backward in the browser history via Alt and the left or right arrow keys.

Even worse, the functionality offered with these methods is dependent on scripting support. It is up to you to decide if the preceding method—creating the links invoking these methods, which is probably the cleanest way to deal with the issue—is worth the effort, or if you should just allow the user to decide how to trigger browser functionality. Generating links also has the effect of changing the browser history. In this case, you are not navigating to pages that are in the browser history, you are adding new pages to the history.

Alternatives to Opening New Windows: Layer Ads

Sometimes there is no way to avoid pop-up windows, because the site design or functionality requires them, and you just cannot make them work because of the browser issues and options explained earlier. One workaround is *layer ads*, which are basically absolutely positioned page elements put on top of the main content.

Let's try an example of those. Imagine your company wants to advertise its latest offers quite obviously when the page is loaded. The easiest way to do this is to add the information at the end of the document and use a script to turn it into a layer ad. When you use this approach, visitors without JavaScript will still get the information, but they won't get anything that covers the content without giving them a chance to get rid of it. The HTML can be a simple DIV with an ID (the real links have been replaced with "#" for the sake of brevity):

exampleLayerAd.html (excerpt)

```
<div id="layerad">
  <h2>We've got some special offers!</h2>
  <ul>
    <li><a href="#">TDK DVD-R 8x 50 pack $12</a></li>
    <li><a href="#">Datawrite DVD-R 16x 100 pack $50</a></li>
    <li><a href="#">NEC 3500A DVD-RW 16x $30</a></li>
  </ul>
</div>
```

The CSS designer can style the ad for the non-JavaScript version, and the script will add a class to allow the ad to show up above the main content. If you call the class dyn, the CSS might look like this:

layerAd.css (excerpt)

```css
#layerad{
  margin:.5em;
  padding:.5em;
}
#layerad.dyn{
  position:absolute;
  top:1em;
  left:1em;
  background:#eef;
  border:1px solid #999;
}
#layerad.dyn a.adclose{
  display:block;
  text-align:right;
}
```

The last selector is a style for a dynamic link that the script will add to the ad, allowing the user to remove it.

The script itself does not contain any surprises. First, define the ID of the ad, the dynamic class, and the class and the text content of the "close" link as properties:

layerAd.js

```javascript
ad = {
  adID : 'layerad',
  adDynamicClass : 'dyn',
  closeLinkClass : 'adclose',
  closeLinkLabel : 'close',
```

The init() method checks for DOM and for the ad, and it adds the dynamic class to it. It creates a new link and adds the text and the class of the "close" link to it. It adds an event handler to this link pointing to the killAd() method and inserts the new link before the first child node of the ad:

layerAd.js (continued)

```javascript
init : function() {
  if( !document.getElementById || !document.createTextNode ) {
    return;
  }
  ad.offer = document.getElementById( ad.adID );
  if( !ad.offer ) { return; }
  DOMhelp.cssjs('add', ad.offer, ad.adDynamicClass );
  var closeLink = DOMhelp.createLink('#', ad.closeLinkLabel );
  DOMhelp.cssjs('add', closeLink, ad.closeLinkClass );
  DOMhelp.addEvent( closeLink, 'click', ad.killAd,false );
  closeLink.onclick = DOMhelp.safariClickFix;
  ad.offer.insertBefore( closeLink, ad.offer.firstChild );
},
```

The `killAd()` method removes the ad from the document and cancels the link's default behavior:

layerAd.js (continued)

```
  killAd : function( e ) {
    ad.offer.parentNode.removeChild( ad.offer );
    DOMhelp.cancelClick( e );
  }
}
DOMhelp.addEvent( window, 'load', ad.init, false );
```

You can test the effect by opening `exampleLayerAd.html` in a browser. If you have JavaScript-enabled, you'll see the ad covering the content, as shown in Figure 6-16. You can get rid of it by using the "close" link.

Figure 6-16. *An example of a layer ad*

One other common use of pop-up windows is for displaying another document or file without leaving the current page. Classic examples include a long list of boring terms and conditions or a photo. Especially in the case of photos, a pop-up is a suboptimal solution, because you can open a window with the same dimensions as the picture but there will be gaps around the image because the browser's internal styles have padding settings on the body. You could work around this problem by using a blank HTML document with a style sheet that sets the body margins and padding to 0 and adding the image to the document in the window via JavaScript. Another option is to show the photo in a newly generated and positioned element covering the main document. The demo `examplePicturePopup.html` does that; all the script needs is a class with a certain name on a link pointing to the photo:

examplePicturePopup.html (excerpt)

```
<a class="picturepop" href="pictures/thumbs/dog7.jpg">Sleeping Dog</a>
```

The script needs to do something that wasn't explained here before—namely, reading the position of elements. You cover the main document with an element by positioning the element absolutely. Because you don't know where the link pointing to the photo is in the document, you need to read its position and show the photo there.

But that is for later. First up, you need to predefine properties. You need a class that triggers the script, applying a link class to the link when the photo is shown, and another class to the element containing the photo. You also need to define a prefix to be added to the link when the photo is displayed and a property acting as a shortcut reference to the newly created element:

picturePopup.js (excerpt)

```
pop={
  triggerClass:'picturepop',
  openPopupLinkClass:'popuplink',
```

```
popupClass:'popup',
displayPrefix:'Hide',
popContainer:null,
```

The init() method checks for DOM support and loops through all the links of the document, testing whether they have the right CSS class to trigger the pop-up. For those that do, the method adds an event handler pointing to the openPopup() method and then stores the link's innerHTML content in a preset property.

picturePopup.js (continued)

```
init : function() {
  if( !document.getElementById || !document.createTextNode ) {
    return;
  }
  var allLinks = document.getElementsByTagName('a');
  for( var i = 0; i < allLinks.length; i++ ) {
    if( !DOMhelp.cssjs('check', allLinks[i],pop.triggerClass ) ) {
      continue;
    }
    DOMhelp.addEvent( allLinks[i], 'click', pop.openPopup, false );
    allLinks[i].onclick = DOMhelp.safariClickFix;
    allLinks[i].preset = allLinks[i].innerHTML;
  }
},
```

The openPopup() method retrieves the event target and ensures that it is a link. It then tests whether there is already a popContainer, which means that the photo is shown. If this is not the case, the method adds the prefix to the link's content and adds the dynamic class to make the link look different:

picturePopup.js (continued)

```
openPopup : function( e ) {
  var t = DOMhelp.getTarget( e );
  if( t.nodeName.toLowerCase() != 'a') {
    t = t.parentNode;
  }
  if( !pop.popContainer ) {
    t.innerHTML = pop.displayPrefix + t.preset;
    DOMhelp.cssjs('add', pop.popContainer, pop.popupClass );
```

The method then creates a new DIV that acts as the photo container, adds the appropriate class, and adds a new image as a child node of the container DIV. It shows the image by setting the src attribute of the new image to the value of the href attribute of the original link. The newly created photo container is then added to the document (as a child of the body element). Finally, openPopup() calls the positionPopup() method with the link object as a parameter.

picturePopup.js (continued)

```
pop.popContainer = document.createElement('div');
DOMhelp.cssjs('add', t,pop.openPopupLinkClass );
var newimg = document.createElement('img');
pop.popContainer.appendChild( newimg );
```

```
newimg.setAttribute('src', t.getAttribute('href') );
document.body.appendChild( pop.popContainer );
pop.positionPopup( t );
```

If the popContainer already exists, all the method does is call the killPopup() method, reset the link to its original content, and remove the class that indicates that the photo is shown. Calling cancelClick() prevents the link from simply showing the photo in the browser.

picturePopup.js (continued)

```
  } else {
    pop.killPopup();
    t.innerHTML = t.preset;
    DOMhelp.cssjs('remove', t,pop.openPopupLinkClass );
  }
  DOMhelp.cancelClick( e );
},
```

The positionPopup() method defines two variables (x and y), initializes them both to 0, and then reads the height of the element from its offsetHeight property. It next reads the vertical and horizontal position of the element and all its parent elements and adds those to x and y. The result is the position of the element relative to the document. The method then positions the photo container below the original link by adding the height of the link to the vertical variable y and altering the popContainer style properties:

picturePopup.js (continued)

```
positionPopup : function( o ) {
  var x = 0;
  var y = 0;
  var h = o.offsetHeight;
  while ( o != null ) {
    x += o.offsetLeft;
    y += o.offsetTop;
    o = o.offsetParent;
  }
  pop.popContainer.style.left = x + 'px';
  pop.popContainer.style.top = y + h + 'px';
},
```

The killPopup() method removes the popContainer from the document—clearing the property by setting its value to null—and prevents the default link action from taking place by calling cancelClick().

■ **Note** You can remove a node from the document by calling the removeChild() method of its parent node, with the node itself as the child node to remove. However, because you use a property that points to the node rather than checking for the node itself, you also need to set this property to null.

---

picturePopup.js (continued)

```
  killPopup : function( e ) {
    pop.popContainer.parentNode.removeChild( pop.popContainer );
    pop.popContainer = null;
    DOMhelp.cancelClick( e );
  }
}
DOMhelp.addEvent( window, 'load', pop.init, false );
```

The result is that you can click any image pointing to a photo with the correct class, and it'll show the image below it. Figure 6-17 shows an example.

Figure 6-17. *An example of a dynamically displayed photo*

The beauty of this approach is that it is not only limited to photos. With just a simple modification, you can display other documents inside the current one. The trick is to dynamically add an IFRAME element to the photoContainer and set its src attribute to the document you want to embed. The demonstration exampleIframeForPopup.html does exactly that to show a lengthy terms-and-conditions document inside the main one.

The only differences (apart from different property names, because the method does not show a photo) are in the openPopup method, where you add the new IFRAME:

iframeForPopup.js (excerpt)

```
var ifr = document.createElement('iframe');
pop.ifrContainer.appendChild( ifr );
ifr.setAttribute('src', t.getAttribute('href') );
```

Figure 6-18 shows what this could look like.

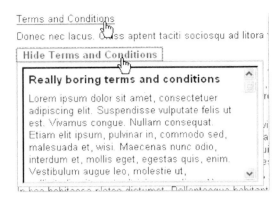

Figure 6-18. *An example of a dynamically included and displayed document*

Including other documents via IFRAME elements is an easy and well-supported method, but it is not the most accessible way. What you could do instead is use a server-side language like PHP to retrieve the content of the document and include it in the current one, and use the same trick the layer ad example earlier uses. For more modern browsers, you can also do this "on the fly" using Ajax, but that will be explained in its own chapter, Chapter 8.

Summary: Windows and JavaScript

Controlling the current window and opening new ones has traditionally been a large part of JavaScript development, especially when it comes to web application development. In recent years, however, due to an increase in restrictions fueled by concerns about browser security and web surfers simply being fed with lots of pop-ups and installing blocking software, it has become progressively harder to use new windows—even if you want to use them for a good cause. These and accessibility concerns make using multiple browser windows an increasingly unreliable method of web communication. Thanks to some of the replacement techniques discussed here (as well as Ajax, to which I devote Chapter 8) and good frameworks like Twitter Bootstrap, there is hardly any need for them any longer. Here are a few key things to remember about Windows and JavaScript:

- Test, test, and test again whether the window you have opened really exists before you try to do anything to it.

- Always remember that although the windows are on the same screen, they are completely separate instances of the browser. You need to go via the window.opener if you want to reach one pop-up from another or a function in the main script from any of the pop-ups you opened.

- Refrain from trying to control windows by taking away toolbars, moving them around the screen, or showing and hiding them via blur() and focus(). Most of these capabilities are still available now, but they are very likely to be blocked in future browsers.

- You can simulate a lot of browser behavior or interactive elements with the window object methods—like closing and printing a window or moving back in the browser history. However, it might be better to leave this choice to the user. If you want to offer your own controls to the user, create these with JavaScript, too. Otherwise, the user will get a promise you can't keep when JavaScript is unavailable.

- If you use pop-up windows, tell visitors in the link opening the window that there will be a new window. This informs visitors with user agents that don't necessarily support multiple windows that there might be a change they have to deal with; it also prevents visitors from accidentally closing the window your web site needs. Years of unsolicited advertising and pop-ups have conditioned web surfers to immediately close new windows without even glancing at them.

- Employing timed execution of code via the window methods `setTimeout()` and `setInterval()` is a bit like using makeup: as a girl you learn how to put it on; as a woman you learn when to take it off. You can use both of these methods—and they are tempting to create all kinds of snazzy effects—but you should think of your users, and ask yourself, "Is there really a need for animation when a static interface might lead much more quickly to the same result?"

Summary

Well done! You have reached the end of this chapter and should be well equipped now to create your own JavaScript solutions with images and windows, or—even better—window replacement techniques.

If some of the examples were a bit tough to wrap your head around, don't get frustrated, because this is a feeling you'll experience often as a JavaScript developer. And it does not mean that you don't get it. Dozens of ways exist to solve any given problem in JavaScript. Although there are much easier ways than those explained here, getting used to this kind of scripting should make you well equipped for more advanced scripting tasks like using third-party APIs or web application development.

In the next chapter, you have the chance to become better acquainted with event and property handling, as we discuss navigation and forms.

■ ■ ■

CHAPTER 7

JavaScript and User Interaction: Navigation and Forms

In this chapter, I will talk about two more common uses of JavaScript: navigation and forms. Both involve a lot of user interaction and therefore need to be planned and executed thoughtfully. The success of a web site stands and falls with the ease of its navigation, and there is nothing more frustrating on the Web than a form that is hard to use or impossible to fill out.

■ **Note** This chapter consists of a lot of code examples, and you will be asked to open some of them in a browser to test the functionality for yourself. So if you haven't been to `http://www.beginningjavascript.com` yet to download the code examples for this book, it might be a good time to do so now. I am a firm believer in hands-on training when it comes to coding, and it'll be easier for you to understand some of the functionality when you can experience it firsthand or—better yet—fiddle around with it in your own editor.

Navigation and JavaScript

Spicing up web-site navigation has been one of the main tasks of DHTML since browsers first began supporting dynamic changes to the look and feel of page elements. The era of animated and fading navigation started with DHTML. The idea seemed to be that if the web page's navigation was very slick, tech-y, and looked and acted remotely like the LCARS interfaces on the starship *Enterprise*, the site must be great. A lot of times, visitors disagreed, and they would use a site search option, assuming one was provided, once they got bored with the navigation.

I won't talk about flashy navigation here; instead, I'll give you examples of what you can do with JavaScript to make page and site navigation more intuitive and less cumbersome while keeping it as accessible as possible.

The Fear of the Page Reload

A lot of JavaScript enhancements to forms and web navigation are made to prevent visitors from having to reload the page or load a lot of pages before reaching the information they came for. This is an admirable idea and can work wonderfully; however, let's not forget that JavaScript can reach elements of the page only when the whole document is loaded and it can deal with what is already in the document (that is, unless you use Ajax to load other content on the fly—more about that in the next chapter).

This means you can create a slick interface that shows only a slice of the overall page content with JavaScript, but it also means that visitors without JavaScript will have to deal with the entire amount of data in the document. Before you go completely nuts on enhancing pages, turn off JavaScript from time to time and see whether you'd be able to cope with the amount of data available in the document.

The benefit of smaller documents with only a bit of specialized information in them is that you can use the whole toolkit the browser offers the user: going forward and backward, bookmarking and printing. This is functionality you might break when you use JavaScript for navigation or pagination. The less desirable effect is that you have to maintain a lot more documents and visitors have to load each separately—thus also increasing the server traffic.

It is not evil to use JavaScript to enhance web sites; it is all a matter of moderation and knowing your audience.

Basics of Navigation and JavaScript

The most basic idea of navigation and JavaScript is that you don't rely on JavaScript to make your navigation work. Depending on JavaScript, page or site navigation will block out users who don't have JavaScript at their disposal and will also block out search engines.

Tip The latter is a good argument if you ever have to explain to a nontechnical person why a bunch of `javascript:navigate('page2')` links are not a good idea. The notion of site visitors who have JavaScript disabled as a target group that is worth thinking about is not easy to explain to someone who doesn't even know how to turn it off in his browser. Explaining to him that the "big, blind millionaire" Google won't index his site is an easier selling point.

A classic example of using JavaScript seemingly to make navigation easier but with the potential of alienating quite a large a group of visitors is the use of a select box for navigation. Select boxes are great because they let you offer a lot of options without wasting screen space. Figure 7-1 shows an open select box; the closed one uses up only one line for all these options.

Figure 7-1. *Using a select box for navigation*

Open the demo page `exampleSelectNavigation.html`, and select one of the options from the drop-down menu. If you are connected to the Web and have JavaScript enabled, you will be immediately sent to the address you choose. Unfortunately, if you've chosen the wrong option, you don't get a chance to undo your choice. Without JavaScript, you can select an option, but nothing happens.

exampleSelectNavigation.html

```
<form>
<p>
  <select onchange="window.location = this.options[this.selectedIndex].value">
    <option value="#">Please select</option>
    <option value="http://www.apress.com">The publisher</option>
```

```
    <option value="http://wait-till-i.com">The author's blog</option>
    <option value="http://icant.co.uk">The author's other articles</option>
    <option value="http://onlinetools.org">Scripts and tools by the author</option>
  </select>
</p>
</form>
```

Keyboard access is another problem: you normally use the Tab key to access a select box and press the up and down keys to select the choice you want. In this example, you won't get that chance though, because you will be sent to the first option as soon as you press the down arrow key. The workaround is to press the Alt and down arrow keys together to expand the whole list. You can then choose your option with the up arrow and down arrow keys and press Enter to select it. But did you know that?

The easiest solution to these problems is to never use a change, mouseover, or focus event to send data to the server or the user to a different web location. It is not accessible for a lot of visitors and can cause a lot of frustration. It is especially frustrating if there is no indicator that data is being sent and that the page will change.

Instead, offer a real Submit button, a script that does the same redirection on the server side, and a submit handler to redirect via JavaScript when and if it is available.

exampleSaferSelectNavigation.html (excerpt)

```
<form method="post" action="redir.php">
<p>
  <label for="url">Please select your destination:</label>
  <select id="url" name="url">
    <option value="http://www.apress.com">The publisher</option>
    <option value="http://wait-till-i.com">The author's blog</option>
    <option value="http://icant.co.uk">The author's other articles</option>
    <option value="http://onlinetools.org">Scripts and tools by the author</option>
  </select>
  <input type="submit" value="Make it so!">
</p>
</form>
```

The script is pretty straightforward: you apply an event handler to the first form on submit that triggers a method. That method reads what choice the user made from the selectedIndex of the options list with the ID url and redirects the browser there via the window.location object. You'll read more about the window.location object in the next section and all about the selectedIndex and form objects in the "Forms and JavaScript" section of this chapter.

exampleSaferSelectNavigation.js

```
send = {
  init : function() {
    DOMhelp.addEvent(document.forms[0], 'submit', send.redirect, false);
  },
  redirect : function(e){
    var t = DOMhelp.getTarget(e);
    var url = t.elements['url'];
    window.location.href = url.options[url.selectedIndex].value;
    DOMhelp.cancelClick(e);
  }
}
DOMhelp.addEvent(window, 'load', send.init, false);
```

The server-side script to send non-JavaScript users to the other URI could be a simple header redirect in PHP:

```php
<?php header('Location: ' . $_POST['url']); ?>
```

If the user has JavaScript enabled, she won't have to do the round-trip to the server; instead, she'll get sent to the other web site immediately. You do this by setting the `window.location.href` property, which is one part of the built-in browser navigation.

Browser Navigation

Browsers give you several objects you can use for automatic redirection or navigation around the browser's history. You already encountered the `window.back()` method in the last chapter. The `window` object also provides the properties `window.location` and `window.history`.

The `window.location` object stores the URI of the current element and has the following properties (in parentheses, you see the return value provided if the URI were `http://www.example.com:8080/index.php?s=JavaScript#search results`):

- hash: The name of the anchor in the URI (#searchresults)

- host: The domain name part of the URI (www.example.com)

- hostname: The domain name, including subdomains and port numbers (www.example.com:8080)

- href: The whole URI string (http://www.example.com:8080/index.php?s=JavaScript#searchresults)

- pathname: The path name of the URI (/index.php)

- port: The port of the URI (8080)

- protocol: The protocol of the URI (http:)

- search: The search parameters (?s=JavaScript)

All of these properties can be read and written. For example, if you want the search to change to DOM scripting, you can do this via `window.location.search='?DOM scripting'`. The browser will automatically URL-encode the string to DOM%20scripting. You can also send the user's browser to another location by changing the `window.location.href` property.

In addition to these properties, the `window.location` has two methods:

- reload(): Reloads the current document (the same effect as clicking the Reload button or pressing F5 or the Ctrl and R keys simultaneously).

- replace(URI): Sends the user to the URI, and replaces the current URI with the other one. The current URI will not be part of the browser history any longer.

■ **Caution**   Notice that this is different from the `replace()` method of the `String` object, which replaces one part of a string with another.

You can use `reload()` to refresh the page in an interval to load new content from the back end without the user clicking the Reload button. This functionality is quite common in JavaScript-based chat systems.

Using replace() can be quite annoying, because you break the user's Back button functionality. She cannot go back to the current page when she doesn't like the one you sent her to.

The list of pages the user visited before reaching the current one is stored in the window.history object. This object has only one single property, called length, which stores the number of already visited pages. It has a few methods you can use (with the last two in the following list added as part of HTML5):

- back(): Go back one page in the browser history.

- forward(): Go forward one page in the browser history.

- go(n): Go *n* steps forward or back in the browser history depending on whether *n* is positive or negative. You can also reload the same page via history.go(0).

- pushState (state, title, url): This method pushes data into the session history, where state represents an object full of data, title represents the page title, and url represents the URL added to the history.

- replaceState (state, title, url): This method works in the same way pushState() does, but it modifies data instead of adding new data to the browser's history.

The history object allows you only to navigate to the other pages—not read out their URIs or change them. The exception to the rule is the current page, which gets wiped from the browser history when you use replace().

As already explained in the previous chapter, you effectively simulate browser functionality by sending the user to other pages via JavaScript, which might be superfluous or thoroughly confuse the user.

In-Page Navigation

You can use JavaScript to make navigation within the same page more interesting and less screen-space consuming. In HTML, you can provide in-page navigation via anchors and targets, both defined with the <a> tag, either with an href attribute for an anchor or a name or id attribute for a target.

▦ **Note** The name attribute for anchors is deprecated in HTML5, and it actually is enough to provide an ID to link an anchor and target pair. However, to ensure compatibility with older browsers, it might be a good idea to use it as you will in the following example.

Let's take a list of internal links in a table of contents linked to different targets further down the page as an example for in-page navigation:

exampleLinkedAnchors.html (excerpt)

```
<h1>X - a tool that does Y</h1>
<div id="toolinfo">
  <ul id="toolinfotoc">
    <li><a href="#info">Information</a></li>
    <li><a href="#demo">Demo</a></li>
    <li><a href="#installation">Installation</a></li>
    <li><a href="#use">Use</a></li>
    <li><a href="#license">License</a></li>
    <li><a href="#download">Download</a></li>
  </ul>
  <div class="infoblock">
```

```
  <h2><a id="info" name="info">Information about X</a></h2>
  [... content ...]
  <p class="back">
    <a href="#toolinfotoc">Back to <acronym title="Table of Contents">TOC</acronym></a>
  </p>
</div>
<div class="infoblock">
  <h2><a id="demo" name="demo">Demonstration of what X can do</a></h2>
  [... content ...]
  <p class="back">
    <a href="#toolinfotoc">Back to <acronym title="Table of Contents">TOC</acronym></a>
  </p>
</div>
[.... more sections ...]
</div>
```

You might be thinking that the DIV elements with the class infoblock are not necessary for this in-page navigation to work. That is only partly true, because Microsoft Internet Explorer (IE) has a very annoying bug when it comes to named anchors and keyboard navigation.

If you open the demo page exampleLinkedAnchors.html in Internet Explorer, navigate through the different menu items by pressing the Tab key, and choose the section you want by pressing the Enter key, the browser gets sent to the anchor you choose. However, Internet Explorer does not send the keyboard focus to this anchor. If you press the Tab key again, you don't get to the next link in the document; instead, you get sent back to the menu.

You can fix this problem by—among other tricks—nesting the anchor in an element that has a defined width. This is what the DIVs are for. You can test this out on the demo page exampleLinkedAnchorsFixed.html. The practical upshot is that you can use these elements—in this case the DIVs—for CSS styling.

Tip By default, the accessibility features might be turned off in different browsers. For example, to turn it back on in Safari on MacOS, go to Preferences, Advanced, Accessibility. Select the Press Tab To Highlight Each Item On A Webpage option.

Now let's replicate and improve this functionality with a script. What the script should do is show the menu, but hide all the sections, and show only the one you choose to keep the page shorter and less overwhelming. The logic is pretty easy:

- Loop through the links in the menu, and add click event handlers to show the sections connected with the menu item.

- In the event listener method, hide the previously shown section and show the current one.

- When initializing the page, hide all the sections and show the first one.

However, this does not take another aspect of in-page navigation into consideration: the page could have been requested with a predefined target coming from another link. Try it out by adding an anchor to the URI—for example, exampleLinkedAnchorsFixed.html#use—in your browser. You'll automatically scroll down to the Using section. Your script should take this use case into consideration.

Let's start by defining the skeleton of the script. The main object of the script is called iv, for *inner navigation*—because in is a reserved word in JavaScript, and you want to keep it short. You'll need several properties:

- A CSS class to define when the menu is JavaScript enhanced
- A CSS class to highlight the current link in the menu
- A CSS class to show the current section

Tip You don't need to hide the sections via JavaScript, but you can use the CSS parent class trick described in the previous chapter.

You'll need to define properties for the parent element to add the CSS class to and the ID of the menu to be able to loop through the links.

Two more properties are needed: one to store the currently shown section, and one to store the currently highlighted link.

In terms of methods, you'll need an init() method, an event listener to get the current section, and a method to hide the previous section and show the current section.

innerNav.js (skeleton)

```
iv = {
  // CSS classes
  dynamicClass : 'dyn',
  currentLinkClass : 'current',
  showClass : 'show',

  // IDs
  parentID : 'toolinfo',
  tocID : 'toolinfotoc',

  // Global properties
  current : null,
  currentLink : null,

  init : function(){ },
  getSection : function(e){ },
  showSection : function(o){ }
DOMhelp.addEvent(window, 'load', iv.init, false);
```

The init() method begins with checking whether DOM is supported and all necessary elements are available. Only then do you add the class to the parent element to hide all the section elements automatically, via CSS.

innerNav.js (excerpt)

```
init : function(){
  if(!document.getElementById || !document.createTextNode) {
    return;
  }
```

```
iv.parent = document.getElementById(iv.parentID);
iv.toc = document.getElementById(iv.tocID);
if(!iv.parent || !iv.toc) { return; }
DOMhelp.cssjs('add', iv.parent, iv.dynamicClass);
```

Store a possible URL hash in the variable loc, and start looping through all the links in the menu. Replacing the # in the hash value makes it easier to use it later on, because you can use the name in a getElementById() without having to remove the hash.

innerNav.js (continued)

```
var loc = window.location.hash.replace('#', ' ');
var toclinks = iv.toc.getElementsByTagName('a');
for(var i = 0; i < toclinks.length; i++) {
```

Compare the current link's href attribute with loc and store the link in the currentLink property if they are the same. The string replace() method used here deletes anything except the anchor name from the href property. This is necessary because getAttribute('href') in some browsers like Internet Explorer returns the entire link location including the file path (this has been fixed in IE 8), not only what is inside the HTML href attribute.

innerNav.js (continued)

```
if(toclinks[i].getAttribute('href').replace(/.*#/, ' ') == loc){
  iv.currentLink = toclinks[i];
}
```

Next, add a click event pointing to getSection(). Notice that in this example script you don't need to stop the default event—on the contrary, allowing the browser to jump to the section will also change the URI in the location bar, and that in turn allows the user to bookmark the section.

innerNav.js (continued)

```
DOMhelp.addEvent(toclinks[i], 'click', iv.getSection, false);
}
```

The currentLink property is defined only when one of the links is the same as the hash in the URI. This means that if the URI has no hash, or it has one that points to an anchor that isn't there, you need to define currentLink as the first anchor in the menu instead. The init() method finishes by calling the showSection() method with the currentLink as a parameter.

innerNav.js (continued)

```
  if(!iv.currentLink) {
    iv.currentLink = toclinks[0];
  }
  iv.showSection(iv.currentLink);
},
```

The event listener method getSection() does not need to do much; all it needs to do is determine which link was clicked and send it to showSection() as a parameter. If it weren't for the need to access window.location.hash, these two lines could have been part of the showSection() method.

innerNav.js (continued)

```
getSection : function(e) {
  var t = DOMhelp.getTarget(e);
  iv.showSection(t);
},
```

The showSection() method retrieves the link object that was either clicked or defined in the init() method as the parameter o. The first task is to read the href attribute of this link and retrieve the anchor name by deleting everything before and including the hash sign via a regular expression. You then retrieve the section to show by reading the element with the anchor ID and going up two nodes in the node tree.

innerNav.js (continued)

```
showSection : function(o) {
  var targetName = o.getAttribute('href').replace(/.*#/,'');
  var section = document.getElementById(targetName).parentNode.parentNode;
```

Why two nodes up? If you remember the HTML, you nested the links inside headings and nested the headings and the rest of the section inside DIV elements:

exampleLinkedAnchors.html (excerpt)

```
<li><a href="#demo">Demo</a></li>
[... code snipped ...]
<div class="infoblock">
  <h2><a id="demo" name="demo">Demonstration of what X can do</a></h2>
```

Because getElementById('demo') gives you the link, one node up is the H2 and another one up is the DIV.

You then need to check whether there is an old section shown and a link highlighted, and then remove the highlight and hide the section by removing the appropriate classes. Then add the classes for the current link and the current section, and set the properties current and currentLink, making sure that the next time showSection() is called it undoes what you did now.

innerNav.js (continued)

```
      if(iv.current != null){
        DOMhelp.cssjs('remove', iv.current, iv.showClass);
        DOMhelp.cssjs('remove', iv.currentLink, iv.currentLinkClass);
      }
      DOMhelp.cssjs('add', section, iv.showClass);
      DOMhelp.cssjs('add', o,iv.currentLinkClass);
      iv.current = section;
      iv.currentLink = o;
  }
}
DOMhelp.addEvent(window, 'load', iv.init, false);
```

If you apply this script to the demo HTML page and add an appropriate style sheet, you get a much shorter page showing the different sections when you click the links. You can see this for yourself by opening exampleLinkedAnchorsPanel.html in a browser. On MacOS in Firefox 17.0.1, the page looks like what you see in Figure 7-2.

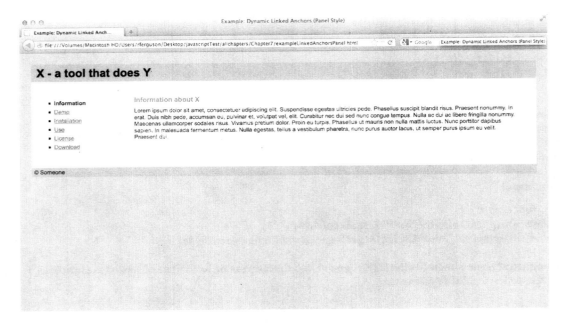

Figure 7-2. *A panel interface created from an anchor—target list*

Simply applying a different style sheet turns the page into a tabbed interface, as you can see in exampleLinkedAnchorsTabs.html and in Figure 7-3.

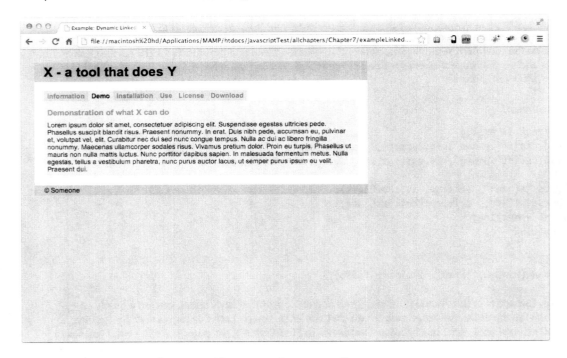

Figure 7-3. *A tabbed interface created from an anchor—target list*

This is pretty neat for a short script; however, cleaning up the link href and retrieving the section every time the user clicks one of the options seems repetitive.

A different approach to accomplishing the same task is to store the links and the sections in two associative arrays and simply provide showSection() with the name of the anchor to show and highlight. The demo exampleLinkedAnchorsTabsNamed.html uses this technique and shows how to apply a mouseover handler for the same effect at the same time.

innerNavNamed.js

```
iv = {
  // CSS classes
  dynamicClass : 'dyn',
  currentLinkClass : 'current',
  showClass : 'show',

  // IDs
  parentID : 'toolinfo',
  tocID : 'toolinfotoc',
```

The first change is that you need only one current property as well as two new array properties, called sections and sectionLinks, which will store the sections and links later on.

innerNavNamed.js (continued)

```
// Global properties
current : null,
sections : [],
sectionLinks : [],
init : function() {
  var targetName,targetElement;
  if(!document.getElementById || !document.createTextNode){
    return;
  }
  var parent = document.getElementById(iv.parentID);
  var toc = document.getElementById(iv.tocID);
  if(!parent || !toc) { return; }
  DOMhelp.cssjs('add', parent, iv.dynamicClass);
  var toclinks = toc.getElementsByTagName('a');
  for(var i = 0; i < toclinks.length; i++){
```

Add a mouseover handler in addition to the click, and store the href attribute in a property called targetName for each of the links in the menu.

innerNavNamed.js (continued)

```
DOMhelp.addEvent(toclinks[i], 'click', iv.getSection, false);
DOMhelp.addEvent(toclinks[i], 'mouseover', iv.getSection,false);
targetName = toclinks[i].getAttribute('href').replace(/.*#/,'');
toclinks[i].targetName = targetName;
```

Define the first link as the currently active link by storing it in the presetLink variable, and determine whether the anchor points to an existing element. If it does, store the element in the sections array and the link in the sectionLinks array. Note that this results in an associative array, which means you can reach the first section via section['info'].

innerNavNamed.js (continued)

```
  if(i == 0){ var presetLink = targetName; }
  targetElement = document.getElementById(targetName);
  if(targetElement) {
    iv.sections[targetName] = targetElement.parentNode.parentNode;
    iv.sectionLinks[targetName] = toclinks[i];
  }
}
```

Then you can obtain a possible anchor name from the URI hash and call showSection() initially either with that anchor name or with the one stored in presetLink.

innerNavNamed.js (continued)

```
  var loc = window.location.hash.replace('#', ' ');
  loc = document.getElementById(loc) ? loc : presetLink;
  iv.showSection(loc);
},
```

The getSection() event calls showSection() with the value of the targetName property of the link. This property was set in the init() method earlier.

innerNavNamed.js (continued)

```
getSection:function(e){
  var t = DOMhelp.getTarget(e);
  iv.showSection(t.targetName);
},
```

All of this makes showSection() a piece of cake, because all it needs to do to reset the last link and section and set the current ones is to use the arrays to reach the right elements and add or remove the CSS classes. The current section gets stored in one single property, called current, instead of properties for both the section and the link.

innerNavNamed.js (continued)

```
  showSection : function(sectionName){
    if(iv.current != null){
      DOMhelp.cssjs('remove', iv.sections[iv.current], iv.showClass);
      DOMhelp.cssjs('remove', iv.sectionLinks[iv.current], iv.currentLinkClass);
    }
    DOMhelp.cssjs('add', iv.sections[sectionName], iv.showClass);
    DOMhelp.cssjs('add', iv.sectionLinks[sectionName], iv.currentLinkClass);
    iv.current = sectionName;
  }
}
DOMhelp.addEvent(window, 'load', iv.init, false);
```

There are more options for in-page navigation—for example, you could offer "previous" and "next" links instead of "back" links to go through the options. If you want to see a script that does that and also offers several tabbed navigations per page, you can check out DOMtab at http://onlinetools.org/tools/domtabdata/.

Site Navigation

Web-site navigation is a different kettle of fish from page internal navigation. You must be tired of reading it by now, but there is just no good argument for navigation that is dependent on JavaScript. Yes, you can use JavaScript to send the user to other locations automatically, but it is not a safe method, because browsers like Opera and Mozilla allow users to prevent that. (Malicious web sites used redirection in the past to send the user to spam sites.) Furthermore, it strips you, as the site maintainer, of the opportunity to use site metrics software that counts hits and records how your visitors travel around the site, because not all metrics packages count JavaScript redirects.

For these reasons, site navigation is basically constrained to enhancing the functionality of the HTML structure of the menu and adding functionality to it via event handlers. The real redirection of the user to other pages still needs to happen via links or form submission.

One very logical HTML construct for a web-site menu is a nested list:

exampleSiteNavigation.html (excerpt)

```
<ul id="nav">
  <li><a href="#">Home</a></li>
  <li><a href="#">Products</a>
    <ul>
      <li><a href="#">CMS solutions</a>
        <ul>
          <li><a href="#">Mini CMS</a></li>
          <li><a href="#">Enterprise CMS</a></li>
        </ul>
      </li>
      <li><a href="#">Company Portal</a></li>
      <li><a href="#">eMail Solutions</a>
        <ul>
          <li><a href="#">Private POP3/SMTP</a></li>
          <li><a href="#">Listservers</a></li>
        </ul>
      </li>
    </ul>
  </li>
  <li><a href="#">Services</a>
    <ul>
      <li><a href="#">Employee Training</a></li>
      <li><a href="#">Auditing</a></li>
      <li><a href="#">Bulk sending/email campaigns</a></li>
    </ul>
  </li>
  <li><a href="#">Pricing</a></li>
  <li><a href="#">About Us</a>
    <ul>
      <li><a href="#">Our offices</a></li>
      <li><a href="#">Our people</a></li>
      <li><a href="#">Jobs</a></li>
```

```
      <li><a href="#">Industry Partners</a></li>
    </ul>
  </li>
  <li><a href="#">Contact Us</a>
    <ul>
      <li><a href="#">Postal Addresses</a></li>
      <li><a href="#">Arrange Callback</a></li>
    </ul>
  </li>
</ul>
```

The reason is that, even without any style sheet, the structure and the hierarchy of the navigation are obvious to the visitor. You can also style the navigation without much hassle, because all elements are contained in those higher up in the hierarchy, which allows for contextual selectors.

■ **Note** We're not going to discuss here whether it makes sense to offer every page of the site in the navigation (because this is traditionally the job of a site map). In the next chapter, we will revisit this topic and offer it as a choice to the user.

Basic web-site usability and common sense dictate that the currently shown page should not link to itself. To keep this from happening, replace the current page link with a STRONG element, which also means that users without CSS understand where they are in the navigation, and you get a chance to style the current page differently as part of the navigation without having to resort to CSS classes. Using a STRONG element instead of a SPAN also means that users without CSS get an obvious indicator of which item is the current one.

For example, on the Mini CMS page, the navigation would be as follows:

exampleHighlightedSiteNavigation.html (excerpt)

```
<ul id="nav">
  <li><a href="#">Home</a></li>
  <li><a href="#">Products</a>
    <ul>
      <li><a href="#">CMS solutions</a>
        <ul>
          <li><strong>Mini CMS</strong></li>
          <li><a href="#">Enterprise CMS</a></li>
        </ul>
      </li>
    </ul>
  </li>
```

You have to do this on the server side, because it wouldn't make sense to highlight the current page in JavaScript (which, of course, wouldn't be hard to do by comparing all the link href attributes with the window.location.href).

Expecting this HTML structure allows you to create an Explorer-like expanding and collapsing menu. A menu item that contains other items should show or hide its child items when you click it. However, the logic of the script is probably a bit different from what you'd expect. For starters, you don't have to loop through all the links of the menu. Instead, you do the following:

1. Add a CSS class to the main navigation item that hides all nested lists.

2. Loop through all UL items in the navigation (because those are the nested submenus).

3. Add a CSS class indicating that this list item contains other lists to the parent node of each UL.

4. Add a click event on the first link inside the parent node.

5. Test whether the parent node contains any STRONG elements, and add the class to show the UL if there is one—thus preventing the submenu the current page is in from being hidden. You replace the parent class with an open one to show that this section is already expanded.

6. The click event listener method needs to check whether the first nested UL of the parent node has the show class and remove it if that is the case. It should also replace the open class with the parent class. If there is no show class, it should do the exact opposite.

The demo document exampleDynamicSiteNavigation.html does this, with the Mini CMS page defined as the current page to show the effect. Figure 7-4 shows how this looks in Firefox 17.0.1 on MacOS.

Figure 7-4. *A tree menu with JavaScript and CSS*

The script's skeleton is rather short; you define all the necessary CSS classes as properties, the ID of the navigation as another property, and init() and changeSection() methods to apply the overall functionality and expand or collapse the sections accordingly.

siteNavigation.js (skeleton)

```
sn = {
  dynamicClass : 'dyn',
  showClass : 'show',
  parentClass : 'parent',
  openClass : 'open',
  navID : 'nav',
  init : function() {},
  changeSection : function(e) {}
}
DOMhelp.addEvent(window, 'load', sn.init, false);
```

The init() method defines a variable called triggerLink and checks for DOM support and whether the necessary navigation element is available before applying the dynamic class to hide the nested elements.

siteNavigation.js (excerpt)

```
init : function() {
  var triggerLink;
  if(!document.getElementById || !document.createTextNode) {
    return;
  }
  var nav = document.getElementById(sn.navID);
  if(!nav){ return; }
  DOMhelp.cssjs('add', nav, sn.dynamicClass);
```

It then loops through all the nested UL elements and stores a reference to the first link inside the parent node as triggerLink. It applies a click event calling the changeSection() method and adds the parent class to the parent node.

siteNavigation.js (continued)

```
var nested = nav.getElementsByTagName('ul');
for(var i = 0; i < nested.length; i++){
  triggerLink = nested[i].parentNode.getElementsByTagName('a')[0];
  DOMhelp.addEvent(triggerLink, 'click', sn.changeSection, false);
  DOMhelp.cssjs('add', triggerLink.parentNode, sn.parentClass);
  triggerLink.onclick = DOMhelp.safariClickFix;
```

The code tests whether the parent node contains a STRONG element and adds the show class to the UL and the open class to the parent node if that is the case. This prevents the current section from being hidden.

siteNavigation.js (continued)

```
    if(nested[i].parentNode.getElementsByTagName('strong').length > 0){
      DOMhelp.cssjs('add', triggerLink.parentNode, sn.openClass);
      DOMhelp.cssjs('add', nested[i], sn.showClass);
    }
  }
},
```

All the event listener method changeSection() needs to do is get the event target, test whether the first nested UL of the parent node has the show class applied to it, and remove that UL if that is the case. Furthermore, it needs to change the open class of the parent node to parent and vice versa.

siteNavigation.js (continued)

```
changeSection : function(e){
  var t = DOMhelp.getTarget(e);
  var firstList = t.parentNode.getElementsByTagName('ul')[0];
  if(DOMhelp.cssjs('check', firstList, sn.showClass)) {
    DOMhelp.cssjs('remove', firstList, sn.showClass)
    DOMhelp.cssjs('swap', t.parentNode, sn.openClass, sn.parentClass);
  } else {
    DOMhelp.cssjs('add', firstList,sn.showClass)
    DOMhelp.cssjs('swap', t.parentNode, sn.openClass, sn.parentClass);
  }
  DOMhelp.cancelClick(e);
  }
}
DOMhelp.addEvent(window, 'load', sn.init,false);
```

This script, applied to the right HTML and styled with an appropriate style sheet, will give you the expanding and collapsing navigation. The relevant parts of the CSS are as follows:

siteNavigation.css (excerpt)

```
#nav.dyn li ul{
  display:none;
}
#nav.dyn li ul.show{
  display:block;
}
#nav.dyn li{
  padding-left:15px;
}
#nav.dyn li.parent{
  background:url(plus.gif) 0 5px no-repeat #fff;
}
#nav.dyn li.open{
  background:url(minus.gif) 0 5px no-repeat #fff;
}
```

You can show and hide the nested UL elements by setting the values of their display properties to block and none, respectively. This also takes the contained links out of the normal tabbing order: keyboard users won't have to tab through all the links in the nested lists if they want to reach the next element on the same hierarchical level without expanding the section. If they press Enter first to expand the section, they will be able to navigate through the submenu links with the Tab key.

All LI elements get a left padding to allow for an indicator image to show that the section has child links or that it is open. The LI elements with the class open or parent get a background image to indicate their state.

All of this is pretty nice, but what if you want to provide a link to the parent pages of the nested sections? The solution is to add a new linked image before each of the parent links that does the showing and hiding and leaving the link as it is.

The demo page `exampleIndicatorSiteNavigation.html` shows what this looks like and how it works. The script does not have to change that much:

siteNavigationIndicator.js (excerpt)

```
sn = {
  dynamicClass : 'dyn',
  showClass : 'show',
  parentClass : 'parent',
  openClass : 'open',
```

The first change is that you need two new properties that provide the images to be added to the parent nodes of the nested lists. These will be added via `innerHTML` to make it easy for the maintainer to replace them with other images or even text if desired.

siteNavigationIndicator.js (continued)

```
parentIndicator : '<img src="plus.gif" alt="open section" title="open section">',
openIndicator: '<img src="minus.gif" alt="close section" title="close section">',
navID : 'nav',
init : function() {
  var parentLI, triggerLink;
  if(!document.getElementById || !document.createTextNode){
    return;
  }
  var nav = document.getElementById(sn.navID);
  if(!nav){ return; }
  DOMhelp.cssjs('add', nav,sn.dynamicClass);
  var nested = nav.getElementsByTagName('ul');
  for(var i = 0; i < nested.length; i++) {
```

Instead of taking the first link in the parent node as the trigger link, you create a new link element, set its `href` attribute to a simple hash to make it clickable, and add the parent indicator image defined earlier as its content. Then insert the linked image as the first child of the parent node.

siteNavigationIndicator.js (continued)

```
parentLI = nested[i].parentNode;
triggerLink = document.createElement('a');
triggerLink.setAttribute('href', '#')
triggerLink.innerHTML = sn.parentIndicator;
parentLI.insertBefore(triggerLink, parentLI.firstChild);
```

The rest of the `init()` method stays almost as it was, with the difference being that you not only apply the classes when the parent node contains a `STRONG` element, but also replace the "parent" indicator image with the "open" one.

siteNavigationIndicator.js (continued)

```
    DOMhelp.addEvent(triggerLink, 'click', sn.changeSection, false);
    triggerLink.onclick = DOMhelp.safariClickFix;
    DOMhelp.cssjs('add', parentLI, sn.parentClass);
```

```
    if(parentLI.getElementsByTagName('strong').length > 0) {
      DOMhelp.cssjs('add', parentLI, sn.openClass);
      DOMhelp.cssjs('add', nested[i], sn.showClass);
      parentLI.getElementsByTagName('a')[0].innerHTML = sn.openIndicator
    }
  }
},
```

The difference in the changeSection() method is that you need to ensure that the event target was a link and not the image by comparing the node name of the target with A.

siteNavigationIndicator.js (continued)

```
changeSection : function(e){
  var t = DOMhelp.getTarget(e);
  while(t.nodeName.toLowerCase() != 'a') {
    t = t.parentNode;
  }
```

The rest of the method stays the same with one difference—you change the content of the link in addition to applying the different classes.

siteNavigationIndicator.js (continued)

```
    var firstList = t.parentNode.getElementsByTagName('ul')[0];
    if(DOMhelp.cssjs('check', firstList, sn.showClass)) {
      DOMhelp.cssjs('remove', firstList, sn.showClass);
      DOMhelp.cssjs('swap', t.parentNode, sn.openClass, sn.parentClass);
      t.innerHTML = sn.parentIndicator;
    } else {
      DOMhelp.cssjs('add', firstList, sn.showClass)
      DOMhelp.cssjs('swap', t.parentNode, sn.openClass, sn.parentClass);
      t.innerHTML = sn.openIndicator;
    }
    DOMhelp.cancelClick(e);
  }
}
DOMhelp.addEvent(window, 'load', sn.init, false);
```

All of this is just one example of enhanced site navigation, and it is probably the easiest one to use. Making a multilevel drop-down navigation menu accessible, for example, that also works for mouse and keyboard users alike is an immense task that is not within the scope of this book, because it is very advanced DOM scripting.

Pagination

Pagination means that you cut down a large set of data into several pages. This is normally done on the back end, but you can use JavaScript to make it quicker to check a long list of elements.

A demo of pagination is examplePagination.html, which appears in Firefox 19.0.2 on MacOS as shown in Figure 7-5.

previous **1 to 5 of 22** next

ID	Artist	Album	Comment
1	Depeche Mode	Playing the Angel	They are back and finally up to speed again
2	Monty Python	The final Rip-Off	Double CD with all the songs
3	Ms Kittin	l.com	Good electronica
4	Bad Religion	No control	My first Concert ever
5	Skinny Puppy	Digital Brap	Massive Digipack with live songs and videos

previous **1 to 5 of 22** next

Figure 7-5. Paginating a large set of data rows

The content to be manipulated consists of a set of rows of the same HTML table, which has the class paginated.

examplePagination.html (excerpt)

```
<table class="paginated">
<thead>
  <tr>
    <th scope="col">ID</th>
    <th scope="col">Artist</th>
    <th scope="col">Album</th>
    <th scope="col">Comment</th>
  </tr>
</thead>
<tbody>
  <tr>
    <th>1</th>
    <td>Depeche Mode</td>
    <td>Playing the Angel</td>
    <td>They are back and finally up to speed again</td>
  </tr>
```

```
<tr>
  <th>2</th>
  <td>Monty Python</td>
  <td>The final Rip-Off</td>
  <td>Double CD with all the songs</td>
</tr>
[... and so on ...]
</tbody>
</table>
```

You used pagination in the last chapter in the slide-show example, although the example showed one item at a time. The logic of pagination with several items is much more complex, but this example should give you an insight to the tricks you can use:

- You hide all the table rows via CSS.

- You define how many rows should be shown on each page.

- You show the first rows and generate the pagination menu.

- This menu has a "previous" link and a "next" link, and it has a counter telling the user which slice of the data is to be shown and how many items there are in total.

- If the current slice is the first, the "previous" link should be inactive; if it is the last, the "next" link should be inactive.

- The "next" link increases the start value of the slice by the amount defined, and the "previous" link decreases the start value.

You will use several properties and five methods in this example. It is a good idea to comment the properties to make it easier for future maintainers to alter them to their needs.

pagination.js (skeleton)

```
pn = {
  // CSS classes
  paginationClass : 'paginated',
  dynamicClass : 'dynamic',
  showClass : 'show',
  paginationNavClass : 'paginatedNav',
  // Pagination counter properties
  // Number of elements shown on one page
  Increase : 5,
  // Counter: _x_ will become the current start position
  //          _y_ the current end position and
  //          _z_ the number of all data rows
  Counter : ' _x_ to _y_ of _z_  ',
  // "previous" and "next" links, only text is allowed
  nextLabel : 'next',
  previousLabel : 'previous',
```

You use one method to initialize the script, one to generate the extra links and elements that you need, one to navigate around the "pages" (that is, hide the current result set and show the next), one to show the current page, and one to alter the pagination menu.

```
  init : function(){},
  createPaginationNav : function(table){},
  navigate : function(e){},
  showSection : function(table, start){},
  changePaginationNav : function(table, start){}
}
DOMhelp.addEvent(window, 'load', pn.init, false);
```

Grab a coffee and some cookies, because this is quite a script ahead of you. Don't worry though—most of it is simple logic.

The init() method checks whether DOM is supported and starts looping through all table elements in the document. It tests whether the table has the right class (defined in the pn.paginationClass property) and whether it has more rows than you want to show on each "page" (defined in the pn.increase property). If one of these is not the case, it skips the rest of the method—effectively not adding any menu.

pagination.js (excerpt)

```
init : function() {
  var tablebody;
  if(!document.getElementById || !document.createTextNode){
    return;
  }
  var ts = document.getElementsByTagName('table');
  for(var i = 0;i < ts.length; i++){
    if(!DOMhelp.cssjs('check', ts[i], pn.paginationClass)){
      continue;
    }
    if(ts[i].getElementsByTagName('tr').length < pn.increase+1){
      continue;
    }
```

Because the data rows you want to hide don't include the header row, but only those contained in the table body, you need to tell the other methods this.

The easiest option is to store only the relevant rows in a property of the table. You grab the first TBODY in the table and store all of its rows in a datarows property. You also store the number of all rows in datarowsize and initialize the current property as null.

This property will store the start of the page you want to show. By storing the rows and the number of rows as properties, you make it easier for other methods to retrieve information from the table without having to read out this information again from the DOM.

pagination.js (excerpt)

```
tablebody = ts[i].getElementsByTagName('tbody')[0];
ts[i].datarows = tablebody.getElementsByTagName('tr');
ts[i].datarowsize = ts[i].datarows.length;
ts[i].current = null;
```

Apply the dynamic class to the table and thus hide all the table rows. Call the createPaginationNav() method with a reference to the current table as a parameter to add the "previous" and "next" links, and call showSection() with the table reference and 0 as parameters to show the first result set.

pagination.js (excerpt)

```
    DOMhelp.cssjs('add', ts[i], pn.dynamicClass);
    pn.createPaginationNav(ts[i]);
    pn.showSection(ts[i], 0);
  }
},
```

The createPaginationNav() method does not contain any surprises; all it does is create the links and the counter and add the event handlers pointing to the navigate() method. You start by creating a new paragraph element and adding the pagination menu class to it.

pagination.js (excerpt)

```
createPaginationNav : function(table){
  var navBefore, navAfter;
  navBefore = document.createElement('p');
  DOMhelp.cssjs('add', navBefore, pn.paginationMenuClass);
```

Add a new link to the paragraph with the previousLabel property value as the text content and a new SPAN element that will display the number of the current result set in between the "previous" and "next" links. You preset the counter with 1 as the start value, the number of elements shown on each page as defined in pn.increase as the end value, and the number of all data rows as the total number. The last element to add to the new paragraph is the "next" link. You add the new paragraph immediately before the table via parentNode and insertBefore().

pagination.js (excerpt)

```
navBefore.appendChild(DOMhelp.createLink('#', pn.previousLabel));
navBefore.appendChild(document.createElement('span'));
counter=pn.counter.replace('_x_', 1);
counter=counter.replace('_y_', pn.increase);
counter=counter.replace('_z_', table.datarowsize-1);
navBefore.getElementsByTagName('span')[0].innerHTML = counter;
navBefore.appendChild(DOMhelp.createLink('#', pn.nextLabel));
table.parentNode.insertBefore(navBefore, table);
```

It would be good to show the same menu below the table as well. Instead of re-creating all these elements once more, it is enough to clone the paragraph and insert it after the table via parentNode, insertBefore(), and nextSibling. Then store the "previous" and "next" links of each paragraph as their own table properties to make it easier to change them in other methods.

pagination.js (excerpt)

```
navAfter = navBefore.cloneNode(true);

table.parentNode.insertBefore(navAfter, table.nextSibling);
table.topPrev = navBefore.getElementsByTagName('a')[0];
table.topNext = navBefore.getElementsByTagName('a')[1];
table.bottomPrev = navAfter.getElementsByTagName('a')[0];
table.bottomNext = navAfter.getElementsByTagName('a')[1];
```

You couldn't apply the event handlers earlier, because cloneNode() does not clone any handlers. Now you can apply all the handlers and the fixes for old versions of Safari to each of the links. The last change for this method is to store the counters in properties to make it easier for the other methods to update them.

pagination.js (excerpt)

```
    DOMhelp.addEvent(table.topPrev, 'click', pn.navigate, false);
    DOMhelp.addEvent(table.bottomPrev, 'click', pn.navigate, false);
    DOMhelp.addEvent(table.topNext, 'click', pn.navigate, false);
    DOMhelp.addEvent(table.bottomNext, 'click', pn.navigate, false);
    table.bottomNext.onclick = DOMhelp.safariClickFix;
    table.topPrev.onclick = DOMhelp.safariClickFix;
    table.bottomPrev.onclick = DOMhelp.safariClickFix;
    table.topNext.onclick = DOMhelp.safariClickFix;
    table.topCounter = navBefore.getElementsByTagName('span')[0];
    table.bottomCounter = navAfter.getElementsByTagName('span')[0];
},
```

The event listener method navigate() needs to check which link invoked it. The first step is to retrieve the event target via getTarget() and make sure it is a link by comparing its node name with A. (Remember, Safari likes to send the text node inside the link as the event target instead.)

pagination.js (excerpt)

```
navigate : function(e){
  var start, table;
  var t = DOMhelp.getTarget(e);
  while(t.nodeName.toLowerCase() != 'a'){
    t = t.parentNode;
  }
```

It then needs to check whether the link is active or not by testing whether it has an href attribute. (You will later turn the "next" or "previous" link off by removing the href attribute.) If there is none, it shouldn't do anything. The next task is to find the table from the link that is activated. Because there is navigation above and below the table, you need to check whether either the previous or next sibling node has the node name of table and define the variable table accordingly.

pagination.js (excerpt)

```
if(t.getAttribute('href') == null || t.getAttribute('href') == ' '){ return; }
if(t.parentNode.previousSibling && t.parentNode.previousSibling.nodeName.toLowerCase() == 'table') {
  table = t.parentNode.previousSibling;
} else {
  table = t.parentNode.nextSibling;
}
```

Then determine whether the activated link was either one of the "next" links or one of the "previous" links, and define start as the current property of the table plus or minus the defined increase accordingly. You call showSection() with the retrieved table and the start values as parameters.

pagination.js (excerpt)

```
  if(t == table.topNext || t == table.bottomNext){
    start = table.current + pn.increase;
  } else if (t == table.topPrev || t == table.bottomPrev){
    start = table.current - pn.increase;
  }
  pn.showSection(table, start);
},
```

The showSection() method calls the changePaginationNav() method to update the links and the counter and tests whether there is already a current parameter on the table. If there is one, this means data rows exist that need to be removed. You get rid of them by looping through the section of the data rows stored in the datarows property and removing the CSS class defined in showClass().

pagination.js (excerpt)

```
showSection : function(table, start){
  var i;
  pn.changePaginationNav(table, start);
  if(table.current != null){
    for(i=table.current; i < table.current+pn.increase; i++){
      if(table.datarows[i]) {
        DOMhelp.cssjs('remove', table.datarows[i], pn.showClass);
      }
    }
  }
```

You then loop from start to start plus the predefined increase, and you add the CSS class to show these rows in the table. Notice that you need to test whether these rows exist; otherwise, you might try to reach rows that aren't there on the last page. (Imagine a list of 22 elements; clicking the "next" link on the 16–20 page would try to show elements 21 to 25.) To make sure the right slice gets shown the next time the method gets called, all that is left is to define the current property as the start value.

pagination.js (excerpt)

```
  for(i = start; i < start + pn.increase; i++){
    if(table.datarows[i]) {
      DOMhelp.cssjs('add', table.datarows[i], pn.showClass);
    }
  }
  table.current = start;
},
```

As hinted earlier, the changePaginationNav() method renders the "previous" link on the first page and the "next" link on the last page inactive. The trick to making links appear but not clickable is to remove the href attribute.

On the first page, the start value minus the predefined increase would result in a negative number, which is easy to test. When the number is larger than 0, you add the href attribute again.

pagination.js (excerpt)

```
changePaginationNav : function(table, start){
  if(start - pn.increase < 0) {
    table.bottomPrev.removeAttribute('href');
    table.topPrev.removeAttribute('href');
  } else {
    table.bottomPrev.setAttribute('href', '#');
    table.topPrev.setAttribute('href', '#');
  }
```

If start plus the increase is bigger than the number of rows, you need to remove the "next" link; otherwise, you need to make it active.

pagination.js (excerpt)

```
if(start + pn.increase > table.rowsize - 2) {
  table.bottomNext.removeAttribute('href');
  table.topNext.removeAttribute('href');
} else {
  table.bottomNext.setAttribute('href', '#');
  table.topNext.setAttribute('href', '#');
}
```

Update the counter with the appropriate values. (Keep in mind that start needs a 1 added to it to make it easier to understand for humans, and you need to test that the last value is not larger than the number of existing rows). At this point, you have created a paginated interface from a normal data table.

pagination.js (excerpt)

```
    var counter = pn.counter.replace('_x_', start+1);
    var last = start + pn.increase;
    if(last > table.datarowsize){ last = table.datarowsize; }
    counter = counter.replace('_y_', last)
    counter = counter.replace('_z_', table.datarowsize)
    table.topCounter.innerHTML = counter;
    table.bottomCounter.innerHTML = counter;
  }
}
DOMhelp.addEvent(window, 'load', pn.init, false);
```

The logic of pagination stays the same, even if you decide to show and hide list items or other HTML constructs. You can make it even more complex by showing numbered steps in between the "previous" and "next" links instead of the counter, but I leave that to you to have a go at it.

Summary of Navigation with JavaScript

Powering a site's navigation with JavaScript is a very tempting use of your skills, because it is "out there" and still quite amazing for wowing clients with a fancy interface. The main thing to remember is that you should turn off JavaScript from time to time and see whether your interface still works. The same applies to not using your mouse but trying the keyboard instead.

You can use JavaScript to make large amounts of data, like deeply nested navigation menus, easier to grasp and presented to the user in bite-size chunks. However, don't forget that some users will get all of the navigation without your script cutting it up into smaller servings. It might be a good idea to make menu interfaces that use the whole site map as their data source optional rather than a given. We will take a look at how to do that in the next chapter.

The things you need to remember about JavaScript navigation are:

- Don't send the user to another location or send form data without the user clicking or activating an interface element. It is more confusing than helpful and might even be considered a security threat. (If you can do it, anyone else also can send the user to a site.)

- Hiding data does not make it disappear. Although you can make a lot of data easy to digest with a slick interface, some users will still get the whole lot in one serving, and all users—including those on slow connections—will have to download all of the data.

- It is much safer to piggyback on existing web-navigation patterns than to invent new ones. For example, it was quite easy, using links and anchors, to turn a working in-page navigation into a tabbed interface. Creating all the necessary tabs via JavaScript would have been a lot more hassle.

Forms and JavaScript

On the following pages, you'll learn how to access, read, and change forms and their elements. I will not go into the details of validating forms here, because I devoted Chapter 9 to the topic of data validation.

I will, however, touch on basic form usability, as well as some bad practices and why they should be avoided. First of all, let's take a look at the form used in some examples in this chapter and later on in the book:

exampleForm.html (excerpt)

```
<form method="post" action="send.php">
<fieldset>
  <legend>About You</legend>
  <p><label for="Name">Your Name</label></p>
  <p><input type="text" id="Name" name="Name" /></p>
  <p><label for="Surname">Your Surname</label></p>
  <p><input type="text" id="Surname" name="Surname" /></p>
  <p><label for="email">Your email</label></p>
  <p><input type="email" id="email" value="you@example.com" name="email"></p>
</fieldset>
<fieldset>
  <legend>Your message</legend>
  <p><label for="subject">Subject</label>
  <select id="subject" name="subject">
    <option value="generalEnquiry" selected="selected">General question</option>
    <option value="Webdesign">Webdesign</option>
    <option value="Hosting">Hosting</option>
    <option value="Training">Training</option>
    <option value="Partnership">Partnership</option>
    <option value="other">Other</option>
  </select></p>
  <p><label for="otherSubject">specify other subject</label>
  <input type="text" id="otherSubject" name="otherSubject" /></p>
```

```
  <p><label for="Message">Your Message</label></p>
  <p><textarea id="Message" name="Message" cols="20" rows="5"></textarea></p>
</fieldset>
<fieldset>
  <legend>Email options</legend>
  <p><input type="checkbox" name="copyMeIn" id="copyMeIn">
  <label for="copyMeIn">Send me a copy of this email to the above address</label></p>
  <p><input type="checkbox" name="newsletter" value="yes" id="newsletter">
  <label for="newsletter">Sign me up for the newsletter</label></p>
  <p>Newsletter format:
  <input type="radio" name="newsletterFormat" id="newsHtml" value="html" checked="checked">
  <label for="newsHTML">HTML</label>
  <input type="radio" name="newsletterFormat" id="newsPlain" value="plain">
  <label for="newsPlain">Text</label></p>
  <p class="submit"><input type="submit" value="Send Form"></p>
</fieldset>
</form>
```

■ **Note** As you can see, this is a valid form for an HTML 4 STRICT document, and all elements are closed for XHTML compliance if you want to go that way. Notice also that in XML-compliant HTML you need to write single attributes like `selected` and `checked` as `selected="selected"` and `checked="checked"`, respectively.

The form features fieldsets for grouping elements into logical units and labels for connecting explanation texts with specific form elements. This helps a lot with form accessibility, because it provides logical organization and avoids ambiguity.

Basics of Forms with JavaScript

Reaching and altering forms in JavaScript can be achieved in several ways. As always, there is the DOM scripting way of simply reaching the forms and their elements via `getElementsByTagName()` and `getElementById()`, but there is also an object called `forms` that contains all the forms in the current document.

This object allows you to reach the forms in the document in three ways:

- In an array where the index is an integer—for example, `document.forms[2]` for the third form.

- Via their name defined in the name attribute as an object—for example, `document.forms.myForm`.

- The same form array can also be accessed as an associative array or hash—for example, `document.forms['myForm']`. This is necessary when the name contains special characters or spaces, and you cannot notate it as an object.

Form Properties

The `forms` object itself has only one property, `length`, and it stores the number of forms in the document.

Each of the forms, however, has more properties you can use, all of which can be read and changed:

- `action`: The script the form data is sent to when the form is submitted

- `encoding`: The encoding of the form as defined in the `enctype` attribute of the FORM element

- method: The submission method of the form—either POST or GET

- name: The name of the form as defined in the name attribute (not in the id!)

- target: The target the form data should be sent to (which is important if you use frames or multiple windows)

Form Methods

The Form object has only two methods:

- reset(): Resets the form to its initial state, which means that all the entries and choices the user made get undone, and the form shows the initial values defined in the value, selected, or checked attributes of the individual elements. Be aware of the difference—reset() does not clear the form, but restores it to its initial state. This is the same effect a user gets when he activates a Reset button in the form.

- submit(): Submits the form.

Both methods simulate browser functionality—namely, activating a Reset or Submit button—and you should make sure that you don't use them to take away necessary interactivity from the user. There is a good reason that forms get submitted when the user clicks a Submit button or presses Enter on the keyboard—it is the most accessible way, and if you hijack this functionality and submit the form when users interact with other elements, you might force them to submit the form prematurely.

Form Elements

Every form in the forms collection has as a property called elements, which in essence is an array of all the form elements inside this form (as opposed to all HTML elements). You can reach the elements the same way you initially reach the forms, via the index number, via the object name, or as an associative array:

- var elm = document.forms[0].elements[2];

- var elm = document.forms.myForm.elements.myElement;

- var elm = document.forms.myForm.elements['myElement'];

As you can see in the preceding example, you can mix and match the notations. You can also use variables instead of the index numbers or the strings inside the brackets.

The elements collection itself has one read-only property called length. You could, for example, use this property to loop through all elements in a form and read out their type:

```
var myForm = document.forms[0];
var formElements = myForm.elements;
var all = formElements.length;
for(var i = 0; i < all; i++) {
  alert(formElements[i].type);
}
```

Each element inside the collection has several properties; which ones are supported is dependent on the type of the element. I'll now list all the properties and list the elements that support this property in parentheses. We'll go through the different elements in detail later on in this chapter:

- `checked`: Boolean indicating whether or not the element was selected (buttons, check boxes, radio buttons)

- `defaultChecked`: Boolean indicating whether or not the element was initially selected (check boxes, radio buttons)

- `value`: The value of the element as defined in the `value` attribute (all elements except select boxes)

- `defaultValue`: The initial value of the element (text boxes, text areas)

- `form`: The form the element resides in (read only—all elements)

- `name`: Name of the element (all elements)

- `type`: The type of the element (read only—all elements)

One special element type is the select box, which comes with a collection of its own, a property called `options`—but more on this later. Each element has a range of methods that is also dependent on the type of element. None of these methods expect any parameters.

- `blur()`: Takes the focus of the user agent away from the element (all elements)

- `focus()`: Puts the focus of the user agent on the element (all elements)

- `click()`: Simulates the user clicking the element (buttons, check boxes, file upload fields, Reset and Submit buttons)

- `select()`: Selects and highlights the text content of the element (password fields, text fields, and text areas)

Note   Notice that `click()` seems at first a bit odd, but it can be really helpful if you work on web applications, and the middle tier of your development environment does things to the submitting process of forms like Java Spring and .NET do. This is not a JS beginner's environment, though, so it falls outside the scope of this book.

HTML Attributes Not Contained in the Elements Collection

In addition to using the properties of the `elements` collection, you can read and set (browser settings permitting, of course) the attributes of the element in question once you reach it via the `forms` and `elements` collections. For example, you could change the size of a text field by changing its `cols` and `rows` attributes:

```
var myTextBox = document.forms[0].elements[2];
if (myTextBox.type == 'textarea'){
  myTextBox.rows = 10;
  myTextBox.cols = 30;
}
```

Tip It is a good idea to check the type of the element you are manipulating before trying to set attributes on it, in case they are not available for this element. A SELECT element, for example, does not have cols or rows attributes.

Globally Supported Properties

All form elements initially supported the type, name, form, and value properties. One recent change is that file upload fields do not support setting value any longer, because it would allow a malicious scripter to inject her own files to upload to your server when a user on an infected computer uploads something.

Using form can be quite handy to reach the parent form when you access an element directly via DOM methods. For example, by accessing the e-mail field in the example form via the DOM:

```
var mail = document.getElementById('email');
```

You can reach the form to change one of its properties or submit it either via mail.form or via mail.parentNode.parentNode.parentNode.

exampleForm.html (excerpt)

```
<form method="post" action="send.php">
<fieldset>
  [... code snipped ...]
  <p><input type="text" id="email" value="you@example.com" name="email"></p>
</fieldset>
  [... code snipped ...]
</form>
```

Depending how deep the element is nested in the form, using form can save you a lot of trouble when counting the nodes and actually makes the script easier to maintain because you are independent of the HTML. If you want to use node traversal exclusively, you could also use a recursive loop that checks the nodeName of the parent node to achieve the same independence of the HTML markup:

```
var mail = document.getElementById('email');
parentForm = mail.parentNode;
while(parentForm.nodeName.toLowerCase() != 'form') {
  parentForm = parentForm.parentNode;
}
```

Using blur() and focus()

You can use blur() to take the user agent's focus away from an element or use focus() to set it. The danger of this is that blur() does not take any target it should set the focus to, which means that user agents might focus on the next element, the location bar of the browser, or whatever else they please. For a sighted user with a mouse, this is not much of an issue; however, blind users relying on assistive technology or keyboard users will have a problem finding their way around the document again.

You might encounter something like this when you look through the code of some web sites:

```
<a href="#" onclick="dothings();" onfocus="this.blur()">Home</a>
```

Developers used to do this to stop browsers from showing a blue box or a dotted border around the current link. This is a very bad idea, because a keyboard user wouldn't know which element she is currently able to reach when pressing Enter.

There are some legitimate reasons to use focus(); however, in most cases, it is not a good idea to alter the automatic order of form entry. Not every user can see the form, and even users who can see might not look at it.

Especially with longer forms that require a lot of different data to be entered, you'll find that people don't look at the screen, but touch-type as they read the data from a printout or their credit card, passports, and so on. It is pretty frustrating to check the form in between and realize you didn't fill out the right fields or you are still stuck at an error message that popped up earlier.

Text Fields, Text Areas, Hidden Fields, and Password Fields

Text fields, text areas, hidden fields, and password fields are probably the most common fields you will have to deal with, because they are the ones that users enter text content in.

In addition to supporting the global form element properties, they also support the element properties value and defaultValue. The difference is that if a user changes the content of the element, it changes the value property but not the defaultValue. This also means that when you change the value of the field, the change is visible, but when you change the defaultValue, it isn't. If you want to change the element's default value and make it visible, you need to call the reset() method immediately afterward. In the example document, you have a default value on the e-mail field:

```
<p><input type="text" id="email" value="you@example.com"  name="email"></p>
```

You could read the value and the default value like this:

```
var mail= document.getElementById('email');
alert(mail.defaultValue);
alert(mail.value);
```

When the user hasn't changed anything on the field, both values would be you@example.com. However, if the user enters me@otherexample.com in the field, the two values become different.

It is tricky to find an example for defaultValue that does not require you to do something with JavaScript that should be the job of the back end. One example is to test whether the current domain is German and change the default of the e-mail field to a German e-mail address. The following code should be executed when the document has loaded:

```
var mail = document.getElementById('email');
if(window.location.host.indexOf('.de') != -1) {
  mail.defaultValue = 'email@adresse.de';
  mail.form.reset();
}
```

Notice that you need to call reset() to make the change visible. You can see the change happening in exampleFormGermanPreset.html. (I cheated there to make it visible by excluding the host test.)

■ **Note** For TEXTAREA elements, you read and write the value and defaultValue just like for any other form text element. However, the HTML tag has no value attribute—the initial value and the changed value is the text contained in between the opening and closing tags.

Text elements allow for a method called `select()`, which highlights all the text inside them to make it easier to copy and paste text examples. This is often seen as a feature in webzines or online documentation systems.

Check Boxes

Check boxes are a great way to offer an unambiguous "yes" or "no" choice. They are very easy to read out on the server side. (The form sends the name of the box with the value of the check box if there is one, or it uses "on" if there is none, and it doesn't send the name at all when the user hasn't selected the box.) It's much easier to use than, for example, a radio button group or a select box with "yes" and "no" options.

In addition to having the global element properties described earlier, check boxes have the properties `checked` and `defaultChecked`, which are both Boolean values indicating whether the option was chosen. You can read and write both of these properties, but you need to reset the form to make changes to `defaultChecked` visible.

One common use of JavaScript in connection with check boxes is offering the user the opportunity to select all check boxes or reverse the choices made in a lot of check boxes—one example is how they are used in web-based e-mail systems, as shown in Figure 7-6. The logic of these functions is pretty simple: you loop through all elements, test the `type` of each one, and change the `checked` attribute accordingly. You can see a demo of this in `exampleFormCheckboxes.html`.

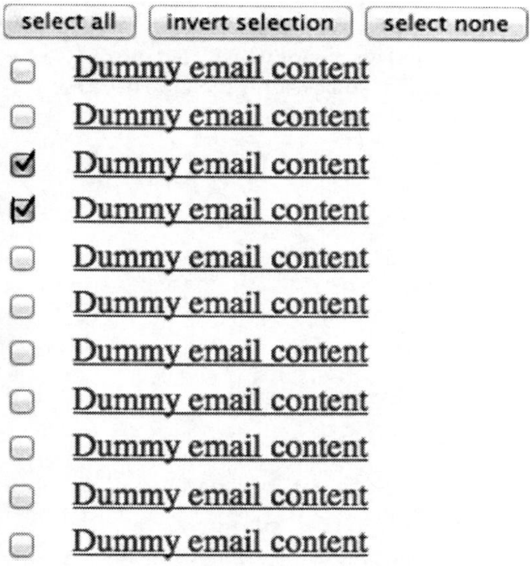

Figure 7-6. Bulk changing of check boxes via JavaScript

There are three buttons in the example that call the same function—`changeBoxes()`—when the user clicks them. Each button supplies a different numeric value for the function's sole parameter—1 for select all, -1 for invert, and 0 for select none.

exampleFormCheckboxes.html (excerpt)

```
<input type="button" onclick="changeBoxes(1)" value="select all">
<input type="button" onclick="changeBoxes(-1)" value="invert selection">
<input type="button" onclick="changeBoxes(0)" value="select none">
```

This allows you to keep the function to change the check boxes simple. Simply loop through all the elements in the first form found in the page. If the element type is not checkbox, continue the loop without executing the rest of it.

If the element is a check box, determine whether action is smaller than 0 and reverse the check-box state by changing checked to false when it is true and vice versa. If the action is 0 or larger, simply set the checked property to the value of action.

exampleFormCheckboxes.js (excerpt)

```
function changeBoxes(action) {
  var f = document.forms[0];
  var elms = f.elements;
  for(var i = 0; i < elms.length; i++) {
    if(elms[i].type != 'checkbox'){ continue; }
    if(action < 0){
      elms[i].checked = elms[i].checked ? 0 : 1;
    } else {
      elms[i].checked = action;
    }
  }
}
```

If this is confusing, remember that the checked property is a Boolean value. This means when it is true or 1, the check box is selected, and when it is false or 0, the check box is not selected. If you use only the true or false keywords, you have to add another case in the else condition (via the ternary notation in this case):

```
function changeBoxes(action) {
  var f = document.forms[0];
  var elms = f.elements;
  for(var i = 0; i < elms.length; i++){
    if(elms[i].type != 'checkbox'){ continue; }
    if(action < 0){
      elms[i].checked = elms[i].checked ? false : true;
    } else {
      elms[i].checked = action == 1 ? true : false;
    }
  }
}
```

Using the ternary operator, you could even reduce the whole check-box logic part of the script to one line:

```
function changeBoxes(action) {
  var f = document.forms[0];
  var elms = f.elements;
  for(var i = 0; i < elms.length; i++){
    if(elms[i].type != 'checkbox'){ continue; }
    elms[i].checked = action < 0 ? (elms[i].checked ? 0 : 1) :action;
  }
}
```

Because a lot of complex form code is not necessarily created by client-side-oriented developers, there is a high likelihood you will encounter this type of construct, which is why I took the opportunity here to show it to you.

Radio Buttons

Radio buttons are called that because they look like the dials on old radios, in case you wondered. They act like check boxes, with the difference being that they belong to one group with the same name, and the user can choose only one. Radio buttons are very easy to use for mouse and keyboard users alike, and they are a good replacement for short select boxes in case you ever run into problems using a select box.

They have the same Boolean checked and defaultChecked properties as check boxes, but they will automatically set the checked property of the other choices to false when you set one. Again, you can read and write both checked and defaultChecked, and you need to reset the form to make changes to defaultChecked appear visually. Because the example HTML has a radio group of only two options, let's use a different example:

exampleFormRadioGroup.html (excerpt)

```
<form method="post" action="send.php">
  <fieldset>
    <legend>Step 1 of 3 - Your favourite Character </legend>
     <p>
       <input type="radio" name="character" id="charC" value="Calvin" checked="checked">
       <label for="charC">Calvin</label>
     </p>
     <p>
       <input type="radio" name="character" id="charH" value="Hobbes">
       <label for="charH">Hobbes</label>
   </p>
   <p>
       <input type="radio" name="character" id="charSd" value="Susie Derkins">
       <label for="charSd">Susie Derkins</label>
   </p>
   <p>
     <input type="radio" name="character" id="charS" value="Spaceman Spiff">
     <label for="charS">Spaceman Spiff</label>
   </p>
   <p>
     <input type="radio" name="character" id="charSm" value="Stupendous Man">
     <label for="charSm">Stupendous Man</label>
   </p>
  </fieldset>
  <p class="submit"><input type="submit" value="Next Step"></p>
</form>
```

> **Note** This is also a good opportunity to show the difference between name and id. Although a group of radio buttons all share the same name (in this case, character), they each must get a unique id to allow the labels to be connected with them. Labels are handy not only for assistive technology like screen readers, but they also make the form much easier to use, because users can click the names next to the check boxes to select them.

The demo HTML includes some buttons to show the output of the JavaScript; you can test it out by opening it in a browser. The script shows how you can deal with radio buttons:

formRadioGroup.js

```
function setChoice(n) {
  var f = document.forms[0];
  f.character[n].checked = true;
}
function getChoice() {
  var f = document.forms[0];
  var choices = f.elements.character;
  for(var i = 0; i < choices.length; i++){
    if(choices[i].checked){ break; }
  }
  alert('Favourite Character is: ' + choices[i].value);
}
```

You can access the radio button group as an array with the shared name (in this case, character). Setting an option of a radio group is pretty straightforward: the setChoice() function takes a number as a parameter (n), reads the first form (forms[0]), and sets the checked property of the n-th character item to true.

formRadioGroup.js (excerpt)

```
function setChoice(n) {
  var f = document.forms[0];
  f.character[n].checked = true;
}
```

If you click the Set Choice To Hobbes button in the example, you see that the highlighted radio button changes, as shown in Figure 7-7.

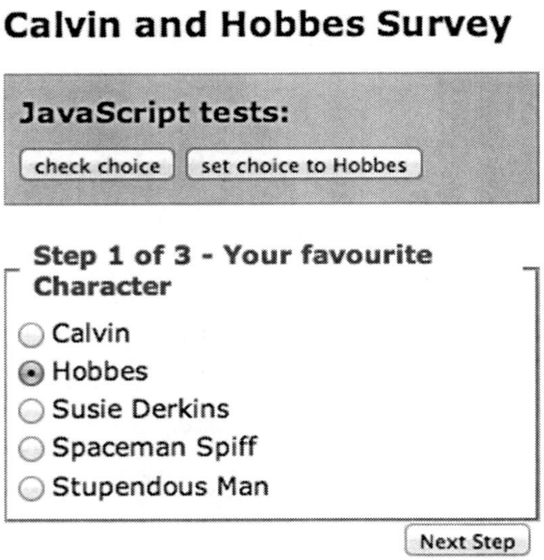

Calvin and Hobbes Survey

JavaScript tests:

[check choice] [set choice to Hobbes]

Step 1 of 3 - Your favourite Character

○ Calvin
◉ Hobbes
○ Susie Derkins
○ Spaceman Spiff
○ Stupendous Man

[Next Step]

Figure 7-7. *Changing the selected option in a radio group*

Reading the currently selected choice is just as easy: you select the first form, store the characters list in a new variable called choices, and loop through it. Then you test the checked property of each of the elements in the array and break the loop when you find one that returns true. This is the currently selected radio choice: there can be only one that is selected in any group of radio buttons sharing the same name.

formRadioGroup.js (continued)

```
function getChoice() {
  var f = document.forms[0];
  var choices = f.elements.character;
  for(var i = 0; i < choices.length; i++) {
    if(choices[i].checked){ break; }
  }
  alert('Favourite Character is: ' + choices[i].value);
}
```

Buttons

There are three kinds of buttons in HTML: two that work without scripting, and one that was included in the specifications to work only in conjunction with scripts.

Authors may create three types of buttons:

submit buttons: When activated, a submit button submits a form. A form may contain more than one submit button.

reset buttons: When activated, a reset button resets all controls to their initial values.

push buttons: Push buttons have no default behavior. Each push button may have client-side scripts associated with the element's event attributes. When an event occurs (e.g., the user presses the button, releases it, etc.), the associated script is triggered.

—http://www.w3.org/TR/REC-html40/interact/forms.html#buttons

This makes "push buttons"—which are either the input-type button or the button element—the perfect trigger element for JavaScript-only functionality.

The Reset and Submit buttons, on the other hand, are very important parts of the form and shouldn't be tampered with unless you really have a good reason for the change. One recurring request is to change the value or the state of the Submit button when the form is submitted to prevent impatient users from clicking the button twice. You could do this via a click handler; however, the better option is to use a submit handler on the form, because this also triggers the change when the form is submitted via the Enter key. Figure 7-8 shows how this might look.

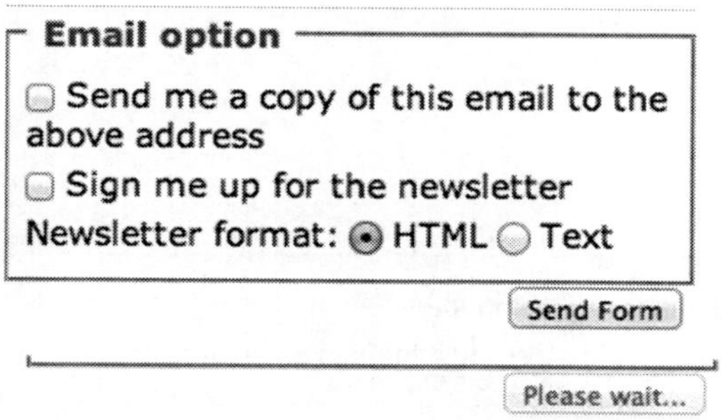

Figure 7-8. Changing the style and text content of a Submit button when the form gets sent

All you need to do to achieve this functionality is assign an event handler to the window that calls an `init()` function and another one that calls a `change()` function when the form is submitted.

This function loops through all the form elements (after retrieving the form via `getTarget()`) and checks whether the element is an image or a Submit button. If this is the case, it disables the button via the `disabled` attribute and changes the button value to `Please wait`:

exampleChangeSubmitButton.js

```
submitChange = {
  init : function() {
    DOMhelp.addEvent(document.forms[0], 'submit', submitChange.change,false);
  },
  change : function(e){
    var t = DOMhelp.getTarget(e);
    for(var i = 0; i < t.elements.length; i++){
      if(!/submit|image/.test(t.elements[i].type)) { continue; }
        t.elements[i].disabled = true;
        t.elements[i].value = 'Please wait... ';
    }
  }
}
DOMhelp.addEvent(window, 'load', submitChange.init ,false);
```

An image button defined via `<input type="image">` acts like a Submit button, the only difference is that it doesn't submit its name to the back end but two sets of name-value pairs, consisting of the original name followed by `.x` and `.y` and the coordinates the user clicked as the values. That way, you can perform different actions depending on where the button is clicked. This information is not readable via JavaScript, only on the back end.

From a JavaScript point of view, there is not much more you can do with an image input, except that you can provide a rollover state for it.

Select Boxes

Select boxes are probably the most complex and versatile of form elements. Designers love them because they can use select boxes to store a lot of options for the user to choose from in a small screen space.

Each select box has a list object called `options` that has several properties:

- `length`: The number of all options inside this select box.

- `selected`: Boolean if the option is selected by the user.

- `selectedIndex`: The index number of the selected element. If no element was selected, this returns −1 (which actually is a property of the `SELECT` element but is appropriate to mention here).

- `text`: The text content of the option.

- `value`: The value of the option.

Note Notice that `text` and `value` are properties of each of the options contained in the select box; you cannot read out the chosen value by reading the value property of the select box object itself—because there is no such thing.

There are two kinds of select boxes: single-choice select boxes that allow one exclusive choice, and multiple-choice select boxes that allow the user to choose more than one option by holding down Ctrl and highlighting the options desired.

Note Multiple-choice select boxes are a nightmare to use for users with assistive technology or keyboard users, which is why you might want to consider using a list of check boxes instead. This will also make it easier to read out the choice on the server side.

Reading out single-choice select boxes is pretty easy. For example, take the select box in the demo form:

exampleSelectChoice.html (excerpt)

```
<p>
  <label for="subject">Subject</label>
  <select id="subject" name="subject">
    <option value="generalEnquiry" selected="selected">General question</option>
    <option value="Webdesign">Webdesign</option>
    <option value="Hosting">Hosting</option>
    <option value="Training">Training</option>
    <option value="Partnership">Partnership</option>
    <option value="other">Other</option>
  </select>
</p>
```

The quickest way to reach the select box is to use the name of the element instead of the index. The reason is that the element type of select boxes could be either select-one or select-multiple, depending on whether or not the multiple attribute is set. Once you get to the correct object, you can use its selectedIndex property to read out the chosen option and display the value or the text of the option by using the selectedIndex as the list counter:

exampleSelectChoice.js (excerpt)

```
function checkSingle() {
  var f = document.forms[0];
  var selectBox = f.elements['subject'];
  var choice = selectBox.selectedIndex;
  alert('You chose ' + selectBox.options[choice].text)
}
```

In the case of multiple-choice select boxes, this isn't enough, because the user might have chosen more than one option (selectedIndex will return only the first choice).

Instead of using selectedIndex, you'll have to loop through all the options and test the selected property of each one:

exampleSelectChoice.js (excerpt)

```
function checkMultiple() {
  var f = document.forms[0];
  var selectBox = f.elements['multisubject'];
  var choices=[];
  for(var i = 0; i < selectBox.options.length; i++) {
```

```
      if(selectBox.options[i].selected == 1) {
        choices.push(selectBox.options[i].text);
      }
    }
  }
  alert(choices.join(', '));
}
```

You can reach the select box via its name in the elements collection and create a new array called choices. (The [] is a shortcut notation for new Array().) Loop through each of the options of the select box, and check whether its selected property is true. Where that is the case, push the option's text value as a new array item into choices. Then convert the array to a string using the array's join() method and display it.

This way of reading the values also works with a single-choice select box; however, it might be overkill depending on the number of options available. You can put both methods together in a more generic function by reading out the choices, depending on the type of the element:

exampleSelectChoice.js (excerpt)

```
function getSelectValue(fieldName) {
  var f = document.forms[0];
  var selectBox = f.elements[fieldName];
  if(selectBox.type == 'select-one') {
    var choice = selectBox.selectedIndex;
    alert('You chose ' + selectBox.options[choice].text);
  } else {
    var choices = [];
    for(var i = 0;i < selectBox.options.length; i++){
      if(selectBox.options[i].selected == 1) {
        choices.push(selectBox.options[i].text);
      }
    }
    choices.join(', ');
    alert(choices);
  }
}
```

Adding Options in a Select Box

Select boxes are unique as form elements go, because you can use them to add or remove options programmatically. You can add a new option by using the Option constructor and including it in the list of options:

```
extraOption = new Option(value, text, defaultSelected, selected);
```

If, for example, you want to add "DOM scripting" as a subject to the list, you can do so like this:

exampleSelectChoice.js (excerpt)

```
function addOption(fieldName) {
  var f = document.forms[0];
  var selectBox = f.elements[fieldName];
  var extraOption = new Option('DOM scripting', 'domscripting', 0, 0);
  selectBox.options[ selectBox.options.length ] = extraOption;
}
```

Removing and Replacing Options in a Select Box

You can remove an option by setting it equal to null:

exampleSelectChoice.js (excerpt)

```
function removeOption(fieldName,i) {
  var f = document.forms[0];
  var selectBox = f.elements[fieldName];
  selectBox.options[i] = null;
}
```

Replacing options is just as easy; simply set the old option to the new one:

exampleSelectChoice.js (excerpt)

```
function replaceOption(fieldName, i) {
  var f = document.forms[0];
  var selectBox = f.elements[fieldName];
  var extraOption = new Option('DOM scripting', 'domscripting', 0 ,0);
  selectBox.options[i] = extraOption;
}
```

Inserting an option before another option is a bit more problematic, because you need to copy all the options before you rewrite the options collection. The function insertBeforeOption() takes two parameters: the name of the form element and the index of the option you want to insert the new option before. You start by defining two loop counters, called i and j, and a blank array called opts before finding the select box and creating the new option.

exampleSelectChoice.js (excerpt)

```
function insertBeforeOption(fieldName, n) {
  var i = 0, j = 0, opts = [],
  var f = document.forms[0];
  var selectBox = f.elements[fieldName];
  var extraOption = new Option('DOM scripting', 'domscripting', 0,0);
```

Then store the options of the select box in a variable called old and loop through them, creating a new option for each of them and assigning their properties to the new option.

exampleSelectChoice.js (continued)

```
var old = selectBox.options;
for(i = 0; i < old.length; i++) {
  opts[i] = new Option(old[i].text, old[i].value, old[i].defaultSelected, old[i].selected);
}
```

The new list will be one element longer, which is why you increase the length property before looping through the new list. You test whether the loop counter is the same as the parameter sent to the function and insert the new option if this is the case.

exampleSelectChoice.js (continued)

```
old.length++;
for(i = 0; i < old.length; i++) {
  if(i == n) {
    old[i] = extraOption;
```

Otherwise, you set the option to the old option and increase the j counter variable. Notice you need a second counter here because you cannot change the variable i during the loop. Because the new option list will be one item bigger, you need to use j to get the value stored in the opts array.

exampleSelectChoice.js (continued)

```
    } else {
      old[i] = opts[j];
      j++;
    }
  }
}
```

Depending on the number of options in the select box, this could become a rather slow and demanding script. You can achieve the same effect a lot quicker and with less code by using the DOM:

exampleSelectChoice.js (excerpt)

```
function insertBeforeOptionDOM(fieldName, i) {
  var selectBox = document.getElementById(fieldName);
  if(!selectBox){ return false; }
  var opt = selectBox.getElementsByTagName('option');
  var extraOption = document.createElement('option');
  extraOption.setAttribute('value', 'domscripting');
  extraOption.appendChild(document.createTextNode('DOM Scripting'));
  selectBox.insertBefore(extraOption, selectBox.options[i]);
}
```

Select boxes are a big part of web application development and have traditionally been the interface for sorting two lists by moving elements back and forth.

Interactive Forms: Hiding and Showing Dependent Elements

One really cool thing about JavaScript and forms is that you can make forms a lot more engaging and dynamic than they are out of the box. It is tempting to make everything interact with each other and immediately send a form without expecting the user to click a Submit button or press Enter. The danger of this is not only do you sacrifice support for user agents other than visual ones, but also users might send data prematurely.

When it comes to simply changing the interface or the number of options displayed in a form, it is quite safe to use change handlers. Let's use the demo form as an example. You might have noticed that there are some fields that have a logical connection: the "other subject" text field makes sense only when the Other option has been selected, and the choice to receive the newsletter as HTML or plain text comes into play only when the user has chosen to subscribe to the newsletter.

exampleDynamicForm.html (excerpt)

```
<form method="post" action="send.php">
  [... code snipped ...]
  <p><label for="subject">Subject</label>
  <select id="subject" name="subject">
    <option value="generalEnquiry" selected="selected">General question</option>
    <option value="Webdesign">Webdesign</option>
    <option value="Hosting">Hosting</option>
    <option value="Training">Training</option>
    <option value="Partnership">Partnership</option>
    <option value="other">Other</option>
  </select></p>
  <p><label for="otherSubject">specify other subject</label>
  <input type="text" id="otherSubject" name="otherSubject"></p>
  [... code snipped ...]
  <p><input type="checkbox" name="newsletter" value="yes" id="newsletter">
  <label for="newsletter">Sign me up for the newsletter</label></p>
  <p>Newsletter format:
  <input type="radio" name="newsletterFormat" id="newsHtml" value="html" checked="checked">
  <label for="newsHTML">HTML</label>
  <input type="radio" name="newsletterFormat" id="newsPlain"  value="plain">
  <label for="newsPlain">Text</label></p>
```

With a script, you can hide these options and make them appear only when the user selects the appropriate option. Figure 7-9 shows how that looks in a browser.

Figure 7-9. Showing and hiding form elements based on user choices

241

You define a class to apply to the elements you want to hide and the IDs of the two dynamic elements as properties of a main object called df.

dynamicForm.js

```
df = {
  hideClass : 'hide',
  letterOption : 'newsletter',
  subjectOption : 'subject',
```

The init() method checks for DOM support and whether the necessary elements are available.

dynamicForm.js (continued)

```
init : function() {
  if(!document.getElementById || !document.createTextNode){
   return;
  }
  df.news = document.getElementById(df.letterOption);
  df.subject = document.getElementById(df.subjectOption);
  if(!df.subject || !df.news){ return; }
```

Next you need to find the elements to hide. By using the DOMhelp method closestSibling(), you can make sure you don't try to hide line breaks but that you hide the elements you actually want to reach. Store the elements in properties of the main object to make them accessible to the event handler methods.

You can hide the elements by adding the hiding class to them and assign a click event handler to the check box called letterChange() and a change handler to the select box called subjectChange().dynamicForm.js (continued)

```
  df.newsOpt = DOMhelp.closestSibling(df.news.parentNode, 1);
  df.subjectOpt = DOMhelp.closestSibling(df.subject.parentNode, 1);
  DOMhelp.cssjs('add', df.newsOpt, df.hideClass);
  DOMhelp.cssjs('add', df.subjectOpt, df.hideClass);
  DOMhelp.addEvent(df.news, 'click', df.letterChange, false);
  DOMhelp.addEvent(df.subject, 'change', df.subjectChange, false);
},
```

You retrieve the check box via getTarget() in the letterChange() method before testing its checked property. If the property is checked, you remove the hiding class; otherwise, you add it.

dynamicForm.js (continued)

```
letterChange : function(e){
  var t = DOMhelp.getTarget(e);
  var action = t.checked ? 'remove' : 'add';
  DOMhelp.cssjs(action, df.newsOpt, df.hideClass);
},
```

The subjectChange() method works the same way: you retrieve the target and check whether the fifth option is the selected one (that is, whether selectedIndex is equal to 4). If it is, you remove the hiding class from the optional element; otherwise,, you add it. As an extra, the method sets the focus of the browser to the newly shown element so that users can immediately start typing.

dynamicForm.js (continued)

```
  subjectChange : function(e) {
    var t = DOMhelp.getTarget(e);
    var action = t.selectedIndex == 5 ? 'remove' : 'add';
    DOMhelp.cssjs(action, df.subjectOpt, df.hideClass);
    if(action == 'remove') {
      df.subjectOpt.getElementsByTagName('input')[0].focus();
    }
  }
}
DOMhelp.addEvent(window, 'load', df.init, false);
```

Showing and hiding the connected elements is one way to connect parts of a form to other options. A different approach is to keep them visible but add a `disabled` attribute. This makes them impossible to change for the user, and the browser shows them grayed out.

This is a bit less versatile than just hiding elements, because the `disabled` attribute is only applicable to `input`, `textarea`, `select`, `option`, `optgroup`, and `button`. Figure 7-10 shows how the form looks with disabled elements in Firefox on Windows.

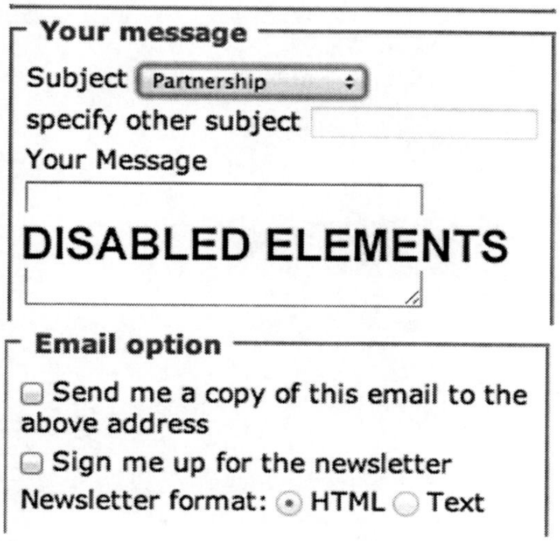

Figure 7-10. *Disabling elements instead of hiding them*

The main difference in the script is that you have to target each `input` element you want to disable individually. In the case of the radio buttons, this means that you have to go through a loop. The changes in the script are highlighted in bold and should be self-explanatory:

dynamicFormDisable.js

```
df = {
  hideClass : 'hide',
  letterOption : 'newsletter',
  subjectOption : 'subject',
```

243

```
  init : function() {
    if(!document.getElementById || !document.createTextNode){
     return;
    }
    df.news = document.getElementById(df.letterOption);
    df.subject = document.getElementById(df.subjectOption);
    if(!df.subject || !df.news){ return; }
    df.newsOpt = DOMhelp.closestSibling(df.news.parentNode, 1);
    df.newsOpt = df.newsOpt.getElementsByTagName('input');
    for(var i = 0; i < df.newsOpt.length; i++){
      df.newsOpt[i].disabled = 1;
    }
    df.subjectOpt = DOMhelp.closestSibling(df.subject.parentNode, 1);
    df.subjectOpt = df.subjectOpt.getElementsByTagName('input')[0];
    df.subjectOpt.disabled = 1;
    DOMhelp.addEvent(df.news, 'click', df.letterChange, false);
    DOMhelp.addEvent(df.subject, 'change', df.subjectChange, false);
  },
  letterChange : function(e){
    var i;
    var t = DOMhelp.getTarget(e);
    var disable = t.checked ? false: true ;
    for(i = 0; i < df.newsOpt.length; i++) {
      df.newsOpt[i].disabled = disable;
    }
  },
  subjectChange : function(e){
    var t = DOMhelp.getTarget(e);
    if(t.selectedIndex == 5) {
      df.subjectOpt.disabled = null;
      df.subjectOpt.focus();
    } else {
      df.subjectOpt.disabled = 1;
    }
  }
}
DOMhelp.addEvent(window, 'load', df.init, false);
```

The practical upshot of using `disabled` is that these elements cannot be reached via tabbing any longer either—something that is still possible with elements that are hidden (unless you hide them by setting `display` to none as shown earlier in the site-navigation section).

Custom Form Elements

Given enough skill and testing time, you can use JavaScript to extend the normal form controls browsers provide, thereby giving the users your own custom controls, and even make them keyboard accessible. Especially in web application development, this might be a true necessity.

HTML5 has added new input types that give forms much more functionality. Some of the types include `tel`, `search`, and `email`. Validation has also become much better with options like the `required` attribute for `input`, `select`, and `textarea` tags.

Summary of Forms and JavaScript

I hope this chapter gave you insight as to what is possible with forms and JavaScript. You learned about the different properties and methods of forms themselves and each of the elements that they might contain with their individual properties and methods. You saw in detail how to deal with select boxes and how you could make a form more dynamic by hiding elements that are dependent on others and showing them only when the other elements are activated or have the right value.

The main things to remember about forms and JavaScript are:

- Try not to go overboard with what you do with forms. See whether the form is still usable with a keyboard once you're done spicing it up. In particular, longer forms are more likely to be filled out by tabbing from field to field rather than by clicking the different elements and then editing them.

- Don't automatically submit a form with an event handler—forms can be submitted by having the user click the Submit button or press Enter. Don't take these options away from the user.

- Although the older form collections forms and elements are not up-to-date DOM scripting techniques (because they are HTML dependent, whereas all the other DOM methods could also be applied to an XML string), they might be the easier options to use on generic or generated forms where you cannot control the IDs or the number of elements. Looping through one elements list is a lot easier than looping through all child elements of a form and comparing them with the possible element names or looping through the input, textarea, and select element collections individually.

Summary

You now should be able to handle the most common uses of JavaScript. You can come back to this chapter and the previous one when you need to refresh your memory about how to deal with images, windows, navigation, and forms.

In the next chapter, we will leave the world of browser and client-side scripting and focus on how we can make JavaScript talk to the back end and server-side scripts. This will also enable you to take a look at Ajax.

■ ■ ■

CHAPTER 8

Back-End Interaction with Ajax and Node.js

You finally reached the chapter where I talk about Ajax. The good news is you can use Ajax to create really nice, slick interfaces, and you can extend JavaScript's reach much further than the browser and the currently displayed document.

The not-so-good news is that Ajax depends on the XMLHTTPRequest object (or XHR for short) or its Microsoft equivalent, and that one has "HTTP" written all over it. What this means is that you cannot use any Ajax examples without a server. Furthermore, you need some basic knowledge of server-side scripting to use Ajax (unless you use one of the out-of-the-box packages available—more on those in the "Summary" section of the chapter).

It also means that using Ajax robs JavaScript of one of its strengths: the ability to create interfaces that work offline and on the file system of a computer, or even from a CD or memory stick. However, the benefits of Ajax make up for this.

The other part of this chapter is an introduction to *Node.js*, or *Node*. Node gives the JavaScript developer the ability to write code on the server side. Similar to Ruby or PHP, Node lets you talk to the database and send information to the client side of your application. In the example in this chapter, you will create an HTTP server entirely from JavaScript.

To get started, you need to set up a local server, because the Ajax examples are using PHP as their server-side language. This is not as tough as it seems because there are a lot of prepackaged servers available.

My favorite is XAMPP, which can be downloaded at http://www.apachefriends.org/. You can get an installer and follow the instructions to have your own server up and running in a matter of minutes.

XAMPP installs Apache 2, MySQL, PHP, and all the add-ons you will ever need and is available for many platforms. It also comes with an FTP and e-mail server, a statistics package, and many more options, and it is constantly kept up to date by the maintainers of Apache Friends (http://www.apachefriends.org). Oh and yes, it is free, of course.

■ **Tip**   Again, to avoid frustration when working with the rest of the chapter, you should try out for yourself the many code examples in this chapter to see what I am talking about. The difference compared to the other chapters is that the code examples will not work locally on a computer on the file system; they require a server, because Ajax needs the HTTP protocol to work. If you don't want to install a server but you are online, you can go to this book's home page at http://www.beginningjavascript.com/, where you'll be able to see all the code examples in action.

When you install XAMMP, you can unpack the chapter examples in a directory—called, for example, jsbook—in the htdocs directory of the server installation, which could be c:\xammp\htdocs\. To see the examples, you open a browser and type in http://localhost/jsbook/ as the location.

■ **Tip** In addition to reading the official help FAQs at http://www.apachefriends.org/en/faq-xampp.html, Mac users can use MAMP, which does the same thing. You can download MAMP at http://www.mamp.info.

Household Cleaning Liquid, Football Club, or Flash Gordon's Spacecraft: What Is Ajax?

Ajax originally stood for *Asynchronous JavaScript and XML*, a term that was coined by Jesse James Garrett at Adaptive Path in February 2005 (http://www.adaptivepath.com/publications/essays/archives/000385.php). It describes a methodology of developing web applications that's different from the traditional one.

As explained in the article, traditional web apps and sites work synchronously—every time you follow a link or submit a form, the browser sends the data to the server, the server (hopefully) responds, and the whole page gets refreshed.

Ajax applications work *asynchronously*, which means that you send data back and forth between the user agent and the server without reloading the whole page. You replace only the parts of the page that change. You can also send several requests and go on scrolling and using the page while the other parts load in the background.

One good comparison is that Ajax is to traditional web pages what instant messaging is to e-mail messages: immediate feedback, with no long waiting times and with more options to communicate. Figure 8-1 shows the flow of Ajax applications compared to traditional web sites and web applications.

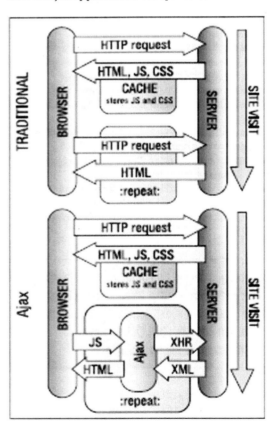

Figure 8-1. *Ajax vs. traditional request*

At first glance, this appears to add an extra layer of complexity to the whole matter. However, the really cool thing about it is that the communication between the Ajax engine and the browser is triggered via JavaScript and not via page reloads.

In practical terms, the end user spends less time waiting for pages to load and render and interacts more easily with the page, because she can request data and still read the text or look at the other content on the page. This makes for a much slicker interface, because you could, for example, give feedback on a login form without changing the whole site, while being able to test for the right entries on the server or in a database.

Let's have a go at a simple example. The demo file exampleXHR.html uses Ajax (well, without the X, because there is no XML involved) to load and display files from the server when the user clicks a link, as shown in Figure 8-2.

Figure 8-2. *Loading external files via Ajax*

The magic wand behind all of this is an object I introduced earlier called XMLHttpRequest. This is a nonstandard object because it is not part of an official standard on the World Wide Web Consortium (W3C) web site. (It is a working draft at the moment; for more detail see http://www.w3.org/TR/XMLHttpRequest/.) However, it is supported across all modern browsers. If you need to support Internet Explorer 6, you should look for the ActiveXObject that will do the same thing: ActiveXObject("Microsoft.XMLHTTP").

■ **Caution**   The problem with this is when a user has JavaScript enabled but ActiveX disabled in Microsoft Internet Explorer, he won't be able to experience your Ajax efforts. Keep this in mind if you create Ajax solutions and get user bug reports.

Let's go through the example step by step so that you can see what the different parts do. The HTML contains links pointing to text files and calls the simplexhr.doxhr method with two parameters: an ID of an HTML element to send the text to and the URL of the text.

exampleXHR.html (excerpt)

```
<li>
    <a href="perfect_day.txt"
       onclick="simplexhr.doxhr('txtcontainer1', this.href ); return false;">Perfect Day</a>
</li>
<li>
    <a href="great_adventure.txt"
       onclick="simplexhr.doxhr('txtcontainer1', this.href ); return false;">Great Adventure</a>
</li>
```

▪ **Note** These links are not totally unobtrusive and up to the standard of the rest of the code examples in this book, but at least they work without JavaScript—the browser will simply show the text files when scripting is not available. It is very tempting, especially when using out-of-the-box Ajax libraries, to create scripting-dependent links. No matter how cool the technology is, this is never a good idea.

simpleXHR.js

```
simplexhr = {
  doxhr : function( container, url ) {
    if( !document.getElementById || !document.createTextNode) {
      return;
    }
    simplexhr.outputContainer = document.getElementById( container );
    if( !simplexhr.outputContainer ){ return; }
```

The script starts by checking for the DOM and checking whether the element you want to write content into is available. If the element is available, it gets stored in a property called outputContainer to make it available for all other methods in the script.

simpleXHR.js (continued)

```
var request;
try{
  request = new XMLHttpRequest();
} catch ( error ) {
  try {
    request = new ActiveXObject("Microsoft.XMLHTTP" );
  } catch ( error ) {
    return true;
  }
}
```

Define a new variable called request and use the try and catch construct to see which XHR version is supported. Try assigning a new XMLHttpRequest. If that is not supported, an error occurs that triggers the catch statement. (You can learn more about try and catch() in the appendix of this book.) This one tries to assign the Microsoft ActiveX object instead. If that is not available either, the method returns true, which means the browser will just follow the link and show the text in the browser.

If the assignment was successful, you have a new XMLHttpRequest object at your disposal.

▪ **Note** For a complete list of methods, handlers, and properties of the XMLHttpRequest object, you can consult the documentation at the W3C site: http://www.w3.org/TR/XMLHttpRequest/. You can also refer to the Mozilla Developer Network at https://developer.mozilla.org/en-US/docs/DOM/XMLHttprequest or the Microsoft web site at http://msdn.microsoft.com/en-us/library/ms535874%28v=vs.85%29.aspx.

The first step is to call the open() method to start the connection with the server and retrieve or send data. The open() method takes five parameters, three of which are optional:

```
request = open(requestMethod, url[, sync, [name, [password]]]);
```

- The requestMethod parameter (among some other options beyond the scope of this chapter) can be either GET or POST and corresponds to HTTP methods.
- The url parameter is the location of the file on your server.

▓ **Note** XMLHttpRequest does not allow you to load content from other servers, because that would be a big security problem. Imagine any JavaScript embedded in an e-mail or web site being able to send off any data from your computer or retrieve more code from a server. There are solutions to this problem. One is to load third-party content by using a proxy script on the server. Another is to enable cross-origin resource sharing (CORS) on the server. Information about CORS can be found on the W3C site at http://www.w3.org/TR/cors/.

- The sync parameter is optional and is a Boolean that defines whether the request should be sent asynchronously or synchronously. It is hard-wired to true—which means the request will be sent asynchronously. Synchronous requests would lock up the browser.
- The name and password parameters are optional and necessary only when the file you try to call requires user authentication.

In this case, you will retrieve files only from the server. To do that, you use GET as the request method and the file's location as the url parameter, omitting the optional parameters.

simpleXHR.js (continued)

```
request.open('get', url );
```

The readyState property of the request object contains a numeric value that describes what is happening to the request. It is incremented throughout the request and response. The different possible values for readyState and their corresponding request states are as follows:

- **0:** The object was created, but the open method has not been called yet.
- **1:** The send method was not been called yet.
- **2:** The send method was called, but the data isn't available yet.
- **3:** The server is sending data.
- **4:** The connection is complete—the data was sent and retrieved.

Every time the status changes, XHR triggers a readystatechange event. You can use the corresponding onreadystatechange event handler to invoke a function in which you can test against the possible values of readyState and take the appropriate action.

simpleXHR.js (continued)

```
request.onreadystatechange = function() {
  if( request.readyState == 1 ) {
    simplexhr.outputContainer.innerHTML = 'loading... ';
  }
```

Once the request is initialized (readyState equals 1), it is a very good idea to give the user some feedback that there are things happening in the background. In this example, the script displays a "loading..." message inside the HTML output element, as shown in Figure 8-3.

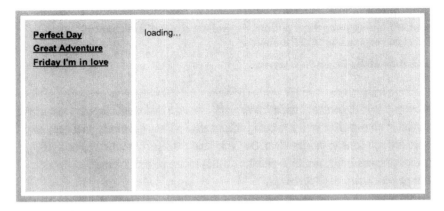

Figure 8-3. *Notifying the user that the request was sent and is under way*

The other states cannot be read safely cross-browser, which is why you skip 2 and 3 and check whether the request was finished by comparing readyState with 4.

simpleXHR.js (continued)

```
if( request.readyState == 4 ) {
  if ( /200|304/.test( request.status ) ) {
    simplexhr.retrieved(request);
  } else {
    simplexhr.failed(request);
  }
}
```

When the request is complete, you check another property called status, which stores the status of the request. The status is the standard HTTP response status code of the response. It is 0 when the connection cannot be established, in other error conditions, or when the request has been cancelled, and it is 404 when the file is not found.

Note For a complete list of standard HTTP response status codes, see
http://www.w3.org/Protocols/rfc2616-sec10.html.

If the status is either 200 (all OK) or 304 (not modified), the file has been retrieved and you can do something with it. In the case of this demo script, you call the retrieved() method. If the status is any other value, you call failed().

simpleXHR.js (continued)

```
  }
  request.send( null );
  return false;
},
```

The `send()` method sends your request to the server and can take request parameters to send to the server-side script being invoked. If you don't have any parameters to send, it is safest to set it to `null`. (Internet Explorer accepts `send()` without any parameters, but this can cause problems in older Mozilla browsers.) Finally, setting the method's `return` value to `false` stops the link from being followed.

simpleXHR.js (continued)

```
failed : function( requester ) {
  alert('The XMLHttpRequest failed. Status: ' + requester.status );
  return true;
},
```

If the request didn't succeed, the `failed()` method shows an `alert()` dialog telling the user about the problem. (This is not very clever or pretty, but it should do for the moment.) Returning `true` after the user clicks the dialog's OK button causes the link to be followed. You can test this by opening the file `exampleXHR.html` locally in a browser (without the `http://protocol`) and clicking the links. Because there is no HTTP transmission, any request will fail with code 0, as shown in Figure 8-4.

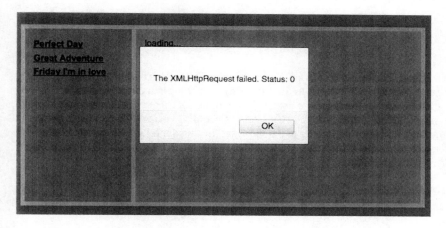

Figure 8-4. *Notifying the user that the XMLHttpRequest failed*

However, if all went well with the request, the method `retrieved()` takes over.

simpleXHR.js (continued)

```
  retrieved : function( requester ) {
    var data = requester.responseText;
    data = data.replace( /\n/g, '<br>' );
    simplexhr.outputContainer.innerHTML = data;
    return false;
  }
}
```

This method enables you to obtain and use the data sent back from the XMLHttpRequest. The data can be read out in a few different formats based on responseType. Two text-based formats are responseText and responseXML. The difference between these is the type of output—responseText returns a string, and responseXML returns an XML object. You can use all the usual string properties and methods on responseText, such as length, indexof(), replace(), and so on, and you can use all the DOM methods on responseXML, such as getElementsByTagName(), getAttribute(), and so on. In addition to returning text-based responses, you can receive binary data using returnType blob or arrayBuffer.

In this example, you merely retrieve text and use the String.replace() method to convert all line breaks, \n, into BR elements. Then you can write out the changed string as innerHTML to the outputContainer and return false to stop the normal link behavior.

In many cases, it is sufficient to use responseText and write out data via innerHTML. It is also a lot quicker and less work for the user's browser and CPU than using XML and DOM to convert the objects back into HTML.

■ **Note** The Ajax acronym doesn't really work for these examples, because the process lacks the XML component. For this reason, this approach is known as *Asynchronous HTML and HTTP (AHAH)* and is defined as a *microformat* with code examples at http://microformats.org/wiki/rest/ahah.

Et Tu, Cache?

Normally, the browser cache is your friend. The browser stores downloaded files in it, which means the user doesn't have to download your scripts over and over again. However, in the case of Ajax, caching can cause problems.

Safari is the main offender, because it caches the response status() and does not trigger the changes any longer. (Remember that the status returns the HTTP code 200, 304, or 404.) However, avoiding issues with caching is pretty simple: before calling the send() method, add another header to the request. This header tells the browser to test whether the data has changed since a certain date. Which date you set doesn't matter, as long as it is in the past—for example, at the time of this writing is written as follows:

```
request.setRequestHeader( 'If-Modified-Since', 'Mon, 12 Jan 2013 00:00:00 GMT' );
request.send( null );
```

Putting the X Back into Ajax

If you use responseXML, you can use DOM methods to turn the received XML into HTML. The demo exampleXMLxhr.html does this. As a data source, take the album collection used in the pagination example in the last chapter in XML format.

albums.xml (excerpt)

```
<?xml version="1.0" encoding="utf-8"?>
<albums>
  <album>
    <id>1</id>
    <artist>Depeche Mode</artist>
    <title>Playing the Angel</title>
    <comment>They are back and finally up to speed again</comment>
  </album>
  <album>
```

```
    <id>2</id>
    <artist>Monty Python</artist>
    <title>The final Rip-Off</title>
    <comment>Double CD with all the songs</comment>
  </album>
  [... more albums snipped ...]
</albums>
```

You want to retrieve this data via XHR and display it as a table in the page. Figure 8-5 shows the different stages of the request.

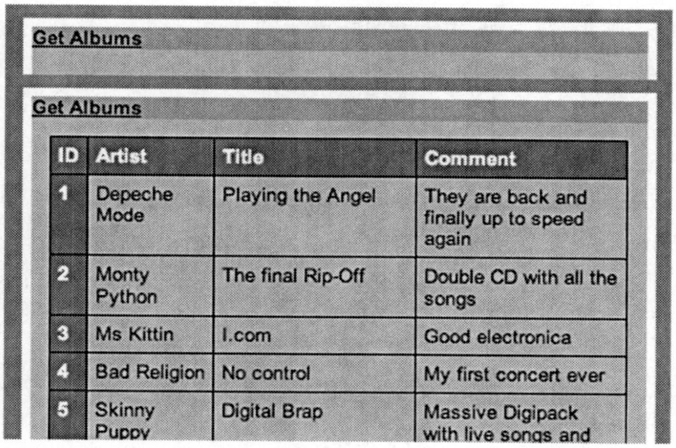

Figure 8-5. *Retrieving and showing XML data as a table*

The main part of the script does not have to change.

simpleXMLxhr.js

```
simplexhr = {
  doxhr : function( container, url ) {
    if( !document.getElementById || !document.createTextNode ){
      return;
    }
    simplexhr.outputContainer = document.getElementById( container );
    if( !simplexhr.outputContainer ) { return; }
    var request;
    try {
      request = new XMLHttpRequest();
    } catch( error ) {
      try {
        request = new ActiveXObject("Microsoft.XMLHTTP" );
      } catch ( error ) {
        return true;
      }
    }
    request.open('get', url,true );
```

```
    request.onreadystatechange = function() {
      if(request.readyState == 1) {
        simplexhr.outputContainer.innerHTML = 'loading... ';
      }
      if(request.readyState == 4) {
        if( request.status && /200|304/.test( request.status ) ) {
          simplexhr.retrieved( request );
        } else {
          simplexhr.failed( request );
        }
      }
    }
    request.setRequestHeader('If-Modified-Since', 'Mon, 12 Jan 2013 00:00:00 GMT');
    request.send( null );
    return false;
  },
```

The difference is in the retrieved() method that reads the data via responseXML and writes out a data table using the XML as the source of content. Remove the loading message, and use the DOM createElement() and createTextNode() methods to create the main table.

simpleXMLxhr.js (continued)

```
retrieved : function( requester ) {
  var data = requester.responseXML;
  simplexhr.outputContainer.removeChild(simplexhr.outputContainer.firstChild);
  var i, albumId, artist, albumTitle, comment, td, tr, th;
  var table = document.createElement('table' );
  var tablehead = document.createElement('thead');
  table.appendChild( tablehead );
  tr = document.createElement('tr');
  th = document.createElement('th');
  th.appendChild( document.createTextNode('ID'));
  tr.appendChild( th );
  th=document.createElement('th');
  th.appendChild( document.createTextNode('Artist'));
  tr.appendChild( th );
  th = document.createElement('th');
  th.appendChild( document.createTextNode('Title'));
  tr.appendChild( th );
  th=document.createElement('th');
  th.appendChild( document.createTextNode('Comment'));
  tr.appendChild( th );
  tablehead.appendChild( tr );
  var tablebody = document.createElement('tbody');
  table.appendChild( tablebody );
```

Notice that when you create tables on the fly, Internet Explorer will not display them unless you nest the rows and cells in a TBODY element. Firefox won't mind.

Next, loop over all the album elements of the data that was retrieved.

simpleXMLxhr.js (continued)

```
var albums = data.getElementsByTagName('album');

for( i = 0 ; i < albums.length; i++ ) {
```

For each album, you read the contents of the XML nodes by their tag name and retrieve their text content via firstChild.nodeValue.

simpleXMLxhr.js (continued)

```
tr = document.createElement('tr');
albumId = data.getElementsByTagName('id')[i].firstChild.nodeValue;
artist = data.getElementsByTagName('artist')[i].firstChild.nodeValue;
albumTitle = data.getElementsByTagName('title')[i].firstChild.nodeValue;
comment = data.getElementsByTagName('comment')[i].firstChild.nodeValue;
```

You use this information to add the data cells to the table via createElement(), createTextNode(), and appendChild().

simpleXMLxhr.js (continued)

```
  td = document.createElement('th');
  td.appendChild( document.createTextNode( albumId ) );
  tr.appendChild( td );
  td = document.createElement('td');
  td.appendChild( document.createTextNode( artist ) );
  tr.appendChild( td );
  td = document.createElement('td');
  td.appendChild( document.createTextNode( albumTitle ) );
  tr.appendChild( td );
  td = document.createElement('td');
  td.appendChild( document.createTextNode( comment ) );
  tr.appendChild( td );
  tablebody.appendChild( tr );
}
```

Add the resulting table as a new child element to the output container, and return false to stop the link from loading the XML as a new document. The failed() method stays the same.

simpleXMLxhr.js (continued)

```
    simplexhr.outputContainer.appendChild( table );
    return false;
  },
  failed : function( requester ) {
    alert('The XMLHttpRequest failed. Status: ' + requester.status );
    return true;
  }
}
```

You can see that by doing the "right thing" in terms of DOM scripting, scripts can get rather convoluted. You could cut down the amount of code by using tool methods to create the table rows, but that means even more processing because the methods have to be called from within a loop.

If you know the XML structure like you do in this example, it is probably a lot faster and easier to use innerHTML and string methods to convert the data. The demo exampleXHRxmlCheat.html does exactly that. Most of the script stays the same, but the retrieved() method is a lot shorter.

simpleXMLxhrCheat.js (excerpt)

```
retrieved : function( requester ){
  var data = requester.responseText;
  simplexhr.outputContainer.removeChild(simplexhr.outputContainer.firstChild);
  var headrow = '<tr><th>ID</th><th>Artist</th><th>Title</th><th>Comment</th></tr>';
  data = data.replace( /<\?.*\?>/g, ' ' )
  data = data.replace( /<(\/*)id>/g, '<$1th>' )
  data = data.replace( /<(\/*)(artist|title|comment)>/g, '<$1td>' )
  data = data.replace( /<(\/*)albums>/g, '<$1table>' )
  data = data.replace( /<(\/*)album>/g, '<$1tr>' );
  data = data.replace( /<table>/g, '<table>' + headrow );
  simplexhr.outputContainer.innerHTML = data;
  return false;
},
```

You retrieve the data as responseText, remove the "loading…" message, and then create a header table row as a string and store it in the variable headrow. Because responseText is a string, you can use the String.replace() method to change the XML elements.

Start by removing the XML prologue by deleting anything beginning with <? and ending with ?>.

■ **Note** This example uses regular expressions, which you might not know yet, but which we will talk about in more detail in the next chapter. It suffices to say that regular expressions are delimited with slashes and match a certain pattern of text. If there are parentheses inside the slashes, these strings will be stored in variables starting with $; these can be used in the replacement string to stand in for the substrings that match the pattern. For example, the regular expression pattern /<(\/*)id>/g matches everything that starts with a <, followed by an optional / (which is stored as $1 if it is found), followed by the string id and the closing > character. The second parameter, <$1th>, writes out either <th> or </th>, depending on the original id tag being the opening or closing tag. Rather than use regular expressions, you could perform simple string replacement instead:

```
data = data.replace('<id>', '<th>');
data = data.replace('</id>', '</th>');
```

Replace the other elements according to this scheme: every albums element becomes a table, every album a tr, every id a th; artist, title, and comment become a td each. Append the headrow string to <table> and store the end result in the outputContainer element using innerHTML.

Replacing XML with JSON

Although XML is a popular method of data transfer formats—it is text based and you can ensure validity and systems being able to talk to each other via DTDs, XML Schemata, or RELAX NG. Ajax fans have become more and more aware that it can be quite a drag to convert XML to JavaScript objects.

Instead of reading an XML file as XML and parsing it via the DOM or reading it as text and using regular expressions, it would be a lot easier and less straining to the system to have the data in a format that JavaScript can use directly. This format is called **JSON** (http://json.org/). It allows a dataset to be expressed in an object literal notation. The demo exampleJSONxhr.html uses the XML of the earlier example as JSON:

```
<albums>
  <album>
    <id>1</id>
    <artist>Depeche Mode</artist>
    <title>Playing the Angel</title>
    <comment>They are back and finally up to speed again</comment>
 </album>
  <album>
    <id>2</id>
    <artist>Monty Python</artist>
    <title>The final Rip-Off</title>
    <comment>Double CD with all the songs</comment>
  </album>
  <album>
    <id>3</id>
    <artist>Ms Kittin</artist>
    <title>I.com</title>
    <comment>Good electronica</comment>
  </album>
</albums>
```

Converted to JSON, this is as follows:

albums.json

```
{
  "album":
   [
    {
      "id" : "1",
      "artist" : "Depeche Mode",
      "title" : "Playing the Angel",
      "comment" : "They are back and finally up to speed again"
    },
    {
      "id" : "2",
      "artist" : "Monty Python",
      "title" : "The final Rip-Off",
      "comment" : "Double CD wiid all the songs"
    },
```

```
    {
      "id" : "3",
      "artist" : "Ms Kittin",
      "title" : "I.com",
      "comment" : "Good electronica"
    }
  ]
}
```

The benefit is that the data is already in a format that JavaScript can understand. All you need to do to convert it to objects to display is to use the eval method on the string.

exampleJSONxhr.js (excerpt)

```
retrieved : function( requester ) {
  var content = '<table><thead>';
  content += '<tr><th>ID</th><th>Artist</th>';
  content += '<th>Title</th><th>Comment</th>';
  content += '</tr></thead><tbody>';
  var data = JSON.parse(' (' + requester.responseText + ') ' );
```

This gives you all the content as objects you can access via either property notation or associative array notation (the latter is shown in the id example, the former in all the others):

exampleJSONxhr.js (excerpt)

```
  var albums = data.album;
  for( var i = 0; i < albums.length; i++ ) {
    content += '<tr><td>' + albums[i]['id'] + '</td>';
    content += '<td>' + albums[i].artist + '</td>';
    content += '<td>' + albums[i].title + '</td>';
    content += '<td>' + albums[i].comment + '</td></tr>';
  }
  Content += '</tbody></table>';
  simplexhr.outputContainer.innerHTML = content;
  return false;
},
```

For files on your own server, using JSON instead of XML is a lot quicker. (In tests, it proved to be up to ten times faster.) However, using eval() can be dangerous if you use JSON from a third- party server, because it executes any JavaScript code, not only JSON data.

You can avoid this danger by using a parser that makes sure that only data gets converted into objects and malicious code does not get executed. An open source version is available at http://www.json.org/js.html. We'll come back to JSON in Chapter 11.

Using Server-Side Scripts to Reach Third-Party Content

As mentioned earlier, it is difficult for security reasons to use to XHR load content from other servers. If you want to retrieve, for example, RSS feeds from other servers, you can use a server-side script that loads them for you or connect to a CORS-enabled server.

> **Note** This is a common myth about Ajax: it does not replace server-side code but is backed up by it and offers a slicker interface to it. XHR by itself can retrieve data only from the same server or send information to server-side scripts. You can't, for example, access a database in JavaScript—unless you use a method called JSONP (JSON with padding), the database provider offers an output as JavaScript, and you include it in its own script tag. There is an example of this in Chapter 11.

The server-side component is a pass-through or proxy script that takes a URL, loads the content of the document, and sends it back to the XHR. The script needs to set the right header to tell the XHR that the data it returns is XML. If the file cannot be found, the script returns an XML error string instead. The following example uses PHP, but any server-side language can perform the same task.

loadrss.php

```php
<?php
// Set the XML header
header('Content-type: text/xml');
// Define an error message in case the feed cannot be found
$error='<?xml version="1.0"?><error>Cannot find feed</error>';
// Clear the contents
$contents = '';
// Read the url variable from the GET request
$rssurl = $_GET['url'];
// Test if the url starts with http to prevent surfers
// from calling and displaying local files
if( preg_match('/^http:/', $rssurl ) ) {
  // Open the remove file, and store its contents
  $handle = @fopen( $rssurl, "rb" );
    if( $handle == true ){
      while ( !feof($handle ) ) {
        $contents .= fread( $handle, 8192 );
      }
      fclose( $handle );
    }
}
// If the file has no channel element, delete contents
if( !preg_match('/<channel/', $contents ) ){ $contents = ''; }
// Return either the contents or the error
echo $contents == '' ? $error : $contents;
?>
```

The demo `exampleExternalRSS.html` uses this script to retrieve the latest headlines in RSS format from the Yahoo web site.

The relevant part in the HTML is the link that calls the `doxhr()` method with the element to output the news in and the RSS URI as parameters.

exampleExternalRSS.html (excerpt)

```
<p>
  <a href="http://rss.news.yahoo.com/rss/topstories"
     onclick="return readrss.doxhr('newsContainer',this.href)">
     Get Yahoo news
  </a>
</p>
<div id="newsContainer"></div>
```

■ **Note**   RSS is an acronym for Really Simple Syndication. In essence, it is XML with content in it that you want to share with the world—typically, news headlines. The specifications for RSS are available at `http://blogs.law.harvard.edu/tech/rss`, and you can read more about its benefits at Wikipedia: `http://en.wikipedia.org/wiki/RSS`.

The important detail in this example is that RSS is a standardized format, and you know the XML structure—even if you get it from a third-party web site. Every valid RSS document contains—among many other things—an `items` element with nested `item` elements. Each of these contains at least a `title` describing and a `link` pointing to the full piece of information. You can use these to show a list of clickable headlines that send the user to the Yahoo site where she can read the full news article, as shown in Figure 8-6.

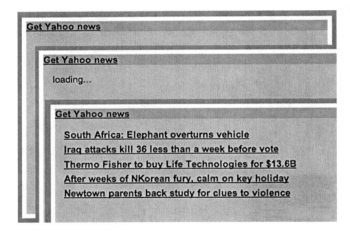

Figure 8-6. *Retrieving and showing RSS feed data*

The script is once again a simple XHR. The difference is that instead of linking to the URL directly, you pass it to the PHP script as a GET parameter:

externalRSS.js

```
readrss = {
  doxhr:function( container, url ) {
    [... code snipped as it is the same as in the last example ...]
    request.open('get', 'loadrss.php?url=' + encodeURI( url ) );
    request.setRequestHeader('If-Modified-Since', 'Mon, 12 Jan 2013 00:00:00 GMT' );
```

```
    request.send( null );
    return false;
},
```

The `retrieved()` function needs to change. First, it deletes the "loading…" message from the output container and retrieves the data in XML format using `responseXML`. Because the PHP script returns an error message in XML format, you need to test whether the returned XML contains an `error` element. If this is the case, read the node value of the first child of the first error element and write it to the `outputContainer` surrounded by a paragraph tag.

externalRSS.js (continued)

```
retrieved : function( requester ) {
  readrss.outputContainer.innerHTML = '';
  var data = requester.responseXML;
  if( data.getElementsByTagName('error').length > 0 ) {
    var error = data.getElementsByTagName('error')[0].firstChild.nodeValue;
    readrss.outputContainer.innerHTML = '<p>' + error + '</p>';
```

If there is no `error` element, retrieve all the `item` elements contained in the returned XML and check the length of the resulting list. If there is less than one `item`, return from the method and allow the link to load the XML document in the browser. This is a necessary step to ensure that the RSS returned was valid—because you didn't check this in the server-side script.

externalRSS.js (continued)

```
} else {
var items = data.getElementsByTagName('item');
var end = items.length;
if( end < 1 ){ return; }
```

If there are items to be displayed, you define the necessary variables and loop through them. Because some RSS feeds have lots of entries, it makes sense to constrain how many you display; in this case, you choose 5. You read the `link` and the `title` for each `item` and add a new list item with an embedded link with this information as its `href` attribute and text content, respectively. Notice that this example simply assembles a string of HTML; you could, of course, go the "cleaner" way and create elements and apply text nodes.

externalRSS.js (continued)

```
var item, feedlink, name, description, content = '';
for( var i = 0; i < 5; i++ ) {
  feedlink = items[i].getElementsByTagName('link').item(0).firstChild.nodeValue;
  name = items[i].getElementsByTagName('title').item(0).firstChild.nodeValue;
  item = '<li><a href="' + feedlink+'">' + name + '</a></li>';
  content += item;
}
```

Insert the final content string inside a UL tag within the `outputContainer`, and you have clickable headlines with fresh Yahoo news.

externalRSS.js (continued)

```
    readrss.outputContainer.innerHTML = '<ul>' + content + '</ul>';
    return false;
}
```

The rest of the script remains unchanged; the failed() method displays an alert only when the XHR doesn't succeed.

externalRSS.js (continued)

```
    },
    failed : function( requester ) {
      alert('The XMLHttpRequest failed. Status: ' + requester.status );
      return true;
    }
}
```

XHR on Slow Connections

One problem that might occur is that the connection of an XHR can take a long time, and the user sees a loading message with nothing happening at all. You can avoid this issue by using window.timeout() to stop the execution after a certain amount of time. The demo exampleXHRtimeout.html shows an example using this technique. In addition to using the Window object, XHR Level 2 includes a timeout property and an ontimeout event. At this time, Chrome and Safari do not support XHR timeouts, while Opera, Firefox, and Internet Explorer 10 do.

The default setting for the request is 10 milliseconds, which causes the timeout as shown in Figure 8-7. You can use the second link in the example to set the timeout to 10 seconds and try again, and—if your connection is not dead slow or Yahoo isn't down—you will get the headlines.

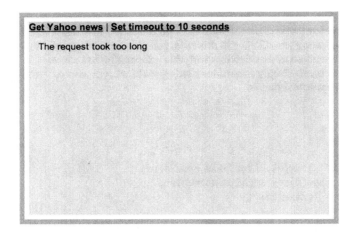

Figure 8-7. *Allowing an XHR connection to time out*

The differences in the script are that you need a property to define how long to wait before a timeout is triggered, one to store the `window.timeout`, and a Boolean property that defines whether there was a timeout or not. The Boolean has to be inside the `doxhr()` method because it needs to get initialized every time `doxhr()` is called.

XHRtimeout.js

```
readrss = {
  timeOutDuration : 10,
  toolong : false,
  doxhr : function( container, url ) {
    readrss.timedout = false;
    if( !document.getElementById || !document.createTextNode ){
      return;
    }
    readrss.outputContainer = document.getElementById( container );
    if( !readrss.outputContainer ){ return; }
    var request;
    try {
      request = new XMLHttpRequest();
    } catch( error ) {
      try {
        request = new ActiveXObject("Microsoft.XMLHTTP");
      } catch( error ) {
        return true;
      }
    }
```

In the onreadystatechange event listener, you add the timeout and assign it to the `toolong` property of the main object. Inside the timeout, you define an anonymous function that checks the `readystate` and compares it with 1. This is the scenario when the defined time has passed and the request is still on the first stage rather than the fourth and final one. When this happens, call the `abort()` method of the request, set the `timedout` property to `true`, and write out a message to the display element that the request took too long.

XHRtimeout.js (continued)

```
request.onreadystatechange = function() {
  if( request.readyState == 1) {
      readrss.toolong = window.setTimeout( function(){
        if( request.readyState == 1 ) {
          readrss.timedout = true;
          request.abort(); // Stop
          readrss.outputContainer.innerHTML = 'The request took too long';
        }
      },
      readrss.timeOutDuration
    );
    readrss.outputContainer.innerHTML = 'loading... ';
}
```

When the request has successfully ended and there wasn't any timeout (which is stored in the `timedout` property), you clear the timeout.

XHRtimeout.js (continued)

```
       if( request.readyState == 4 && !readrss.timedout ) {
       window.clearTimeout( readrss.toolong );
       if( /200|304/.test( request.status ) ) {
           readrss.retrieved( request );
         } else {
           readrss.failed( request );
         }
       }
     }
     request.open('get', 'loadrss.php?url='+encodeURI( url ) );
     request.setRequestHeader('If-Modified-Since', 'Mon, 12 Jan 2013 00:00:00 GMT' );
     request.send( null );
     return false;
},
```

The rest of the script stays the same.

A Larger Ajax Example: Connected Select Boxes

Let's take a look at a larger Ajax example—I call it that although you won't be using XML. Connected select boxes are a classic example of what JavaScript can do for you to make an interface faster. One common use for them is the flight offer web site, where you choose one airport in a select box and the page immediately shows you the destination airports that are available from this airport in a second select box. Traditionally, this is achieved by keeping all the airport connection data in JavaScript arrays and manipulating the options arrays of the select elements. Changing the first airport select box automatically changes the second one to the available destinations.

This is very nice when you have a mouse and you have JavaScript available; however, it can be pretty frustrating when one of the two is missing, or even impossible when neither is available. This example will show how you can create interdependent select boxes that work without a mouse and JavaScript and will not reload the whole page when JavaScript is available.

The trick is to make the functionality work on the server side and then add the JavaScript and XHR tricks to stop the whole page from reloading. Because you don't know whether the user really can cope with this, you can even make it optional instead of a given.

■ **Note** This approach to Ajax is more accessibility aware than the original one. The reason is that you don't want to make the biggest DHTML mistake once again—using a technology without considering those who cannot deal with it. Jeremy Keith coined this approach *HIJAX* in his DOM scripting book, but so far it hasn't gotten as much public awareness as the Ajax term has.

The first step is to create a server-side script that does all the functionality. Because this is not a book about PHP, we won't get into too much detail here. It suffices to say that the main document exampleSelectBoxes.php includes a smaller PHP script, selectBoxes.php. The latter contains all the airport data as arrays (but could as easily go to a database to retrieve them) and writes out the different states of the interface based on the user selecting a choice and sending the form, as shown in Figure 8-8.

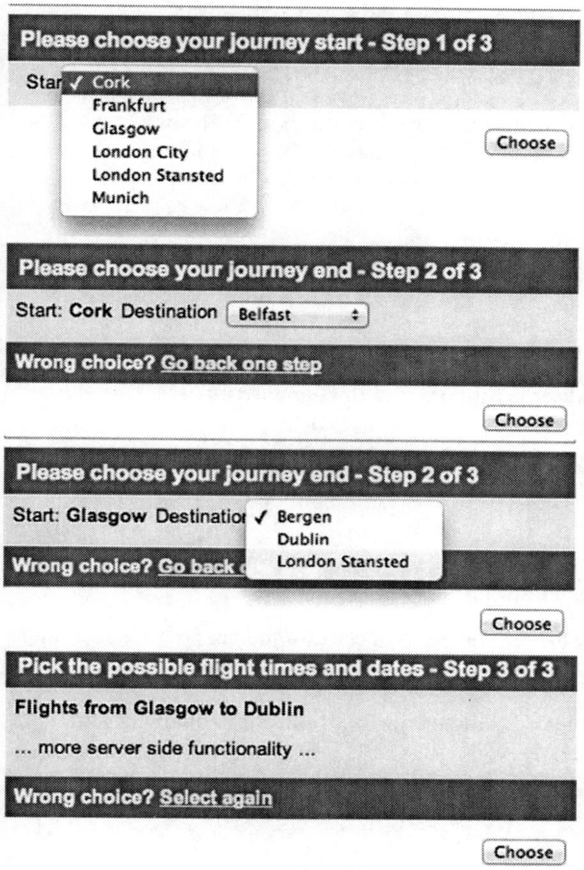

Figure 8-8. Connected select boxes

The main page features the form with a DIV with an id you can use for the XHR output.

exampleSelectBoxes.php (excerpt)

```
<form action="exampleSelectBoxes.php" method="post">
  <div id="formOutput">
   <?php include('selectBoxes.php');?>
  </div>
  <p class="submit"><input type="submit" name="select" id="select" value="Choose" /></p>
</form>
```

■ **Note**   This example uses POST as the method to send the data.

The PHP script returns an HTML interface you can hook into at each stage of the process:

- If there hasn't been any form data sent yet, it displays one select box with the ID airport listing all the airports in the dataset.

- If there was an airport chosen and sent to the server, the script displays the chosen airport inside a strong element and as a hidden form field. It also displays the possible destination airports for this choice as a select box with the ID destination. Furthermore, it creates a link pointing back to the main document to start a new selection with the ID back.

- If the user chooses an airport and a destination and sends them back to the server, the script just hints at more functionality because you don't need more for this example. However, it offers the link back to the initial page.

If JavaScript is available, the script should do the following:

- Create a new check box in the form that allows to user to turn on Ajax functionality—in this case, only reloading the section of the form that is created by selectBoxes.php.

- If that check box has been selected, the script should override the normal submit process of the form with a function called by an event handler. As a loading indicator, it should change the text of the Submit button to "loading."

- It should also add a search parameter to the link back to the first stage to ensure that when the user clicks that link, he won't have to select the check box again.

Let's start with the skeleton of the script. You need a label for the check box, a class for the paragraph containing it (not really necessary, but it allows for styling), and the IDs of the form elements container and the link back to the start of the process.

As methods, you need an init() method, the main XHR method with the retrieval and failure handlers, and cancelClick() and addEvent() for event handling.

selectBoxes.js (skeleton)

```
dynSelect = {
  AJAXlabel : 'Reload only the results, not the whole page',
  AJAXofferClass : 'ajax',
  containerID : 'formOutput',
  backlinkID : 'back',
  init : function(){},
  doxhr : function( e ){},
  retrieved : function( requester, e ){},
  failed : function( requester ){},
  cancelClick : function( e ){},
  addEvent : function(elm, evType, fn, useCapture ){}
}
dynSelect.addEvent( window, 'load', dynSelect.init, false );
```

Now start to flesh out the skeleton.

selectBoxes.js

```
dynSelect = {
  AJAXlabel : 'Only reload the results, not the whole page',
  AJAXofferClass : 'ajax',
  containerID : 'formOutput',
  backlinkID : 'back',
```

The init() method tests whether the W3C DOM is supported, retrieves the first form, and stores the Submit button with the ID select in a property—this is necessary to remove the button on the last step. It then creates a new paragraph and applies the class for the Ajax trigger defined earlier.

selectBoxes.js (continued)

```
init : function(){
  if( !document.getElementById || !document.createTextNode ){
   return;
  }
  var f = document.getElementsByTagName('form')[0];
  dynSelect.selectButton = document.getElementById('select');
  var p = document.createElement('p');
  p.className = dynSelect.AJAXofferClass;
```

Next on the agenda is the check box to offer the option to turn on Ajax. Set the name and ID of the check box to xhr and determine whether the current URI already has the ?ajax search string. If it has, preset the check box to already selected. (This is necessary to ensure that the link back to the first step does not stop the Ajax enhancements from working.)

selectBoxes.js (continued)

```
dynSelect.cb = document.createElement('input');
dynSelect.cb.setAttribute('type', 'checkbox');
dynSelect.cb.setAttribute('name', 'xhr');
dynSelect.cb.setAttribute('id', 'xhr');
if( window.location.search != '' ) {
  dynSelect.cb.setAttribute('defaultChecked', 'checked' );
  dynSelect.cb.setAttribute('checked', 'checked');
}
```

Add the check box to the new paragraph, and add a label with the appropriate text following it. The new paragraph becomes the first child node of the form, and you apply an event handler that triggers the dohxhr() method when the form is submitted.

selectBoxes.js (continued)

```
  p.appendChild( dynSelect.cb );
  var lbl = document.createElement('label');
  lbl.htmlFor = 'xhr';
  lbl.appendChild( document.createTextNode( dynSelect.AJAXlabel ) );
  p.appendChild( lbl );
  f.insertBefore( p, f.firstChild );
  dynSelect.addEvent(f, 'submit', dynSelect.doxhr, false );
},
```

The dohxr() method tests whether the check box has been ticked and simply returns when it isn't. If it is, you define two variables for the current airport and the current destination and store the output element in a property. You test whether the output container exists and return if it doesn't.

selectBoxes.js (continued)

```
doxhr : function( e ) {
  if( !dynSelect.cb.checked ){ return; }
```

```
var airportValue, destinationValue;
dynSelect.outputContainer = document.getElementById(dynSelect.containerID );
if( !dynSelect.outputContainer ){ return; }
```

Here is the XHR code, which defines the correct object and sets the onreadystatechange event listener.

selectBoxes.js (continued)

```
var request;
try {
  request = new XMLHttpRequest();
} catch( error ) {
  try {
    request = new ActiveXObject("Microsoft.XMLHTTP");
  } catch( error ) {
    return true;
  }
}
request.onreadystatechange = function() {
  if( request.readyState == 1 ) {
    dynSelect.selectButton.value = 'loading... ';
  }
  if( request.readyState == 4 ) {
    if( request.status && /200|304/.test( request.status ) ) {
      dynSelect.retrieved( request );
    } else{
      dynSelect.failed( request );
    }
  }
}
```

Determine whether the document contains the airport and destination select boxes; if so, store their current states in the variables airportValue and destinationValue. Notice that you need to check the type of the airport field in the second stage of the flight selection process because it is a hidden field.

selectBoxes.js (continued)

```
var airport = document.getElementById('airport');
if( airport != undefined ) {
  if( airport.nodeName.toLowerCase() == 'select' ) {
    airportValue = airport.options[airport.selectedIndex].value;
  } else {
    airportValue = airport.value;
  }
}
var destination = document.getElementById('destination');
if( destination ) {
  destinationValue = destination.options[destination.selectedIndex].value;
}
```

Because the form is sent using POST and not GET, you need to define the request a bit differently. First of all, you need to assemble the request parameters as a string. (This is the trail of variables on the URI when the send method is GET—for example, `http://www.example.com/index.php?search+DOM&values=20&start=10`.)

selectBoxes.js (continued)

```
var parameters = 'airport=' + airportValue;
if( destinationValue != undefined ) {
  parameters += '&destination=' + destinationValue;
}
```

Next, open the request. In addition to using the modified header to prevent caching, you also need to tell the server that the content type is `application/x-www-form-urlencoded`; then you transmit the length of all the request parameters as the value to accompany `Content-length`. You also need to tell the server to close the connection once it has finished retrieving all the data. Unlike GET requests, `send()` needs a parameter when you POST, which is the URI-encoded parameters.

selectBoxes.js (continued)

```
request.open('POST', 'selectBoxes.php');
request.setRequestHeader('If-Modified-Since', 'Mon, 12 Jan 2013 00:00:00 GMT');
request.setRequestHeader('Content-type', 'application/x-www-form-urlencoded');
request.setRequestHeader('Content-length', parameters.length );
request.setRequestHeader('Connection', 'close');
request.send( encodeURI( parameters ) );
```

■ **Note** Don't beat yourself up if you don't know all that is going on here; after all, it is server and HTTP code, and you are just starting with JavaScript. Chances are you will never really have to grasp what all that means, as long as you use it this way.

If you are on the page before the last one and both an airport and a destination are available, remove the Submit button to prevent errors.

■ **Note** This is a cosmetic step for this example. A real application should work through the following steps, too, but you don't need to go that far now.

Finally, invoke `cancelClick()` to prevent normal form submission.

selectBoxes.js (continued)

```
  if( airport && destination ) {
    var sendButton = document.getElementById('select');
    sendButton.parentNode.removeChild( sendButton );
  }
  dynSelect.cancelClick( e );
},
```

The `retrieved()` method doesn't differ much from the other examples. Undo what you did in the previous step by changing the Submit button's value back to `Select` before retrieving the `responseText` of the request and replacing the old form elements with the new ones. Add `?ajax` to the `href` of the link pointing back to the first step to make sure that activating this link will not turn off the previously selected functionality. (By now, you know the user wants the Ajax interface.)

selectBoxes.js (continued)

```
retrieved : function( requester, e ) {
  dynSelect.selectButton.value = 'Select';
  var content = requester.responseText;
  dynSelect.outputContainer.innerHTML = content;
  var backlink = document.getElementById( dynSelect.backlinkID );
  if( backlink ) {
    var url = backlink.getAttribute('href');
    backlink.setAttribute('href', url+'?ajax');
  }
  dynSelect.cancelClick( e );
},
```

The rest of the script consists of the familiar `failed()`, `cancelClick()`, and `addEvent()` utility methods.

selectBoxes.js (continued)

```
  failed : function( requester ){
    alert('The XMLHttpRequest failed. Status: ' + requester.status);
    return true;
  },
  cancelClick : function( e ){
    [... code snipped ...]
  },
  addEvent: function( elm, evType, fn, useCapture ){
    [... code snipped ...]
  }
}
dynSelect.addEvent( window, 'load', dynSelect.init, false );
```

This example shows that Ajax is very dependent on server code. If you know what you will get back, it is easy to create a useful and attractive interface.

You can also use the Ajax approach in an unobtrusive and optional manner to make older effects more eye-catching and targeted better to those who want them.

Node.js

We spent the majority of this book talking about how to use JavaScript on the client side and how to enhance your web application with it. This will be a short introduction to using your newly acquired skills to develop applications that will run on the server. Because this is not running in your browser, it would first be helpful to explain a little of what is going on and get set up.

Node.js is built on top of Google's Chrome JavaScript engine called V8. Because of this, Node lets you create a web server just by using JavaScript, with no need for installing any other server software.

Created by Ryan Dahl with the goal of making a web application like Gmail, Node is an open source project that can run in multiple environments and can be hosted by companies like Heroku, Amazon's AWS, Nodejitsu, and Joynet, which is also a sponsor of the project. Most famously LinkedIn uses Node for its mobile app.

Installing Node.js and Getting Started

You can get started quickly by going to `http://www.nodejs.org/download` and then downloading and installing Node on your system. After that, you should be ready to do a few quick examples.

We are going to jump right in and make sure things are working. First let's make sure Node is installed and check the current version. As of this writing, I'm using version 0.10.2. You can try this out for yourself by going to the command line and typing `node—version`.

At this point, you should have Node installed and you should be ready to go. Let's skip the "Hello World" example and go straight to the other example you will see in every Node tutorial: how to make a web server.

httpServer.js

```
var http = require('http');

var server = http.createServer(function (request, response){
    response.writeHead(200,{"Content-Type": "text/plain"});
    response.end("It's the information age!");
});
server.listen(8080);
```

From a pure code perspective, it looks like regular JavaScript. So how can this create a web server? Let's dig into the details.

First you need the HTTP module. Modules add functionality to your application. The HTTP module is built into Node; however, there is a Node package manager (npm) that lets you install other modules. The next variable created is called `server`, which is an instance of `HttpServer`, returned by the call to `createServer` on the `http` object. The `createServer` method accepts an anonymous function that can accept two parameters, `request` and `response`.

Before we talk about the two lines let's talk about the last line in this code:

```
server.listen(8080);
```

This tells the server to listen to port 8080. That means if you typed in your browser "localhost:8080," it directs you to your currently running server. When that happens, the server has to make a response. This is invoked each time a request is made to the server. It is passed a request object, which contains details of that request, and also a response object, which is used to make the response once the handler processes the request. In this case, the request handler unconditionally responds to each request with a status code of 200 (the "OK" status code, indicating success) and a response body containing a string.

Modules

We spoke of modules giving you the ability to add functions to your Node-based application. They also give you the ability to keep your own files organized. Let's take the current file and make a module out of it.

httpServerModule.js

```
var http = require('http');
```

```
function startUp(){
    function onRequest(request, response){
        response.writeHead(200,{"Content-Type": "text/plain"});
        response.end("It's the information age!");
    }
        http.createServer(onRequest).listen(8080);
}
exports.startup = startUp;
```

Now let's make an index.js file to start it up.

index.js

```
var server = require("./httpServerModule");
server.startup();
```

You can see that the module is mostly the same. The main thing to look out for is the last line:

```
exports.startup = startUp;
```

Here you are adding the property startUp to the object exports. This object is available to anyone who uses require() to access a module. Variables in the module scope that are not added to exports remain private to the module.

The other file Index.js is similar to our original project. You require the module to be loaded. The ./ tells Node to look for the module relative to the directory containing the current file. If it's not found, Node first searches in core modules and then looks in other folders to find a match. You can find a full description on the Node site (http://nodejs.org/api/modules.html#loading_from_node_modules_Folders). The second line just calls your startup function, and the module does the work. If you like, you can also run this from the command line using REPL (Read-Eval-Print-Loop). At the command line, just type in **node**, and then you can run each line just as you would in the index file. Then check your browser.

In concept, it is similar to creating objects to hold your functions. This way, you don't have too many variables in the global namespace.

Callbacks

In the previous example, you had anonymous functions that handled the results of your requests. This works fine, but it could be difficult to read if there were a lot of things going on. Callbacks let you separate some of the functions in a way that makes it easy to read. The next example shows how you can use Node to make a request to a web server and use callbacks to display the results in the command line.

Here you create a module similar to the one you created before. This time, when making the HTTP request you assign two things. The first are the options describing the host server and the path on that server you are interested in. Next is the callback function. This function receives a response back from the server and has two events assigned to the response.

httpRequest.js

```
var http = require('http');

var options = {
```

```
          host: 'www.apress.com',
          path: '/9781430250920'
    };
      callback = function(response) {
        var str = ''
          response.on('data', function (chunk) {
          str += chunk;
    });

    response.on('end', function () {
      console.log(str);
    });
}

function client (){
    var req = http.request(options, callback);
          req.end();
}

exports.client = client;
```

This is similar to the event listeners in regular JavaScript. You look for the "data" event and grab the data returning from the server. In this example, you append it to the str variable.

The second event end lets you know that the stream of data coming from the server has ended. The result in your command line is a long string made up of the contents of the web page you just made a request for.

Because this is a module, you can access it from here.

serverRequestIndex.js

```
var server = require("./httpRequest");
server.client ();
```

Debugging

The last part of your short intro to Node is to talk about how to debug your app. The quickest way to run the debugger is at the command line node -debug filename.js. Inside your code, you add the debugger command where you want to check your code. This might not be the most intuitive way to debug your application. IDEs like Eclipse, JetBrain's IntelliJ Idea, and WebStorm products have debugging options where you can set breakpoints and work with Node.js in the same way you would work with other server-side languages. You can find detailed instructions for Eclipse on gitHub: https://github.com/joyent/node/wiki/Using-Eclipse-as-Node-Applications-Debugger. You can find the details for JetBrain's products here: http://www.jetbrains.com/idea/webhelp/running-and-debugging-node-js.html.

Another way of working with Node is to install the node-inspector. Be aware that, as of this writing, it is no longer being maintained. However, if you want to try it, go to the command line and type in **npm install –g node-inspector**. The –g flag will make sure it's a global install.

After it is installed, you will need two command-line windows to make this work. In the first window, you can type in **node –debug filename.js** or **node –debug-brk filename.js**. The second option told the debugger to use a breakpoint at the beginning of the program.

In your second window, type **node-inspector**. You will get the message "visit http://0.0.0.0:8080/debug?port=5858." Copy and paste that into Chrome, and you will get the Chrome debugger with your breakpoint ready to go. (See Figure 8-9.) If you don't get that and instead get "connect ECONNREFUSED," make sure you don't have any other programs running on port 5858. You might need to close whichever app has the port open.

Figure 8-10 shows the editing features in JetBrain's IntelliJIdea.

Figure 8-9. *Chrome Debugger used to debug Node.js applications*

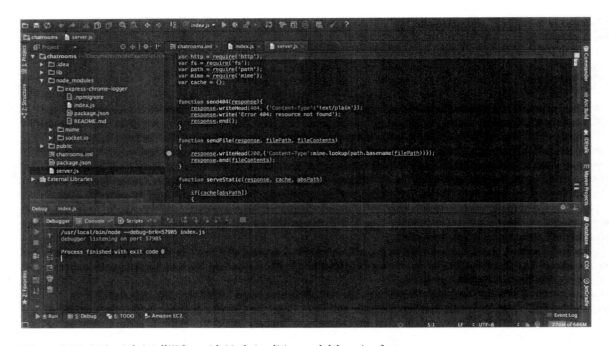

Figure 8-10. *JetBrain's IntelliJIdea with Node.js editing and debugging features*

Summary

I hope this has given you an insight into what can be done with JavaScript and XMLHttpRequest to create dynamic connections between the back end and the browser without reloading the page. Also, I hope this chapter helped you understand how you can take your JavaScript skill to the server side with Node.js.

As cool as Ajax is, there are some things to keep in mind:

- Primarily, Ajax was invented as a methodology to develop web applications, not web sites. It might be overkill to "Ajax-ify" every small form and menu.

- Ajax is a connector between client-side scripting and the back end; it is only as powerful as the back-end script or the information is.

- Ajax can be used to connect to data sources on the same server as the script using it. You can also use a script on the server to connect to a different server, or you can have a third-party service that offers data in JSON format. Finally, if the server supports CORS, you can connect to data on servers other than yours.

- It is very tempting and easy to create an Ajax application that looks impressive but is obtrusive—relying on the mouse and on JavaScript being available. Creating an Ajax interface that is accessible is a much harder task.

Ajax can be very useful, and a lot of gifted developers are working on frameworks and libraries that can help you to create Ajax applications quickly without having to know all the ins and outs of it—using them might even prevent you from repeating mistakes these developers have made themselves in the past. The number of libraries available is staggering, and it can be hard to tell which one is the right one for the task at hand.

Node.js is not a framework in itself like Rails is for Ruby. It does give you low-level access to develop any kind of application you like using JavaScript. There are frameworks that are available to help you organize your code and build large-scale applications like express (http://expressjs.com/).

In the next chapter, we will finally take a closer look at regular expressions and how to use them to validate data. You will learn how to create a contact form as an example application and maybe reuse some of the XHR functionality achieved here to make it slicker than a run-of-the-mill contact form.

CHAPTER 9

Data Validation Techniques

In this chapter, you will learn about using JavaScript to validate data entered by the user or coming from other systems. You already heard a lot about this in Chapter 2, which dealt with decisions involving data, and we will use some of that knowledge and extend it here.

Data validation has gone though some changes with the introduction of HTML5. Before, JavaScript was the first line of defense against having bad data possibly sent to the database. Now new features built into the browser help developers by removing a lot of the heavy lifting because the browser does a large part of the validation itself.

This is not to say that there should not be any server-side validation. There are a lot of server-side frameworks that have validation built in, so there isn't a good reason not to have your data checked a second time before committing it to a database.

HTML5 introduces a concept called *constraint validation*, which involves giving your data certain rules or constraints to live by. This way, the browser can check against the rules you set out and make sure the data is correct.

Pros and Cons of Client-Side Validation

Validating user entries on the client is great for several reasons:

- It saves the user a page reload when he enters incorrect data; and you can save the state of the variables, so the user does not have to enter all the data again, just the incorrect data.

- It cuts down on server traffic because there is no round-trip to the back end in case of an error.

- It makes the interface more responsive because it gives the user immediate feedback.

On the other hand, validating on the client has several issues:

- It cannot be trusted as the one and only means of validation. (JavaScript might not be available or could even be deliberately turned off to circumvent your validation measures. This would occur in cases where JavaScript is the only way to validate the data.)

- It could happen that the user agent does not notify the user of dynamic changes to the document—this is the case with very old screen readers for users with visual impairments.

- If you don't want to make your validation rules visible—say, to prevent spam or for authentication purposes—there is no way to do that in JavaScript.

A Quick Reminder About Protecting Content with JavaScript

Validation is one thing, protecting content with a password or obfuscating it via encryption is another. If you look around the web, you will find a lot of examples that promise that you can protect a web page from being available with a JavaScript password. Normally, these scripts are something like this:

examplePassword.html

```
var pw = prompt('Enter Password', ' ');
if(pw != 'password123') {
  alert('Wrong password');
  window.location = 'boo.html' ;
} else {
  window.location = 'creditCardNumbers.html';
}
```

The one and only cracking skill needed to work around this protection is to look at the page source, or—if the protection is in its own JavaScript file—open that in a browser or text editor. In some cases, where there is no redirection to the correct page, but only to the wrong one, simply turning off JavaScript will get you through.

There are seemingly more clever protection methods that use the password as a part of the file name:

```
var pw = prompt('Enter Password' , ' ');
window.location = 'page' + pw + '.html';
```

These can be cracked by finding out which files are available on the server—because either the directory listing hasn't been turned off (which is amazingly often the case—for proof just perform a Google search on "index of /mp3"—including the quotation marks) or the page can be found in counter statistics or in the cache of either the browser or Google.

The same applies to obfuscating (making something unreadable by encrypting or replacing words) content and scripts. Anything that was protected by JavaScript can be cracked with it—given enough time and determination. Just don't waste your time with it.

■ **Note** JavaScript is a language that is executed on the client computer most of the time, which makes it far too easy for a malicious attacker to work around your protection methods. In the case of right-click prevention scripts to protect images and text from being copied, you will most likely alienate normal visitors and get nothing but a dry chuckle out of real attackers.

Packing JavaScript with something like Dean Edward's packer (`http://dean.edwards.name/packer/`) to make really heavy scripts shorter is another issue, though, and might be a good idea at times—for example, if you want to use a large library script on a high-traffic site. Although packing JavaScript might make the file smaller, you might incur a performance hit uncompressing the file on the client side. Yahoo also has a tool to compress both JavaScript and CSS at `http://yui.github.com/yuicompressor/`.

Regular Expressions

Regular expressions help you match a string against a character pattern and are great for validating user entry or changing document content. They are not confined to JavaScript and are present in other languages, like Perl, PHP, and UNIX server scripts. They are amazingly powerful, and if you talk to Perl or PHP enthusiasts and server administrators, you'll be amazed how often they can replace a 50-line *switch/case* or *if/else* construct you wrote in JavaScript with a single regular expression. Many editing environments also feature "find" and "search and replace" functionality, allowing the use of regular expressions.

Regular expressions are the cat's pajamas once you get your head around them; however, at first sight a construct like /^[\w]+(\.[\w]+)*@([\w]+\.)+[a-z]{2,7}$/i (which checks whether a string is a valid e-mail syntax) can strike fear into the faint of heart. The good news is that it is not as tough as it looks.

Syntax and Attributes

Imagine you want to search for the string cat in text. You can define this as a regular expression in two different formats:

```
// Expression literals; notice that you must not use quotation marks!
var searchTerm = /cat/;
// Object constructor
var searchTerm = new RegExp('cat');
```

If you use this expression on a string via the match(), search(), exec(), or test() method, it'll return anything that has "cat" in it—regardless of the location in the string—like *catalog*, *concatenation*, or *scat*.

If you want to match only the word "cat" as a string without anything else around it, you need to use a ^ to indicate the start and a $ for the end:

```
var searchTerm = /^cat$/;
var searchTerm = new RegExp('^cat$');
```

You can also omit either the start indicator, ^, or the end indicator, $. This would match *cat*, *cat*alog, or *cat*astrophe:

```
var searchTerm = /^cat/;
var searchTerm = new RegExp('^cat');
```

The following code would find *polecat* or *wildcat*:

```
var searchTerm = /cat$/;
var searchTerm = new RegExp('cat$');
```

If you want to find "cat" regardless of case—for example, to match *cat*, *Catherine*, or *CAT*—you need to use the i attribute following the second slash. This causes the case to be ignored:

```
var searchTerm=/cat/i;
var searchTerm=new RegExp('cat', 'i');
```

If you have a string that could have the word "cat" in it several times, and you want to get all matches as an array, you need to add the parameter g for *global*:

```
var searchTerm = /cat/g;
var searchTerm = new RegExp('cat', 'g');
```

By default, regular expressions match patterns only in single-line strings. If you want to match a pattern in a multiline string, use the parameter m for *multiline*. You can also mix them, and the order is not important:

```
var searchTerm = /cat/gim;
var searchTerm = new RegExp('cat', 'mig');
```

Wildcard Searches, Constraining Scope, and Alternatives

The period character (.) plays the role of the joker card in regular expressions; it stands for "any character." (This can be confusing, because in advanced web searches or on the DOS and UNIX command line, it is the asterisk, *.)

```
var searchTerm = /c.t/gim;
var searchTerm = new RegExp('c.t', 'mig');
```

This matches *cat, cot, CRT,* and even nonsense strings like *c#t* and *c!T,* or those including spaces like *c T* or *c\tt.* (Remember that \t is the tab character.)

This might be too much flexibility for your needs, which is why you can use square brackets to limit the scope of the choices only to those you want to offer:

```
var searchTerm = /c[aou]t/gim;
var searchTerm = new RegExp('c[aou]t', 'mig');
```

You can match *cat, cot,* or *cut* in all uppercase and lowercase versions with this regular expression. You can also provide ranges like a-z within the brackets to match all lowercase letters, A-Z to match all uppercase letters, and 0-9 to match digits.

▥ **Caution**   Notice that regular expressions match the characters of the numbers, not their value. A regular expression with [0-9] would return 0200 as a valid four-digit number.

If you want to find, for example, a single lowercase letter followed immediately by a single uppercase letter, you'll use

```
var searchTerm = /[a-z][A-Z]/g;
var searchTerm = new RegExp(' [a-z][A-Z] ', 'g');
```

You can use the ^ character inside the brackets to exclude an option from the search. If you want to avoid "cut," for example, you can use

```
var searchTerm = /c[^u]t/g;
var searchTerm = new RegExp('c[^u]t', 'g');
```

Brackets match only one character at a time, which is why you can't match something like *cost, coast,* or *cast* with this expression. If you want to match several options, you can use the pipe character (|) inside parentheses, which functions like a logical OR:

```
var searchTerm = /c(^u|a|o|os|oas|as)t/g;
var searchTerm = new RegExp('c(^u|a|o|os|oas|as)t', 'g');
```

This now matches *cat, cot, cost, coast,* and *cast,* but not *cut* (because of the ^u).

Restricting the Number of Characters with Quantifiers

In many cases, you want to allow for a range of characters, like a to z, but you want to restrict their number. For this, you can use **quantifiers** in regular expressions, as listed in Table 9-1.

Table 9-1. *Quantifier Notations in Regular Expressions*

Notation	Number of Times Possible
*	0 or 1 time(s)
+	1 or more time(s)
?	0 or 1 time(s)
{n}	n times
{n,m}	n to m times

■ **Note** Adding the question mark (?) after each of these means that the regular expression should match them but as few times as possible.

For example, if you want to match the syntax of a serial number that consists of two groups of four characters, each separated with dashes, you use

```
var searchTerm = /[a-z|0-9]{4}\-[a-z|0-9]{4}/gim;
var searchTerm = new RegExp(' [a-z|0-9]{4}\-[a-z|0-9]{4}', 'mig');
```

■ **Note** You need to escape characters that are to be used literally, and not with any special meaning they might have in a regular expression pattern, like the dash in this case. You can do this by preceding the character with a backslash, \. Characters that need to be escaped are -, +, /, (,), [,], *, {, }, and ?. For example, /c.t/ matches *cat* or *cot* or *c4t*, whereas /c\.t/ only matches *c.t*.

Word Boundaries, Whitespace, and Other Shortcuts

All of these different options can result in pretty convoluted regular expressions, which is why there are some shortcut notations available. You might remember the special character notation for whitespace in Chapter 2, like \n for a line break and \t for a tab character. The same are available for regular expressions, as Table 9-2 shows.

Table 9-2. *Shortcut Notations for Regular Expressions*

Notation	Equivalent Notation	Meaning
\d	[0-9]	Only digits (integers)
\D	[^0-9]	All characters but digits (integers)
\w	[a-zA-Z0-9_]	All alphanumeric characters and the underscore
\W	[^a-zA-Z0-9_]	All nonalphanumeric characters
\b	N/A	Word boundary
\B	N/A	Not word boundary
\s	[\t\n\r\f\v]	All whitespace
\S	[^\t\n\r\f\v]	No whitespace

For example, if you want to test for a US Social Security number, which is a nine-digit number with dashes following the third and the fifth digits (for example, 456-33-1234), you can use the following regular expression, with optional dashes (using the ? quantifier), because the user might not enter them:

```
var searchTerm = /[0-9]{3}\-?[0-9]{2}\-?[0-9]{4}/;
var searchTerm = new RegExp('[0-9]{3}\-?[0-9]{2}\-?[0-9]{4}', ");
```

Alternatively, you can use the shortcut notation for digits:

```
var searchTerm = /\d{3}\-?\d{2}\-?\d{4}/;
var searchTerm = new RegExp('\\d{3}\-?\\d{2}\-?\\d{4}', ");
```

Be aware that if you use the shortcut notations inside quotation marks or in the constructor notation, you need to precede them with double backslashes, not single ones, because you need to escape them! With this knowledge, you should be well equipped to write your own regular expressions. As proof, let's go back to the example in the beginning paragraph of this section:

```
var validEmail = /^[\w]+(\.[\w]+)*@([\w]+\.)+[a-z]{2,7}$/i
```

E-mails can be pretty straightforward, like me@example.com, or more complex, like chris.heilmann.webdev@example.museum. This regular expression should return both as valid e-mails.

It tests whether the string starts with a group of one or more word characters, ^[\w]+, followed by a group of 0 or more word characters preceded by a period, (\.[\w]+)*, before the @ sign. After the @ sign, the string might have one or more groups of one or more word characters followed by a period, ([\w]+\.)+, and it'll end in a string that has between two and seven characters. This last string is the domain, which could be something short like de or longer like name or museum. Notice that by allowing several words followed by a period, you also make sure that e-mails like user@open.ac.uk are recognized.

Methods Using Regular Expressions

There are several methods that take regular expressions as parameters. The expression itself—the things inside the slashes or the RegExp constructor—is called a **pattern**, because it matches what you want to retrieve or test for.

- instance.test(string): Tests whether the string matches the pattern, and returns true or false.

- instance.exec(string): Matches the string and the pattern one time, and returns an array of matches or null.

- instance.match(pattern): Matches the string and the pattern, and returns the resulting matches as an array of strings or null.

- instance.search(pattern): Matches the string and the pattern, and returns the positions of the positive matches. If the string does not match any of the pattern, the search returns –1.

- instance.replace(pattern, replaceString): Matches the string against the pattern, and replaces every positive match with replaceString.

- instance.split(pattern, limit): Matches the string against the pattern, and splits it into an array with the substrings surrounding the pattern matches as array items. The optional limit parameter cuts down the number of array elements.

The Power of Parentheses Grouping

You might remember that to group an expression, you use parentheses, (). This not only groups the pattern, but also stores the results in special variables you can use later on. This is especially handy when you use it in conjunction with the replace() method. The results are stored in variables named $1 through $9, which means you can use up to nine parenthetical groupings in each regular expression. If you want to exclude a group from this, you precede it with ?:.

For example, if you have a list of names in the format *Surname, Name* and you want to convert each entry in the list into *Name Surname* format, you can do the following:

exampleNameOrder.html

```
names=[
  'Reznor, Trent',
  'Eldritch, Andrew',
  'Clark, Anne',
  'Almond,Marc'
];
for(i = 0; i < names.length; i++) {
  alert(names[i].replace(/(\w+)+,\s?(\w+)/g, '$2 $1'));
}
```

The pattern matches any word preceding the comma (followed by an optional whitespace character) and the following word, and stores both in variables. The replacement string reverses the order by using the $ variables.

A more complex example is to print the URL of every external link of a content area behind the link:

exampleShowURL.html

```
showURLs = function(){
  var ct = document.getElementById('content');
  var searchTerm = '(<a href="((?:http|https|ftp):\/\/ ';
  searchTerm    += '(?:[\\w]+\.)+[a-z]{2,7})">';
  searchTerm    += '(?:\\w|\\s|\\.)+<\/a>)';
  var pattern = new RegExp(searchTerm, 'mgi');
  ct.innerHTML = ct.innerHTML.replace(pattern, '$1 ($2) ');
}
```

You start the pattern with a set of parentheses to store the whole construct in the variable $1 and match the start of a link <a href=". You follow up with a set of parentheses surrounding what is inside the href attribute, which is a URL starting with either http, https, or ftp, not storing this group in a variable (because this set of parentheses is preceded by ?:), followed by a colon and two slashes (that need to be escaped), followed by a URL ending in a domain. (This is the same pattern used in the e-mail checking example.)

You close the parentheses, storing everything inside the link's href attribute in $2, and match everything inside the link element (which could be one or more words, whitespace, or a period) but don't store it in a variable. Then close the main group after the closing </a> and use replace to replace every link with the pattern matches, which in effect will turn <a href=http://www.example.com">example</a> into
<a href=http://www.example.com">example</a> (http://www.example.com).

Regular Expression Resources

As with any programming language, there are dozens of ways to reach the same goal. I don't want to just give examples to copy and paste when getting your head around regular expressions will get you so much further.

There are many online resources that list patterns according to their task:

- The Regular Expression Library (`http://regexlib.com/`) has a searchable database of patterns.

- At Regular-Expressions.info (`http://www.regular-expressions.info/`), you'll find a very extensive tutorial on regular expressions.

- RegEx Advice (`http://regexadvice.com/`) has a good forum and blogs on regular expressions.

In terms of books, there's *Introducing Regular Expressions* by Michael Fitzgerald (O'Reilly, 2012), *Regular Expressions Pocket Reference* by Tony Stubblebine (O'Reilly, 2007), and the very extensive *Mastering Regular Expressions* by Jeffrey Friedl (O'Reilly, 2006).

For the more UNIX-inclined user, there is *Regular Expression Recipes: A Problem-Solution Approach* by Nathan A. Good (Apress, 2005).

Summary of Validation Methods

In real-life scripting situations, you are never likely to stick to one of the preceding methods, but use a mixture of them all to reach your goal as quickly as possible. There are no fixed rules for what to use when, but some hints and benefits might be good to remember:

- Regular expressions only match characters; you cannot do calculations with them (at least not in JavaScript; PHP offers the e switch, which evaluates matches as PHP code).

- Regular expressions have the benefit of being language independent—you can use the same rules on the server and the client side. Both the string and the mathematical methods are fixed to JavaScript and might not be the same in other languages.

- It is very easy to match large ranges of options in regular expressions, with strings that can get messy very quickly, unless the ranges are following a simple rule, like A to Z or 0 to 9.

- If you have to validate numbers, most of the time it is not worth the effort using string or regular expression validation; just stick to testing the values mathematically. Strings are too forgiving, because you cannot compare values and do calculations with them. The only options you have are determining the string length and testing for special characters.

- There is no shame in using out-of-the-box patterns and methods developed by others. Many of these have been tested by dozens of developers in different development environments.

Constraint Validation

We'll now talk about some of the techniques you can use with forms, to spot which fields need validation and to tell the user that something is amiss.

HTML5 adds new input types for forms and new ways of adding validation that does not require JavaScript. It also provides an API (Application Programming Interface) to allow developers to extend the capabilities to better suit their needs. Constraint validation is the method of letting the browser validate the content of web forms.

Designating Mandatory Fields

There have been several methods available for designating form elements as mandatory and requiring validation. HTML5 makes this simple by adding the `required` attribute to your form fields. Internet Explorer (IE) 10+,

Safari 5, Firefox 16, Chrome 23, and Opera 21.1 support this. One of the nice things about constraint validation is that the browser will do the validation for you, displaying a warning when the field is empty.

The input tag has the required attribute:

```
<input type="text" id="firstName" required title="First Name is Required! " >
```

When trying to submit your form, the built-in validation will give you a warning like the one shown in Figure 9-1, depending on your browser.

Figure 9-1. *An example of Chrome displaying a warning for users on fields where the* validate *attribute has been used. Safari 5 and 6 have partial support for the* required *attribute in that it will not display a warning*

Adding the pattern attribute lets you add regular expressions to the field where you might want to do an extra level of validation.

For example, you might want to make sure that the URL provided is only for a certain domain:

```
<input type="url" id="theURL" required title="URL is Required! "
pattern="https?://(?:www\.)?twitter\.com/.+"/>
```

This example lets the user type in her twitter address (http://www.twitter.com/username). Even though the field is required, the pattern attribute gives it additional rules to follow before it is valid.

Additional Validation Attributes

One of the new form input types is Number. You use this type to create a number stepper with a minimum value and a maximum value. (See Figure 9-2.) If you type in a number higher than the max value and then try to submit the form, the built-in validation will occur.

Pick a number between 1 and 10: | 11 ⊕ | Send

⚠ Value must be less than or equal to 10.

Figure 9-2. *Chrome displaying a warning where the value is higher than the* max *attribute*

Here is an example of the number input type:

```
<input type="number" min="1" max="10" step="1">
```

The placeholder attribute does not do any kind of validation, but it is useful when giving users direction on how to fill out a form. Combined with an input type like email, it can be very helpful. (See Figure 9-3.)

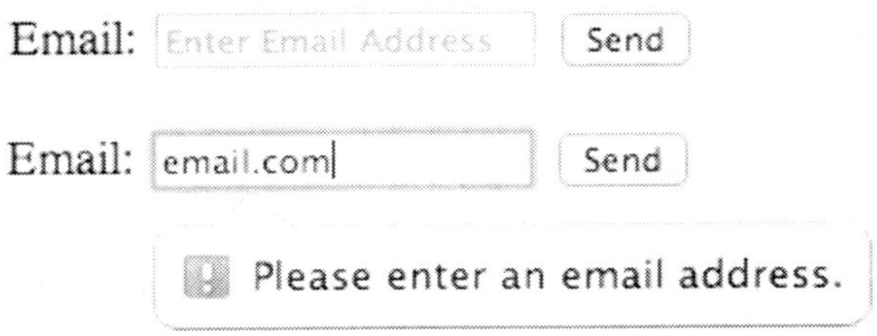

Email: [Enter Email Address]   [Send]

Email: [email.com|]   [Send]

     [🔲 Please enter an email address.]

Figure 9-3. *Chrome displaying both the placeholder text and a warning where the email address is invalid*

Here is an example of the email input type:

```
<input type="email"  placeholder="Enter Email Address">
```

The Novalidate Attribute

In the case that you want to disable the validation of a node on submission, use the following:

```
<form novalidate>
      <input type="text" required >
      <input type="submit" value="Submit">
</form>
```

Adding the formnovalidate attribute to a submit button will keep the form from performing any validation on any of the input nodes:

```
<input type="submit" value="Submit" formnovaidate>
```

Additional User Feedback Using CSS Pseudo Classes

HTML5 brings with it a consistent way of validating form data, but the built-in way of indicating what's wrong to the user is different across browsers. To create a more consistent experience, you can use new Cascading Style Sheet (CSS) classes.

Letting users know visually that a field is mandatory can be done with new pseudo CSS classes.

exampleHTML5Required.html (excerpts)

```
<style>
 input:required{
    border: 1px solid #F00;
}

:optional{
    background:#CCC;
}
</style>
  <label>Your Email
  <input required id="email" type="email" placeholder="Enter Email Address" >
  </label>
```

```
    <label>Message
    <textarea id="message"></textarea>
    </label>
<button>Submit</button>
```

In the preceding example, you can see :required and :optional have been added to CSS. In the first instance, you are making sure that any input tag that has the required attribute receives the style. In the next instance, it could be any field that does not carry the required attribute.

Immediate feedback can also be helpful to users when filling out forms. The :valid and :invalid classes can be used to let someone know the status of the field they just filled out. In this example, you add the class interacted when the user moves on to the next field. In the fields "blur" state, it will run the validation and display a red or green border, depending on if the information is valid.

exampleValidBlur.html (excerpts)

```
<style>
.interacted:invalid{
    border: 1px solid red;
}

.interacted:valid {
    border: 1px solid green;
}
</style>

<script>
        function addInteractedClass(){
    var inputs = document.getElementsByTagName("input");

    for (var I = 0; i< inputs.lengh; i++){
       inputs[i].addEventListener("blur", function(event){
              event.target.classList.add("interacted");
              },false);
                   }
        }

 document.addEventListener("DomContentLoaded", addInteractedClass, false);
</script>

<p><label for="name">Your Name</label></p>
<p><input required id="name" type="text" placeholder="Please Enter Your Name" ></p>

<p><label for="email">Your Email</label></p>
<p><input type="email" id="email" required ></p>

<p><input type="submit" id="send" valie="Send Form" ></p>
```

In addition to the CSS classes used in the last two examples, some other classes are available:

- `in-range`

- `out-of-range`

- `read-only`

- `read-write`

Detecting Support for HTML5 Form Attributes

Not all browsers support every new input type. Browsers that don't do so will ignore the type you give it and act as if the type is set to "text."

To check if the browser supports the attribute you are looking for, you can write two functions. The first one will run when the DOM is loaded and execute an `if` statement. This will call the second function with the attribute name and the field as its parameters.

The second function creates an element based on the field type and returns a value of `true` or `false`, if the attribute is in that element. The result is returned back to the first function, which will complete the conditional statement and know if it should use the built-in browser functions or JavaScript.

```
function initFormCheck(){
    if(testHTML5Attr("required","input")){
    //use built in browser validation
    }else{
            //use JavaScript fall back
    }
}
function testHTML5Attr(attr,elm){
        return attr in document.createElement(elm);
}
document.addEventListener("DOMContentLoaded" initFormCheck, false);
```

Constraint Validation API

Because the browser is doing a lot of the validation work, it becomes easy to check if the information has been entered properly before sending any data to the server. The constraint validation API (http://www.whatwg.org/specs/web-apps/current-work/#constraint-validation) adds properties and methods to DOM nodes that can be used in a pure JavaScript solution.

This is also important because even though Safari 6 supports validation, it does not suppress submitting data when the required attributes are present.

This example uses the valid property of the email fields to check for a correctly formatted email address and checks to see if the addresses match.

exampleCheckEmail.html (excerpts)

```
<script>
    function emailCheck(){
        var email1 = document.getElementById("email1");
        var email2 = document.getElementById("email2");
        var resultDiv = document.getElementById("result");
        var form = document.getElementById("emailForm");
```

```
        form.addEventListener("submit", function(event){
          if(email1.validity.valid && email2.validity.valid && email1.value && email2.value){
            resultDiv.innerHTML = "<p>Email is valid and they match</p>";
          }else{
                resultDiv.innerHTML = "<p>Email is not valid or they do not match</p>";
          }
            event.preventDefault();
        }, false);
    }
  document.addEventListener("DomContentLoaded", addInteractedClass, false);
</script>
```

Showing a List of Erroneous Fields

This method shows the user a list of fields that contain errors. (See Figure 9-4.) In addition to adding a border to visualize if the field is valid, you will loop through the form fields to generate a list of all the invalid fields.

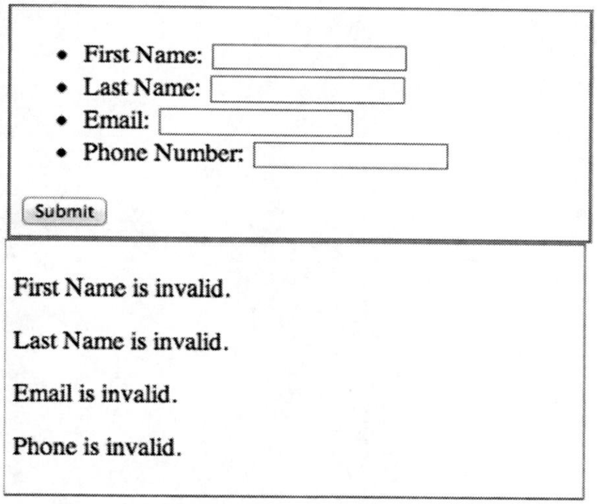

Figure 9-4. Showing a list of erroneous fields

Once the page loads, you add an event listener to the form. When the form is about to submit the data, you stop the form and call the checkInputs function.

The checkInputs function first looks at a div called resultsDiv, where you give the user feedback and empty out any nodes that are in that div. Then it loops though all the input tags and checks for the valid property of each tag.

If the tag is not valid, it then grabs the ID, asks for the properly-formatted name through the reformatName function, and continues to create a paragraph node with text indicating the name of the field is invalid and adds this new node to the resultsDiv.

showInvalidFields.html (excerpts)

```
<script>
    function formCheck(){
        var form = document.getElementById("userForm");
        form.addEventListener("submit", function(event){
```

```
                        checkInputs();
                        event.preventDefault();
                }, false);
    }

function checkInputs(){
    var resultDiv = document.getElementById("result");
        resultDiv.hidden = true;
    var inputs = document.getElementsByTagName("input");

  while(resultDiv.hasChildNodes()){
      resultDiv.removeChild(resultDiv.firstChild);
  }

for(var i = 0; i < inputs.length; i++){
  inputs[i].classList.add("interacted");
  if(!inputs[i].validity.valid){
    var para = document.createElement("p");
    var formatedName = reformatName(inputs[i].id);
    var msg = document.createTextNode(formatedName + " is invalid.");
        para.appendChild(msg);
        resultDiv.appendChild(para);
        resultDiv.hidden = false;
    }
  }
}

function reformatName(oldName){
    switch(oldName){
        case "firstName": return "First Name";
        break;
        case "lastName": return "Last Name";
        break;
        case "email": return "Email";
        break;
        case "phone": return "Phone";
        break;
}

document.addEventListener("DomContentLoaded", formCheck, false);
</script>
```

Other Dynamic Validation Methods

It is very tempting to make every field validate immediately when the user changes it, and you can do a lot with Ajax and the proper back-end datasets or functionality. One great example is to include suggestions of what data is valid while you enter a form.

Google was one of the first examples of web forms to do that. It offers you searches other users have already done with a number of possible results, as shown in Figure 9-5.

Figure 9-5. *Google showing possible results while you type*

Adding autocomplete functionality to your site is made easy with HTML5. First I will go over how it works and then create a JavaScript version that could be updated to pull data from a server.

autoComplete.html (excerpts)

```
<input type="text" name="srch" id="srch" list="datalist1">
<datalist id="datalist1">
  <option value="Bill Gates">
  <option value="Linus Torvalds">
  <option value="Douglas Coupland">
  <option value="Ridley Scott">
  <option value="George Lucas">
  <option value="Dan Akroyd">
  <option value="Sigourney Weaver">
  <option value="Tim Burton">
  <option value="Katie Jane Garside">
  <option value="Winona Ryder">
  <option value="Vince Clarke">
  <option value="Martin Gore">
  <option value="Kurt Harland Larson">
  <option value="Paul Robb">
  <option value="James Cassidy">
  <option value="David Tennant">
</datalist>
```

In this example, a new attribute has been added to the `input` tag. The `list` attribute points to a new `datalist` element. This element holds predefined options that will be displayed as the user starts typing in the field, as shown in Figure 9-6.

Type in a name: VI
                 Vince Clarke

Figure 9-6. *Offering data from the data list*

Now that I have covered the basics, creating a dynamic example is just a matter of using JavaScript to create the datalist for us. If you could use a server-side script to provide data, this example could be adjusted by using some of the AJAX techniques from previous lessons.

dynamicAutoComplete.html (excerpts)

```
<script>
function createDataList(){
    var nameArray = new Array();
            nameArray[0] = "Bill Gates";
            nameArray[1] = "Linus Torvalds";
            nameArray[2] = "Douglas Coupland";
            nameArray[3] = "Ridley Scott";
            nameArray[4] = "George Lucas";
            nameArray[5] = "Dan Akroyd";
            nameArray[6] = "Sigourney Weaver";
            nameArray[7] = "Tim Burton";
            nameArray[8] = "Katie Jane Garside";
            nameArray[9] = "Winona Ryder";
            nameArray[10] = "Martin Gore";
            nameArray[11] = "Kurt Harland Larson";
            nameArray[12] = "Paul Robb";
            nameArray[13] = "James Cassidy";
            nameArray[14] = "David Tennant";

var dataList = document.createElement("datalist");
    dataList.id = "datalist1";
    document.body.appendChild(dataList);

for(var i = 0; i<nameArray.length; i++){
   var option = document.createElement("option");
        option.value = nameArray[i];
        dataList.appendChild(option);
    }
}

document.addEventListener("DOMContentLoaded", createDataList, false);
</script>
```

Browsers That Don't Support Constraint Validation

As you can see, having the browser do the heavy lifting is a good thing. This does leave older browsers out, but there are ways to handle them.

Implementing validation on the server side adds a second level of protection. If your browser doesn't support constraint validation, it won't matter because the server is taking care of it.

Polyfills are JavaScript libraries that let you continue to use the latest browser advancements, and they add support for browsers that don't yet use them natively. There is a long list of polyfills maintained by Paul Irish: https://github.com/Modernizr/Modernizr/wiki/HTML5-Cross-Browser-Polyfills.

Webshims is a collection of polyfills that also includes the constraint validation API. Downloading the webshims library from github (http://afarkas.github.com/webshim/demos/) and adding the JavaScript into your page will give you the ability to add HTML5 syntax to your page and still have older browsers respond properly.

Here is an example of adding webshims to your page:

```
<script src="js/jquery-1.8.2.js"></script>
<script src="js/modernizr-yepnope-custom.js"></script>
<script src="js-webshim/minified/polyfiller.js"></script>
```

```
<script>jQuery.webshims.polyfill('forms');</script>
<form>
    <input type="text" requred>
    <input type="submit" value="submit">

</form>
```

Summary

I hope you feel quite confident writing regular expressions and using constraint validation. HTML5 relieves you of having to write complex scripts to validate the data.

Using the constraint validation API, you can make sure the data is valid and provide visual feedback using new CSS pseudo classes, which can be applied to your form elements in addition to JavaScript.

This does not mean you should not have validation on the server side. Many server-side frameworks have validation built in, so there isn't a good reason not to use it.

Polyfills give you the ability to use the new HTML5 methods on older browsers that don't natively support them. As people upgrade their browsers, the polyfill will leave the new functionality to the browser. So you have a way of creating a consistent experience for a large number of your users.

In the next chapter, we'll take on a larger project and create a dynamic image gallery that's powered by the back end and spiced up with CSS, JavaScript, and Ajax.

CHAPTER 10

Modern JavaScript Case Study: A Dynamic Gallery

In this chapter, you will learn how to develop a JavaScript-enhanced thumbnail gallery backed up by a PHP script. You'll start with learning techniques related to static galleries and how to enhance them. Then you'll move on to a gallery that uses PHP and Ajax to pull images dynamically from the server.

Note You can download the demo code of this chapter or see the results online at `http://www.beginningjavascript.com`. Because the chapter contains image galleries, the download is on the larger side, but it allows you to see all the code—including the server-side PHP—on your local server.

Basics of Thumbnail Galleries

Let's start at the basics and plan our thumbnail gallery. I pondered for a long time whether I should include one in this book, because it has become almost cliché for JavaScript and CSS books to have galleries as examples. However, I wrote this chapter to give an example of how you can spice up a very common solution like a thumbnail gallery with modern scripting and CSS and stay independent of both of them. Many examples—especially CSS-only galleries—look great and work in modern browsers; however, they don't degrade well and don't really deliver what a thumbnail gallery is supposed to deliver.

What Is a Thumbnail Gallery and What Should It Do?

The idea of a thumbnail gallery goes back to the times when browsers started to support images and connection speeds on the Web could be measured in the single kilobits. The job of such a gallery was, and still is, to give an overview of what images are available by providing a smaller preview of each image in the gallery. "Smaller" means smaller in dimensions but also—and most importantly—smaller in file size. This means that a visitor who is only interested in one picture in your gallery does not need to download all images, only the one he is interested in—saving both him time and you server traffic. A lot of CSS-only or JavaScript/HTML thumbnail galleries fail to do this and assume that every user wants to download the lot to see one image. You can offer downloading of all the images, but it should be an option rather than a requirement. The worst thumbnail galleries resize photos via HTML attributes or CSS to thumbnails, thus forcing visitors to download the large images to see them as bad-quality thumbnails. Resizing images by altering their dimensions in CSS, via JavaScript, or by using HTML attributes does not result in good-quality thumbnails; it is simply laziness and a bad idea.

If you want to offer thumbnail galleries in their original sense, you need to generate smaller thumbnail pictures of the large images you want to show. You can do that either as a batch process before you upload the gallery or on the fly via scripting on the server.

■ **Tip** There are a lot of thumbnail-generation and batch-generation tools available. Good—and, most importantly, free—ones are Google's Picasa (available at `http://picasa.google.com/`) and IrfanView (available at `http://www.irfanview.com/`). Generating thumbnails on the server can be easily achieved with PHP and the GD library. I've written an article about how to do that, available at `http://icant.co.uk/articles/phpthumbnails/`, and there is a great premade PHP class called `phpThumb()` available at `http://phpthumb.sourceforge.net/`. Because this is a book about JavaScript, I will not get into the details of image generation via PHP, although it is amazingly handy for online galleries.

Static Thumbnail Galleries

Traditional thumbnail galleries offer the small thumbnail images inside a table or a list. Each of the thumbnails links to a page with the large image that, in return, links back to the thumbnail gallery or offers previous and next image links.

If there are a lot of images, the thumbnail pages can be paginated, showing a certain number of thumbnails at a time and offering navigation forward and backward through the whole collection. With purely static galleries, this means you have to generate all the thumbnail pages, and one for each photo, which is a lot of work initially and a lot of files to transfer to the server on every update of the gallery.

Faking Dynamic Galleries with JavaScript

You can use JavaScript to turn a static thumbnail gallery into a seemingly dynamic gallery by applying event handlers to all the thumbnails. When a thumbnail is clicked, you cover the thumbnails with a new element containing the large image. Keep the gallery accessible to non-JavaScript users by linking the thumbnail to the large picture and simply showing this in the browser:

exampleFakeDynamic.html (excerpt)

```
<ul id="thumbs">
  <li>
    <a href="galleries/animals/dog2.jpg">
      <img src="galleries/animals/tn_dog2.jpg" alt="tn_dog2.jpg">
    </a>
  </li>
  <li>
    <a href="galleries/animals/dog3.jpg">
      <img src="galleries/animals/tn_dog3.jpg" alt="tn_dog3.jpg">
    </a>
  </li>
  <li>
    <a href="galleries/animals/dog4.jpg">
      <img src="galleries/animals/tn_dog4.jpg" alt="tn_dog4.jpg">
    </a>
  </li>
  [... more thumbnails ...]
</ul>
```

■ **Tip**   You might as well use tables or definition lists for thumbnail galleries, as tables degrade better because they remain multicolumn constructs even in non-CSS browsers and definition lists are semantically correct, too. For the examples in this chapter, I used a simple list to keep things easy and allow the thumbnails to take up as much space as is available on the screen.

You can test the effect by opening the demo exampleFakeDynamic.html. Let's go through the functionality step by step, starting with a skeleton for the script:

fakeDynamic.js (skeleton)

```
fakegal = {
  // IDs
  thumbsListID : 'thumbs',
  largeContainerID : 'photo',
  // CSS classes
  closeClass : 'close',
  nextClass : 'next',
  prevClass : 'prev',
  hideClass : 'hide',
  showClass : 'show',
  // Labels
  closeLabel : 'close',
  prevContent : '<img src="last.gif" alt="previous photo" >',
  nextContent : '<img src="next.gif" alt="next photo">',

  init : function(){ },
  createContainer : function(){},
  showPic : function(e){ },
  setPic : function(pic){ },
  navPic : function(e){ }
DOMhelp.addEvent(window, 'load', fakegal.init, false);
```

You need

- The ID of the element containing all the thumbnails
- An ID to assign to the large picture container
- CSS classes for the link to remove the large picture
- The links to navigate through the large pictures
- Classes to show and hide elements
- A label to tell the user that the link hides the large picture
- Labels for the next and previous picture links

In terms of methods, you need

- A method to initialize the functionality
- A utility method that initially creates the image container

- A method to show the picture

- A method to set the picture to be shown

- A method to navigate to the next or previous picture

The method setting the picture to be shown, setPic(), is necessary because both the showing method, showPic(), and the navigation method, navPic(), change the image in the container.

fakeDynamic.js

```
fakegal = {
  // IDs
  thumbsListID : 'thumbs',
  largeContainerID : 'photo',
  // CSS classes
  closeClass : 'close',
  nextClass : 'next',
  prevClass : 'prev',
  hideClass : 'hide',
  showClass : 'show',
  // Labels
  closeLabel : 'close',
  prevContent : '<img src="last.gif" alt="previous photo">',
  nextContent : '<img src="next.gif" alt="next photo" >',
  init:function() {
    if(!document.getElementById || !document.createTextNode) {
      return;
    }
    fakegal.tlist = document.getElementById(fakegal.thumbsListID);
    if(!fakegal.tlist){ return; }
    var thumbsLinks = fakegal.tlist.getElementsByTagName('a');
    fakegal.all = thumbsLinks.length;
    for(var i = 0 ; i < thumbsLinks.length; i++) {
      DOMhelp.addEvent(thumbsLinks[i], 'click', fakegal.showPic, false);
      thumbsLinks[i].onclick = DOMhelp.safariClickFix;
      thumbsLinks[i].i = i;
    }
    fakegal.createContainer();
  },
```

The init() method tests whether DOM is supported and retrieves the element that contains the thumbnails. It then loops through all the links after storing the number of all links in a property called all. (This is necessary later on to avoid a next link on the last image.) It applies an event handler pointing to showPic() to each link in the thumbnail list and stores its index number in a new property called i before calling createContainer() to add the necessary image container element to the document.

fakeDynamic.js (continued)

```
createContainer : function() {
  fakegal.c = document.createElement('div');
  fakegal.c.id = fakegal.largeContainerID;
```

You start the `createContainer()` method by creating a new DIV element, storing it in a property called c, and assigning the large image container ID to it.

fakeDynamic.js (continued)

```
var p = document.createElement('p');
var cl = DOMhelp.createLink('#', fakegal.closeLabel);
cl.className = fakegal.closeClass;
p.appendChild(cl);
DOMhelp.addEvent(cl, 'click', fakegal.setPic, false);
cl.onclick = DOMhelp.safariClickFix;
fakegal.c.appendChild(p);
```

Create a new paragraph and insert a link into it with the `closeLabel` as text content. Assign an event handler pointing to `setPic()` to the link, apply the Safari fix, and add the paragraph to the container element.

fakeDynamic.js (continued)

```
var il = DOMhelp.createLink('#', ' ');
DOMhelp.addEvent(il, 'click', fakegal.setPic, false);
il.onclick = DOMhelp.safariClickFix;
fakegal.c.appendChild(il);
```

Now add another—empty—link to the container with an event handler calling `setPic()`. This link will later surround the large picture, making it clickable and thus possible for keyboard users to get rid of it.

fakeDynamic.js (continued)

```
fakegal.next = DOMhelp.createLink('#', ' ');
fakegal.next.innerHTML = fakegal.nextContent;
fakegal.next.className = fakegal.nextClass;
DOMhelp.addEvent(fakegal.next, 'click', fakegal.navPic, false);
fakegal.next.onclick = DOMhelp.safariClickFix;
fakegal.c.appendChild(fakegal.next);

fakegal.prev = DOMhelp.createLink('#', ' ');
fakegal.prev.innerHTML = fakegal.prevContent;
fakegal.prev.className = fakegal.prevClass;
DOMhelp.addEvent(fakegal.prev, 'click', fakegal.navPic, false);
fakegal.prev.onclick = DOMhelp.safariClickFix;
fakegal.c.appendChild(fakegal.prev);
```

Two more links need to be added to show the previous and the next image, respectively, both with event handlers pointing to `navPic()`.

fakeDynamic.js (continued)

```
  fakegal.tlist.parentNode.appendChild(fakegal.c);
}
```

Add the new container to the parent node of the thumbnail list, and the show can begin.

fakeDynamic.js (continued)

```
showPic : function(e) {
  var t = DOMhelp.getTarget(e);
  if(t.nodeName.toLowerCase() != 'a') {
    t = t.parentNode;
  }
  fakegal.current = t.i;
  var largePic = t.getAttribute('href');
  fakegal.setPic(largePic);
  DOMhelp.cancelClick(e);
},
```

In the event listener method showPic(), retrieve the target and determine whether it really is a link by testing the nodeName. Then store the i property that was assigned to each thumbnail link in the init() method as the value of a new property, current, of the main object to tell all other methods which picture is currently shown. Retrieve the link's href attribute and call the setPic() method with the href as a parameter before stopping the browser from following the link via cancelClick().

fakeDynamic.js (continued)

```
setPic : function(pic) {
  var a;
  var picLink = fakegal.c.getElementsByTagName('a')[1];
  picLink.innerHTML = ' ';
```

The setPic() method takes the second link inside the image container (which is the link after the closing link) and removes any content that this link might have by setting its innerHTML property to an empty string. This is necessary to avoid having more than one picture show at a time.

fakeDynamic.js (continued)

```
if(typeof pic == 'string') {
    fakegal.c.className = fakegal.showClass;
    var i = document.createElement('img');
    i.setAttribute('src' , pic);
    picLink.appendChild(i);
```

You compare the type of the parameter pic with string, because the method can be called with a URL as the parameter or without it. If there is a parameter that is a valid string, you add the show class to the container to show it to the user and add a new image to it with the pic parameter as its source.

fakeDynamic.js (continued)

```
} else {
  fakegal.c.className = ' ';
}
```

If there isn't a parameter of the type string, you remove any class from the picture container, thus hiding it.

fakeDynamic.js (continued)

```
a = fakegal.current == 0 ? 'add' : 'remove';
  DOMhelp.cssjs(a, fakegal.prev, fakegal.hideClass);
  a = fakegal.current == fakegal.all-1 ? 'add' : 'remove';
  DOMhelp.cssjs(a, fakegal.next, fakegal.hideClass);
},
```

Test to see whether the current property of the main object is equal to 0, and hide the previous picture link if this is the case. Do the same with the next picture link, and compare current with the number of all thumbnails (stored in all). Hide or show each link by adding or removing the hide class.

fakeDynamic.js (continued)

```
  navPic : function(e) {
    var t = DOMhelp.getTarget(e);
    if(t.nodeName.toLowerCase() != 'a') {
      t = t.parentNode;
    }
    var c = fakegal.current;
    if(t == fakegal.prev) {
      c -= 1;
    } else {
      c += 1;
    }
    fakegal.current = c;
    var pic = fakegal.tlist.getElementsByTagName('a')[c];
    fakegal.setPic(pic.getAttribute('href'));
    DOMhelp.cancelClick(e);
  }
}
DOMhelp.addEvent(window, 'load', fakegal.init, false);
```

Retrieve a reference to the link that was clicked (by getting the event target via DOMhelp's getTarget() and ensuring the nodeName is A), and determine whether the link is the previous link by comparing this node to the one stored in the prev property. Increment or decrement current depending on which link was activated. Then call setPic() with the href attribute of the new current link, and prevent the browser from following the activated link by calling cancelClick().

All that is left is to add a style sheet; the result might appear as shown in Figure 10-1.

Figure 10-1. Using JavaScript to simulate a server-controlled dynamic image gallery

Displaying Captions

Thumbnail galleries are visual constructs, but it is still a good idea to think about alternative text and image captioning. Not only will these make your gallery accessible to blind users, but they also allow for searching the thumbnail data and indexing it through search engines.

Many tools, like Google's Picasa, allow for dynamic captioning and the addition of alternative text. You could use XHR to create something similar, but because this is a book about JavaScript, and how to store the entered data on the server would need some explanation, it is not a relevant example. Instead, let's modify the "fake" gallery so that it displays captions.

You'll use the image's `title` attribute as a caption for the image; this means that the static HTML needs proper alternative text and title data.

exampleFakeDynamicAlt.html (excerpt)

```
<ul id="thumbs">
  <li>
    <a href="galleries/animals/dog2.jpg">
      <img src="galleries/animals/tn_dog2.jpg" title="This square is mine" alt="Dog in a shady square">
    </a>
  </li>
  <li>
    <a href="galleries/animals/dog3.jpg">
      <img src="galleries/animals/tn_dog3.jpg" title="Sleepy bouncer" alt="Dog on the steps of a shop">
    </a>
  </li>
  [... More thumbnails ...]
</ul>
```

The script itself does not have to change much; all it needs is an extra paragraph in the generated image container and alterations of the methods to send the caption and alternative text data to the large image container.

fakeDynamicAlt.js

```
fakegal = {
  // IDs
  thumbsListID : 'thumbs',
  largeContainerID : 'photo',
  // CSS classes
  closeClass : 'close',
  nextClass : 'next',
  prevClass : 'prev',
  hideClass : 'hide',
  closeLabel : 'close',
  captionClass : 'caption',
  // Labels
  showClass : 'show',
  prevContent : '<img src="last.gif" alt="previous photo">',
  nextContent : '<img src="next.gif" alt="next photo">',
```

The first change is a cosmetic one: you add a new CSS class that will be applied to the caption.

fakeDynamicAlt.js (continued)

```
init : function() {
  if(!document.getElementById || !document.createTextNode) {
    return;
  }
  fakegal.tlist = document.getElementById(fakegal.thumbsListID);
  if(!fakegal.tlist) { return; }
  var thumbsLinks = fakegal.tlist.getElementsByTagName('a');
  fakegal.all = thumbsLinks.length;
  for(var i = 0; i < thumbsLinks.length; i++) {
    DOMhelp.addEvent(thumbsLinks[i], 'click', fakegal.showPic, false);
```

```
    thumbsLinks[i].onclick = DOMhelp.safariClickFix;
    thumbsLinks[i].i = i;
  }
  fakegal.createContainer();
},
showPic : function(e) {
  var t = DOMhelp.getTarget(e);
  if(t.nodeName.toLowerCase() != 'a') {
    t = t.parentNode;
  }
  fakegal.current = t.i;
  var largePic = t.getAttribute('href');
  var img = t.getElementsByTagName('img')[0];
  var alternative = img.getAttribute('alt');
  var caption = img.getAttribute('title');
  fakegal.setPic(largePic, caption, alternative);
  DOMhelp.cancelClick(e);
},
```

The init() method remains unchanged, but the showPic() method needs to read the alternative text and the title attribute of the image, in addition to the href attribute of the link, and send all three of them as parameters to setPic().

fakeDynamicAlt.js (continued)

```
setPic : function(pic, caption, alternative) {
  var a;
  var picLink = fakegal.c.getElementsByTagName('a')[1];
  picLink.innerHTML = ' ';
  fakegal.caption.innerHTML = ' ';
  if(typeof pic == 'string') {
    fakegal.c.className = fakegal.showClass;
    var i = document.createElement('img');
    i.setAttribute('src', pic);
    i.setAttribute('alt' ,alternative);
    picLink.appendChild(I);
  } else {
    fakegal.c.className = ' ';
  }
  a = fakegal.current == 0 ? 'add' : 'remove';
  DOMhelp.cssjs(a, fakegal.prev, fakegal.hideClass);
  a = fakegal.current == fakegal.all-1 ? 'add' : 'remove';
  DOMhelp.cssjs(a, fakegal.next, fakegal.hideClass);
  if(caption != ' ') {
   var ctext = document.createTextNode(caption);
    fakegal.caption.appendChild(ctext);
  }
},
```

The setPic() method now takes three parameters instead of one—the source of the large picture, the caption, and the alternative text. The method needs to delete any caption that might already be visible, set the alternative text attribute of the large picture, and display the new caption.

fakeDynamicAlt.js (continued)

```
navPic : function(e) {
  var t = DOMhelp.getTarget(e);
  if(t.nodeName.toLowerCase() != 'a') {
    t = t.parentNode;
  }
  var c = fakegal.current;
  if(t == fakegal.prev) {
    c -= 1;
  } else {
    C += 1;
  }
  fakegal.current = c;
  var pic = fakegal.tlist.getElementsByTagName('a')[c];
  var img = pic.getElementsByTagName('img')[0];
  var caption = img.getAttribute('title');
  var alternative = img.getAttribute('alt');
  fakegal.setPic(pic.getAttribute('href'), caption, alternative);
  DOMhelp.cancelClick(e);
},
```

The navPic() method, just like the init() method, needs to retrieve the alternative text, the caption, and the source of the large picture and send them to setPic().

fakeDynamicAlt.js (continued)

```
createContainer : function() {
  fakegal.c = document.createElement('div');
  fakegal.c.id = fakegal.largeContainerID;

  var p = document.createElement('p');
  var cl = DOMhelp.createLink('#', fakegal.closeLabel);
  cl.className = fakegal.closeClass;
  p.appendChild(cl);
  DOMhelp.addEvent(cl, 'click', fakegal.setPic, false);
  cl.onclick = DOMhelp.safariClickFix;
  fakegal.c.appendChild(p);

  var il = DOMhelp.createLink('#', ' ');
  DOMhelp.addEvent(il, 'click', fakegal.setPic, false);
  il.onclick = DOMhelp.safariClickFix;
  fakegal.c.appendChild(il);

  fakegal.next = DOMhelp.createLink('#', ' ');
  fakegal.next.innerHTML = fakegal.nextContent;
  fakegal.next.className = fakegal.nextClass;
  DOMhelp.addEvent(fakegal.next, 'click', fakegal.navPic, false);
  fakegal.next.onclick = DOMhelp.safariClickFix;
  fakegal.c.appendChild(fakegal.next);
```

```
      fakegal.prev = DOMhelp.createLink('#', ' ');
      fakegal.prev.innerHTML = fakegal.prevContent;
      fakegal.prev.className = fakegal.prevClass;
      DOMhelp.addEvent(fakegal.prev, 'click', fakegal.navPic, false);
      fakegal.prev.onclick = DOMhelp.safariClickFix;
      fakegal.c.appendChild(fakegal.prev);

      fakegal.caption = document.createElement('p');
      fakegal.caption.className = fakegal.captionClass;
      fakegal.c.appendChild(fakegal.caption);

      fakegal.tlist.parentNode.appendChild(fakegal.c);
    }
  }
DOMhelp.addEvent(window, 'load', fakegal.init, false);
```

The `createContainer()` method needs only one small change, which is creating a new paragraph in the container to host the caption.

As you can see, creating dynamic galleries with JavaScript means generating a lot of HTML elements and reading and writing a lot of attributes. It is up to you to decide whether it is worth the hassle or not. This gets even worse when you want to offer pagination of the thumbnails.

Instead of doing all of this in JavaScript, you could do it on the back end (for example, with PHP or Ruby on Rails or Node.js) and offer a fully functional gallery to all users, and only improve it via XHR and JavaScript.

Dynamic Thumbnail Galleries

Real dynamic thumbnail galleries use URL parameters, instead of lots of static pages, and create the pagination and show the thumbnails or the large images depending on these parameters.

The demo examplePHPgallery.php works that way, and Figure 10-2 shows what this might look like.

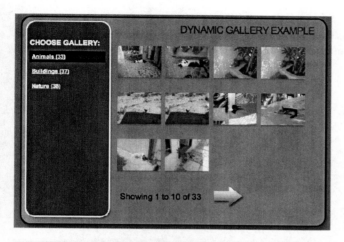

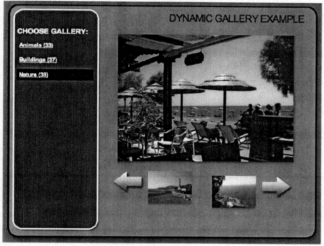

Figure 10-2. *A dynamic PHP-driven thumbnail gallery example with thumbnail pagination and previous and next image preview on the large picture page*

This gallery is fully functional and accessible without JavaScript, but you might not want to reload the whole page every time the user clicks a thumbnail. Using XHR, you can offer both. Instead of using the original PHP document, you use a cut-down version that generates only the content you need—in this case, `gallerytools.php`. I won't go into details of the PHP script; it suffices to say that it does the following for you:

- It reads the contents of a folder that the link in the main menu points to, checks it for images, and returns ten at a time as an HTML list with thumbnails linked to the large images.

- It adds a pagination menu that shows which ten of however many images in total are displayed and offers previous and next links.

- If any thumbnail is clicked, it returns the HTML of the large image and a menu showing the next and the previous thumbnails.

You use this output to overwrite the HTML output of the original PHP script as shown in the demo examplePHPXHRgallery.php. Without JavaScript, it does the same as examplePHPgallery.php; however, when JavaScript is available, it will not reload the whole document, but only refresh the gallery itself. You achieve this by replacing the links in the content section with links to gallerytools.php and XHR calls instead of reloading the whole page.

dyngal_xhr.js

```
dyngal = {
  contentID : 'content',
  originalPHP : 'examplePHPXHRgallery.php',
  dynamicPHP : 'gallerytools.php',
   init : function() {
     if(!document.getElementById || !document.createTextNode) {
       return;
     }
     dyngal.assignHandlers(dyngal.contentID);
  },
```

You start by defining your properties:

- The ID of the element that contains the content that should be replaced with the HTML returned from gallerytools.php

- The file name of the original script

- The file name of the script that returns the data you call via XHR

The init() method tests for DOM support and calls the assignHandlers() method with the content element ID as a parameter.

■ **Note**   In this case, you replace only one content element; however, because there might be situations where you want to replace numerous sections of the page, it is a good idea to create separate methods for tasks like these.

---

dyngal_xhr.js (continued)

```
assignHandlers : function(o) {
  if(!document.getElementById(o)){ return; }
  o = document.getElementById(o);
  var gLinks = o.getElementsByTagName('a');
  for(var i = 0; i < gLinks.length; i++) {
    DOMhelp.addEvent(gLinks[i], 'click', dyngal.load, false);
    gLinks[i].onclick = DOMhelp.safariClickFix;
  }
},
```

The assignHandlers() method tests whether the element with the ID that was sent as a parameter exists, and then loops through all the links in the element. Next, it adds an event handler pointing to the load method and applies the Safari fix to prevent that browser from following the original link. (Remember—the preventDefault() method used in cancelClick() is supported by Safari, but it does not stop the link from being followed due to a bug in Safari.)

dyngal_xhr.js (continued)

```
load : function(e) {
  var t = DOMhelp.getTarget(e);
  if(t.nodeName.toLowerCase() != 'a') {
    t = t.parentNode;
  }
  var h = t.getAttribute('href');
  h = h.replace(dyngal.originalPHP, dyngal.dynamicPHP);
  dyngal.doxhr(h, dyngal.contentID);
  DOMhelp.cancelClick(e);
},
```

In the load method, you retrieve the event target and make sure it is a link. You then read the href attribute of the link and replace the original PHP script name with the dynamic one that returns only the content you need. You call the doxhr() method with the href value and the content element ID as parameters and stop the link propagation by calling cancelClick().

dyngal_xhr.js (continued)

```
  doxhr : function(url, container) {
    var request;
    try{
      request = new XMLHttpRequest();
    } catch(error) {
      try {
        request = new ActiveXObject("Microsoft.XMLHTTP");
      } catch (error) {
        return true;
      }
    }
    request.open('get', url, true);
    request.onreadystatechange = function() {
      if(request.readyState == 1) {
        container.innerHTML = 'Loading... ';
      }
      if(request.readyState == 4) {
        if(request.status && /200|304/.test(request.status)) {
          dyngal.retrieved(request, container);
        } else {
          dyngal.failed(request);
        }
      }
    }
    request.setRequestHeader('If-Modified-Since', 'Wed, 05 Apr 2013 00:00:00 GMT');
    request.send(null);
    return false;
  },
  retrieved : function(request, container) {
    var data = request.responseText;
    document.getElementById(container).innerHTML = data;
    dyngal.assignHandlers(container);
  },
```

```
    failed : function(request) {
      alert('The XMLHttpRequest failed. Status: ' + requester.status);
      return true;
    }
  }
}
DOMhelp.addEvent(window, 'load', dyngal.init, false);
```

The XHR methods are the same as those you used in Chapter 8. The only difference is that you need to call the `assignHandlers()` method again, because you replaced the original content and, as a result, lost the event handlers on the links.

■ **Note** Having a server-side language and JavaScript is a powerful combination. Once you have mastered JavaScript, it might be a good idea to look into languages like PHP or Node.js, because without knowledge of a server-side language Ajax is less fun. Server-side languages can do what JavaScript cannot, like reach files on the server and read their names and properties, and even reach content from third-party servers. PHP syntax is similar to that of JavaScript in some respects, and Node.js is JavaScript.

Creating an Image Badge from a Folder

Let's have a go at another small gallery example using PHP and JavaScript/XHR before we look at some ready-made third-party code and online services in the next chapter.

This exercise will allow the user to navigate through the thumbnails with previous and next links and show the large photo by clicking the thumbnail. The demo `exampleBadge.html` does this, and Figure 10-3 shows how it looks with two badge galleries.

Figure 10-3. *Two image folders as badge galleries*

When creating scripts like these, it is a good idea to keep the HTML as easy as possible. The less you expect from the maintainer, the more likely it is that people will use your script. In this case, all the maintainer needs to do to add a badge gallery to the HTML document is add an element with the class badge and a link pointing to the folder containing the images:

exampleBadge.html (excerpt)

```
<p class="badge"><a href="galleries/animals/">Animals</a></p>
<p class="badge"><a href="galleries/buildings/">Buildings</a></p>
```

Because JavaScript cannot check a folder on the server for files, you need a PHP script to do this for you. The file badge.php does so and returns thumbnails as list items.

Note The following is a quick explanation of the PHP script. This is not JavaScript, but I hope you appreciate some insight into the workings of the tools the upcoming badge script uses.

---

badge.php

```php
<?php
$c = preg_match('/\d+/', $_GET['c']) ? $_GET['c'] : 5;
$s = preg_match('/\d+/', $_GET['s']) ? $_GET['s'] : 0;
$cd = is_dir($_GET['cd']) ? $_GET['cd'] : ' ';
```

You define three variables: $c, which stores the number of thumbnails to be shown; $s, which is the index of what is currently the first thumbnail in the list of all thumbnails; and $cd, which is the folder URL on the server. The $_GET array of PHP stores all the parameters of the URL, which means that if the URL was badge.php?c=3&s=0&cd=animals, $_GET['c'] would be 3, $_GET['s'] would be 0, and $_GET['cd'] would be animals. You can use regular expressions to make sure that $c and $s are integers and preset to 5 and 0, respectively, and use the is_dir() function of PHP to make sure that $cd really is an available folder.

badge.php (continued)

```php
if($cd != ' ') {
  $handle = opendir($cd);
    if(preg_match('/^tn_.*(jpg|jpe|jpeg)$/i', $file)) {
       $images[] = $file;
    }
  }
  closedir($handle);
```

If the folder is available, you start reading out each file in the folder with the opendir() method and test whether the file is a thumbnail by matching its name with the pattern ^tn_.*(jpg|jpe|jpeg)$ (starts with tn_ and ends with either jpg, jpe, or jpeg). If the file is a thumbnail, add it to the images array. When there are no files left in the folder, close the folder by calling the closedir() method.

badge.php (continued)

```php
$imgs = array_slice($images, $s, $c);
if($s > 0) {
  echo '<li class="badgeprev"> ';
  echo '<a href="badge.php?c='.$c;
  echo '&amp;s=' . ($s-$c) . '&amp;cd='.$cd. ' ">';
  echo 'previous</a></li>';
} else {
  echo '<li class="badgeprev"><span>previous</span></li>';
}
```

You use the array_slice() method of PHP to reduce the array down to the chosen images ($c images starting at $s) and test whether $s is larger than 0. If it is, write out a list element with the class badgeprev that has the right parameters in the link's href attribute. If it isn't, write out a SPAN inside the list item instead of a link.

badge.php (continued)

```php
for($i=0; $i<sizeof($imgs); $i++) {
  echo '<li><a href="'.str_replace('tn_', ' ',$cd.$imgs[$i]). ' "> '.
  '<img src="' . $cd . $imgs[$i] . ' " alt="' . $imgs[$i] . ' " /></a></li>';
}
```

Loop through the images and display an IMG element inside a link pointing to the large image for each array item. You can retrieve the link to the large image by removing the tn_ string of the array element's value with str_replace().

badge.php (continued)

```
  if(($c+$s) <= sizeof($images)) {
    echo '<li class="badgenext">';
    echo '<a href="badge.php?c=' . $c . '&amp;s=' . ($s + $c);
    echo '&amp;cd=' . $cd . '">next</a></li>';
  } else {
    echo '<li class="badgenext"><span>next</span></li>';
  }
}
?>
```

Test whether $c and $s together are less than the number of all images in the folder, and display a link if it is or a SPAN if it isn't.

As you can see, the programming syntax and logic of JavaScript and PHP is pretty similar, which is one of the reasons for the success of PHP. Let's now create the JavaScript that uses this PHP script to turn the links into image badges.

badge.js

```
badge = {
  badgeClass : 'badge',
  containerID : 'badgecontainer',
```

You define the CSS class used to specify the badge links and the ID of the image container showing the large picture as properties of the main object badge.

badge.js (continued)

```
init : function() {
  var newUL, parent, dir, loc;
  if(!document.getElementById || !document.createTextNode) {
    return;
  }
  var links = document.getElementsByTagName('a');
  for(var i = 0; i < links.length; i++) {
    parent = links[i].parentNode;
    if(!DOMhelp.cssjs('check', parent, badge.badgeClass)) {
      continue;
    }
```

You test for DOM support and loop through all links in the document, testing whether a particular link's parent node has the badge class assigned to it. If it doesn't, you skip this link.

badge.js (continued)

```
  newUL = document.createElement('ul');
  newUL.className = badge.badgeClass;
  dir=links[i].getAttribute('href');
  loc = window.location.toString().match(/(^.*\/)/g);
  dir = dir.replace(loc, ' ');
```

```
        badge.doxhr('badge.php?cd=' + dir, newUL);
        parent.parentNode.insertBefore(newUL, parent);
        parent.parentNode.removeChild(parent);
        i--;
}
```

You create a new list element and add the badge class to it. You retrieve the link's href attribute, read the window location, and remove anything in the window.location before the last / from the href attribute value.

You call the doxhr() method with the correct URL and the newly created list as parameters, and add the list before the parent element of the current link. You then remove the link's parent element with the DOM method removeChild() and decrease the loop counter by one. (You loop through all the links of the document, which means that when you remove one of them, the counter needs to decrease to stop the loop from skipping the following link.)

badge.js (continued)

```
        badge.container = document.createElement('div');
        badge.container.id = badge.containerID;
        document.body.appendChild(badge.container);
},
```

You create a new DIV as the container for the large image, set its ID, and add it to the body of the document.

badge.js (continued)

```
doxhr : function(url, container) {
    var request;
    try {
        request = new XMLHttpRequest();
    } catch (error) {
        try {
            request = new ActiveXObject("Microsoft.XMLHTTP");
        } catch (error) {
            return true;
        }
    }
    request.open('get', url, true);
    request.onreadystatechange = function() {
        if(request.readyState == 1) {
        }
        if(request.readyState == 4) {
            if(request.status && /200|304/.test(request.status)) {
                badge.retrieved(request, container);
            } else{
                badge.failed(request);
            }
        }
    }
    request.setRequestHeader('If-Modified-Since', 'Wed, 02 Jan 2013 00:00:00 GMT');
    request.send(null);
    return false;
},
```

```
retrieved : function(request, container) {
  var data = request.responseText;
  container.innerHTML = data;
  badge.assignHandlers(container);
},
failed : function(requester) {
  alert('The XMLHttpRequest failed. Status: ' + requester.status);
  return true;
},
```

The Ajax/XHR methods remain largely unchanged, the only difference is that when the data is successfully retrieved, the assignHandlers() method is called with the list item as a parameter.

badge.js (continued)

```
assignHandlers : function(o) {
  var links = o.getElementsByTagName('a');
  for(var i = 0; i < links.length; i++) {
    links[i].parent = o;
    if(/badgeprev|badgenext/.test(links[i].parentNode.className)) {
      DOMhelp.addEvent(links[i], 'click', badge.load, false);
    } else {
      DOMhelp.addEvent(links[i], 'click', badge.show, false);
    }
  }
},
```

The assignHandlers() method loops through all the links in the element sent as the parameter o. It stores this element as a new property in each link called parent and tests whether the link has the class badgeprev or badgenext, which, as you might remember, are added by badge.php to the previous and next links. If the CSS class is there, assignHandlers() adds an event handler pointing to the load method; otherwise, it adds an event handler pointing to the show method, because some links need to navigate through the thumbnails and others need to show the large image.

badge.js (continued)

```
load : function(e) {
  var t = DOMhelp.getTarget(e);
  if(t.nodeName.toLowerCase() != 'a') {
    t = t.parentNode;
  }
  var dir = t.getAttribute('href');
  var loc = window.location.toString().match(/(^.*\/)/g);
  dir = dir.replace(loc, ' ');
  badge.doxhr('badge.php?cd=' + dir, t.parent);
  DOMhelp.cancelClick(e);
},
```

The load method retrieves the event target and makes sure it is a link. It retrieves the href attribute value of the event target and cleans it up before calling the doxhr method with the element stored in the link's parent property as the output container. You stop the link from being followed by calling DOMhelp's cancelClick().

badge.js (continued)

```
show : function(e) {
  var t = DOMhelp.getTarget(e);
  if(t.nodeName.toLowerCase() != 'a') {
    t = t.parentNode;
  }
  var y = 0;
  if(self.pageYOffset) {
    y = self.pageYOffset;
  } else if (document.documentElement && document.documentElement.scrollTop) {
    y = document.documentElement.scrollTop;
  } else if(document.body) {
    y = document.body.scrollTop;
  }
  badge.container.style.top = y + 'px';
  badge.container.style.left = 0 + 'px';
```

In the show method, you once again retrieve the event target and test that it is a link. You then position the large image container on the screen. Because you don't know where in the document the badge will be, the safest method to show the image is to read out the scroll position of the document. To achieve this, you need to do a bit of object detection for different browsers.

■ **Note**   The current vertical scrolling position is a property of the window object called pageYOffset. This is supported in all browsers except Internet Explorer (IE) before version 9. If no HTML DOCTYPE is specified in the document, the scrollTop property is found in the body element of the document object in IE, Firefox Opera, Chrome, and Safari.

You test for all these eventualities and position the image container accordingly by setting the left and top properties of its style attribute collection. This way, you can always be sure that the large image will be visible in the user's browser window.

badge.js (continued)

```
  var source = t.getAttribute('href');
  var newImg = document.createElement('img');
  badge.deletePic();
  newImg.setAttribute('src', source);
  badge.container.appendChild(newImg);
  DOMhelp.addEvent(badge.container, 'click', badge.deletePic, false);
  DOMhelp.cancelClick(e);
},
```

You read the href attribute of the link and create a new IMG element. You remove any large image that might already be shown by calling the deletePic() method and set the new image's src attribute to the href of the link. You add the new image as a child node to the image container, apply an event handler that calls deletePic() when the user clicks the image, and stop the link from being followed by calling cancelClick().

badge.js (continued)

```
  deletePic : function() {
    badge.container.innerHTML = ' ';
  }
}
DOMhelp.addEvent(window, 'load', badge.init, false);
```

All the `deletePic` method needs to do is to set the `innerHTML` property of the container element to an empty string, thus removing the large image.

Summary

In this chapter, you learned how to enhance already existing HTML structures or dynamic server-side scripts for thumbnail galleries with JavaScript either to become dynamic or to appear more dynamic by not loading the whole document when the user chooses another image or thumbnail subset.

Galleries are always fun to create, and coming up with new and flashier solutions for them is also enjoyable. I hope that by learning some of the tricks presented in this chapter you feel confident to play around with them and come up with your own gallery ideas.

CHAPTER 11

Using Third-Party JavaScript

As you probably gathered by now, when you create a JavaScript application, you don't need to reinvent the wheel and recode all the functionality from scratch every time—JavaScript has many, many functions available for you to use, and you can create your own reusable functions and objects, too. But it goes even further than that—you can also make use of third-party code libraries and APIs, and there are many available on the Web these days. Knowing where, why, and how to use them is the key, and that's where this chapter comes in.

In this chapter, we will take a look at jQuery—a well-known and powerful JavaScript library that can help you do your work faster. We will also look at how to retrieve data from Twitter using Twitter's REST API. In addition, we will use the Google Maps API and, finally, look at Twitter Bootstrap.

What the Web Offers You

We're living in pretty exciting times as developers. Over the last few years, the attitude companies have about sharing content and technology has changed drastically. In the past, every company guarded its content and code as if it were made of platinum, and getting any information about the workings of a system or how to communicate with it was a long and painful process that included price negotiations, nonworking demonstrations, PowerPoint presentations, preview code, and other marketing collateral.

A lot of this has changed. Just about every company now has some kind of public/private partnership to court developers. For example, Adobe has an open source HTML editor called *brackets*, where all the source code is available on GitHub (https://github.com/adobe/brackets). A fork of this code is used to make Adobe Edge Code, which is part of the company's creative cloud package.

In addition to making software available for developers, companies now boast about making data available. Giving developers access to data can foster innovation and loyalty to a company, especially if developers can find ways to make some money. An additional benefit for a company is the opportunity to attract talent that could be hired at a later stage.

The Web is also littered with countless third-party JavaScript libraries, which can be downloaded and plugged into your applications, allowing you access to a lot of powerful functionality with very little effort. You'll see some examples of these later in the chapter when we look at jQuery, Google Maps, and Twitter Bootstrap.

REST APIs and Libraries

Note An application programming interface (API) (http://en.wikipedia.org/wiki/Application_programming_interface) is a set of routines and tools for building software applications. Basically, you have a set of methods, objects, and properties you use to piggyback on the functionality of another program or even operating system. In a sense, you've used an API in this book a lot—the browser API you use to access the window object with all its methods and the DOM, which allows you to alter and read the document.

One example of a REST API is from Twitter (details can be found at (`https://dev.twitter.com/`), which allows you to put together a URL to search for tweets by a certain user. The results are returned in the JSON format. In this example, %40 is the URL endoded code for the @ symbol:
`http://search.twitter.com/search.json?q=%40twitterapi`.

Here are other examples of how to use the API:

- This URL searches for tweets about "@twitterapi" but limits the results to two pages (about 3000 results): `http://search.twitter.com/search.json?q=%40twitterapi&page=2`.

- This URL returns any tweets with the word "Brooklyn" in them:
  `http://search.twitter.com/search.json?q=brooklyn`.

- And this example returns tweets about the JavaScript in Japanese with one page of results:
  `http://search.twitter.com/search.json?q=javascript&lang=ja&page=1`.

I could fill an entire book by going into detail about REST, so a detailed discussion is out of scope here. If you are interested, you can read up on it at Wikipedia (`http://en.wikipedia.org/wiki/Representational_State_Transfer`). What REST APIs do is allow you to define in the URL whatever kind of information you want. This could be as simple as adding different data to the URL, for example, to reach different entries of Wikipedia:

- `http://en.wikipedia.org/wiki/Javascript`

- `http://en.wikipedia.org/wiki/DOM_scripting`

You can use this information directly in JavaScript by sending a callback function name as a parameter to the API:

twitterSearch.html (excerpt)

```
<script>
  function results(d) {
          var resultArray = new Array()
          resultArray = d.results;
      for(var i = 0; i< resultArray.length; i++) {
              document.write( resultArray[i].from_user +"<br>" )
              document.write("<img src="+resultArray[i].profile_image_url +"><br>");
              document.write( resultArray[i].text +"<br><br>" )
      }
  }
}
</script>
<script src="http://search.twitter.com/search.json?q=brooklyn&callback=results"></script>
```

In short, you can use a REST API to retrieve information from a system in the easiest form (by assembling a static URL) and in the most complex form (to send parameters to customize the output format of that data and call different methods to retrieve different kind of data).

Using a Library: Short, Shorter, jQuery

One of the main reasons for having code libraries is that developers want to make it easier for other developers to achieve day-to-day coding tasks. You've done that in this book with the DOMhelp library by creating utility methods to work around browser inconsistencies and solve recurring tasks. What you haven't done is provide your own coding syntax or any other means of reaching elements in the page other than the DOM. If you had done that, you could have come up with much shorter code, but you also would have sacrificed the recognition effect of "normal" JavaScript syntax and made development dependent on having knowledge of the library.

jQuery (`http://jquery.com/`) comprises a single JavaScript file, weighing in at only 32K, which you add to the head of your documents. It provides you with an amazing amount of utility methods to achieve web-specific tasks. The code you have to write to work with jQuery is very confusing to JavaScript beginners or developers who haven't dabbled in languages like Ruby, Python, or Java yet. However, you'll find it to be very powerful once you get your head around it.

The concept of jQuery is to offer quick access to any element of the document, and to get this access you have a utility method called $ (of all things) that takes either of the following:

- A DOM construct—, for example, `$(document.body)`

- A CSS selector—for example, `$('p a')`, which is every link inside a paragraph in the document

- An XPath expression—, for example, `$(" //a[@rel='nofollow'] ")`, which matches every link in the document with an attribute called `rel` that has the value of `nofollow`

■ **Note**   XPath is a World Wide Web Consortium (W3C) standard language designed to reach parts of an XML document. It's normally used in connection with XSLT or XPOINTER (`http://www.w3.org/TR/xpath`). Because modern HTML should conform to XML syntax rules (all tags closed, all elements lowercase, attribute values in quotation marks, and single attributes defined as name/value pairs), you can use XPath to find parts of the HTML document, too. Together with XSLT, it is a very powerful tool to convert one XML format to another.

The other trick jQuery has up its sleeve to achieve very short code is a concept called *chainable methods,* which you already know from the DOM. You can add each method to the last one by concatenating them with a full stop. Instead of

```
$p = $('p');
$p.addClass('test');
$p.show();
$p.html('example' );
```

you can use

```
$( 'p' ).addClass( 'test' ).show().html( 'example' );
```

Both of these examples do the same thing: they take every paragraph of the document, add a CSS class called `test`, show the paragraph (in case it was hidden), and change the HTML content of the paragraph to "example". What jQuery provides you with is an amazing number of these very short-named methods that are tailored to fulfill day-to-day web application development tasks. There is good documentation and examples available on the jQuery site (`http://api.jquery.com/`).

Let's take a look at an example. If you are a developer and you write tutorials, you often have to show code examples in HTML pages. You wrap them in PRE and CODE elements to make whitespace in the code appear in the right format, like this:

exampleJQuery.html (excerpt)

```
<h1>Showing and hiding a code example with jQuery</h1>
<p>The code</p>
<pre><code>
```

```
  [... code example ...]
</code></pre>
<p>The CSS</p>
<pre><code>
  [... code example ...]
</code></pre>
```

Let's now write a script in jQuery that generates links preceding the code examples that allow for expanding and collapsing the examples instead of simply showing them, as demonstrated in Figure 11-1.

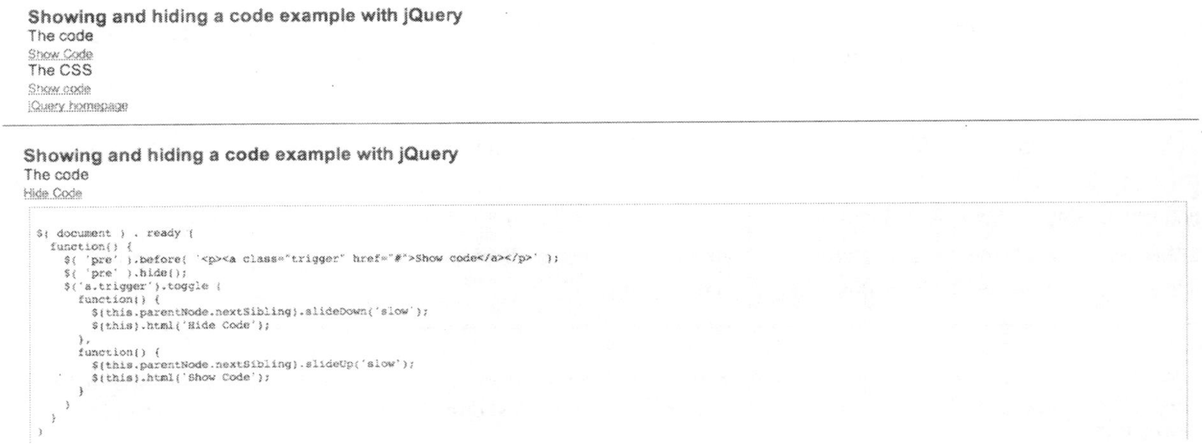

Showing and hiding a code example with jQuery
The code
Show Code
The CSS
Show code
jQuery homepage

Showing and hiding a code example with jQuery
The code
Hide Code

```
$( document ) . ready (
  function() {
    $( 'pre' ).before( '<p><a class="trigger" href="#">Show code</a></p>' );
    $( 'pre' ).hide();
    $('a.trigger').toggle (
      function() {
        $(this.parentNode.nextSibling).slideDown('slow');
        $(this).html('Hide Code');
      },
      function() {
        $(this.parentNode.nextSibling).slideUp('slow');
        $(this).html('Show Code');
      }
    )
  }
)
```

Figure 11-1. *Showing and hiding code examples with jQuery*

jqueryTest.js

```javascript
$(document).ready (
  function() {
    $('pre').before('<p><a class="trigger" href="#">Show code</a></p>');
    $('pre').hide();
    $('a.trigger').toggle (
      function() {
        $(this.parentNode.nextSibling).slideDown('slow');
        $(this).html('Hide Code');
      },
      function() {
        $(this.parentNode.nextSibling).slideUp('slow');
        $(this).html('Show Code');
      }
    )
  }
)
```

As you can see, the code is amazingly short, but it's also rather complex in terms of syntax. Let's go through the example bit by bit so that you can understand what is going on:

jqueryTest.js (excerpt)

```
$(document).ready (
  function() {
```

The $(document).ready () method is an event handler that calls the function provided as a parameter (in this case, an anonymous function) when the document is ready to be manipulated. This means that everything that follows in this script is executed when the document has loaded—and that means only the document and not all the embedded assets in it (like images). As you might remember, we talked in Chapter 5 about the ugly effect of the page content showing up before you can hide it. This method works around that problem.

jqueryTest.js (continued)

```
$('pre').before('<p><a class="trigger" href="#">Show code</a></p>');
$('pre').hide();
```

You take every PRE element in the document and use the before() method to add a string of HTML in the DOM tree before this element—in this case, a paragraph with an embedded link with the class trigger. You use the hide() method of jQuery to hide all PRE elements. (hide() sets the CSS attribute display to none .)

jqueryTest.js (continued)

```
$('a.trigger').toggle (
```

You use the CSS selector a.trigger to match all links with the class trigger (which should be only the ones the script added via the before() method) and use the toggle() method. This method alternately executes the two functions provided as parameters when the user clicks the element. The first parameter is an anonymous function that shows the previously hidden code example and changes the link text to "Hide Code" and vice versa.

jqueryTest.js (continued)

```
function() {
  $(this.parentNode.nextSibling).slideDown('slow');
  $(this).html('Hide Code');
},
```

You can use several jQuery methods to show and hide elements, the most basic being show() and hide(). A more advanced effect is produced using slideDown() and slideUp(), which show the element in a line-by-line animation. Both of these methods take a parameter that indicates the speed of the animation, which can be slow, normal, or fast. To reach the PRE element to show or hide, you need to use the $(this) construct, which returns the event target of toggle(). This means you can use this.parentNode.nextSibling to reach the PRE, because the links are nested in a paragraph. You can change the content of the link itself via $(this) and the html() method, which takes a string of HTML as the sole parameter and changes the element's innerHTML property.

jqueryTest.js (continued)

```
      function() {
        $(this.parentNode.nextSibling).slideUp('slow');
        $(this).html('Show Code');
      }
    )
  }
)
```

The other case of `toggle()` in this example uses `slideUp()` to slowly hide the code example and changes the text of the link back to "Show Code".

jQuery also allows for simple Ajax requests. jQuery uses the `load()`, `$.get()`, and `$.post()` methods as explained at `http://api.jquery.com/category/ajax/`. For example, if you want to create the PRE elements and load the real code examples into them when the user clicks a link, this is pretty easy to do. Check the demo `exampleJQueryAjax.html` to see the following script in action:

jqueryTestAjax.js

```
$(document).ready (
  function() {
    $('a.codeExample').each (
      function( i ) {
        $(this).after('<pre class="codeExample"><code></code></pre>');
      }
    )
    $('pre.codeExample').hide();
    $('a.codeExample').toggle (
      function() {
        if(!this.old){
          this.old = $(this).html();
        }
        $(this).html('Hide Code');
        parseCode(this);
      },
      function() {
        $(this).html(this.old);
        $(this.nextSibling).hide();
      }
    )
    function parseCode(o){
      if(!o.nextSibling.hascode){
        $.get (o.href,
          function(code){
            code=code.replace(/&/mg,'&#38;');
            code=code.replace(/</mg,'&#60;');
            code=code.replace(/>/mg,'&#62;');
            code=code.replace(/\"/mg,'&#34;');
            code=code.replace(/\r?\n/g,'<br>');
            code=code.replace(/<br><br>/g,'<br>');
```

```
                code=code.replace(/ /g,' ');
                o.nextSibling.innerHTML='<code>'+code+'</code>';
                o.nextSibling.hascode=true;
            }
        );
    }
    $(o.nextSibling).show();
  }
 }
)
```

Let's go through this script step by step:

jqueryTestAjax.js (excerpt)

```
$(document).ready (
  function() {
```

You start once again with the ready() method and an anonymous function. (You might as well create a named function and call it via the ready() method.)

jqueryTestAjax.js (continued)

```
$('a.codeExample').each (
  function(i) {
    $(this).after( '<pre class="codeExample"><code></code></pre>' );
  }
)
$('pre.codeExample').hide();
```

You use one of jQuery's iterator methods, each(), to loop through all links that have the CSS class codeExample. You then create PRE elements with the class codeExample and embedded CODE elements after each of these links via the after() method and the $(this) selector before hiding all PRE elements with the codeExample class using jQuery's hide() method.

jqueryTestAjax.js (continued)

```
$('a.codeExample').toggle (
  function() {
    if(!this.old){
      this.old = $(this).html();
    }
    $(this).html('Hide Code');
    parseCode(this);
  },
  function() {
    $(this).html(this.old);
    $(this.nextSibling).hide();
  }
)
```

You use `toggle()` to show and hide the code examples; however, unlike what you did with the last script, you store the original text of the link in a property called `old` when you show the code and replace the link text with "Hide Code". You then invoke the function `parseCode()` with the link as a parameter when you show the code. When you hide the code, you restore the original link text by setting the link text back to the value stored in the `old` parameter before hiding the PRE element with jQuery's `hide()` method.

jqueryTestAjax.js (continued)

```
function parseCode(o){
  if(!o.nextSibling.hascode){
      $.get (o.href,
        function(code){
```

This function tests whether the PRE element following the link (which is its next sibling) has a property called `hascode`, which you will set once the code has been loaded for the first time. This is necessary to avoid the script loading the code every time the user clicks the link—instead, loading it only once. You then use the `$.get()` method with the link's `href` attribute value and an anonymous function as parameters. This effectively sends an request that loads the linked document and invokes the function once the document has been loaded. You send a parameter called `code`, which contains the content of the document that was loaded via XHR.

jqueryTestAjax.js (continued)

```
code=code.replace( /&/mg, '&#38;' );
code=code.replace( /</mg, '&#60;' );
code=code.replace( />/mg, '&#62;' );
code=code.replace( /\"/mg, '&#34;' );
code=code.replace( /\r?\n/g, '<br>' );
code=code.replace( /<br><br>/g, '<br>' );
code=code.replace( / /g, ' ' );
o.nextSibling.innerHTML = '<code>'+code+'</code>';
o.nextSibling.hascode = true;
```

You then use regular expressions to replace all ampersands, tag brackets, and quotation marks with their numbered HTML entities, line breaks with `<br>`, and spaces with their HTML entity before adding the result inside a CODE element as the `innerHTML` property of the PRE element. You set the `hascode` property to `true` to ensure that the next time the user clicks the link to show the code, the `$.get()` construct is skipped.

jqueryTestAjax.js (continued)

```
          }
        );
      }
      $(o.nextSibling).show();
    }
  }
)
```

All that is left to do is show the PRE element using jQuery's `show()` method. Notice that you need to do that outside `$.get()` the construct to make sure the code gets shown the second and subsequent times the user chooses to show the code.

Dangers of jQuery and Other Libraries Using Their Own Syntax

It is amazing how many day-to-day web-application and web-development tasks you can perform easily and quickly with jQuery. However, if you handed this document over to a third-party developer for maintenance, she'd have to know about jQuery or she would be completely lost. This is one of the dangers of using libraries. Instead of relying on JavaScript syntax and rules, you add an extra layer of necessary knowledge to the process. It is up to you to decide whether the benefits the library offers are worth that.

Libraries are there to make the development process quicker and easier, not make us dependent on them or repeat mistakes we've made with libraries in the past already—creating applications and web sites that don't work without JavaScript.

Next we'll look at using the Google Maps API to create mapping applications.

Using an API: Adding a Map to Your Site with Google Maps

Google Maps (http://maps.google.com) is probably the web application that got the whole Ajax craze rolling. It provides the user with maps that can be moved around, zoomed, and—the implementation permitting—even annotated. You can show the location you want to see as maps, as satellite pictures, or as a mixture of both.

Google allows web developers to use Google Maps on their own web sites by means of an API. To use the API, you need to sign up for a free developer key at its homepage:https://developers.google.com/maps/. Here you will also find the documentation and many examples of how to use Google Maps. The key will enable you to use maps on a single domain or subfolder in this domain. The examples in this chapter use a key that works with localhost, which means you need to run them in your local server via http://localhost/ and not from the file system.

Once you have obtained the developer key, you can link to the JavaScript that contains all the map's code in the head of your document. The "your key" shown in bold should be replaced with the key you obtained from Google:

```
<script src="https://maps.googleapis.com/maps/api/js?key=your
key&sensor=true&callback=initialize " type="text/javascript">
</script>
```

Caution   This URL might change in the future, so be sure to check the API home page if your examples fail to work out all of a sudden.

The next step you need to take is to get the latitude and longitude values of the location you want to display. If you type the location you are interested in into Google and then add the word "latitude" (for example "Saitama Japan latitude"), you can get the information you need to add to your map code.

When you have the information, you can start adding your own map to your web site. As an example for an international location, let's use Saitama Prefecture in Japan. The coordinates are 35.8617° latitude and 139.6453° longitude. Using this information and the methods provided for you by the API, it is easy to show a map of a nice place near Tokyo.

You start with an HTML element to contain the map. You can add content in this element that is displayed when JavaScript is not available or when the browser isn't supported. This content could be any HTML, text, or even a static image of the same map. The static image is a nice option to ensure backward compatibility; you just need to be sure not to tell the user anywhere in the text that the map is dynamic, because it might not be.

exampleGoogleMaps.html (excerpt)

```
<div id="map_canvas" style="width:100%; height:100%">
  <p>Here you should see an interactive map, but you
  either have scripting disabled or your browser
  is not supported by Google Maps.</p>
</div>
```

The sample CSS code that Google provides will make your map full screen.

googleMaps.css

```
html { height: 100% }
body { height: 100%; margin: 0; padding: 0 }
#map_canvas { height: 100% }
```

Next you need to add the JavaScript that will put the map in the document:

googleMaps.js

```
function loadMapAPI(){
var script = document.createElement("script");
    script.type = "text/javascript";
    script.src = "https://maps.googleapis.com/maps/api/js?key=YOUR_API_KEY&sensor=true&callback=ini
tialize";
};
  document.body.appendChild(script);
}

function initialize() {
var mapOptions = {
        center: new google.maps.LatLng(35.8617, 139.6453 ),
        zoom: 8,
      mapTypeId: google.maps.MapTypeId.ROADMAP
      var map = new google.maps.Map(document.getElementById("map_canvas"),mapOptions);
  }
}

document.addEventListener("DOMContentLoaded", loadMapAPI,false);
```

The event listener calls the loadMapAPI function once the DOM is loaded. This function then creates a script element and adds the type and source attributes. The source in this case is the URL for the map API. Notice in the URL there is the callback parameter, which tells the browser where to return the results—in our case, the initialize function.

The initialize function creates the mapOptions object literal. Inside this object, you can add options like the ability to center your map on a specific point and zoom, which sets the resolution of your map (0 would be a view of the earth). The map type property tells Google what kind of map it should display:

- ROADMAP—Default 2D map
- SATELLITE—Photographic tiles
- HYBRID—Mix of both roadmap and satellite for prominent features like roads and cities
- TERRAIN—Displays elevation and water features like mountains and rivers

Finally, the map object is created. When creating a map instance, you need to specify a `div` element in your HTML document that will contain the map. In addition, you pass the `mapOptions` object that contains the parameters to customize the map. The code in the above example should give you a map of Sitama Prefecture, as shown in Figure 11-2.

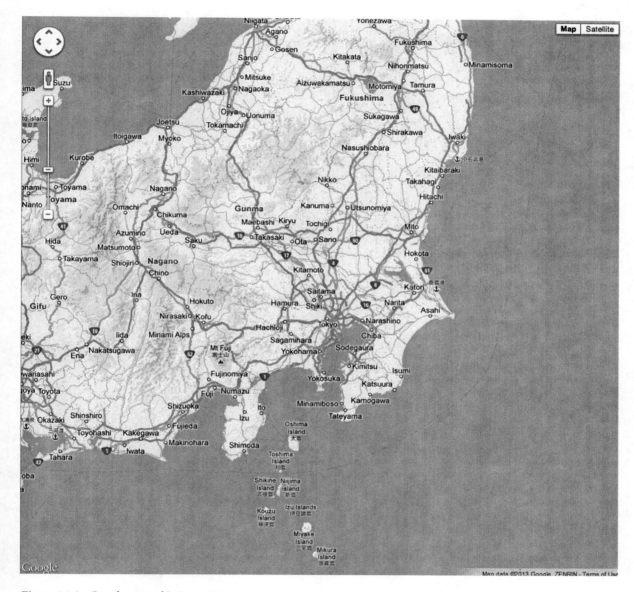

Figure 11-2. *Google map of Saitama Japan*

The map is working, but with the current view it is hard to tell exactly what you should be paying attention to. To fix this, you need to add a marker. Creating a marker is similar to creating the map. You create a marker object and, in the constructor, add an object literal that has all the properties you want this marker to have:

googleMapsMarker.js (excerpt)

```
function initialize() {
var myLatlng = new google.maps.LatLng(35.8617, 139.6453 );
var mapOptions = {
    center: myLatlng,
    zoom: 8,
    mapTypeId: google.maps.MapTypeId.ROADMAP
};
    var map = new google.maps.Map(document.getElementById("map_canvas"),mapOptions);
    var marker = new google.maps.Marker({
        position: myLatlng,
        animation: google.maps.Animation.DROP,
        map: map
    });
}
```

This change creates a red marker icon at the location you defined, as shown in Figure 11-3. The code also adds the animation parameter so that the marker has a bounce when it is displayed.

Figure 11-3. *A map with a marker*

You also can use the API to display windows that will appear when the marker is clicked on. This can help to provide necessary information to the user in addition to links to related sites. In this example, you create a variable called `contentString`. Inside this variable, you add a string of HTML-formatted text. This will be rendered properly in the information window.

The next few steps are similar to the steps you used to create the marker object. You create an `InfoWindow` object and pass an object literal with the property `content`, which will have the value of your variable. Finally, you add a listener to the marker you made previously. So when the marker receives a click, a call to the open method on the `InfoWindow` object is made and you pass over the map and marker this window is associated with. An example of this is shown in Figure 11-4.

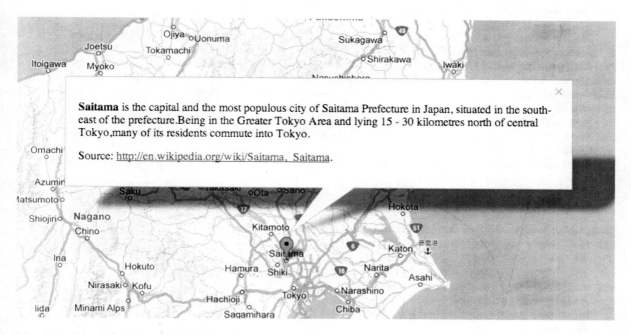

Figure 11-4. A map with a marker and an information window

exampleGoogleMapsMarkerEvent.js (excerpt)

```
var contentString = '<div id="content">'+
    '<p><b>Saitama</b> is the capital and the most populous city '+
    'of Saitama Prefecture in Japan, situated in the south-east of  the prefecture. '+
    'Being in the Greater Tokyo Area and lying 15 - 30 kilometres north of central Tokyo,'+
    'many of its residents commute into Tokyo.</p>'+
    '<p>Source: <a href="http://en.wikipedia.org/wiki/Saitama,_Saitama">'+
    'http://en.wikipedia.org/wiki/Saitama,_Saitama</a>.</p>'+
    '</div>';

var infowindow = new google.maps.InfoWindow({
content: contentString
});
```

```
      var marker = new google.maps.Marker({
        position: myLatlng,
        animation: google.maps.Animation.DROP,
      map: map
});
google.maps.event.addListener(marker, 'click', function() {
    infowindow.open(map,marker);
 });
}
document.addEventListener("DOMContentLoaded", loadMapAPI, false);
```

The last feature you will add is the ability to pan to another location. In this example, once you close the infoWindow, the map object uses the panTo() method to move the map to another location.

First, you need to add a listener to the infoWindow object as you did with the marker. When clicked, the listener calls a function that creates a new object called newLating that holds the new position you want to move the map to. Then you talk to the map object and call its panTo() method. Inside the panTo method, you pass over a new position using the newLating object.

Next you create a newContentString variable with the paragraph stating, "Welcome to Akita Prefecture". The newInfoWindow object will be created. It also will have an object literal with a property called content that references the newContentString variable.

At the end, you have an event added to the newMarker object. When clicked, it will talk to the newInfoWindow object, and it uses its open method to show the new info window:

googleMapsPan.js

```
google.maps.event.addListener(infowindow, 'closeclick', function() {
var newLatLng = new google.maps.LatLng(39.7158,140.1058);
    map.panTo(newLatLng);

var newMarker = new google.maps.Marker({
    position: newLatLng,
    animation: google.maps.Animation.DROP,
    map: map
    });
var newContentString= '<p>Welcome to Akita Prefecture</p>';

var newInfoWindow = new google.maps.InfoWindow({
    content: newContentString
    });

google.maps.event.addListener(newMarker, 'click', function() {
    newInfoWindow.open(map,newMarker);
    });

 });
```

The result is shown in Figure 11-5.

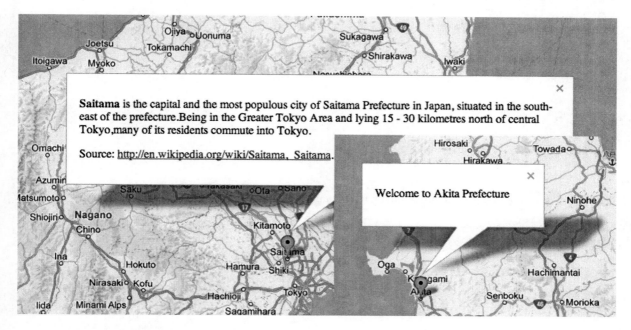

Figure 11-5. *Panning from one map location to a different one*

Full Service: Introducing Twitter Bootstrap

Early in the chapter, you took at look at part of Twitter's REST API. In addition to the REST API, which provides access to its data, Twitter has released Twitter Bootstrap (found at `http://twitter.github.com/bootstrap/`). Bootstrap is a free collection of tools for creating both web sites and applications using HTML, CSS, and optional JavaScript extensions. Bootstrap is the most popular project on GitHub and is used by large companies and start-ups alike.

Some of the features of Twitter Bootstrap include the following:

- Sets up global typography

- Uses a grid system for page layout, and supports responsive design

- Includes styles for HTML elements such as forms, buttons, and tables

- Provides built-in icons

- Provides reusable UI components

Adding bootstrap code to your HTML document is simple. Download the .zip file, and let's look at its contents.

Adding Bootstrap to Your Site

When you unzip bootstrap.zip, you find a file structure similar to how you would organize your own web site. Figure 11-6 shows what this looks like.

```
bootstrap/
├── css/
│   ├── bootstrap.css
│   ├── bootstrap.min.css
├── js/
│   ├── bootstrap.js
│   ├── bootstrap.min.js
└── img/
    ├── glyphicons-halflings.png
    └── glyphicons-halflings-white.png
```

Figure 11-6. A screen shot of the folder layout after unzipping Twitter Bootstrap from the bootstrap page

These files can be copied into your site and referenced in your HTML documents. To get started, use the following code:

exampleBootstrapTemplate.html

```
<!doctype html>
<html>
  <head>
  <title>Bootstrap Template</title>
    <meta name="viewport" content="width=device-width, initial-scale=1.0">
    <link href="css/bootstrap.min.css" rel="stylesheet" media="screen">
    <script src="http://code.jquery.com/jquery.js"></script>
    <script src="js/bootstrap.min.js"></script>
  </head>
  <body>
        <h1>This is my header</h1>
  </body>
</html>
```

When looking at your page in a browser, you should see that the font for your h1 tag is different. It now uses helvetica as the default font. We can see that the h1 tag is flush left, because bootstrap removes all the default margin space in the body of the document. Figure 11-7 shows you what your app should look like at this point.

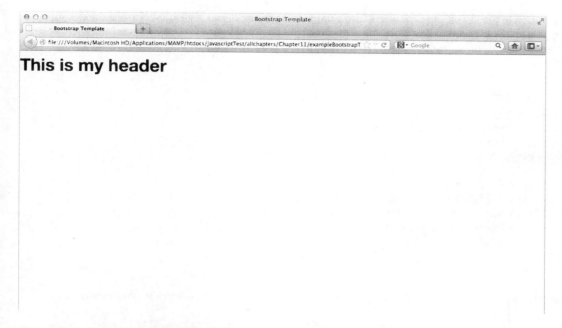

Figure 11-7. *Helvetica is the default font for the page once bootstrap starts working*

Now that you know bootstrap is working, you can use some of its features. First you can put the header inside a `div` that uses the `container` class. Next you can add a paragraph declaring that what comes next is your button. Inside this paragraph, you use the `text-info` class to give it style. After that, you can add a button element with the `btn` class. When looking at this in a browser, you should have your text moved over from the left and your new copy and button ready to go.

exampleBootstrapButton.html

```html
<!doctype html>
<html>
  <head>
  <title>Bootstrap Template</title>
    <meta name="viewport" content="width=device-width, initial-scale=1.0">
    <link href="css/bootstrap.min.css" rel="stylesheet" media="screen">
    <script src="http://code.jquery.com/jquery.js"></script>
    <script src="js/bootstrap.min.js"></script>
  </head>
    <body>
        <div class="container">
            <h1>This is my header</h1>
            <p class="text-info">This is my Button</p>
            <button class="btn">Click Me</button>
        </div>
    </body>
</html>
```

With the button in place, you can now turn it into a drop-down menu. Because you downloaded the default bootstrap .zip file, you don't need to download the drop-down plugin. The plugins for Bootstrap are made to work with jQuery, and because you also added that to your document, this should work by only adding the necessary HTML and CSS.

exampleBootstrapDropdown.html (excerpt)

```
<div class="btn-group">
    <button class="btn ">Click Me</button>
    <button class="btn dropdown-toggle" data-toggle="dropdown ">
        <span class="caret "></span>
    </button>
        <ul class="dropdown-menu">
            <li><a href="#">Depeche Mode</a></li>
            <li><a href="#">Information Society</a></li>
        <li><a href="#">The Cure</a></li>
    <li><a href="#">Erasure</a></li>
</ul>
</div>
```

In Figure 11-8, you can see a drop-down menu powered by Twitter Bootstrap. No extra JavaScript was written.

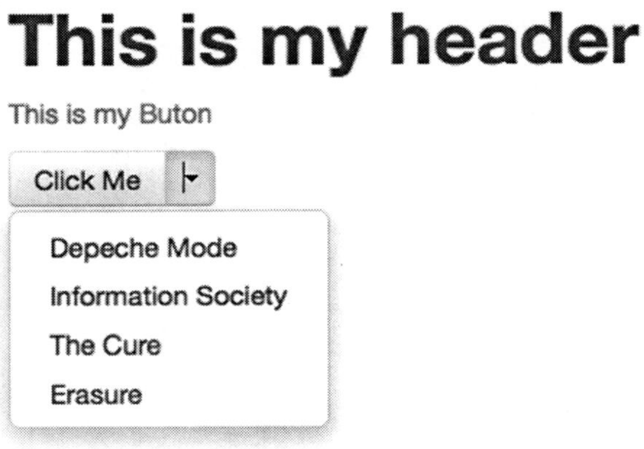

This is my header

This is my Buton

Click Me ⌄

Depeche Mode

Information Society

The Cure

Erasure

Figure 11-8. Drop-down menu powered by Twitter Bootstrap

As you can see, one of the nice things about Bootstrap is that you don't need to add JavaScript to make things work. In case you want to have more control over your documents, you can add your own JavaScript. In this example, you'll add a modal window just using the built-in code.

exampleBootstrapModalNoJs.html (excerpt)

```
<button type="button" data-toggle="modal" data-target="#myModal">Launch modal</button>
    <div id="myModal" class="modal hide fade">
        <div class="modal-header">
            <button type="button" class="close" data-dismiss="modal" aria-hidden="true">x</button>
            <h3 id="myModalLabel">My Modal header</h3>
        </div>
```

```
    <div class="modal-body">
    <p>The body of the window</p>
    </div>
    <div class="modal-footer">
        <button class="btn" data-dismiss="modal" aria-hidden="true">Close</button>
        <button class="btn btn-primary">Save changes</button>
    </div>
```

This makes a modal window pop up. The button tag has a data-target attribute that points to the ID myModal. By using the attribute, the modal window will work without any additional code. To disable the data API, add one line to your code that will look at the document and disable all references to the data API. This can be done for individual components as well. After that, you need to use the jQuery plugin to have the model work. In this example, you add some jQuery code to first disable the data API and then detect when the button now called *launchButton* (using the ID attribute) is clicked on. When launchButton is clicked, myModal will come up as before.

exampleBootstrapModal.html (excerpt)

```
<button type="button" data-toggle="modal" id="launchButton" data-target="#myModal">
Launch modal</button>
```

```
    exampleBootstrapModal.js
    $(document).ready(function(e) {
      $(document).off('.data-api');
      $('#launchButton').click(function(){
            $('#myModal').modal({ show: true});   //if you comment this out, the modal will not work
      });
});
```

By controlling the modal this way, you can have more control over how things work. For example, if you want to have some form validation before the modal comes up, you can run the form validation code and then display the window with a custom message. To control an accordion, you have similar code.

exampleBootstrapAccordion.html (excerpt)

```
<div class="accordion-heading">
  <a class="accordion-toggle" data-toggle="collapse" data-parent="#accordion2"
href="#collapseOne" id="header1">
            Menu Item 1
  </a>
</div>
...
    <div class="accordion-heading">
        <a class="accordion-toggle" data-toggle="collapse" data-parent="#accordion2"
href="#collapseTwo" id="header2">
          Menu Item 2
      </a>
</div>
```

exampleBootstrapAccordion.js

```
  $(document).ready(function(e) {
    $(document).off('.data-api');
```

```
        $('#header1').click(function(){
            $('#collapseOne').collapse('toggle');
        });

    $('#header2').click(function(){
        $('#collapseTwo').collapse('toggle');
        });
});
```

Here you turn off the data API. Then you assign click events to two HTML elements, called header1 and header2. When either element is clicked, you can use the bootstrap API and call the collapse method. This method can receive a few different values. In this case, you send toggle. This automatically expands or collapses the content for you. The next example shows how to control a carousel using the bootstrap API.

exampleBootstrapCarousel.js

```
        $(document).ready(function(e) {
          $(document).off('.data-api');

          $('.carousel-control').click(function(e){

              switch(e.target.getAttribute("data-slide")){
                  case 'prev':
                    $('.carousel').carousel('prev');
          break;
          case "next":
          $('.carousel').carousel('next');
          break;
              }
});

$('.carousel-indicators').click( function(e){

      switch(e.target.getAttribute("data-slide-to")){
          case '0':
          $('.carousel').carousel(0);
          break;
          case '1':
          $('.carousel').carousel(1);
          break;
          case '2':
          $('.carousel').carousel(2);
          break;
      }
    });
});
```

Here you have two functions that each look for CSS classes that the carousel is using to work. In each case, they are looking for detailed information about the attributes in the HTML tags that are being used. The first one is looking at the data-slide attribute in the HTML tags.

exampleBootstrapCarousel.html (excerpt)

```
<a class="carousel-control left" href="#myCarousel" data-slide="prev">&lsaquo;</a>
<a class="carousel-control right" href="#myCarousel" data-slide="next">&rsaquo;</a>
```

In the HTML document, this attribute is associated with the anchor tags that are being used to move the carousel forward or backward. When either of these elements is clicked, JavaScript checks for the value inside a switch statement. Once it finds a match, it calls the carousel method and passes a value of either *"prev"* or *"next"*.

The second function works in a similar way. It looks for when an element using the CSS class ".carousel-indicators" has been clicked. The HTML document has a list that uses this class:

exampleBootstrapCarousel.html (excerpt)

```
<ol class="carousel-indicators">
  <li data-target="#myCarousel" data-slide-to="0" class="active"></li>
  <li data-target="#myCarousel" data-slide-to="1"></li>
  <li data-target="#myCarousel" data-slide-to="2"></li>
</ol>
```

The switch statement looks for the value of data-slide-to. As with the previous switch statement, once the value is found the carousel method is called, with the number (the image count acts like an array starting with 0) passed to make that visible image. The finished carousel is shown in Figure 11-9.

Figure 11-9. *The finished carousel*

Summary

This chapter has given you a taste of some of the services aviaible to you at the moment, and I am sure that this is simply the beginning of a longer experience you'll have with using shared content, information, and services. Many developers spend a lot of time creating wonderful code just to realize that there is already another product out there that does exactly the same, but better. However, that is not much of a problem—it is through communication and trial and error that we become better in what we do.

You can learn a lot and help the development community a great deal by keeping your eyes open and looking at the services available. It's especially important to give feedback as to how easy some services or libraries are to use. It is far too tempting to consider one's own code perfect, and it is sometimes not until someone else shows you how to break it that you realize it's not. This works both ways. And you shouldn't be put off by your shortcomings—keep at it, and you will get better. Don't be shy—keep participating in the JavaScript community.

■ ■ ■

Debugging JavaScript

In this appendix, I will introduce you to some tricks and tools to debug your JavaScript code. It is very important to get acquainted with debugging tools, because programming consists to a large extent of trying to find out what went wrong a particular time. Some browsers help you with this problem; others make it harder by having their debugging tools hidden away or by returning cryptic error messages that confuse more than they help. Some of my favorites include philosophical works like "Undefined is not defined" or the Microsoft Internet Explorer (IE) standard "Object doesn't support this property or method."

Common JavaScript Mistakes

Let's start with some common mistakes that probably every JavaScript developer has made. Having these in the back of your head when you check a failing script might make it a lot quicker to spot the problem.

Misspellings and Case-Sensitivity Issues

The easiest mistakes to spot are misspellings of JavaScript method names or properties. Classics include `getElementByTagName()` instead of `getElementsByTagname()`, `getElementByID()` instead of `getElementById()`, and `node.style.colour` (for the British English writers). A lot of times the problem could also be case sensitivity—for example, writing keywords in mixed case instead of lowercase.

```
If( elm.href ) {
  var url = elm.href;
}
```

There is no keyword called `If`, but there is one called `if`. The same problem of case sensitivity applies to variable names:

```
var FamilyGuy = 'Peter';
var FamilyGuyWife = 'Lois';
alert('The Griffins:\n'+ familyGuy + ' and ' + FamilyGuyWife );
```

This results in an error message stating "familyGuy is not defined," because there is a variable called `FamilyGuy` but none called `familyGuy`.

Trying to Access Undefined Variables

I talked about it in the second chapter of the book: you define variables either by declaring them with or without an additional var keyword. (The latter is necessary to define the scope of the variable.) Keep in mind that strict mode will prevent you from implicitly declaring variables (variables without the var keyword). Because of this, it is recommended that you use the var keyword for every variable.

```
Stewie = "Son of Peter and Lois";
var Chris = "Older Son of Peter and Lois";
```

If you try to access a variable that hasn't been defined yet, you'll get an error. The alert() in the following script throws an error because Meg is not defined yet:

```
Peter = "The Family Guy";
Lois = "The Family Guy's Wife";
Brian = "The Dog";
Stewie = "Son of Peter and Lois";
Chris = "Older Son of Peter and Lois";
alert( Meg );
Meg = "The Daughter of Peter and Lois";
```

This is easy when it is an obvious example like this one, but how about trying to guess where the bug in the following example is?

exampleFamilies.html

```
function getFamilyData( outptID, isTree, familyName ) {
  var father, mother, child;
  switch( familyName ) {
    case 'Griffin':
      father = "Peter";
      mother = "Lois";
      child = "Chris";
    break;
    case 'Flintstone':
      father = "Fred";
      mother = "Wilma";
      child = "Pebbles";
    break;
  }
  var out = document.getElementById( outputID );
  if( isTree ) {
    var newUL = document.createElement( 'ul' );
    newUL.appendChild( makeLI( father ) );
    newUL.appendChild( makeLI( mother ) );
    newUL.appendChild( makeLI( child ) );
    out.appendChild( newUL );
  } else {
    var str = father + ' ' + mother + ' ' + child;
    out.appendChild( document.createTextNode( str ) );
  }
}
getFamilyData( 'tree', true, 'Griffin' );
```

Chrome's developer tools will tell you that there is an error in line 23—" 'outputID' is not defined," as shown in Figure A-1.

Figure A-1. *Chrome showing an error on line 23*

However, if you look at the code in line 23 as shown in Figure A-2, nothing seems to be wrong.

```
9      function getFamilyData(outptID,isTree,familyName){
10        var father,mother,child;
11        switch(familyName){
12          case 'Griffin':
13            father = "Peter";
14            mother = "Lois";
15            child = "Chris";
16          break;
17          case 'Flintstone':
18            father = "Fred";
19            mother = "Wilma";
20            child = "Pebbles";
21          break;
22        }
23 ▼      var out=document.getElementById(outputID);
24        if(isTree){
25          var newUL=document.createElement('ul');
26          newUL.appendChild(makeListElement(father));
27          newUL.appendChild(makeListElement(mother));
28          newUL.appendChild(makeListElement(child));
29          out.appendChild(newUL);
30        } else {
31          var str=father+' '+mother+' '+child;
32          out.appendChild(document.createTextNode(str));
33        }
34      }
```

Figure A-2. *The code shown with a highlight on line 23*

The culprit is a typo in the function parameter, highlighted in Figure A-3, which means that outputID is not defined but outptID is.

```
function getFamilyData(outptID,isTree,familyName){
  var father,mother,child;
  switch(familyName){
    case 'Griffin':
      father = "Peter";
      mother = "Lois";
      child = "Chris";
    break;
    case 'Flintstone':
      father = "Fred";
      mother = "Wilma";
      child = "Pebbles";
    break;
  }
  var out=document.getElementById(outputID);
  if(isTree){
    var newUL=document.createElement('ul');
    newUL.appendChild(makeListElement(father));
    newUL.appendChild(makeListElement(mother));
    newUL.appendChild(makeListElement(child));
    out.appendChild(newUL);
  } else {
    var str=father+' '+mother+' '+child;
    out.appendChild(document.createTextNode(str));
  }
}
```

Figure A-3. *The misspelled function parameter that caused the error*

Typos in parameters are a very confusing bug, because browsers tell you the error occurred in the line where the variable is used and not where you made the mistake.

Incorrect Number of Closing Braces and Parentheses

Another common mistake is not closing curly braces or keeping an orphaned closing brace in the code when deleting some lines. Say, for example, you don't need the isTree option any longer and you remove it from the code:

exampleCurly.html

```
function getFamilyData( outputID, familyName ) {
  var father, mother, child;
  switch( familyName ) {
    case 'Griffin':
      father = "Peter";
      mother = "Lois";
      child = "Chris";
    break;
```

```
    case 'Flintstone':
      father = "Fred";
      mother = "Wilma";
      child = "Pebbles";
    break;
  }
  var out = document.getElementById( outputID );
  var newUL = document.createElement( 'ul' );
  newUL.appendChild( makeListElement( father ) );
  newUL.appendChild( makeListElement( mother ) );
  newUL.appendChild( makeListElement( child ) );
  out.appendChild( newUL );
  }
}
getFamilyData( 'tree', true, 'Griffin' );
```

The orphan closing brace causes an "Uncaught SyntaxError: Unexpected token" error in Chrome. The same problem occurs when you don't close all the braces in a construct, a mistake that can easily happen when you don't indent your code:

exampleMissingCurly.html

```
function testRange( x, start, end ) {
if( x <= end && x >= start ) {
if( x == start ) {
alert( x + ' is the start of the range');
}
if( x == end ) {
alert(x + ' is the end of the range');
}
if( x! = start && x != end ) {
alert(x + ' is in the range');
} else {
alert(x + ' is not in the range');
}
}
```

Running this example causes an "Uncaught SyntaxError: Unexpected end of input" error, which is the last line of the script block. This means that somewhere inside the conditional construct you forgot to add a closing curly brace. Where the missing brace is supposed to be is rather hard to find, but it's a lot easier to find when the code is properly indented.

exampleMissingCurlyFixed.html

```
function testRange( x, start, end ) {

  if( x <= end && x >= start ) {
    if( x == start ) {
      alert(x + ' is the start of the range');
    }
```

```
      if( x == end ) {
        alert(x + ' is the end of the range');
      }
      if( x != start && x != end ) {
        alert(x + ' is in the range');
      }
  } else {
    alert( x + ' is not in the range' );
  }
}
```

The previously missing curly brace is shown in bold (following the "is in the range" alert() message).

Missing/superlative parentheses is another common problem. This happens when you nest functions in if() conditions and later on delete some of them. For example:

```
if (all = parseInt(getTotal()){ doStuff(); }
```

This causes an error because you forgot to close the opening parenthesis of the condition itself. It should look like this:

```
if (all = parseInt(getTotal())){ ... }
```

It can also happen when you nest too many methods and returns:

```
var elm=grab(get(file).match(/<id>(\w+)<\/id>/)[1];
```

This one lacks the closing parenthesis after the [1]:

```
var elm=grab(get(file).match(/<id>(\w+)<\/id>/)[1]);
```

In general, this kind of concatenation of functions is not good coding style, but there are situations where you will encounter examples like this one. The trick is to count the opening and the closing parentheses from left to right—good editors also highlight opening and closing parentheses automatically. Some editors will add the closing parenthesis, curly brace, or quote for you; others don't, so just be aware as you type.

You could also write a utility function to do this for you, which in itself is a test of your attention to detail when it comes to coding syntax:

exampleTestingCodeLine.html

```
function testCodeLine( c ) {
  if( c.match( /\(/g ).length !=
      c.match( /\)/g) .length ) {
    alert( 'closing ) missing' );
  }
}
c = "var elm=grab(get('demo.xml')" +
  ".match( /<id>(\w+)<\/id>/ )[1] );";
testCodeLine( c );
```

Concatenation Gone Wrong

Concatenation is happening a lot when you use JavaScript to output HTML. Make sure that you don't forget the plus (+) signs in between the different parts to concatenate to a whole:

```
father = "Peter";
mother = "Lois";
child = "Chris";
family = father+" "+mother+" "child;
```

The preceding code lacks one plus sign before the child variable. Instead, it should look like the following:

```
father = "Peter";
mother = "Lois";
child = "Chris";
family = father+" "+mother+" "+child;
```

Another obstacle is to make sure you don't concatenate the wrong data types:

```
father = "Peter";
fAge = 40;
mother = "Lois";
mAge = 38;
child = "Chris";
cAge = 12;
family = father + ", " + mother +   " and " + child + " Total Age: " + fAge + mAge + cAge;
alert( family );
```

This will not show the desired result. Instead, it will show this:

```
Peter, Lois and Chris Total Age: 403812
```

The mistake is that you concatenated strings and numbers because the · operator works from left to right. You need to add parentheses around the age term:

```
father = "Peter";
fAge = 40;
mother = "Lois";
mAge = 38;
child = "Chris";
cAge = 12;
family = father + ", " + mother + " and " + child + " Total Age: " + (fAge + mAge + cAge);
alert(family);
```

This results in the desired outcome:

```
Peter, Lois and Chris Total Age: 90
```

Assigning Instead of Testing the Value of a Variable

When testing the value of a variable, it is all too easy to assign it instead of testing it: all you need to do is forget an equal sign:

```
if(Stewie = "talking") {
  Brian.hear();
}
```

This code entices Brian to hear all the time, not only when Stewie has something to say; however, adding one equal sign does make Brian hear only when Stewie talks:

```
if(Stewie == "talking") {
  Brian.hear();
}
```

Tracing Errors with alert() and "Console" Elements

The easiest way to trace errors is to use `alert()` wherever you want to test a certain value. The `alert()` method stops the script execution (with the exception of Ajax calls that might still be going on in the background) and provides you with information about the value of a certain variable. You can deduce if that value is correct or if it is the cause of the error. In some instances, using an `alert()` is not the right option—for example, if you want to trace the change of several values while looping through an array. Depending on the size of the array, this can become tedious, because you need to press Enter every time you want to get rid of the `alert()` and commence to the next array item.

A workaround for this problem is coming up with your own debugging console or logging elements, or using the debugging features in the browser. The DOMhelp library we put together in this book contains debugging features. You can use the `initDebug()`, `setDebug()` and `stopDebug()` methods to simulate a debugging console. Simply add a style for the element with the ID `DOMhelpDebug` and use the methods to show the element and write content to it. For example:

exampleDebugTest.html (excerpt)

```
#DOMhelpdebug{
  position:absolute;
  top:0;
  right:0;
  width:300px;
  height:200px;
  overflow:scroll;
  background:#000;
  color:#0F9;
  white-space:pre;
  font-family:courier,monospace;
  padding:1em;
}
html>body #DOMhelpdebug{
  position:fixed;
  min-height:200px;
  height:200px;
  overflow:auto;
}
```

exampleDebugTest.html (excerpt)

```
<script type="text/javascript"
 src="../DOMhelp.js"></script>
<script type="text/javascript">
  function DOMDebugTest(){
    DOMhelp.initDebug();
    for(var i = 0; i < 300; i++ ) {
      DOMhelp.setDebug( i + ' : ' + ( i % 3 == 0 ) + '\n' );
    }
  }
  DOMhelp.addEvent( window, 'load', DOMDebugTest, false );
</script>
```

This example loops through the numbers 0 to 299 and displays whether the number can be divided by 3 without resulting in a floating-point number. Instead of pressing Enter 300 times, all you need to do to see the results is scroll in the "console window" you created with the earlier styles.

Error Handling with try and catch()

You can test scripts using the `try ... catch` construct. Simply add the code you want to test inside a `try` condition and if there is an error, the code inside `catch()` will be executed. For example:

exampleTryCatch.js

```
try{
  isNaN(age);
} catch(error) {
    console.log(error);
    console.log(error.message);
    console.log(error.name);
    console.log(error.fileName);
    console.log(error.lineNumber);
}
```

The `catch()` method retrieves an `Exception` object as a parameter when an error occurs inside the `try` statement. You can give this object any variable name; in this example, we call it `error`. Depending on the error and the browser, this object will have different properties, and the properties that are the same across browsers will have different values. For example, the `message` property in Chrome, Firefox, IE, and Safari all return a value, but in the case of Safari it has a different result. To see the results, make sure to open the console panel in your developer tools. We will provide more detail about the developer tools later in the appendix.

```
Chrome:  age is not defined

Firefox: age is not defined

IE: 'age' is undefined

Safari: Can't find variable: age
```

Using `try` and `catch` in a debugging process can be very helpful, Depending on the browser, you can easily spot the problem using them.

Sequential Uncommenting

Another easy way to trace an error is to comment out the whole script and uncomment it function by function or—if it is a single function—line by line. Test the script every time you uncomment a line by reloading it in a browser, and you will quickly get to the one that causes the error. This can take time, though, and it would be much easier to know roughly where the error occurs, which is why you need to rely on your browser to give you this information.

Built in Developer Tools

Debugging code in browsers has been greatly improved. Now all browsers have developer tools built in that give you the ability to inspect, update, and save code directly from the browser. But first, how do you access the developer tools in each browser.

Microsoft Internet Explorer

Internet Explorer exposes its developer tools if you click on the gear icon on the top-right corner of the browser and then select "F12 developer tools." You can also press F12 on your keyboard to get the tools to appear. (See Figure A-4.)

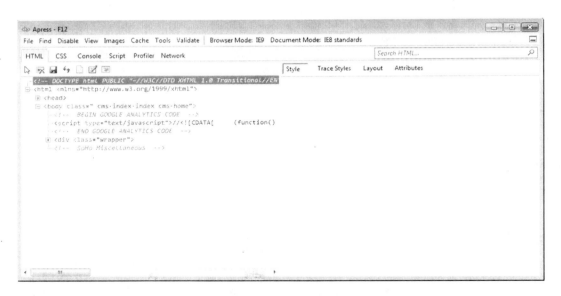

Figure A-4. *The F12 developer tools in Microsoft Internet Explorer*

One thing you will notice with the built-in tools is that they have many similar features. These features include a panel to inspect each part of your page, HTML, CSS, and JavaScript, as well as a profiler and a network monitor. In addition to all of these features is the console where you can write JavaScript directly.

Safari

The debugging tools in Safari are not available by default. To turn them on, go to Safari, Preferences, Advance and then select "Show Develop menu in menu bar."

This enables the Develop drop-down menu. Some of the features available allow you to do things like quickly turn off JavaScript or change the user agent to test what your page would look like using another browser. (See Figure A-5.) Safari also has developer tools. By selecting Develop, Show Web Inspector, you can turn on the developer tools.

Figure A-5. *The debugging menu of Safari*

Opera

The debugging tools in Opera are called Dragonfly. (See Figure A-6.) To access them go to Tools, Advanced, Opera Dragonfly. Another way of accessing them is to go to View, Developer Tools, Opera Dragonfly.

Figure A-6. *Showing the Dragonfly developer tools in Opera*

Firefox

Firefox works a little differently. The tools are there, but they look very different than other browsers, which can cause a little confusion. To get to them, go to Tools, Web Developer, Developer Toolbar. (See Figure A-7.) Once you turn on the toolbar, it will show up at the bottom of the screen. From here, you can inspect the HTML in your document by clicking the Inspect button. To inspect the CSS or the JavaScript, click the Web Console button. You can click the Debugger button to set breakpoints in your JavaScript.

Figure A-7. *Showing the JavaScript console in Firefox*

Chrome

Chrome has its tools under View, Developer, Developer Tools. (See Figure A-8.)

Figure A-8. *Showing the developer tools in Chrome*

Inspecting and Debugging Your Code

In all of these browsers, you have the ability to dig in and look at the code. When trying to single something out in your page, you can right-click (or control-click) on something in your browser and select "Inspect Element." This opens the debugging tools in most browsers and brings you right to the HTML element you are interested in.

You can also update the HTML directly in the developer tools. By double-clicking on any of the HTML elements, you can update text, add CSS, add or remove HTML elements, or do anything else you want to do and get live results in your browser. (See Figure A-9.)

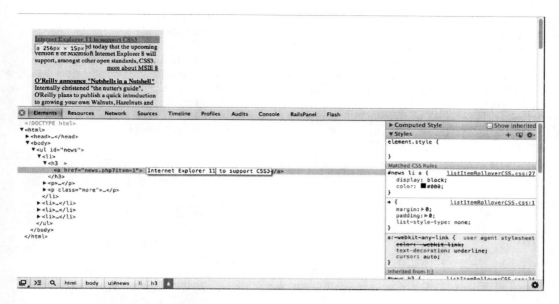

Figure A-9. *Editing HTML directly in Chrome*

The same is true for CSS. By using the Styles panel on the right side (as shown in Figure A-10), you can turn off, edit, or add CSS directly in the browser and see the results instantly.

Figure A-10. *Editing CSS directly in Chrome using the Styles panel*

As these changes are being made, you are updating only the code that is currently loaded in your browser. The original code in your editor is not being updated. To override that code, you can save (control/command–S) and override the original files with your updated ones.

Because the focus of this book is on JavaScript, let's take a look at the some of the debugging features.

Setting breakpoints in your code gives you the ability to see what's going on in real time. When fixing a problem, you'll find that it helps a great deal to have the browser stop in the middle of what it's doing and explain to you things like the current value of a variable.

By selecting Sources in Chrome (or selecting Debugger in Firefox, selecting the file in Safari's debugger), you get a view of the JavaScript code. On the left side, you have line numbers, and if you click on any one of them, you get a breakpoint. (See Figure A-11.)

Figure A-11. *Setting breakpoints in Chrome*

When you refresh the page, the debugger then runs all the JavaScript up to that point and stops. The tools can then help you see what the current value of a variable is or let you see all the function calls that brought you up to that point using the Call Stack. It also has a lot of other features that were not previously available to developers without extensions.

Console

By looking at all of these browsers, you might have run into the console already. You referenced it in the try/catch example, and now you are going to take a deeper dive into it.

What makes the console interesting is that you can think of it as command-line JavaScript—no need for editors or external files. You can just test something real quick on your page and see if it works as expected. In addition, the console has a code-completion feature (as shown in Figure A-12). If you have an idea of how something should work but do not remember exactly what to write, you can use the console to help.

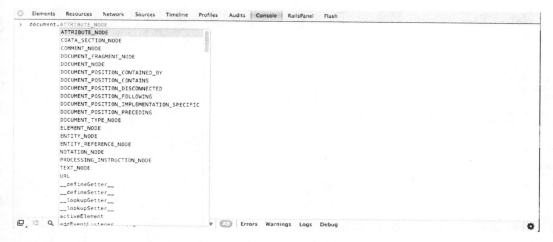

Figure A-12. *The console has code-completion features just like an editor*

From the console, you have access to all the JavaScript code that is in your document. Every object that is built into the browser and every object that you wrote in your code are available and can be executed from the console.

For example, using one of the files from Chapter 5, suppose I wrote the following:

```
sc.init
```

The code that makes up that function gets printed in the console.

However, suppose that I typed the following:

```
sc.init();
```

Here, the code gets executed in the browser at that moment.

You add event listeners, create alert windows, create and change the value of variables all on demand. (See Figure A-13.)

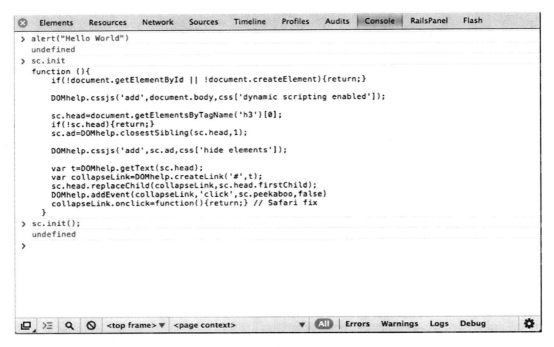

Figure A-13. You can use the console to inspect JavaScript that has been loaded from your site

As you write JavaScript, there is one command you might use more than any other to make sure that things are working the way you think they should:

```
console.log();
```

You used this in the try/catch example. If you have the console open, you can see the results of those statements printed in the console. In other languages, this would be a *print* statement, or *trace* in ActionScript. What this gives you is the ability to print messages.

For example, suppose you need to know your code executed up to a certain point or the current value of a variable (showing image *x* of 10). You can do this without stopping the application from running, as you would do if you were using a breakpoint.

JSLint and Jasmine

Some browser-independent tools are available that also can help you with JavaScript development. One is the online JavaScript verifier JSLint by Douglas Crockford, which is available at http://www.jslint.com/lint.html. JSLint is a tool written in JavaScript that verifies scripts in terms of syntactical validity and tries to ensure good coding style. Because "good coding style" is a subjective matter, you might want to take JSLint reports with a grain of salt. JavaScript development happens mostly in browser environments, and from time to time you need to bend the rules or cut corners to make a script work faster or work around browser issues. That being said, it is still a great tool to use to find ways to optimize your scripts in terms of cleanliness of code if you don't have to cut corners. The great thing about JSLint is that it gives you a full analysis of your script, including reports on global variables and how many times different functions have been called.

If you come from a back-end coding environment, you might have already used or at least heard about *unit testing*(http://en.wikipedia.org/wiki/Unit_testing). In a nutshell, unit testing means that you write test cases for all your methods and functions, and you use a testing harness to run all these tests in succession when you press a button. This way, you can ensure that your code works as you define the test cases it has to fulfill before you develop the code. Unit testing frameworks are available for a lot of different languages, including Java, PHP, ActionScript, and JavaScript.

Pivotal Labs created a testing framework named Jasmine, which does not rely on browsers. You can get information about Jasmine from gitHub:

```
http://pivotal.github.io/jasmine/.
```

There is also a tutorial on unit testing with Jasmine on the Adobe Developer Connection at
http://www.adobe.com/devnet/html5/articles/unit-test-javascript-applications-with-jasmine.html.

Lastly

All in all, debugging JavaScript is much easier these days than it was some years ago. Developer tools built into the browser makes the process a lot easier when you're trying to track down why something is not working.

There are also editors that will try to point out potential problems as you are writing your code.

There is an excellent hands-on course developed by Code School, sponsored by Google, that teaches you how to use the developer tools in Chrome. The course is located at http://discover-devtools.codeschool.com/, and it's free.

Debugging for mobile developers has also improved. Weinre (pronounced *wine-er* or *winery*) lets you remotely debug the browser in your mobile devices on your desktop. Information can be found at http://prople.apache.org/~pmuellr/weinre/docs/latest/. Adobe has a similar product, called Edge Inspect, that also lets you debug your site in multiple devices. You can find it at http://html.adobe.com/edge/inspect/.

Index

T, U, V

W, X, Y, Z

Centennial College Libraries

CPSIA information can be obtained at www.ICGtesting.com
Printed in the USA
LVOW09s0405080114

368545LV00007B/127/P